Western Persia Mission

WESTERN PERSIA
Mission

A Biography of Annie Rhea Wilson (1861-1952)

KATHRYN MCLANE

XULON PRESS

Xulon Press
2301 Lucien Way #415
Maitland, FL 32751
407.339.4217
www.xulonpress.com

Paperback ISBN-13: 978-1-6628-4377-8
Ebook ISBN-13: 978-1-6628-4378-5

To My Great-Grandparents
Annie Dwight Rhea Wilson
(1861-1952)
and
Samuel Graham Wilson
(1858-1916)

PERSIA

A land of barren plains
And mountains bleak and bare,
Deprived of summer rains
To keep it green and fair;

Yet in this desert land,
Where'er a river flows,
Gardens bloom on either hand,
All fragrant with the rose.

The river at its source
Is fed by mountain snows,
And in its winding course
Brings life where'er it goes.

So, like a band of green
Across the desert plain
A line of trees is seen,
And fields of waving grain.

Thus in the prophet's dream
From out the Holy Place
Came forth a living stream,
The river of God's Grace.

Oh river, deep and grand,
Flow through this land of woes
And make its desert sand
To blossom as the rose!

by Annie Dwight Rhea Wilson

INTRODUCTION

THE PRESBYTERIAN BOARD OF THE UNITED STATES OVERSAW
two missions in Persia (Iran) from 1871 until 1941 when the
Iranian government under Reza Shah Pahlavi bought the mission
properties — the Western Persia and Eastern Persia Missions. The
Western Persia Mission was comprised of the stations of Urmia
(1835), Tabriz (1873) and Salmas (1886), and the Eastern Persia
Mission was comprised of the Tehran (1872) and Hamadan (1881)
stations (founding dates in parentheses). The work of the missionaries at these stations is described in the Annual Reports to the
Presbyterian Board, the primary reference used in this compilation.
The early history of the Western Persia Mission was published in
1896 by Samuel Graham Wilson. The present work refers to and
expands on the original historical scope.

The story focuses on the personal accounts of two missionaries of the Tabriz station — Annie Rhea Wilson (1861-1952) and
Samuel Graham Wilson (1858-1916). They devoted over thirty
years of their lives as missionaries educating young Persians at
the Memorial Boys' School. Their relationships with other missionaries and Persians are brought to life through Annie Wilson,
who tells their story in first person.

The period covers important political events in Iran including
the assassination of Nasar al-Din Shah in 1896, the Persian

Constitutional Revolution of 1905-1909, the Russian invasion of Tabriz in 1911, and the subsequent "Reign of Terror" under Samad Khan. During World War I Persian villages were raided by Turkish and Kurdish forces and the mission compounds provided refuge from massacre for thousands of villagers. Missionaries provided firsthand accounts of the Armenian and Assyrian genocides and the mass exodus to the Caucasus. The letters and reports from Samuel Wilson while working in the Caucasus for Near East Relief document the compassionate response to the refugees.

At the end of this work is an Appendix containing a glossary of foreign terms, short biographies, a list of references by chapter, and selected original letters and writings by the Wilsons.

CHAPTER 1

December 1862, Presbyterian Mission, Urmia, Persia

MOTHER NEVER TOOK ME WITH HER DOWN INTO THE CELLAR. This time I stopped playing with my doll and watched her feel for each step with her feet, unable to see over her pregnant belly. She was gone from sight for a few moments, then reappeared holding a bowl of flour and a pitcher of milk. When she tried to close the door by pushing it with her buttocks, it did not close all the way. *Mother left the cellar door ajar.*

As I toddled past Father's study, he did not look up, focusing on the evening sermon he would deliver in the mission church. After pushing my body through the crack of the open cellar door, I teetered, lost my balance, and fell, hitting my head on the stone steps. I landed face down on the dirt floor, sucking dust into my nostrils. The cellar was cold and dark, and I was clammy with fear. At first stunned, the pain of my bruises brought me into full consciousness and my shrill screams reverberated on the brick walls.

The strong arms of Father scooped me up and gently carried me out of the cellar. He sat down on a chair in his study and hoisted me up on his lap. He cleaned my dusty, tear-streaked face with his handkerchief. The screams and shower of tears became a whimper and a sniffle.

"You are an adventurous one, my little Annie," Father said. "We will not tell Mother about your mishap, or she will fret about her carelessness. However, God knows. 'Oh God thou knowest my folly; the wrongs I have done are not hidden from thee.' That is Psalms 69:5. Hopefully you will learn from your bruises and be a righteous daughter in the eyes of God."

My parents were missionaries at the Presbyterian Mission in Urmia, Persia. Father was Rev. Samuel Audley Rhea, a pioneer missionary. Mother's name was Sarah Jane Foster Rhea, but Father called her "Sallie." I was their first child, born on Saturday, August 24, 1861.

The Mission to the Nestorians, as the Urmia Mission was called, was founded by Rev. Justin Perkins in 1835. The other families at the Mission were those of Dr. Austin Wright, Rev. George Coan, Rev. John Shedd, Rev. Joseph Cochran and Rev. Benjamin Labaree. My playmates were six mission children within two years of my age — two of the Coan boys, Frank and Freddie, my brother Foster, Emma Cochran and George Labaree.

In July 1865, Father announced that the family was going to Tabriz for the month of August. Daniel and Guergis, our Nestorian helpers, lifted Foster and me into *cajavahs*, large baskets on either side of Daniel's horse, our transportation for the four-day journey. Mother and Father rode on horseback and the *charvadar* led the mules carrying our loads. We arrived Saturday in Ali Shah, where Father kept a small house that he used while touring the villages, and we spent Sabbath resting and reading the Bible. On Monday when we reached Tabriz, Father took us to the famous Bazaar with five thousand shops and bought us multi-colored wooden tops.

The last week of August Father and I became sick with fever, vomiting and diarrhea. A cold breeze from the Caspian Sea descended on Tabriz and I alternated between sweating with fever and shivering with cold. Mother found a German doctor, who visited us three times and gave us large doses of quinine. "We must get out of these crowded quarters," Mother lamented, "We must go home."

"They will soon be better," the doctor assured Mother.

Father, feeling better after the quinine, was anxious to start the long ride home. When we stopped in Myan at a *caravanserai*, a travelers' inn, Father was seized with severe abdominal pains and became violently ill. The water in Myan contained sulfur and was too bitter to drink. "I am so thirsty," I wailed, "Please, give me water."

"Rev. Rhea's house in Ali Shah is four hours from here," Daniel said. "There is drinkable water there. We can ride at night to avoid further dehydration."

Father initially rode his horse, but after an hour, he could no longer sit up. Daniel and Guergis tied bedding on top of his horse and strapped Father on top. Foster and I cried from thirst and Father groaned with pain until we arrived at the house in Ali Shah.

When Daniel and Guergis lifted Father onto a bed in the house, he heaved a long sigh. Daniel filled a jug with water, and we passed it around, gulping as water spilled over our chins. Mother took the jug to Father and lifted his head. "Try to drink slowly," she said to him as she moistened his lips. "Sam?" She put the jug down and put her ear to his mouth and nose. Then she felt Father's wrists and his chest.

"Say something, Sam," she said quietly, and then repeated her words over and over, each time more frantically. "You cannot be dead; you did not say goodbye."

In the morning Mother wrote to the English Consul in Tabriz, asking him to send a coffin. "When it arrives, we will be on our way to Urmia and away from this house of death," she said.

The coffin did not arrive for two days. As we waited Foster wept and I lay in bed with a fever and abdominal pain. Daniel and Guergis gently placed Father's body in the coffin, surrounded it with charcoal and sealed it. Fearing that I would succumb, Mother chose to travel by night, and the *charvadar* proceeded ahead of us with the coffin. "I wanted to be with Sam on his last journey home," Mother cried.

As we approached Urmia, we were met by Rev. George Coan who took Mother into his arms and comforted us. "The coffin arrived on Thursday morning," he said. "Rev. Perkins buried it in the cemetery in Seir before noon."

Two weeks after reaching Urmia, my illness abated, and Mother took me to visit Father's grave. It was a peaceful site with a view of the valley below. "Father left us so suddenly," I said. At four years old, I was too young to realize my loss. I did not understand that the rest of my life I would hunger for the love of my father.

Eight months after Father's death Mother told Foster and I that she was going to have another baby. How a baby could come into this world without a father, I did not know. Foster and I stood in the study and held on tight to each other until the screaming stopped and Mrs. Cochran came to get us.

My sister Sophea was a pretty baby. As an infant she had a mass of curly blond hair and big blue eyes. "A blessing sent from Samuel," Mother said. "He is telling me not to mourn for him anymore."

For four years Mother taught classes at the Fiske Girls' School and continued missionary work with women in the Nestorian community. Susan Rice, the principal of the Girls' School, and Rev. Justin Perkins, the old mission founder, moved into our house, and we called them "Aunt Susan" and "Grandpa Perkins."

With the other missionary children, Foster and I attended school in the Cochran house. One year, Frank Coan while flying a kite walked backward and fell off the roof of their house, breaking his leg. Another spring, Sophea fell into the watercourse that ran through the yard, and Daniel dragged her out by her heels.

The winter of 1868 was brutally cold, and the horses were frisky after months standing in the stable. The first spring day Mother asked Daniel to take the family on a wagon ride up Mount Seir. Foster sat on the front seat of the wagon with Daniel, and Mother, Sophea and I sat on the back seat. Halfway up Mount Seir, Foster grew sleepy, and his head bobbed from side to side. Daniel stopped the wagon to arrange Foster on the seat to take a nap and the reigns fell from his hand. The horses, sensing their freedom, started to run.

Daniel and Mother jumped out of the wagon to stop the horses as they neared a fork in the road by a steep precipice. Foster, Sophea and I remained in the swaying wagon, still moving along the edge of the cliff. I closed my eyes and prayed to God to send an angel to save us from falling down the mountain. When the wagon came to a stop, I looked up expecting to see an angel with white wings, but instead a Persian peasant held the reins. That God did not answer my prayers and send a glowing white angel was a crushing disappointment to me.

In 1869 twenty-year-old Mary Cochran fell off a horse and hurt her back and she needed to return to America for medical treatment. Susan Rice and Rev. Perkins decided to go back with her and convinced Mother to take the family back to America. "We will live with your Grandmother Cunningham in Jonesborough, Tennessee," she told us. "It will be fun going to school with your cousins. Your father's family lives nearby."

On May 28th we left Persia. Mother, Aunt Susan and Rev. Perkins rode in the wagon, Foster and Sophea traveled in *caja-vahs*, and I accompanied Mary Cochran in a *takheravan*, a chair suspended on horizontal poles carried by one horse in front and another behind. The *charvadars* drove the mules with our baggage, tents and camping gear. Each night we set up camp near a village to get fodder for the donkeys and horses and milk, bread, eggs and chickens for our meals. In the morning we woke at three to the barking of village dogs, and by five our caravan was on its way. I remember our journey as a continuous picnic, and at every stop running through the fields and picking wildflowers.

After we crossed the Aras River a snow-capped mountain with double peaks loomed in front of us. "That is Mount Ararat," Rev. Perkins said. "Noah's Ark landed there after floating one hundred and fifty days. It is a sacred mountain."

"The Ark with the animals, two-by-two?" Foster asked.

"Yes, the Ark that saved all the animals," Rev. Perkins replied.

In two weeks, we reached a summit where we caught sight of an expanse of water. "It is the Black Sea, a milestone in our journey," Rev Perkins said. "Now we will travel by ship and train."

Foster and I had never been on a train or a ship and could barely sleep with anticipation.

Rhea Family, 1864 (left to right) Rev. Samuel Audley Rhea,
Annie Dwight Rhea, Foster Audley Rhea, Sarah Jane Foster Rhea

CHAPTER 2

Arriving in America

OUR SHIP ENTERED NEW YORK HARBOR THE MORNING OF August 24th, my 8th birthday. Aunt Susan woke me saying, "Come on deck and see your birthday present." My present was a view of the New York Harbor with many ships, some with great masts and others with stacks and only accessory sails. We descended the plank and followed thousands of ship passengers into Castle Garden, a large round brownstone building. As we queued under a huge skylight waiting to reach the inspector stations, the cacophony of people speaking in many different languages was disorienting. Feeling faint in the stuffy room, I held Foster's and Sophea's hands with a firm grip.

"Your Uncle John and Uncle Brainerd will arrive tomorrow and take us to Blountville, Tennessee," Mother said.

"Who are Uncle John and Uncle Brainerd?" Foster asked.

"Father's half-brothers," Mother replied. "His mother died shortly after he was born. Father's stepmother had ten children."

Uncle John and Uncle Brainerd met us at the train station and joined us in our cabin. The train whistle blew signaling the start of our journey to Tennessee.

"I cannot tell you how Sam and I worried about you and your brothers fighting in the war," Mother said. "Sam told me that thinking about his relatives fighting against one another brought him great despair. Most of my relatives were on the side of the Union."

"Most of the Rheas had no allegiance to the Confederacy," Uncle Brainerd said, "but when they passed the Conscription Act of 1861, all able-bodied white men between nineteen and thirty-five were liable for three years of service in the Confederate Army. You would be lynched if you didn't comply."

When we arrived at Grandmother Rhea's house, she was waiting on the front porch with two young women. "It is the joy of my life to finally see these little angels," she said. Grandmother Rhea gave Mother a big hug and kissed each of us on the cheek.

"Nine long years and you have not changed a bit," Mother said.

"The war put a fair bit of age on me I am afraid. You of course remember, Maggie and Ellen, my girls."

"Mother, we are young women in our twenties, not girls," Aunt Maggie said. "Sallie, my dear, I am so happy to have you here. We of course wish Sam was still with you, but little Foster is the spit and image of his father. It is almost like having him with us."

"Be ready to leave in the morning for Jonesborough," Mother told us.

"Why are we going to Jonesborough?" Foster asked. "It is fine right here."

"Your Grandmother Cunningham lives in Jonesborough," Mother replied. "You will not be of want for playmates in Jonesborough. Uncle Sam, my half-brother, has three children your age, and so does Aunt Fannie, your father's half-sister. You will go to school together."

The train arrived midday in Jonesborough and Grandmother Cunningham and Aunt Sophie were there to meet us.

"Oh, my beautiful little Sophea," Aunt Sophie exclaimed. "Such beautiful golden curly hair and beautiful blue eyes. I don't deserve to have you named after me; you are so precious." She bent down and took Sophea in her arms and gave her a big hug. "I am glad to meet you too finally, Annie and Foster."

Mother hugged her mother and they wept happy tears. Then Grandmother Cunningham took Foster and me by the hand. "I meet my grandchildren at last."

Grandmother Cunningham lived in a large red brick house with a row of maple trees in front. A brook ran between the house and the street with a small bridge leading to the front yard. "Afton Hall," Mother murmured. "It came through the war unscathed. How I feared it would be damaged."

"The Lord protected us," Grandmother Cunningham said cheerily. "Even the Yankee boys were sensitive enough to avoid destroying the church with their shelling and the house being right across the street was spared as well."

"Why do you call this house Afton Hall?" I asked.

"We named it after an old Scottish song called *Flow Gently, Sweet Afton*," Grandmother replied. "The song is about a murmuring stream, like the brook that runs in front of the house."

As we picked flowers in the garden, Grandmother and Mother watched us and chatted. Sophea and Foster picked a large bouquet of daisies for Aunt Sophie, and I picked sweet peas for Grandmother.

"I like it here," Foster said. "I wonder where we will sleep tomorrow."

Grandmother rushed over and gathered Foster in her arms, "You are staying here, of course" she said. "This is your home."

"Our home?" Foster exclaimed.

"Our journey is over," Mother said.

At last.

Monday, September 20th

"Wake up, children," Mother cried. "It is your first day of school."

Mother took us up the hill to the two-room schoolhouse, one room for elementary school and the other for high school classes. Foster and I had never been to a regular school and were uncertain what the day would bring. We were relieved to see our cousins, Nellie, John, James and Martha. "Let's take the desks next to Nellie and James," I told Foster. "We can watch what they do."

When Mother took us home for lunch she asked, "How is your first day of school going?"

"The teacher told the other students that we were from Persia and one student asked when we were going back," I said.

"When can we go back?" Foster asked.

"We will try to be happy in America first," Mother replied.

Grandmother Cunningham stopped eating and looked intently at Mother. "What are you saying Sallie? Are you thinking of going back?"

"It is my first day back as a teacher in America," Mother said. "In Persia, I knew I was giving the students something very special. Their sparkling black eyes looked at me with the light of hope and hunger for knowledge. The students today seemed apathetic by comparison. The difference in their motivation to learn dismayed me."

"Give your students here a chance," Grandmother retorted, "and give America a chance."

The Cowan-Rhea Weddings, 1870

"Don't you dare get your church clothes dirty," Mother warned us. "Father's half-brother and half-sister are both getting married in Knoxville, October 26th. Uncle Robert is marrying Bella Cowan and Aunt Maggie is marrying Rev. Perez Cowan, a two brother and sister wedding. The Cowans are from a prominent family in Knoxville."

As the two brides entered the nave with their escorts breathless awes followed them in a wave as they passed by the pews. I was awestruck by the beauty of the brides, their long shimmering white satin gowns, the bustles with folds of fabric and long trains carried by attendants. Their flowing veils made them look like angels. After the service we followed the crowds out of the church. Walking with Mother I said, "I want a wedding like this one."

Mother laughed as though it was the funniest thing she had ever heard. "After I pass away, you will need to marry a wealthy man," she said.

When the bride and groom cut the first piece of cake the children rushed to the table. The sweet white cake melted in my mouth. Sophea decided to forgo her fork and leaned over her plate and bit into her piece of cake getting frosting all over her face.

I concluded that weddings were delightful and worth all the fuss of dressing up.

After their wedding trip, Aunt Maggie and Uncle Perez came through Jonesborough and brought us a book of fairy tales that Foster read ten times. Uncle Perez became the pastor at the Jonesborough Presbyterian Church, and they lived in a wing of Grandmother Cunningham's house. Aunt Maggie played piano and sang songs and entertained us with her funny rhymes. On Saturdays, Uncle Perez held a meeting of the "Band of Young Christians" and entertained us by drawing illustrations of the Scriptures with colored crayons.

"You spend so much attention to teaching Scriptures to children, who are still innocent," Mother said.

"Christ's first command to Peter was 'feed my lambs.' John 21:15,' " Uncle Perez replied.

Aunt Maggie quickly became my favorite Aunt and Uncle Perez my favorite uncle, and this close relationship followed me later in life.

Spring 1873

"The Women's Presbyterian Board of Missions offered me the position of Field Secretary in the Northwest region," Mother said. "I know you love your home in Jonesborough, but I have decided to accept their offer. The family will move to Lake Forest, Illinois outside of Chicago."

"Chicago?" I exclaimed.

"There are good schools, and in the summer the weather will be cooler and not so humid."

"Sallie, be frank about the weather," Grandmother Cunningham scolded. "The winters in Chicago can be brutal; the wind off Lake Michigan can blow you off your feet."

"Last year Chicago had a fire that killed three hundred people and left one hundred thousand homeless," Aunt Sophie added.

"Do we have a choice?" Foster asked.

I already know Mother's answer.

Mother slowly shook her head "No." "It has been decided. We will move there in July."

"I don't want to move," Foster bemoaned.

"But Foster, moving to Lake Forest means a new adventure," I said. "I like new adventures, going to new places, experiencing new things."

July 1873

"It may not be safe to take the train to Chicago," Uncle Sam exclaimed. "A train in Iowa was derailed by Jesse James and his gang. The bandits shot and killed the conductor, the engineer and a passenger before robbing the safe."

"Bandits have never robbed a train before," Aunt Sophie declared.

"It would be better to wait until the bandits are caught," Uncle Sam said.

"Nonsense," Mother said. "This family has been through raids by the Kurds in Persia and survived. I am sure we will survive the James gang."

"Since my mother is taking the train with you, I feel I have a say in the matter," Uncle Sam said.

"Grandma is coming with us?" I exclaimed.

"Yes, your grandmother and I have decided to go with you to Lake Forest," Aunt Sophie said. "I will take care of you while your mother is traveling."

"Where will you be going, Mother?" I asked.

"My work covers the entire Northwest region," Mother replied. "I will be traveling almost every week, giving talks on missions, asking for donations and organizing missionary societies."

On the train from New York to Chicago Foster worried about bandits boarding the train at every stop. When we arrived in Chicago, Foster exclaimed, "We made the whole trip without running into Jesse James."

"How many people live in Lake Forest?" I asked.

"About eight hundred," Mother said, "but with Chicago on our doorstep it will not feel like a small town."

Rev. James Taylor, the pastor of the Presbyterian church, welcomed us to Lake Forest. "Your house is over there by the train station," he said and handed Mother the keys.

Our house was a small white cottage with a kitchen, sitting room and three small bedrooms. "Sallie, it will be noisy and cold here," Grandmother said. "There is only the stove for heat."

"Our warm spirts will make it cozy," Mother replied. "I asked that it be walking distance from the train station, since I will frequently go to the Board office in Chicago and my work will require traveling each week."

"Will you be home for dinner?" I asked.

"Only on the weekends unless I am working in Chicago," Mother replied.

"Where will we go to school?" I asked.

"You and Sophea will attend a girls' school called Ferry Hall," Mother replied. "Foster will go to Lake Forest Academy, the boys' school. Both are a short distance away."

"I will walk with you to school and be there to walk home with you," Aunt Sophie said.

The next day, Mother arranged for a horse and carriage from the livery to take us to the Holt estate. The house of Devillo and Ellen Holt was a massive brick house clad with wood.

Mrs. Holt met us at the door and welcomed us inside. "We call the house 'The Homestead,'" she said. "We have six children; our the oldest, George, is twenty-one and the youngest is Nellie who is three. Anna, Alfred and William are about your ages and are looking forward to playing together. You are welcome here any time."

"Let me show you the garden," Anna Holt said. There were three gardeners working in the plot of land that stretched to meet the road, a full half-block.

"What do you do with all of the flowers?" I asked.

"Every day the gardeners bring bouquets into the house," Anna replied. "Over there is Mother's Conservatory and the stable for my horse, Black Beauty. I am the only girl in Lake Forest who has a horse."

"I wish I had a horse," I said.

"Mother told me your father died, and your mother is a hard-working missionary lady."

"Mother's slogan is 'Live for God and do something good.'"

"I can tell that you are a religious person too and that we will be good friends."

"I would like that."

Anna Holt became my best friend for life.

For two years Grandmother and Aunt Sophie lived with us and kept life merry, but it was the Holt's open generosity that made Lake Forest feel like home. After school Foster and I spent the afternoon at the Holt house. We sat on the floor by the fireplace with the Holt children and listened to their father read from the Bible while he sat in his armchair. When we returned home, a red shawl hanging in the back stoop was the signal that Mother had returned, and we ran to be held in her arms.

CHAPTER 3

1875

WHILE WE WERE IN JONESBOROUGH WITH GRANDMOTHER
Cunningham for the summer Mother received a letter from
the Lake Forest Presbyterian Church. "The Woman's Board of
Missions and the people of Lake Forest are building us a new
house," she exclaimed. "They want to know if we have any specific instructions."

"What will you tell them?" Grandmother asked.

"Just three things," Mother replied. "Make it warm, make it
warm, make it warm."

On August 24th, my fourteenth birthday, we returned to Lake
Forest to find a new furnished house at the corner of Sheridan and
College Roads, conveniently situated across the street from the
Holt's estate. It was a two-storied wood framed house with an attic,
a cellar and a lawn with old oak trees that sloped to a ravine. The
first floor had three rooms divided by folding doors that could be
opened to create one large room for Mother's Thursday Women's
Mission meetings. Upstairs were five bedrooms, heated by a base-
burner in the living room with a heat register in the ceiling.

"Whenever you question the righteousness of humanity,
remember this act of kindness," Mother declared. "It will
uplift you."

In the spring of 1877, before graduating from Ferry Hall, I was uncertain what I would do the following year. Then a letter came from Lake Forest College. When I read it, I screamed for joy; it was a four-year college scholarship.

Mother wept when I told her. "Going to Mount Holyoke was the most influential time of my life," she said. "I wanted you to have the same opportunity to go to college, but never thought you would be able to go on my meager salary. The scholarship is a true blessing."

Classes at Lake Forest College were initially held in the New Hotel, built in 1871 for summer guests and with no heating system. When winter came, we shivered through classes, and the boarding students who lived at the hotel buried themselves in quilts and huddled together to stay warm. At night inexplicable fires sporadically broke out in the building necessitating a patrol.

On December 16th at two in the morning a fire in the cupola sent the dormitory students out on the lawn. An hour later I answered a loud knock on the door, with four shivering girls asking for a place to spend the rest of the night. I welcomed them in to warm by the stove and had them share Mother's bedroom and the guest room, which were unoccupied. In the morning we emerged to find that our college was a heap of ashes.

"Where will we have classes?" I asked, bewildered and forlorn.

"After Christmas, classes will be moved to the Old Hotel by the train tracks," answered one of the teachers.

The new college was being built across the street from the Holt estate, and laborers worked night and day digging clay and baking bricks in kilns. In the fall of 1878 College Hall was completed in time for my sophomore year. Each day when I ascended College Hall's wide staircase, I imagined that with each step I was climbing up a ladder of achievement.

The co-educational environment at Lake Forest College was competitive. Charlotte Skinner and I were the only girls in our class of five. We were out to prove our brains equal to the boys, so we took Latin, Greek, mathematics and science.

The Class of 1881 graduated two women and three men: Charlotte Skinner and I, Arthur Wheeler, Hiram Stanley, and Frederick and Franklin Jewett. Charlotte Skinner was Salutatorian, and I was the Valedictorian. Commencement was a proud day for me, and my family and relatives loaded me with presents and flowers.

Mother had a luncheon that filled the house and when the last guest left, she turned to me and handed me a letter addressed from Aunt Maggie. "I know what it says already," Mother said. "Maggie wanted to know what I thought before she wrote to you. Go ahead, read it."

I gasped after I read a few paragraphs. "Aunt Maggie and Uncle Perez are asking me to come to Wellesley College for a year and stay with them."

"You have been living in Lake Forest for eight years and helping with the children," Mother said. "Sophea and Foster are now old enough to be on their own, so it is time for you to spread your wings and see other parts of the country. Perez and Maggie need a distraction. They have been mourning the loss of their little Margie, who died over a year ago. It will be good for them to have you there."

We spent the summer in Jonesborough visiting Grandmother Cunningham and preparing for Aunt Sophie's wedding; she was marrying Rev. Calvin Duncan, a new pastor at the Presbyterian church. After the wedding I took the train to Boston, my first journey alone. I tried to read a book by the dim kerosene lamp until my eyes were barely open, then I slipped my silver watch under my pillow for safe keeping. I did not realize I had forgotten it until I was on the platform in Boston. I was torn between receiving my Aunt Maggie's open arms and running back to the train.

"Why are you so distressed?" Aunt Maggie asked.

"My watch," I said, "I have forgotten my watch on the train. I need to go back to my cabin."

"Here comes a porter."

To my amazement, the porter approached me and handed me my watch. I was so taken with admiration that I hugged the man and said, "You are the kindest man in the whole world."

Then I noticed my bags were not where I had left them and looked frantically in every direction. "Perez directed the coachman to take your baggage to our carriage," Aunt Maggie said. "We are ready to be off to Wellesley."

The Manse where they lived was a spacious two-story white wood framed New England house with green shutters. Reverend Perez and Aunt Maggie had a bedroom on the first floor "Your room is upstairs," Aunt Maggie said. "It belonged to Margie."

"I was so sad when I heard that she died," I replied. "She was such a beautiful child."

"Fortunately, we bought a bed for an adult, thinking that she would grow into it, but I am afraid the tiny chair and table in the room will not suit you. You will need something for reading and writing. To be honest, I have barely been in this room since she passed. It is so painful to see her things. Perez's cousin Emily wrote, in her odd way, that the furniture has 'lips of dirks to stab us.' She was right."

"How poignant," I said. "I can imagine her little ghost still sitting in the chair."

That night as I was preparing for bed, I opened the small drawer of the nightstand next to the bed to put my watch in a safe place. There was a small book in the memory of Margaret "Margie" McClung Cowan (1876-1879). When I opened it, a two-page letter to Uncle Perez from his Cousin Emily fell out. I had heard so many stories of his odd cousin, the poet, I could not help but read it. There was the line about "the little furniture of loss" that haunted Aunt Maggie. The following line was about her hope that heaven would be warm with so many "barefoot ones." *Very eerie indeed.*

After I took my shoes off the bare floor was painfully cold to my feet. "Yes, I hope heaven is warm," I murmured as I lay down and pulled the comforter up to my chin.

The next day when I returned from my first day at Wellesley College, the child's furniture was gone and replaced with a narrow table and a chair for an adult, and when I prepared for bed and opened the drawer of the nightstand, the memorial book with the letter from Emily Dickinson was gone.

It was a cheery household with frequent guests, Wellesley College faculty or members of the Presbyterian Church. Every evening Aunt Maggie played piano and we sang songs together.

Classes at Wellesley were held in College Hall built in 1875 above Lake Wabon. It held all the classrooms, the dormitory and housing for the faculty, all in a single monstrous building. I took advanced Latin and Greek, and history from Alice Freeman Palmer, who one month later was named acting president of Wellesley. Like the rest of her students, I admired her, a woman six years older than me who was both seriously dedicated and socially engaging. We called her "The Princess." In her first speech to the students after she officially became the college president, she told us. "Women need to attain a college education so that if they need to work, they have the necessary skills to do so." Having such a strong female role model, in addition to Mother, made me feel empowered as a woman. I felt my feet squarely on the ground without the need to lean on a man.

There were two male visitors who came to see me during my stay with Aunt Maggie and Uncle Perez. The first male visitor was Rev. James Boyd Porter from Riceville, Tennessee. Grandmother Cunningham gave him my name and address, and his letter of introduction requested a meeting in late September. He was a tall man with sandy hair. "After attending Princeton Theological Seminary, I worked at the Presbyterian church in Jonesborough," he said. "I stayed at your grandmother's house."

"Beautiful Afton Hall," I murmured. "It is kind of you to stop by to give your regards."

"It is not the only reason," he continued. "Your grandmother thought you might be inclined toward missionary work."

"I may be interested in missionary work after completing a master's degree," I replied.

Rev. Porter seemed disconcerted by what I said, but regained his composure and asked, "What do you think about missionary work in Japan?"

"I hear good things about the missions in Japan from my mother, who is the Field Secretary for the Women's Mission Board of the Northwest."

"Yes, I have heard good things too, and it is why I was pleased when I was given a commission there."

"A commission to Japan? Why congratulations. When are you leaving?"

"In November. That is why I sent my request to meet you with some urgency."

"Goodness, I am flattered. With all the preparations you must have to make for your trip to Japan, meeting me was urgent?"

"Yes, you see I am looking for someone to go with me as my wife. I was hoping that you would be interested."

I was completely discombobulated. "Go as your wife?"

"Yes, I was hoping that you would be interested."

"We have only known each other for an hour," I sputtered.

"If you would like a day or so to think about it, I can wait."

"A day or two will not matter. I am not interested."

"You should think about it before you make a final decision."

"My decision is final; I am not interested."

Rev. Porter stared blankly at me with his mouth open as though he was not expecting the conversation to be over. Then he stood up and made his way to the front door.

Shortly after he left Aunt Maggie entered the parlor with a tea pot and a plate of sugar cookies. "Where is Reverend Porter?" she asked.

"He said everything he had to say and left," I responded.

My other male visitor that spring was George Hubbard Holt, the oldest son of the Holt family that lived across the street from us in Lake Forest. He sent a letter to me in March saying he would be in Boston visiting friends at Harvard and wanted to see me as well. Unlike Reverend Porter, George was a childhood friend, and I had no apprehension about seeing him. It had been almost a year since I had seen anyone from Lake Forest and considered it to be a treat.

Aunt Maggie called upstairs that George was waiting to see me in the parlor. As I passed her at the bottom of the stairs she whispered, "Don't worry about it being Fast Day. You and Mr. Holt will have a fine luncheon while the rest of us starve."

"What is Fast Day?" I exclaimed.

"In New England April 19th is a religious day of fasting. Being from the South I had never heard of it until we moved here," Aunt Maggie said.

George Holt was nine years older than me, a slight man who looked younger than thirty years. He wore a gray suit and black tie and a perfectly groomed red beard and mustache.

"You look so much like a businessman now," I exclaimed.

"Father has me next in line to be President of Holt Lumber Company," George replied, "but I still spend every winter in the woods of Wisconsin and live in the lumber camp."

I laughed thinking of this slight young man next to burly lumberjacks. "We always knew that you would be successful like your father Devillo," I said.

"I have not been successful in all aspects of my life. I do not have much luck with women."

"Someday you will."

Aunt Maggie came in with a tray of sandwiches, lemonade and fruit. "One sandwich accidently fell off the plate and I ate it," she said, smiling slyly. "I will be back later to scold you if any evidence remains."

"Mrs. Cowan, you have out done yourself," George said.

"Classes at Wellesley and living in another part of the country have broadened my perspective," I said.

"What are your plans for next fall?" George asked.

"I have been offered a position at Ferry Hall teaching Greek and Latin."

"Splendid. I was hoping you would return to Lake Forest so we can see more of each other." *So strange for George to be lonely and desperate for companionship.*

Many years later Anna Holt, his sister and my close friend, confided that her mother had suggested that he pay me a visit. "I think Mother hoped that George would take a liking to you and initiate a courtship," Anna said. Whatever George's impression was, he never tried to court me. After his father died, he became the President of Holt Lumber Company and continued to live in the Homestead with his sister Nellie and never married.

A month before I was leaving Wellesley and returning to Lake Forest, I received a telegram from the Presbyterian Board of Foreign Missions. They asked if I would be interested in a teaching position in the Girls' School in Salmas, Persia. Although I found Persia tempting, I had already arranged for a teaching position at Ferry Hall while I completed a master's degree at Lake Forest College. I decided it would not be advisable to change my mind so close to the start of the school year when they could not hire a replacement in time. *Perhaps after I teach for several years at Ferry Hall, I can apply to pursue missionary work.*

My first day as a Greek and Latin teacher at Ferry Hall Girls' School I waited nervously with the other teachers for my turn for an audience with the principal. The line of teachers outside the principal's office barely moved for half an hour. *Why did I not come earlier to get a place near the front of the line?*

When the office door opened and I was ushered in, I tried to appear collected. "I am Annie Dwight Rhea," I said, "Ferry Hall's new Greek and Latin teacher."

"My dear Annie, I remember when you were born in Urmia," Mrs. Thompson said.

"You were at the mission in Urmia?" I exclaimed.

"Yes, I was there from 1860 to 1862," Mrs. Thompson said. "My husband died from typhoid after we had only been there six weeks. It is why I wear a widow's cap and veil. Your father assisted in our wedding ceremony in Amherst before we traveled together with your parents and the Labarees to Persia. I taught in the Fiske School for two years before returning to America."

"You knew my parents in Urmia?"

"Yes, I knew them very well. I am pleased to have you as one of our teachers. Good luck with your classes."

I was about to take my leave when Mrs. Thompson cleared her voice and said, "Annie, it would give me great joy to see you take up missionary work in the future. You have the same deep spiritual aura that your father had."

Esther Thompson mentored me and treated me as her daughter. I called her my "mother-in-love" and vowed that I would name one of my children after her.

In 1883 we had a trying summer in Jonesborough at Afton Hall; Aunt Sophie had her first child, Rhea Duncan, after a difficult pregnancy and she and the baby were not well. Baby Rhea cried at night waking the household and Aunt Sophie was irritable in the hot humid weather, so unlike her. In January Aunt Sophie died of pneumonia, and Grandmother Cunningham tried to provide for baby Rhea, but he died four months later. It was a terrible shock to me. She was only thirty-six years old.

CHAPTER 4

Spring 1886

"YOU ARE IN NO SHAPE TO TRAVEL WITH THAT COLD," I TOLD
Mother. "If you are not careful, you will catch pneumonia."

The annual meeting of the Woman's Board of Presbyterian
Missions was being held in Indianapolis. Mother, who was the
Field Secretary for the Northwest, was presenting a paper at
the conference, just as she had for the past thirteen years. The
day before she was scheduled to take the train from Chicago to
Indianapolis, she caught a severe cold. Dr. Alfred Haven, who
was the only doctor in town, stopped by each day to check on
her. "Give her tea to help with the congestion," he said.

Mother sat up to drink a cup of tea and whispered in a raspy
voice, "Annie, dear, I so want to attend the conference, but my
voice is failing me. You must go in my place and present the paper."

"I will not be a good replacement for you," I said, "but if I can
arrange for a substitute teacher for my classes at Ferry Hall, I can
present your paper."

Annie Brown, one of Mother's coworkers, met me in Chicago
and we took the night train to Indianapolis. From the station we
were taken by carriage to Mrs. Field's house. "She is holding an
afternoon reception in our honor," Annie Brown said. "We will
stay for dinner and spend the night."

The maid directed us to wait in the parlor. When Mrs. Field entered her smile dissolved into an expression of consternation. "Who are you?" she asked. "I was expecting Mrs. Rhea."

"I am Annie, her daughter," I replied. "Mother fell ill."

"Oh, how disappointing," Mrs. Field cried. "Everyone is looking forward to her visit and hearing her speak."

"I have come in her place and will present her paper at the conference," I said.

"Your mother will be sorely missed," Mrs. Field bemoaned. "I know you can read her paper, but…"

"A call for you, Mrs. Field," the maid interjected, and Mrs. Field left the room.

"She certainly could not conceal her disappointment, could she?" I whispered.

"You must understand that since interest in missionary work has swept the nation your mother is a primary draw for attendees to the conference," Annie Brown said.

Other guests arrived for the reception and expressed their dismay that Mother was not attending. They treated me cordially, but with feigned interest.

The conference attendees were primarily women from across the country, but a few men, including representatives of the Presbyterian Mission Board, also attended.

As I sat at a table, waiting nervously to be called to the podium to deliver Mother's paper, one of the conference organizers approached and handed me a calling card. It read "Rev. Samuel G. Wilson, Tabriz, Persia." After agreeing to meet with the missionary from Tabriz, I was escorted to a table in the back of the conference hall, where I found a full-bearded man sitting alone. "Mrs. Rhea?" he said with a surprised tone in his voice.

"No, I am her daughter, Annie," I replied. "Mother is ill and could not attend."

"I was asked to convey greetings to your mother from the missionary families of the Urmia station — the Coans, the Cochrans, the Shedds and the Labarees."

"I will tell her when I return to Lake Forest," I said, "but if you pass through Chicago during your furlough she would enjoy speaking with you personally."

"Were you also at the mission in Urmia?" he asked.

"Only as a child," I replied, "but I know many of the missionaries at the Urmia station. They visit us on furlough. Frank and Fred Coan, and Emma and Joe Cochran were my childhood friends."

After relaying the cheery messages from the Urmia missionaries, Mr. Wilson talked about his missionary work. "Six years ago, I joined the mission in Tabriz as a teacher in the Boys' School. After becoming proficient in the languages, I joined the others on tour to spread the gospel in the villages."

"I thought furlough was granted only after every eight to ten years of missionary service," I said.

"Mother thought ten years was too long, so Father paid my way," Sam said. "I will return in October."

"Where are you originally from, Mr. Wilson?"

"I was born and raised in Indiana, Pennsylvania. At fourteen I went to Princeton and was graduated in 1876. Then I attended Western Theological Seminary in Pittsburgh and returned to Princeton to earn a master's degree. In 1880 after being ordained, I left for Persia. Mother protested as I was only twenty-two years old at the time."

"You are only three years older than me," I exclaimed. "I would have never guessed it. Your beard belies your youth."

"The beard and mustache are customary for priests and teachers in Persia. When Persians refer to someone who is knowledgeable, they say, 'He has a big beard.' The only reason I would shave my beard would be to get married."

His words made me smile. *He is quite handsome, despite the beard.*

My name was announced, and I proceeded to the podium. *Don't be nervous, don't be nervous. It will be over soon.* I cleared my voice and began reading the paper, which I had practically memorized. The words flowed from my mouth as though someone else was speaking, and as I spoke the last words, I heaved a sigh of relief. With sweat moistening my brow, I froze my lips in a smile.

The conference organizer thanked me and asked the audience if there were any questions. There was only one question, that from the young missionary from Tabriz. "What was the name of the school where your mother taught in Urmia?"

I suppose he thinks I do not know. "The Fiske Girls' School," I answered confidently.

When I came back to his table, the young pastor was smiling broadly. "Bravo, Miss Rhea," he exclaimed. "I thought my question might trip you up."

"Not a chance," I replied. "My mother has told me everything about the Urmia station."

For the rest of the conference Mr. Wilson was my assiduous companion. He amused me with his stories about Tabriz and showed great interest in my memories of childhood in Urmia. By the end of the conference, I felt as if I had known him for years.

Before the conference adjourned, Mr. Wilson said, "Next month I will be going to the Presbyterian General Assembly in Milwaukee and will pass through Lake Forest. I will arrange to visit your mother then."

"We do not need to say 'goodbye' then, do we?" I said.

"We will see each other again," he replied with a broad smile. "Of that I am certain."

Mr. Wilson wrote to Mother, and with her usual generosity she invited him to stay a day or two at our house. In May, he visited Lake Forest as promised, and Mother and I found him entertaining. He told stories of his first year in Tabriz and difficulties with the native languages. "Making mistakes with words in Azeri often caused me problems. One day I wanted to buy a rug in the bazaar. I hired a young boy to carry it to my house and he arrived with a samovar. When I told him it was a mistake, he handed me my receipt — I had bought a samovar, not a rug. I kept it, being too embarrassed to return it. Since then, I have learned to enjoy tea."

"I will need some time in the kitchen to prepare dinner," Mother said. "I suggest you and Annie take a walk. The cherry trees along the path to Lake Michigan are in full bloom."

"That would truly be a pleasure," Mr. Wilson responded, and offered me his arm. "Shall we?"

We strolled through the Lake Forest College campus, following a secluded dirt path surrounded by flowering cherry trees. I had become comfortable with Mr. Wilson's presence and felt little apprehension about being alone with him. He talked pleasantly about how glorious the spring was in Tabriz with the blooming almond trees.

Suddenly a man jumped out in front of us from behind a tree.

"Goodness," I gasped, and found myself clinging to Mr. Wilson's arm. It was Mr. Van Beheren, a faculty member and colleague at Ferry Hall.

"Sorry if I alarmed you, Miss Rhea," Mr. Van Beheren said. "I was snooping around to see if you were a Ferry Hall girl making a rendezvous with an Academy boy."

Mr. Wilson laughed loudly as we watched Mr. Van Beheren retreat back into the trees. When I turned, I was surprised to see Mr. Wilson in front of me kneeling on one knee. "What are you doing?" I asked.

"I decided to ask for your hand in marriage," Mr. Wilson said. "This seemed to be as good a time and place as any."

"What?" I exclaimed.

"I came back to America hoping to find a wife to take back to Persia," Mr. Wilson said. "When I met you, I was sure you were the one."

I could hardly believe my ears. "But I don't know you at all," I protested.

"I understand your surprise and hesitation," Mr. Wilson replied. "Would you be willing to keep the question open and correspond with me over the next few months?"

"Yes, we can correspond," I replied, thinking of nothing else I could say. He seemed pleased with my response.

When I told Mother that Mr. Wilson had proposed to me, she said, "Nothing would please me better."

The next day Mr. Wilson left for the General Assembly and sent an elegant box of candy.

His letters began to shower our mailbox, ardent and beautifully written, and I began to look forward to their arrival. On a second visit to Lake Forest, he gave a sermon at the First Presbyterian Church and was invited to a dinner at the Manse. He gave a talk at Ferry Hall on the missionary hospital in Tehran that Mother had secured donations to build. His visit started rumors and raised suspicions. "What does he want?" the people of Lake Forest whispered.

In July I was happy to get away from the gossip and go to Jonesborough, Tennessee with Mother and the family. Mr. Wilson followed me there with the ruse that he came to give sermons at the Jonesborough Presbyterian Church, across the street from Afton Hall. Grandmother Cunningham had the young visiting missionary pastor stay at her house. Mother and I knew he was there to pursue his courtship. *Did Grandmother know too?*

One afternoon Mr. Wilson arranged for us to take a carriage ride. He went to the livery stable beforehand to make sure the buggy was spotless and the horse well-looked after. I still remember the touch of his strong warm hand as he helped me mount the step to the carriage. His touch made me reflective and as we rode through Jonesborough, I quietly listened to his banter.

After we passed through town and reached the countryside, the air smelled of newly cut hay. I took in a deep breath and turned toward Mr. Wilson. "My answer is 'yes,' " I said. "I will be your wife and return with you to Persia."

He stopped the carriage abruptly and reached for my hand. "You have made me the happiest man alive," he said. Then with a laugh, he started the horse on a gallop and shouted, "We are off to Persia." The horse and the carriage sped along the road, kicking up a storm of dust.

That night at dinner we made the announcement to the family. "Did that come about in your few weeks here giving sermons?" Grandmother Cunningham asked.

Before Sam answered, Mother interjected, "She knows better."

Although Grandmother Cunningham and my cousins wanted the wedding to be held at Afton Hall, Mother insisted on having it in Lake Forest. After Mr. Wilson returned to Indiana, Pennsylvania to tell his family, he sent a diamond ring by registered mail, inscribed with S.G.W. to A.D.R. (Samuel Graham Wilson to Annie Dwight Rhea.)

Everything was a whirlwind after that. With only a few weeks in Lake Forest before the wedding, Mother ordered a trousseau from Wanamaker's in Philadelphia and located a dressmaker in Chicago. My best friend, Anna Holt, took the train with me to Chicago to try on the wedding dress.

"I think you were wise to choose a dark color," the dressmaker said as she drew the curtains. "That way you can wear it to other formal occasions."

The dress was a warm brown color with golden overtones. The collar was trimmed with white lace ruffles and long sleeves with matching white ruffles at the wrists. The bodice buttoned up from the waist to the neck with tightly spaced ceramic buttons. From the waist down, the fabric folded and flowed down to the floor, and in the back, there was ample drapery for a small bustle, but no trail.

"Is it too practical looking?" I asked Anna, who was looking at me in solemn surprise.

"Why no," Anna exclaimed. "You look stately."

"Stately? Whatever do you mean?"

"As though you are ready to conquer the world."

On the way back on the train, I looked over and saw a tear running down Anna's cheek. "What is it?" I exclaimed.

"I am so sad that you cannot be the maid of honor for my wedding to Arthur Wheeler in December," she cried. "I do not know who could replace you."

"Oh Anna," I cried, "I will miss you so much. Please promise you will write often."

"I will write you twice a day," she said and smiled mockingly. And we both laughed and cried the rest of the train ride to Lake Forest and walked home, hand in hand.

A week before the wedding, Sam came by train. I almost did not recognize him on the platform with his beard shaven. He was accompanied by his stern-looking brother Robert Dick Wilson, Professor of Hebrew. "Rob can speak forty-six languages, including Syriac," Sam bragged. "He will visit us in Persia when he is researching ancient scriptures in the Middle East."

"I kept up with my Syriac by reading a passage in my Syriac Bible every day," Mother said, not to be out done.

"One of the first translations of the Old Testament was in Syriac," Rob exclaimed. "It was translated in the second century from the original Aramaic version…"

"Rob," Sam interjected. "We can talk about Bible translations later. Mrs. Rhea, please tell us what is planned for the wedding."

"Tomorrow you and Annie will have your photographs taken," Mother said. "A photographer is coming from Chicago."

"What shall we wear?" Sam asked, seemingly surprised.

"Your wedding clothes, of course."

"The day before the wedding there will be a church rehearsal and a dinner for the wedding party at the Holt mansion."

The wedding was September 16th. Sam's brother Rob was the best man, my sister Sophea was the maid of honor, Anna Holt was my only bridesmaid, and my brother Foster gave me away. The church was full of old friends, many coming up from Chicago. The ceremony was presided over by Rev. James McClure, the minister of the Lake Forest Presbyterian Church

After the reception in the chapel, Sam and I stood at the door of the church waiting for the carriage to the train station. "Everything was perfect except now it is raining," I bemoaned.

"In Persia rain on your wedding day is a good omen," Mother interjected.

"What about the wedding presents?" I asked. "We cannot pack them in my trunk."

"Sophea offered to write thank you notes," Mother said. "I will send the presents to Persia."

A carriage, bedecked with flowers, took Sam and I to the six o'clock train. We sat together in our cabin glowing in the aftermath. I was in such a daze that I did not fully realize that I would not see Lake Forest or my family again for another eight years.

Before going to New York to embark on our journey to Persia we spent two weeks in Indiana, Pennsylvania so I could meet Sam's family. Harry, Sam's oldest brother, brought us to the Wilson homestead on the corner of Church and 7th Streets. Andrew Wilkins Wilson, Sam's father, was the first to greet me, a spry sixty-year-old man of medium stature with a long face and beard. "You are welcome here, daughter," he said. "Call this your home."

His words warmed my heart. Most my life I had been father-hungry, having lost my father at such a young age.

Sam's mother, Anna Graham Dick Wilson, was a small, cheerful woman with a sweet smile. Sitting down at the dinner table with ten sons and daughters she said, "I would be lonely if I did not have twelve at the table."

Harry, at thirty-two, was Sam's only married sibling. He had a house nearby with his wife Margaret and their baby, Harry Jr., who they called "Lad." Rob lived in Pittsburg and taught at Western Theological Seminary, Andy was in Law School, and Ella was a senior at Vassar College. The remaining children lived at home: Annie who was eighteen; John who was in his mid-twenties and the four teenagers — Annie, Dick, Jennie, and Agnes. It was a loyal and convivial family. When I accepted Sam's proposal, I had not anticipated the additional joy that belonging to his family would provide me.

Father Wilson took us for a tour around Indiana. We visited his dry goods store, Wilson & Son, at 642 Philadelphia Street, a beautiful red brick building with a rounded decorative cornice. "It was constructed in 1880," he said. "My son Harry is my partner and John is a cashier. My brother Joseph's son Willis works here as well as other relatives. It is a real family business."

After seeing the Wilson store, we visited the Normal School that he co-founded with John Sutton, his late business partner. "I knew that for the community to prosper we needed good schools.

The Normal School attracts the most innovative educators," Father Wilson said. "All of our children have attended the school and the four younger ones are currently enrolled."

"Father taught us to value education," Sam said. "Harry, Robert, Andy and I were graduated from Princeton, and father expects his daughters, in addition to Ella, to attend college."

Our departure at the train station was a sorrowful farewell to the Wilson family. Mother Wilson hugged us with tears flowing down her cheeks. "Let us know that you have arrived safely," Father Wilson said. "Your mother will be worried sick until she hears from you."

Annie Rhea Wilson, 1886   Samuel Graham Wilson, 1886

Wilson family, 1886: back row (left to right) John, Ella, Samuel, Annie; second row (left to right) Dick, Father Wilson, Mother Wilson, Robert, Harry; front (left to right) Agnes, Jenny, Andy.

CHAPTER 5

October 1886 — New York to the Caucasus

ON OCTOBER 2ND, OUR SHIP STEAMED OUT OF NEW YORK harbor for England. As we stood on the deck my heart throbbed in my throat. *The last time I traveled across the Atlantic Ocean I was eight years old. There is no turning back now.*

Sam's warm fingers slipped through mine as though he understood that I needed reassurance. "We are lucky to be traveling alone," he said. "Usually, missionaries travel in groups to and from furlough. On my first trip I sailed with three other new recruits and Mary Jewett, a ten-year veteran. She was tasked with teaching all four of us Azeri, Armenian, and Persian before we reached our destination. After our honeymoon in Europe, I will begin your instruction in the native languages of northern Persia."

This is the first time that we will be alone together, day and night, and in close quarters. I blushed thinking of dressing and undressing in Sam's presence.

When we changed for dinner, I turned quickly unbuttoned and removed my dress with my back toward Sam. Dressed only in my bloomers and corset, I heard him approach. He wrapped his arms around my waist and kissed the top of my head. "Our small cabin is hardly romantic enough for consummation," he whispered. "Besides we have hardly become used to each other's touch."

He is as apprehensive as I am. I turned and smiled, kissing him lightly on the lips. "Yes, I agree, my dear Samuel."

Crossing the Atlantic, we roamed the deck and read in the parlor each day. The middle of the seventh day, we arrived in Liverpool and took a train to London, where we officially initiated our honeymoon in the Hotel L'Europa. We spent the month of October touring London, Paris, Brussels and Berlin. Sam's brother Rob gave us one hundred dollars as a wedding present which afforded us sumptuous meals, such as a dinner in Paris at La Tour d'Argent with a view of Notre Dame from our table.

In November we boarded a ship from Hamburg for St. Petersburg. We were surprised by the snow and sleighs dashing down the Nevsky Prospect, the main street of the city. At the train station I noticed Russians crossing themselves when they passed Christian icons hanging on posts.

"I did not realize how profoundly religious Russians are," I exclaimed.

Sam laughed. "You mean the icons? Russians are highly superstitious and think they will be cursed if they do not cross as they walk by."

"And sitting silently before boarding the train, is that another superstition?"

"Yes, it guarantees their safe journey," Sam replied. "Persians are profoundly superstitious too. They wear amulets called *nazars* to protect them from the 'Evil Eye.' If one is about to embark on a trip and sneezes, it is a sign of bad luck, and the trip is postponed. If someone sneezes in the dispensary when they are handed medicine, they drop the medicine on the floor and run away in terror."

"Perhaps we should cross ourselves in front of the icons to avert a train wreck," I said.

It was three days by train to Nalchik — the first day traveling through a vast monotonous plain of farmland and the second day through rolling hills. Rostov was the first major stop, a charming town with a prominent Russian Orthodox church with a bright turquoise roof and shining gold domes. "One more day by train," Sam said, "then we travel by troika over the Greater Caucasus Mountains to Tiflis."

"What is a troika?" I asked.

"A wagon drawn by three horses abreast," Sam replied. "When moving at top speed of thirty miles per hour, the middle horse trots while the side horses canter. I find it exhilarating."

In the early morning we reached Nalchik and the train screeched to a halt. "This is the end of the line of the Russian railroad," Sam said.

Looking out the window I understood why; the Greater Caucasus Mountains rose abruptly to the south — an imposing, white-capped wall of granite over ten thousand feet high.

"Are we leaving the last vestige of Western civilization and going into the wilderness?" I asked.

"You will be surprised how well the military road is maintained and the number of villages along the way," Sam replied. "This was once where the Silk Road from Asia entered Russia."

Our troika driver was a large, black-bearded man wearing a sheepskin fez, brown trousers, leather boots, and a thick woolen jacket with stripes of red, green, and orange. Sam and I sat behind the driver on seats padded with hay, serving the dual purpose of comfort for passengers and feed for the horses. "Stunning steeds," I said. The large muscular horses seemed to frolic in the foothills on the first segment of our trip to Vladikavkaz. The next day we ascended over three thousand feet, and the troika perilously careened next to a precipice. The memory from my childhood was relived, when our wagon teetered on the edge of a cliff, and I prayed for an angel to save us.

We arrived at the charming village of Stepantsminda on a plateau between Mount Kazbeck and Mount Shani, with peaks reaching over fifteen thousand feet. Needing to stretch our legs, we hiked to a fourteenth century church perched on the mountainside. The rooms at the travelers' inn were dirty and cramped but we easily slept with the fresh mountain air.

We left before dawn and summited the mountain range at Cross Pass, where daylight emerged through a rose-colored sky. The fertile green valley of Transcaucasia stretched far below us, the Caspian Sea reflected the sun to the east, and the Black Sea glimmered to the west. "It is like seeing earth from a far-off star," I murmured.

"Perhaps this is how God sees the Earth," Sam replied.

The descent from the summit was more perilous that the ascent. The troika drivers and horses, having passed over the road many times, were not intimidated by the narrow winding passage and proceeded at a full speed, twice coming to an abrupt halt to negotiate herds of sheep blocking the road.

When we reached Tiflis, my legs were numb from sitting and buckled when I stepped down from the wagon. Sam entered a shop and emerged with two mats, each rolled and tied with a cloth band. "We have another three hundred miles to Persia, then eighty miles to Tabriz," Sam said. "For the rest of the journey we will be sleeping at post houses or in tents on these travel beds."

I squeezed a rolled mat between my fingers. "Are they stuffed with wool?" I asked.

"Yes," Sam replied, "and good insulation from the frozen ground."

From Tiflis, we ascended the foothills of the Lesser Caucasus Mountains, traveling through forests of pine and beech. At seven thousand feet above sea level, we stopped at a lake. "We're at Lake Sevan," Sam said. "The water is pure and refreshing." The troika driver caught trout and cooked them on sticks over a fire. "*Ishkhan*," he said as he handed me a stick of cooked fish.

"*Ishkan* is the Armenian name for the Sevan trout," Sam explained.

The fish had a superbly delicate flavor, and I savored every morsel. After nightfall, we slipped into our tent and slept close together on our mats. The next day we passed through small mountain villages of wood houses with towers of hay on the roofs.

"The hay serves a dual purpose," Sam explained. "Storage of feed for the animals and it deflects the rain and snow."

As we turned a bend in the road, a majestic snow-capped mountain with two peaks appeared.

"*Kuh-e-Nuh* is the Persian name for Mount Ararat," Sam said. "It is a holy place. From the Bible and local legend, the top of Mount Ararat is believed to be the final resting place for Noah's Ark after the one hundred and fifty days of the great flood. To the weary missionary traveling back to Persia, it is a welcome sign. A view of the two peaks of Mount Ararat will be ahead of us for the next two days."

"How high is Mount Ararat?" I asked.

"Greater Ararat is seventeen thousand feet and little Ararat is thirteen thousand feet," Sam replied.

"Has anyone summited Ararat?" I asked.

"Superstitions and stories surround attempts to summit Ararat," Sam said. "A monk named Jacob was determined to find the Ark. On his first attempt he was overcome with sleepiness and awoke to find himself back where he had started. On his second attempt, the result was the same. On his third attempt, an angel appeared and told him that touching the Ark was forbidden but gave him a small piece of wood from the Ark as a reward for his persistence. The piece of the Ark is safely stored in the treasury of the monastery of Etchmiadzin, the world's oldest cathedral."

That afternoon we arrived in Erivan, surrounded by vineyards, fields and orchards. "An oasis on the bleak plain," Sam exclaimed. "Noah lived part of his life in this little paradise."

We took a room in the village posthouse for the night and sitting on our mattresses Sam read Genesis 8:1-5, the story of Noah and the Ark. "How did Noah know the waters had subsided?" Sam asked, testing me.

"He sent forth a dove out of the Ark," I replied. " 'And the dove came back to him in the evening, and lo, in her mouth a freshly plucked olive leaf,' Genesis 8:11."

"The Caucasus is thought to be the original home of the olive tree," Sam said, "which further supports the claim that the Ark landed here."

As we traveled the next day Sam said, "When we have a chance, we will visit the Urmia mission. Your childhood friends Joe Cochran, Fred Coan and Emma Cochran are resident missionaries."

"Mother told me Josie and Fred returned, but I had no idea that Emma had too."

"She returned last year. Did your mother tell you the story about Emma Cochran and the Kurd named Kurdu?"

"No. What happened?"

"Mrs. Cochran was touring the Christian villages of Targawar and brought eight-year-old Emma with her. One night they camped outside the village of Umbi, where Kurdu lived. Emma was lying on a rug next to Mrs. Cochran, who woke in the middle of the night and saw the rug where Emma was lying slowly moving out of the tent. Mrs. Cochran screamed, and Kurdu was frightened away."

"Why did he want to take Emma?" I asked.

"Kurdu saw cute little Emma and decided to abduct her for his harem."

"Do they take girls often?"

"Sometimes they take pupils from the Girls' School in Urmia. More often they see a young couple traveling, kill the husband and take the wife."

My stomach seized, and I looked hard at Sam. He smiled and patted my hand. "They probably would not bother killing me, since I am a sound sleeper, but I might not know you are gone until the morning."

"Would you come after me?"

"Without a rifle? I cannot say that I would."

I gave Sam a swift kick in the leg and pouted. "Some husband you turned out to be."

The next day, an Englishman engaged us in conversation before we were on our way. "Did you hear about the Russian soldier who ran into a band of Kurds last night?"

"No, what happened?" Sam asked.

"They wanted his horse and he resisted so they stripped him of his clothes, his watch and his money. He found his way to the house of the telegraph operator who clothed him and let him stay."

"You see, Annie?" Sam said. "The Kurds are notorious bandits."

"And she will see them for herself," the Englishman added. "The Kurds are camped on a hill outside of town."

My breath became shallow as our troika passed a group of men by the side of the road. They wore wool hats the shape of beehives, coats and long baggie pants tied with wound cloth belts. From their belts hung long curved swords in sheaths. Up the hill was a large encampment of black tents. I hid my face in my hands, not wanting to meet the men's gaze. "They fancy you, Annie," Sam whispered.

The road ahead was treacherous, with cliffs on either side. At one point the troika leaned towards the edge of a hill and barely escaped toppling down the side. Squeezing between the two sides of a rocky passage, a high-pitched sound of scraping metal caused me to wince and the rest of the day the wheel wobbled. I prayed that the wheel would not fall off and was relieved when the walls of a city appeared ahead.

"We have arrived at Nakhchivan," Sam exclaimed, "and none too soon."

CHAPTER 6

November 1886 — Nakhchivan to Tabriz

"THE TROIKA DRIVER ANNOUNCED THAT HE WOULD SEEK repair of the carriage wheel before continuing to Julfa," Sam said.

"I am relieved that the wheel is being fixed even though the delay is disappointing," I said. "How long will we be here?"

Sam laughed. "The pace of life in the Caucasus is that of Asia, not Europe. As Rudyard Kipling said: 'A fool lies here who tried to hustle the East.' "

"I must remember that every time I grow impatient," I said.

"You will not regret our short stay in Nakhchivan; it is an interesting town. The name means 'he descended first.' Legend is that Noah settled here after emerging from the Ark with his wife, Emzara, and his children. His grave is in an Armenian cemetery."

"I would certainly like to see Noah's grave," I exclaimed.

Noah's monument was an unassuming octagonal stone and brick structure built into the side of a small hill, eight feet in diameter and four feet above the ground. The underground vault was accessed from two sides of the monument, each with steps leading down to a heavy wooden door. Inside the vault, a central pillar supported the arches of the ceiling and contained a recessed alter where incense burned. "The pillar is hollow and acts like a flue for the incense smoke," Sam explained.

I noticed a haphazard arrangement of stones of various sizes on the mud-plastered ceiling. "The stones on the ceiling look as though they could fall off at any instant," I exclaimed.

"Oh yes, the stones," Sam said. "Legend is that if a worshipper pushes a stone on the ceiling and it sticks, their prayers will be answered."

"Goodness, I must try it then," I exclaimed.

"We will need to go outside and find a proper stone," Sam replied and led me up the steps. "Pick carefully," he added solemnly.

I wandered off to the side of a hill where rocks had accumulated from erosion. I knelt down and prayed, "Lord, please let me pick the stone that will stick to the ceiling. I will pray for true love with my husband and our happiness together in Persia."

With closed eyes I felt the stones below me and one with jagged edges pricked my palm. "Why this could stick," I whispered. I stood up smiling and returned with Sam to the crypt. My first attempt to get the stone to stick to the ceiling failed, so I turned it over and tried again. After pressing the stone hard against the dried mud, it stayed when I cautiously withdrew my hand, but fell before I could claim victory.

"Try again," Sam said eagerly. "You almost had it."

Determined, I pressed my stone firmly against the ceiling with the fingertips of my right hand and counted out loud to seven. "The flood waters came seven days after Noah entered the Ark," I said as I slowly released the pressure. "Genesis 7:10."

The stone was still on the ceiling when we departed, and my heart welled with pride. "This is the most sacred place that I have ever been," I said. "I will always remember this."

We traveled across a fertile plateau with farms and herds of sheep as we slowly descended to Julfa on the Aras River. "It is time to depart from the troikas and drivers who have been our constant companions for the past six days," Sam said. As we bid them farewell, another party loaded their baggage to head in the opposite direction. "They run a good business," Sam commented. "As for us, tomorrow we will cross the Aras River and be in Persia."

The ferry across the Aras River consisted of a flat wooden platform suspended above the water by large timbers and secured to either side of the river by a long sturdy wire. In the frosty morning air, we huddled together sitting on our pile of baggage as the pilot turned a wheel that slowly propelled the platform seventy-five yards across the river. "This is the same primitive means by which the founder of the mission in Urmia, Rev. Justin Perkins, crossed the river over fifty years ago," Sam said.

"He was with our party in 1869 when Mother returned with us to America," I replied. "I remember that he let us children call him 'Grandpa Perkins.' We must have taken the ferry then, but I cannot remember it."

A Persian official at the dock took our passports and questioned Sam in Azeri. Although I could not comprehend what they were saying, I could sense Sam's exasperation by his brusque responses. *Will we ever get through customs?*

Sam reached in his pocket and handed the customs official a coin and smiles were exchanged. "What was that about?" I asked.

"He asked, 'Are you Persian?' to which I replied, 'No. We are Americans as it says on our passports.' "

"Did he think they were forged?" I asked.

"No. He said, 'I can't read.' Then I asked, 'What is the charge?' and he replied. 'Whatever favor you wish to confer.' I gave him a kran as *anam*."

"*Anam*?"

"Yes, there are three types of payments to Persians, other than for buying goods: a fee or tip for a legitimate service is called '*anam*;' giving money, or alms, to an inferior, say a beggar, is called '*bakshish*;' and a gift to a superior to procure a favor is called '*peeshkesh*.' The latter is how many of the noblemen of Persia receive their titles."

"Not by merit or virtue?"

"No, through *peeshkesh*. Officials with meaningless titles all over Persia and members of the Shah's retinue are experts at demanding graft. *Peeshkesh* and *mudakhil*, official swindling, are both open and universal in Persia."

"Do missionaries also engage in *peeshkesh* and *mudakhil*?"

"Of course not," Sam replied with a sigh, "but it marks us as culturally unintegrated foreigners. Missionaries get into trouble with officials, who expect *peeshkesh*. When they do not receive it they levy a 'fine.'"

For the next four days, I rode in a mule-drawn wagon with our baggage and Sam rode alongside on horseback. My frame was constantly jolted as the wheels of the wagon passed over the rocky riverbed of the Incheh Chai. Towards evening the muleteer stopped at a quadrangular building with thick mud walls and small windows on the second floor. In the central court at least a hundred camels grazed on hay. "Where are we?" I asked.

"In Galin Kaiya," Sam replied. "This is a *caravanserai*, a type of inn, quite minimalistic. It is why we carry traveler beds. We will be lucky if there is an unoccupied room judging by all the camels, sheep and donkeys in the courtyard."

Sam spoke earnestly with the muleteer in Azeri and shook his head as he approached the wagon. "No rooms for the night, but we can sleep in the stable."

"Like Joseph and Mary?" I asked.

"I often sleep in the stable while on tour in the villages," Sam replied. "It is comfortable sleeping on the hay, if it is not infested with fleas."

Sam bought bread and cheese and we ate sitting cross-legged on the hay accompanied by the "music" of oxen snorting and chickens cackling. I was thankful to only wake once in the night to a biting flea.

The second and third nights in Marand and Sufian we found rooms at *caravanserais*. Grotesque frescos of the animals covered the walls, but none were the breathing cackling or snorting kind we slept with in Galin Kaiya. With the temperature at night near freezing, I was glad to find that our rooms were supplied with oval clay braziers containing burning coals. We placed our travel beds on the floor on either side of our brazier and covered ourselves with heavy wool quilts.

"Every day I have tried to learn ten Azeri words," I said, "but I am afraid even with about five hundred words, I have a long way to go."

"Do you remember what *peshwaz* means?" Sam asked.

"It means 'welcome to travelers,' " I said proudly.

"Yes, it is a Persian custom for friends to ride miles out to meet travelers coming from afar. The day after tomorrow, when we near Tabriz, a *peshwaz* will honor our arrival. Do you remember how to greet them?"

"*Salam alakum*," I said. "Peace be with you."

On December 11th, the last day of our journey, frost covered the ground, and the breath of Sam's horse and the mules formed clouds around us. I rocked my feet back and forth on the wagon floor to keep them from going numb with cold. Sam was nervous with anticipation and fixed his eyes on the horizon. "I think I see them," he shouted and galloped ahead, only to return later crest-fallen. "Only a peasant with his oxen."

The muleteer stopped for lunch of bread and hard-boiled eggs and Sam joined me in the wagon. "The mission in Tabriz consists of three other couples and three single women: Dr. George Washington Holmes, our medical missionary, and his wife Eliza; Reverend Jeremiah Oldfather, a pastor in the church, and his wife Felicia; and Reverend Samuel Ward and his wife Irene. The ladies who teach at the Girls' School and visit the Persian women are Mary Jewett, Grettie Holliday and Loretta Van Hook. Reverend William Whipple and his wife Mary are American Bible agents who live across the street from the mission. Although not formally part of the mission the Whipples are included in our social gatherings."

"Are any of the women my age?" I asked.

"They are all ten to fifteen years older than you."

"Goodness, they will all treat me like a child," I responded.

"The men are at least fifteen years older than me and were a great help when I arrived."

Just then a young man came galloping up on his horse. "Yacob," Sam cried. They shouted in Armenian, the young man pointed down the road, and Sam rode off with him. *Who is Yacob? Where are they going?*

I was aghast when Sam returned, galloping toward the wagon with large party of men on horseback — Americans and Europeans, followed by Persians in bright-colored costumes. After many *salaams* our joyous cavalcade continued another three hours to the gates of Tabriz. Sam rode ahead boisterously shouting at the man riding next to him, never looking back to acknowledge his wife in the mule-drawn wagon slowly following behind. *I feel like a piece of baggage.*

Yacob was finally introduced to me when we arrived at the mission. "Yacob was one of my first students," Sam said. "He is now a teacher at the Boys' School. He has agreed to give you lessons in Azeri."

"*Khanum,*" Yacob said with an enchanting smile. "*Salam alakum.*"

CHAPTER 7

December 11th, 1886

IT WAS DARK WHEN THE WAGON DRIVER STOPPED IN FRONT of an adobe house. "This is home," Sam announced. He dismounted his horse and took my hand to help me down from the wagon. An old man wearing baggy trousers, a wool jacket and a round felt hat stood at the open door.

Who is this? When he kissed Sam's cheek I was overcome by a wave of apprehension and held my breath as I approached. The man merely beckoned me inside out of the cold with swift waves of his hand, saying "*Khanum, salaam alakum.*"

The house was warm and fully lit. A woman wearing a full skirt and a handkerchief over her long, braided hair slipped next to the man's side. Contrary to my expectations, Sam and I had not arrived at a house that had been vacant for over a year. *Does another couple live here?*

"Ishak is our general factotum, and his wife Miriam is our cook," Sam said to me in English. "This is Annie, my wife," Sam said in English and then repeated the same in Azeri. The man and woman nodded their heads respectfully. I smiled and nodded back. *How should I greet people with whom we are sharing our house?*

"How long have you lived here?" I asked.

"I have rented this house for the past five years," Sam replied. "It is well suited and enormously convenient; the two-room mission Boys' School is in the front yard by the road. You will see it tomorrow."

The rooms were comfortably furnished with European furniture and Persian rugs. Ishak and his wife Miriam lived down a hallway at the end of the house adjacent to the kitchen. The other end of the hallway opened to a living and dining room on one side and a study and bedroom on the other side. A flight of steps against the outside wall led to a guest room perched on the flat roof.

"How do you like it?" Sam asked, studying my face.

"The house is pleasant," I replied, "only I did not know we would be sharing the house with another couple."

"Ishak and Miriam take care of the house and cooking and will continue to do so," Sam explained. "With teaching classes at the Boys' School and visitations with Persian women, you will not have time for housekeeping."

I feel like a second wife with the household already established and overseen by another woman.

"I will need to learn the native languages in order to perform those functions," I said.

"You will learn quickly given the urgency of being able to communicate in the native languages," Sam said. "Five days a week Yacob will teach you Azeri and Armenian. One day a week a teacher from the Boys' School will give you Persian lessons."

"Why so many days for Azeri and Armenian?" I asked.

"They are the more difficult languages for English speakers, and the ones most used in northern Persia. Many words are similar in sound but different in meaning, for instance *dava* means 'a brawl or fighting,' *daha* means 'more,' and *dua* mean 'prayer.' One missionary woman on tour saw horses kicking and biting and reported that 'the horses are having a *dua*,' a prayer, instead of *dava*, a brawl, which brought her hostler to his knees in hysterical laughter."

The next day was Sunday, December 12th and I was happy to have a day of rest after traveling for ten weeks. Sam and I attended the morning church service led by Rev. Jeremiah Oldfather in Azeri. The church service was well attended by Persians, and I admittedly paid more attention to the congregation than the sermon that I could not comprehend.

"Do you give sermons in the mission church?" I asked.

"I occasionally give a sermon when Rev. Oldfather is sick or away," Sam replied, "but preparing sermons and leading the church service are not aspects of missionary work that best suit me. Teaching at the Boys' School and touring in the outfield are responsibilities that make better use of my aptitudes. Spreading the gospel in the villages is most enjoyable work. I am always intrigued by life outside the large cities of Persia, and I enjoy the long horseback rides in the country."

"How long are you usually away on a tour?" I asked.

"Frequently I will be gone one or two weeks at a time," Sam replied. "When my destinations are five to twelve days journey on horseback, I will be gone longer, usually four to eight weeks."

"Give me an example so I can understand better what it is like to go on tour."

"There is not a wealth of entertainment in Persia, so anything out of the ordinary excites interest. Upon entering a village, word spreads quickly that there is a *tamasha*, an event. Curiosity draws a large crowd to hear what the missionaries have to say and follow them wherever they go."

"*Tamasha*," I said. "What a wonderful word."

"Wait until you become the object of *tamasha*, the spectacle to behold. You might be intimidated, as I was at first."

"Where do you stay on tour?" I asked.

"In the village, we often rent a room in a house, sometimes that means sharing the common room with only a curtain to separate us from the owners. I often prefer to sleep in a stable or in a tent outside of the village."

"Will I accompany you on your trips?"

"When you have a command of Azeri you will join me and share the gospel with the women in the villages while I speak with the men," Sam replied. "When you have learned Armenian, I will take you to Karadagh to the speak to the Armenian women in the mountains, one of my favorite destinations."

"Armenians?" I exclaimed.

"They are the largest minority in northwest Persia," Sam replied. "Of the thirty thousand Armenians in Persia, six thousand reside in Tabriz. The city is divided into twenty-four wards or districts. Our mission is situated in the *Lawala*, between *Ahrab*, a predominantly Muslim district, and *Baron Avak*, where many Persian Armenians reside."

"Are the Persian Armenians Muslims?" I asked.

"Most Persian Armenians belong to the Christian Gregorian Church," Sam replied.

"Why do Presbyterian missionaries evangelize Armenians if they are already Christian?"

"We consider them 'nominally Christian,' " Sam replied. "When I go to an Armenian village and ask, 'Who was Christ?' they answer, 'Christ was born out of the side of Mary and spoke as a newborn. The Jews killed him.' I once asked a Gregorian priest in Karadagh, 'Who was Jesus, and who was Christ?' and he replied, 'They say that Hesous was a brother of Christos.' In the villages a peasant or a blacksmith without religious training can become a priest. They do not know the Scriptures. However, the sign of the cross is of great importance. Boys wear jackets with brightly colored crosses on the back, and when asked what it means they repeat a formula for the Trinity. The church services are ritualistic and omit the teaching of Christian moral principles. The Gregorian priest and bishop speak in ancient Armenian, a language that the congregation does not understand."

"What do you say to the villagers?"

"Whether we are standing by the threshing floors, at the blacksmith shop, or with a crowd under the mulberry trees, we talk about what the Scriptures say about Sin, Righteousness and Salvation. When we talk about Sin, they say, 'We are steeped in sin. We steal, cheat, slander, extort. We do not know how to do otherwise. No one has taught us.' Another man says, 'If my sins were put into the deep valley near the village, they would fill it so that you could walk on the level.' "

"Will converting them change how sinful they are?"

"Our practical goal is to teach Persians the moral messages in the Scriptures, something lacking in the services given by the bishop in the Gregorian Church and the *mullah* in the Islamic Mosque. If our efforts result in their conversion and they join the Presbyterian Church that is an added blessing."

"Doesn't the law of the Qur'an command that one who forsakes their Islam faith be put to death?"

"Yes, the threat remains, but persecution by friends and family is the more typical outcome. The army commander, the *Sipahsalar*, assured me in private that if any Muslim becomes Christian, he would be protected."

"How do the Gregorian bishops react to Presbyterian missionaries spreading the gospel among their Armenian congregations?"

"As you can imagine, the Bishop of the Gregorian Church in Tabriz vehemently opposes our efforts to enlighten the Armenians. He is particularly angered that many Armenians attend the mission church services on Sunday afternoon. He tells his congregation that we have no baptism, no wedlock and that we spit on the picture of the Virgin Mary. One Gregorian bishop in Khoi said, 'By going to the Prots,' meaning Protestants, 'you will become contaminated in two months and become lepers.' "

"Scare tactics. Do Armenian boys attend the mission Boys' School?"

"Yes, most of our students are Armenians. When it comes to education Armenian parents are keen on their boys, and to some extent their girls, being well-educated. They know that the Presbyterian mission schools provide excellent educational training for their children."

"What about the Persian Muslims? Are they prejudiced against us too?"

"Even more so. The Muslims consider Christians to be unclean and consider our touch to be contaminating. Muslim vendors in the bazaars demand that we point to what we want to buy rather than touching their wares. Our medical missionary, Dr. Holmes, is the exception. Regardless of faith, he helps Persians in desperate need of medical treatment and must examine them. Staying overnight in the hospital room, under a 'Christian roof,' however, is usually objectionable to Muslim patients."

"How do you perform your missionary work surrounded by such prejudice and bigotry?"

"With patience and persistence. Every week we see evidence of increasing tolerance and appreciation for our work. The Muslims are curious about our religion and come to the mission church services to listen. On rare occasions the *mullahs* complain to the mayor of Tabriz, the *beglar-begi*, and he has the police arrest Muslims as they exit our church. Then a year or so will go by without interference."

"Do Muslims send their children to the mission schools?"

"The Muslim parents are resistant thus far and the government is capricious, sometimes imposing restrictions. It is due to our requirement that our students take Bible classes. Mary Jewett and I have discussed offering separate departments for Muslims and Armenians, but currently we do not have the resources, either classrooms or teachers, to commit to this. It is my goal to find a way to make our schools accessible to Muslim children."

"I have faith in you," I said. "I am committed to helping you obtain your goal someday."

"We have a formidable task," Sam replied. "I will be glad to have you working by my side."

"Let's go for a walk and I will introduce you to Tabriz, your new home," Sam said.

My home? When will I be able to call it home?

"What should I wear?" I asked.

"Dress warmly and conservatively," Sam replied. "It is below freezing, and the Persian women will find your dress curious, crowd around and try to touch you."

"Where are we going?"

"We are heading for *Kala*, the old district. The streets will become crowded close to the bazaar, and you need to hold my hand, or I will lose you in the crowd."

On our journey from Julfa to Tabriz I saw single-story mud houses in the villages, but somehow expected the houses in Tabriz to be grander. In place of glass many houses had windows covered with oiled paper that reflected the morning sunlight with a strange yellowish glare. Walls, twenty feet high, blocked the view of the yards. "Where are the house entrances?" I asked.

"At the bottom of a small flight of stairs you can see the entry gate surrounded by checkered or multicolored pilasters," Sam said. "The plain house exteriors are deceiving. Inside the gates are often beautiful gardens and separate extravagantly decorated suites for men and women. You will be surprised when you visit Persian homes."

Sam thrust me against a wall. A drove of donkeys careened down the street crowding on one another and over the sidewalks. He laughed as I regained my breath. "Tabriz is donkeys *par excellence*," he declared. "There are donkeys carrying baskets of fruit or firewood, others carrying butchered animals strapped to their back, others with enormous mounds of hay or thorn bushes secured by netting. The ones carrying building materials are most hazardous; bricks falling off and poles dragging behind ready to hit a passerby in the shins."

"My favorite are the white donkeys mounted by white-turbaned men wearing flowing white robes," I said. "How interesting their sandals are with their pointed, turned-up toes. But how do they navigate the ice and snow wearing sandals in the winter?"

"They are the high priests of Islam," Sam said. "*Mullahs*. They are carried on the back of a servant to mount and dismount."

"Who then is a *sayyid*?" I asked.

"*Sayyids* are descendants of Muhammad and regarded as nobility," Sam replied.

"How can you tell a *mullah* from a *sayyid*?" I asked.

"They dress similarly but only the *sayyid* has the privilege of wearing a green turban."

A woman pushed confidently by us enveloped in a dark blue sheet, covering her from head to foot. As she shuffled by, I caught a glimpse of her eyes through small patches of lacework in her veil.

"She moves like a ghost," I whispered.

"She is wearing the traditional Muslim *hijab*, women's street clothes," Sam said. "It consists of *shalwar*, *chuddar* and veil. The *shalwar* is the pair of baggy trousers under which she wears her house dress. The trousers are gathered at the ankles and have stockings attached. The *chuddar* is a two-yard square of cloth, typically dark blue or black, that she wraps over her head and around her torso and lets it flow down below her knees. The veil has lacework in front of the eyes allowing her to see where she is going. A woman's social standing is presumed by the quality of her veil's lacework; the woman who passed had fine needle lacework called *sokmeh-doozy*, which indicates she is of the higher class. This woman is accompanying her husband, although you did not notice him. He is walking on the street some distance ahead."

As we emerged onto a central square, I noticed a man with disheveled hair wearing a skullcap wrapped with colorful bands of cloth. The skin of a fox with the head still intact was flung over one shoulder of his flowing muslin robe. In a loud voice, he beseeched passersby to listen to him waving a club at their face and yelling "*Ya hak, Ya hak.*"

"And who is that?" I exclaimed. "What is he yelling?"

"It is a *dervish*," Sam said. "He is crying, 'Oh Truth, Oh Truth.' They tell stories from the Qur'an or give a street session of poetry by Rumi or Hafez. I find them altogether romantic. They expect to be given *anam* in return for their performance. His collection box is that large Indian nutshell that he is holding from a strap, called a *kashgul*."

The dervish began strutting in front of a small crowd that had assembled. He grew more fervid as he spoke, his eyes flashing with excitement as he reached the climax of his tale. As we passed, the *dervish* lurched toward us and shook his club in my face. Petrified I grabbed onto Sam's waist and hid my face in his chest. We scurried off to the far side of the square.

"We will visit the Grand Bazaar, and get out of the cold," Sam said. "Then I think you will have had enough excitement for the day."

The Grand Bazaar was an extensive brick structure with high vaulted ceilings. Columnar piers at twelve feet intervals supported ceiling arches that spanned thirty feet. Between each pier was a shop with a dealer sitting on a rug with abacus and account books lying beside him. In front of the piers were Armenian silversmiths, each with a showcase of jewelry.

"What are the merchants doing?" I asked. "They do not appear to be tending to customers."

"One is smoking tobacco in a water pipe, called a *qalyan*; another is reading the Qur'an; and another is praying with his head bowed to the floor. They are still aware of the customers and keep an eye on their wares through the corners of their eyes."

Throngs of people rubbed against one another; pushing their way through the crowd. I held tight to Sam's hand to keep from being pushed away in the river of humanity. There was the constant cry "*Khabar-dar!*"

"What does *Khabar-dar* mean?" I asked.

"Literally it means 'Be wakeful,' " Sam said, "but we might translate it as 'Look here.' Are you enjoying this?"

"Yes," I responded, "but all the people, the pushing, the constant din. It makes me quite dizzy. You were right about it being enough excitement for one day."

Sam smiled. "We will come back in the spring when the streets and the bazaar are even more lively."

How could it be livelier? Will I ever be able to adapt to life in Persia?

Donkeys *par excellence* of Tabriz

Chapter 8

The Girls' School Teachers — Loretta Van Hook and
Grettie Holliday

"IF YOU'VE RECOVERED FROM YESTERDAY, I WOULD LIKE
to take you to visit the Girls' School today," Sam said. "It is in the
Gala district, about a mile away."

"Who is in charge of the Girls' School?" I asked.

"Loretta Van Hook and Grettie Holliday run the school and are
regarded with great affection by the pupils."

"What do the girls study?"

"Classes are held in language, literature, science, history, and
music," Sam said. "The girls are taught to read and write in Azeri,
Persian and English by native teachers. They learn needlework
and sell their pieces, bringing in one hundred dollars each year."

"What about religion?"

"The girls attend Bible Class and go with one of the missionary
women to learn practical missionary work."

At the end of a cobbled street, we approached a three-story red
brick building with Vienna-style arched windows and a veranda
running the length of the second floor. "This building houses both
the classrooms and dormitory for the Girls' School," Sam said.
"The school was built in 1882, funded by the Second Presbyterian
Church in Chicago. When digging the foundation, a pot of coins
was unearthed, and the workmen divided it amongst themselves.
Unfortunately, rumors circulated about treasure and all sorts of

scavengers descended on the property. To make matters worse, the government declared that permission had not been granted to build the school and demanded that work on the school be halted."

"What did you do?"

"Reverend Oldfather took matters into his hands and contacted Tehran. After a month's negotiations and payment of a building fee, a substitute for *peeshkesh*, they we were allowed to continue."

"How many girls attend the school?"

"The school was built for thirty girls, but it could likely take in fifty with crowding. The girls are primarily Persian Armenians and Jews. Someday we hope the Muslim girls will come."

On the first floor there was a suite of sunny meeting rooms, one with a steaming samovar. "This is where the missionary women meet for tea," Sam said. "You will soon be joining them."

Reaching the second floor we were met by the shrill voices and laughter of young girls. Grettie Holliday and Loretta Van Hook stood at the front of the meeting room. The girls sat on carpets on the floor, wearing ankle-length blue, green or burgundy dresses and belts covered with silver. Around their necks were necklaces of coral or amber beads. On the top of their heads were embroidered skullcaps with colorful handkerchiefs tied over them, and down their backs hung many thin braids of hair with silver ornaments clasped to the ends.

"What lovely little girls," I exclaimed.

"The girls who attend the school are bright and pretty, with rosy cheeks and sparkling black eyes," Sam replied. "The students at the Boys' School take special interest in them, and the silver belt they wear is their mother's bridal pledge."

Loretta Van Hook nodded her head and smiled acknowledging our presence. "Girls, please welcome Reverend and Mrs. Wilson who have paid us a visit."

"Welcome to our school," the shrill voices cried simultaneously in English.

"Carry on," Sam said and motioned for me to follow him. "There will be plenty for you to do with the students at the Boys' School, but you may find the opportunity to teach a special class for the girls. It may also be useful for you to come and listen to them speaking Azeri, Armenian and Persian. You can accompany Loretta and Grettie to and from the mission when I am teaching."

"What a wonderful idea," I replied. "It would be a good opportunity for me to befriend some women at the mission."

The next Sunday afternoon, I invited Loretta and Grettie to tea after church service. Grettie Holliday was an aggressive woman from Indianapolis, who came to Persia three years ago at the age of forty. Although over age for normal application to the Presbyterian Board for Foreign Missions, she was allowed to work at the mission since she raised her own funding. Loretta Van Hook was a quiet, sad-looking widow. When they arrived, Grettie said, "What a charming house. I wish mine had all the delicate wall murals."

"Thank you," I replied. "I immediately liked them as well."

"No, no, no," Grettie retorted. "That is no way to answer a compliment in Persia. This is the expected response: 'It is your house then, it is mine no longer.'"

"Really?" I mustered. Both Grettie and Loretta laughed at my astonishment.

"This courtesy also extends to the Shah," Grettie continued. "A wealthy man built a beautiful palace, and the Shah came to see it, exclaiming 'I like this house very much. How much did it cost you?' The man told him it cost four times what it had, and the Shah replied, 'I can't take the palace with me, but you can give me the money instead.' It broke the man financially, and in the end the Shah also took the palace."

"I apologize for not knowing the customs," I said. Grettie and Loretta laughed again heartily.

"The most important custom to learn is how a woman should dress and behave outside the mission," Loretta said.

"I ride horseback to the villages in *chuddar* with a veil over my hat," Grettie said. "They think I am a Muslim noblewoman, a *sayyida*, and are surprised when I dismount and unveil to European dress. It is a very effective way to get their attention."

"Do you travel by yourself?" I asked.

"Goodness no," Grettie replied. "I travel with my itinerating party — my translator, Karaput, my armed aide and business manager, Josef, and my cook, Yagoot, who I call 'Ruby.' "

"The First Presbyterian Church in Indianapolis independently funds Grettie's work," Loretta interjected.

"I help with teaching the Persian girls at the school, but my real passion is spreading the gospel in the villages," Grettie added.

"How did you come to Persia to be a missionary?" I asked Loretta.

"I became a teacher when I was fourteen, and teaching has been my passion," Loretta responded, flashing a hint of a smile. "When I married James and moved to Iowa in 1870, I refused to give up teaching, but I became pregnant six months later. Baby Arthur was born the day after Christmas and died a month later. Then six months after my baby's death, my husband James passed away."

"How horrible," I exclaimed. "You must have been devastated."

"My religious faith helped me rise above the sorrow," Loretta said. "I moved to Rockford, Illinois, enrolled in the Female Seminary and graduated in 1875. A year later I sailed to Persia."

"I admire how you took hold of your life despite the setbacks," I said.

"I believe it was God's will," Loretta responded. "His will was for me to help Persian women improve their lot."

"One of the reasons I invited you for tea was to ask if I could help you at the Girls' School while I am learning the native languages," I said. "Do you think there would be something I could do to assist you?"

"There is always a need for extra help," Loretta exclaimed and managed an authentic smile.

"You would also be a relief to me," Grettie said. "I often feel guilty when I leave Loretta to go on tour in the villages."

"Could I start tomorrow?" I asked.

"We will pick you up tomorrow morning at seven-thirty sharp," Grettie declared.

Later I told Sam, "I am so pleased that my first attempt to find a place with the other women at the mission was met with such a positive reception."

"Did you warm up to Loretta?" he asked. "I am sure Grettie only gave you a hard time."

"Loretta has the appearance of a sad frail widow," I said, "but I realized that she has so much passion and determination to better the future for girls in Persia."

"I also admire her as a living example of the Scriptures: 'we rejoice in our sufferings, knowing that suffering produces endurance, and endurance produces hope, and hope does not disappoint us, because God's love has been poured into our hearts.'"

"Romans 5:3-5," I replied.

I spent three days a week at the Girls' School with Loretta Van Hook, accompanied by Grettie Holliday when she was not on tour. The kindergarten, which was started in the home of Eliza Holmes, was transferred to the Girls' School and I took charge of it. I had no experience as a kindergarten teacher, but I did what I could to keep the children stimulated.

Yacob came regularly to teach me Azeri and Armenian. He was patient and encouraging, pronouncing words slowly with his smooth dark lips. He took joy in my successes and laughed at my mistakes with his black eyes sparkling. *Such a handsome young man. My guess is that he is four years younger than me.* I must admit that I developed a bit of a crush on him.

After a month of language lessons Sam said, "To help you learn more quickly, we will stop speaking English at home and I will request that the other missionaries also follow suit when they converse with you."

"I don't think I am ready," I cried.

"One is never ready," Sam replied, "It is not a punishment, it is to help you." I was effectively cut off from my native tongue except on Friday evenings, when the mission church service for the one hundred Europeans in the community was given in English. Sam let me attend with reservations.

January 1887

In January boxes from America arrived with clothes and wedding presents. It was a blessing. In October when we left America, my baggage contained one set of winter clothes and a coat. For a month I longed for more warm clothes to wear.

One of the most precious wedding gifts was from my friends in Lake Forest — a sidesaddle, beautifully crafted in leather with three-pommels and a handkerchief pocket on one side. "Now I only need a fine horse that is worthy to wear this saddle," I told Sam, "Not your typical small, gaunt Persian horse."

Sam's twenty-ninth birthday was on February 11th, and I planned a party. Miriam allowed me into the kitchen to make a cake, which I wanted to be a surprise. While making a list of ingredients for Ishak to purchase from the bazaar, I realized that I did not know the Azeri word for "chocolate." When I asked Grettie to help me, she laughed. "Chocolate is not something that one can buy at the bazaar. Persians do not eat chocolate."

"Whatever shall I do then?" I bemoaned.

"Make a cake with almonds instead," Grettie suggested. "They are plentiful in Persia."

When Ishak returned with the ingredients — flour, milk, butter, eggs, and almonds — I boldly ventured into the kitchen with Miriam. Baffled by the deep fire pit in the floor and the small fireplace on one side, my confidence quickly eroded. *How am I to bake a cake?*

Miriam, in her deeply respectful manner, pointed at the hole in the floor and said, "It is a *tandur*, a Persian oven." A subtle smile played on her lips as she started to assemble ingredients. "Tell me how much."

I found my usefulness as the "supervisor" of cake baking, and Miriam let me test for doneness after lifting the cake out of the *tandur*. The cake baking episode helped me bond with Miriam; my cook was now my friend.

The missionary families — the Oldfathers, the Wards, the Holmes and the Whipples — attended Sam's birthday party; nine children, including four girls between eight and eleven years old and five boys between two and seven years old. It was a lively, noisy party and Sam seemed to enjoy it.

At the end of the party, I gave each child a present of a mason jar of canned peaches or strawberry jam. "Here is something American for each of you," I said. "Sam's mother sent these to us."

As we undressed for bed, Sam asked in a loud voice, "Why did you give away my mother's canned goods? She only sends them to me once a year. We cannot buy canned fruit in the bazaar." I could sense that Sam was quite irritated. *Was this our first marital disagreement? Over preserves?*

"We have plenty left," I said, "and I intend to save them for special occasions. Besides our mainstay should be Persian fare." After all the preparation for Sam's birthday and with my good intentions, I had violated something sacred to him by giving away his mother's mason jars. Crestfallen, I continued to brush my hair until I heard Sam's sonorous sleep sounds before going to bed. With my face turned away from him, I let tears stream down my face. *How I wanted to please him, only to displease. Will our marriage and my life in Tabriz be happy?*

After a night of fitful sleep, I looked haggard in the morning. At breakfast Sam asked, "How are you enjoying Miriam's cooking?"

"It suits me fine," I said with a weak smile. "The Persian kitchen is so foreign to me. It is difficult for me to navigate. I enjoy having the free time to concentrate on my Armenian grammar."

Sam looked up, startled by the sarcastic edge of my voice.

"What do you teach at the Boys' School," I asked Sam.

"Most of the teaching of primary lessons up to algebra and geometry is done by Vahan Tamzarian, a graduate of Harput College in Turkey," Sam replied. "I primarily serve as the principal, and teach some of the advanced classes, such as history, physics, physiology, and geology. I also teach a Bible Class that I hope you might assume someday."

"Do you interact much with the more junior students?" I asked.

"As principal, I take a personal interest in each of the seventy boys at the school. On Sunday afternoons I have the fifteen boarders to the house for Bible lessons."

"Have any of the boys converted?" I asked.

"Three years ago, when the present class was received, only one was a professing Christian," Sam replied. "Spiritual improvement through moral and religious training has been difficult and trying. Their inherited prejudices and home influence constantly work against it, but now nine are members of the church, and the others show marked change in moral character and conduct from studying the Scriptures."

Over a long weekend, Friday through Monday, or during the Boys' School vacation, Sam frequently toured the countryside with Grettie Holliday to spread the gospel. Even though Grettie was twelve years older than Sam, it always gave me pangs of jealousy when he toured with her. I constantly had to remind myself that they traveled as a group of five — Sam, Grettie, and the three members of her itinerating party, Josef, Karaput and Ruby. I was relieved when he returned each time with the same exasperating comment: "Grettie would drive any husband mad; she is so bossy." Still every time he left with her the pangs of jealousy returned.

I must learn the native Persian languages so I can tour with him.

CHAPTER 9

1887 — My First Spring in Tabriz

THE ARG OF ALI SHAH WAS A CONSPICUOUS STRUCTURE
half a mile north of the mission. "I would like to climb the Arg
and get my bearings on the city of Tabriz," I said.

"The climb to the top of the Arg is too treacherous in winter,"
Sam told me. "Wait until spring when the snow and ice have melted."

"What is the Arg?" I asked.

"It was a citadel built in the fourteenth century," Sam replied.
"What remains was part of the mosque."

It was now officially spring; the snow had melted and buds on
the almond trees were flowering.

"With the clear sky we will be able to see Lake Urmia from the
top of the Arg, sixty-five miles to the west," Sam said.

As we climbed one hundred and twenty feet to the top of the
Arg, Sam told me its legends. "A slave of great strength threw each
brick up to a mason and, as the wall became higher and higher,
his throws required greater effort. When completed, the slave's
reward was his freedom. Another story is about a daring youth
who climbed the Arg by slipping his fingers between the bricks
with his back against the wall. When he succeeded in reaching the
top he was arrested and executed."

"Why was he executed?" I asked.

"His successful climb demonstrated that he could have become
the world's greatest thief," Sam replied. "Casting criminals from

the top of the Arg was a form of execution. Even twenty-five years ago, women who were unfaithful in marriage were thrown off the top. One woman escaped death by spreading her skirt and allowing it to balloon, slowing her descent."

"Are any of these stories true?" I asked.

"Persians are great story tellers, and there is surely some truth in everything they say."

Reaching the top of the Arg, a cold blast of air sent me backward, and Sam grabbed my hand. "Come and admire the view," he said.

Sam led me along a corridor running along three sides of the top of the Arg. "To the northeast, you see the army barracks directly below, and the Eynali Mountain Range in the distance. Facing south, you see the mission compound and farther off Mount Sahand with its snow-capped peak. To the west, Lake Urmia is that white streak on the horizon and farther west the Zagros Mountains separating Persia from the Turkish border of the Ottoman Empire."

After we descended to the street I said, "It was worth the climb to see the beautiful snow-covered mountains on all sides of Tabriz. To think that six months ago, I lived in the flat lands of Lake Forest, Illinois."

"In addition to the mountains, I hope you learn to love the Persian people as much as I do," Sam said. "They are an intelligent and vivacious people, lovers of jokes, stories and verbal exchange. Social visits last three to four hours, and the Persians find ample reasons for giving small gifts they call *sogats*."

"I will need to observe and learn the proper Persian social protocols of etiquette."

I felt a hard tug on my skirt and saw a dirty knobby-knuckled hand clinging to my dress. I gasped when I saw the deeply wrinkled face of a woman shivering and sitting cross-legged on the ground with cloth bandages tied to her feet. "*Khanum*, bread money," she cried in Azeri. "*Khanum*." Sam quickly handed her some coins, and she released my skirt.

"Do you have to give them money to be able to be on your way?" I asked.

"Sometimes *bakshish* is the best solution," Sam answered. "She is obviously destitute and deserving. The children who are beggars are the most difficult. There are two little waifs, Ali and Gooli, who all the missionaries know because they follow us endlessly, running in front of us and holding out their hands. When we ride out on tour, they run alongside our caravan crying, '*Sahib*, may your journey be blessed.' When we have a conference at the mission, they follow the arriving guests saying, 'Eid mobarak,' 'May your festival be blessed.' They pester us until we give them *bakshish*."

Further ahead I saw bright colored towels hanging over a low wall. A waft of smoke circled over a dome-shaped structure at street level. As we approached the stench of the smoke became unbearable and I squeezed my nostrils with my fingers to keep the smoke from entering. "What on earth are they burning?" I asked.

"It smells like a mixture of carcasses and manure," Sam said.

"Carcasses and manure?" I exclaimed.

"The smell of the manure will dissipate as the fire gets hot, but I am afraid the smell of the carcasses lingers."

"What is that building?"

"It is the *hammam*, the public bathhouse. See the men queued up to go down into the bath?"

A heavy cloud of steam billowed out of the entrance to the bathhouse each time the door opened. "When the steam clears look at the remarkable painting above the door," Sam said. "It is a scene from the epic poem *Shahnameh* with *Rostam*, the legendary hero of Persia."

"How exquisite," I exclaimed.

A man climbed onto the roof of the bathhouse and blew a long horn, a low bellowing note that made me laugh. "It is the bathkeeper," Sam explained. "He blows the *booq-e javaz* to announce that the bath is ready."

"Do women have separate bathhouses?" I asked.

"Some exist, but more typically women and men are assigned different days or hours."

Further on a group of women sat next to an open stream running along the street. They were washing clothes, beating them on rocks. "Where does the water come from?" I asked.

"The water for Tabriz and the surrounding villages comes from ancient wells that were excavated in the foothills," Sam responded. "Some are three hundred feet deep. Water flows from the wells through underground channels called *karizes* and finally comes to the surface through a hole called a *chesma*."

"The pool around the *chesma* is unprotected. Don't children fall in and drown?"

"Occasionally," Sam replied. "The word *chesma* also refers to a nymph in Turkish mythology that lures children into water where they drown."

"Where does Ishak go to fetch our water?"

"Every day he goes by horseback to a *chesma* and fills two large water jars. After the *chesma* the water runs in an open stream where clothes are washed, and it is no longer safe to drink."

"Do wealthy Persian households fetch water everyday too?"

"No, the wealthy have an *abanbar*, a water tank, in their cellar, and water from a *kariz* is directed into it. Some of the nobles have a wind tunnel attached to the reservoir, which acts to cool the cellar where meat, cheese and milk are stored. It is an ingenious cooling system developed by the ancient Persians."

We stopped at an imposing façade covered with multicolored tiles, predominantly blue. "Even in ruins it is beautiful," I remarked.

"It is the Blue Mosque," Sam said. "Tiles cover it inside and out with verses of the Qur'an running along the bases of the arches."

After Sam handed the doorman some coins as *anam*, we were allowed inside.

"A few years ago, this was a dog kennel," Sam said.

"A dog kennel?" I exclaimed.

"Yes, there are two or three in every ward," Sam replied. "Dogs are the scavengers of the street. One should beware these large fierce curs; they snarl and snap at one's heels as you pass by."

Ahead we saw a crowd of children on roofs looking into the street and heard dogs fighting. I could picture the dogs' foaming mouths and snarling teeth and held tight to Sam's arm as we approached. When we reached the corner, we were surprised to find not dogs, but a small boy imitating the snarls and barks of a dog fight.

We entered a square in the *Kala* district where vendors were selling food and drink. A bare-footed man approached us wearing an embroidered wool *araqchin*, a dome-shaped rimless skullcap. He carried a glass goblet in one hand and a large clay jar hanging from his shoulder by a rope.

"What is he selling?" I asked. "It looks like milk."

"It is buttermilk," Sam replied. "Except for the possibility of contracting disease from the goblet, which was used by his previous customers, the buttermilk is far safer than water." Sam pointed to a man on the other side of the square with a large, stoppered jug tied to his back with ropes. "That is a *sakka*, a water porter, and there is another ahead of us carrying a sheep skin lined bag on his back filled with water."

"It looks heavy," I replied. "See how he leans forward for balance."

Further on we encountered a boy yelling, "*Laboo laboo!*" He carried a basket full of reddish-purple balls over his shoulder. "Boiled beets?" I asked.

"Yes," Sam replied, "*Laboo* is traditional street food."

"What is the old man with the buckets selling?" I asked. "The glass bottles hanging from the rim of the bucket appear to contain syrups, perhaps orange and pomegranate."

"He is selling *sherbet*, which in the East is a fruit-flavored drink made by mixing fruit syrups with water."

We passed a bakery with smoke billowing from a cavernous brick oven. Sheets of bread, *lavash* and *sangak*, were stacked five feet high on racks outside. Birds swarmed underneath to eat crumbs that fell to the street and a man stood outside with a broom shooing them away.

"What is the difference between *lavash* and *sangak*?" I asked.

"*Lavash* is baked on the sides of an oven and *sangak* is baked on a bed of small stones," Sam replied.

In front of the Grand Bazaar, people congregated around various street entertainers. Two men stood on a stoop, one playing a zither and the other tapping the head of a goblet shaped drum. A handsome dervish in a clean white smock sang poetry in a melodious voice. A snake charmer blew on a flute and a cobra swayed to the high-pitched melody.

"The snake charmer is playing a Persian *ney*, a hollow cane," Sam said. "In addition to mesmerizing reptiles, the snake charmer also sells prayers written on small pieces of paper that guarantee protection from snake bites."

"What are the other Persian instruments being played?"

"The *santoor* is a trapezoidal shaped zither with seventy-two strings. The *tonbak* is the goblet shaped drum with a goatskin head."

"It is utterly delightful to be entertained by Persian music and poetry and smell the spices that waft in the breeze from the shop over there."

"It is a fine *chai-khana*, a teahouse. They are popular places for social gathering, similar in social function to pubs in America, except no inebriating beverages are served. They are everywhere in Tabriz in various forms; some are only an outdoor carpeted platform, while others are attractive buildings with chairs, tables and chandeliers."

"There is so much life in the streets this time of year; men in sheepskin hats smoking pipes, a cobbler shoeing horses, a rug weaver stringing their warp, children playing a game of jacks."

"The jacks are sheep knuckles," Sam said. "Have you noticed the perambulating barber?"

"Barber?"

"Yes, see the man with scissors and razors protruding from his girdle? He presents a mirror in front of potential customers, who take the hint and squat down in the street to have their head shaved and their beard trimmed."

Continuing east past the Grand Bazaar we reached the twenty-acre complex of local government buildings. "The local military is based here," Sam said, "the soldier's quarters, drill grounds, the armory and arsenal. The governor-general's residence, the courthouse and royal prison are also situated here. Further on is *Dar-ol-Khalafeh*, the royal compound and palace of the *Vali Ahd*, the Crown Prince and heir apparent to the Shah. On this side is the custom house, the post office and the government school."

"What are the boys playing in the schoolyard?"

"*Ashtook*. It is a game with eight rocks, four for each team. The players try to claim rocks for their team by hitting them with a sheep knuckle."

"The boys are so animated even though it is a simple game with rocks."

"You will see the boys at the mission school playing *Ashtook* and another game called *Haft sang* with seven rocks, where a ball is used to knock out opponents, resembling our dodgeball. I find it refreshing to see the boys enjoy such simple things."

As we walked back to the district of *Lawala*, we passed a group of men, women and children seated in the street on rugs listening to a *sayyid*. "What is he telling them?" I asked.

"He is telling them the eulogies of Islamic martyrs," Sam replied.

"*Khabar-da*r!" a man cried as he approached on a horse. "Make way; the *Vali Ahd* is coming!"

Sam pulled me against a wall and shielded me with his body. As the horseman rode by, he enforced his warning with blows of his baton and the group sitting on rugs scrambled against the wall. "Oh," I gasped as the Crown Prince's carriage ran over and muddied their rugs. "How inconsiderate."

"Alas, one must respect the wishes of *Vali Ahd*, the Crown Prince," Sam said. "He is the heir to the throne, Persia's next Shah."

"What is his name?" I asked.

"Mozaffar ad-Din," Sam replied.

"Walking through the streets of Tabriz during the warm spring days presents such a lively scene in contrast to the cold days of winter. The people frolic so."

Sam smiled and squeezed my hand. "I am pleased to hear that you are falling in love with Tabriz as I have. It is a truly an enchanting city."

My First *Nowruz*

Pretending to read, I stealthily watched Miriam over my book. She methodically placed a mirror, painted eggs, a book and several small bowls on the side table in the dining room. When she went into the kitchen, I ventured over to see what the bowls contained. One was filled with sprouting grass leaves, another with garlic, and others with vinegar, an apple, olives, red berries and a pudding. "What is this for?" I whispered to Sam.

Sam looked up from his book with a quizzical expression. "Why it is the *Haft-sin* table," he replied and went back to reading.

"And what is a *Haft-sin* table for?" I asked.

Sam lowered his book enough for his eyes to be visible and laughed. "You might not remember this traditional Persian custom; the *Haft-sin* table is for *Nowruz*, the Persian New Year celebration on March 21st."

"A New Year celebration in March?" I exclaimed.

"Yes, *Nowruz* is celebrated on the vernal equinox. The twelve months of the Persian calendar start on the twenty-first day of our calendar and end on the twentieth. Persian Muslims also follow the religious Islam calendar. It has 354 or 355 days in a year, so it lags ten or eleven days behind our Gregorian calendar."

"Then what day is it?" I asked.

"Today is March 14th, 1887, by the Gregorian calendar, the 23rd Esfand 1265 by the Persian calendar and 19th of Jumada al-Akhirah 1304 by the religious Islam calendar."

I smirked. "How on earth do you keep track?"

"Every morning, when I am still half asleep in bed, I ask myself, 'What day is it?' and by the time I have figured out the date by all three calendars, I am fully awake."

"Back to the *Haft-sin* table. What are those things meant for?"

"It is a Zoroastrian tradition, the ancient pagan religion of Persia." Sam said. "There are seven dishes with items that begin with the letter *sin*, or 'S' of the Persian alphabet. *Sabze*, sprouting wheat, is a symbol for rebirth; *Samanu*, the wheat germ pudding, symbolizes strength; *Senjed* is the Persian olive which symbolizes love; *Serkeh*, vinegar, is for patience; *Seeb*, an apple, is for beauty; *Seer*, garlic, is for health, and *Somaq*, red sumac berries, are for sunrise."

"What about the other things on the table?"

"The mirror is for self-reflection, the candles for enlightenment and the eggs stand for fertility."

"What a charming custom," I exclaimed. "What is the book?"

"A book of wisdom is always set on the table as well. It could be the Qur'an or the Avesta, the Zoroastrian scriptures. This book is the *Shahnameh* by Ferdowsi, written between 977 and 1010 CE. It is the longest epic poem ever written and the national epic of Persia."

"What should I expect to happen on *Nowruz*?"

"*Nowruz* is celebrated for thirteen days, with visits to families and friends. Dr. Holmes and I will visit the houses of Persian men. The missionary women will visit the Persian ladies and you will be invited to accompany them. Typically, tea, pastries, dried fruit and nuts are served."

"That sounds delightful."

"This Wednesday is *Charshanbe Suri*, 'Festive Wednesday.' In the evening there will be bonfires, firecrackers and fireworks. People dress in disguises and roam the streets banging spoons against plates or bowls. They go door-to-door and receive snacks, like our Halloween."

"Does the mission participate?"

"Yes, some of us stand at the gate and give out packages of dried fruit. The thirteenth day of Nowruz is *Siazdah Be-dar*, 'Nature's Day,' when the Persians picnic outside. *Dorugh-e Sizdah*, 'Lie of the Thirteenth,' is like April Fool's Day; the schoolboys play pranks on the missionary teachers and the principal. One of the boys comes to my office dressed up as a Kurdish sheik with a turban, a sword and a cotton beard and levies a fine on the school. When I give him a healthy *peeshkesh*, he and the other boys run to the bazaar to spend it."

The days before *Nowruz* the bazaars were decorated with garlands and brilliantly colored cloths. Ornaments resembling colorful tops were suspended from arches spanning the streets. A nobleman's servant carried a plate of dried fruit to our door. "This collection of dried fruits and nuts is called *yeddi luvn*," Sam said. "This is the typical present to friends for Nowruz."

On Wednesday, *Charshanbe Suri*, Sam and I watched the parade from the rooftop — clowns with ludicrous masks, minstrels with leashed monkeys beat on tambourines and clanged cymbals, children banged spoons against plates and bowls. "The noise is deafening," I exclaimed, covering my ears with my hands.

Sam put his arm over my shoulder and said, "If I speak the tongues of men and of angels, but have not love, I am but a noisy gong or a clanging cymbal."

"1 Corinthians 13:1," I replied.

After sunset, the smoke from burning incense and small bonfires filled the air. Fireworks exploded from every corner of the city and the chatter of firecrackers echoed in the streets. Men and young boys jumped over the bonfires burning on rooftops and in the roads.

"What are they singing around the bonfire?" I asked. "It repeats over and over."

"They are singing '*Zardi-ye man az toh, sorkhi ye toh az man*,' which means 'My yellow is yours; your red is mine.' It is a Zoroastrian song asking the fire to take away their sickness and other problems, and to replace it with health and energy. Zoroastrians are also called 'fire worshippers.' Early Christians may have been fire worshippers too. 'He will baptize you with the Holy Spirit and fire.' "

"Matthew 3:11," I replied.

The following week, I accompanied Eliza Holmes and Mary Whipple by carriage to a Persian noblewoman's home. The three-story house had Austrian-style arched windows and red-brick accents on the exterior. The noblewoman waved to us from the third story veranda, accompanied by a group of ladies in colorful silk *chuddar*. "The women's apartment, the *anderoon*, is on the third floor," Mary Whipple stated. "We climb up the stairs from the rear women's entrance and leave our shoes at the door."

We entered a large room with an immense carpet where Persian women sat in a circle around a wooden tray covered with pastries and dried fruit. We were served tiny glasses of sweet tea. "Try one of those crescent pastries," Eliza Holmes said. "They are called *ghottab* and are filled with almond and walnuts. I can never resist them."

The pastries were luscious, and I could not resist taking another. Mary and Eliza became immersed in conversation in Azeri, and I had a hard time following their conversation. The Persian noble woman occasionally glanced at me. *I suppose she wonders why I do not speak.*

The time wore on and I stealthily glanced at my watch. *We have been here for over three hours, and I do not know what anyone is saying.*

Finally, Eliza and Mary were thanking our kind hostess and motioned to me to stand up. Mary grabbed my arm as I stumbled. My foot had fallen asleep while sitting on the floor. After stomping on it to get the circulation back I bravely headed down the stairs after Eliza and Mary and made it into the carriage. "Don't worry, sometime soon you will understand the language and be able to speak it," Mary said.

Eliza chuckled. "Annie was too busy eating *ghottab to speak*."

"We will be visiting other Persian women's homes later this week. Would you like to join us?" Mary asked.

"Thank you for including me," I replied. "I will go next year when I have a better grasp of the language."

At dinner, I listened the Sam report on his day with George Holmes. "Our first visit was with the Governor-general, Amir-i-Nizam. He greeted us in stocking feet wearing a hat. Our conversation went like this: '*Salam alakum*' (peace to you), the governor exclaimed. '*Salam alakum*,' we replied. '*Eid mobarak*' (May your feast be blessed). 'May your favor be increased,' he replied. After sitting on chairs drinking tea, we inquired about his Excellency's noble condition. '*Al hamd ul Ullah*' (Praise God),' he replied, 'I am well,' but most of our conversation was about his many ailments."

"He needs to sing and jump over the bonfire," I replied.

"Next, we visited the mayor, the *beglar-begi*. Tea was served in tiny glasses with silver filigree handles. The servant first went to serve the mayor, who declared with a wave of his hand to serve him after the guests. The tea was as sweet as syrup, so I indulged heavily on the little bottles of Shiraz lemon juice and sliced grapefruit to flavor it. After tea, attendants entered with tiny coffee cups of Zenjan silver with exquisite embellishment. The coffee was very thick, black and sweet. Finally, the *qalyan*, or waterpipe, was passed to us. We declined saying, 'It is not our custom.'"

"What does a *qalyan* look like?" I asked.

"The water pipe, or *qalyan*, stands two feet high. It consists of a vase capable of holding a quart of water, a bowl on top for burning charcoal and dampened tobacco, and a twenty-inch mouthpiece. The vase and bowl are glass, china, brass or silver and set with turquoise or other jewels. Both Persian men and women are fond of the *qalyan*. It will be offered to you on your social callings."

"I will remember the phrase 'It is not our custom' when it is offered," I replied. "Our visit with the noblewoman lasted four hours. How do you say 'adieu' on such occasions?"

"The custom is to say, 'Will you command our dismissal?' and the response of the host or hostess is 'Do you withdraw your graciousness?' Then you leave."

Over the next week Sam visited several other Persian men. "We visited a poor household today," Sam said. "We knocked on the outer door, so the women had a chance to conceal themselves, then entered through a long, arched corridor into a half-underground room with a window covered with oiled paper. 'Welcome, you have done me a great favor,' the host exclaimed. 'May your festival be blessed. May your house be blessed,' we replied. 'It is a present to you,' the host replied.

"The other guests rose from the floor and placed their right hand on their heart and then on their forehead and bowed low. We knelt on our knees on calico cushions, our body weight resting on our heels. There was a fish swimming in a pan in front of us. 'At *Nowruz*, the fish always faces towards Mecca,' our host commented. Then he placed before us a few candies, some hard-boiled eggs and pickled grapes. He filled our cups with sugar before adding tea, while he sipped his unsweetened tea through a lump of sugar he held between his teeth."

"The tea is so sweet here," I said, "almost undrinkable."

"Sugar cane was first brought to Persia from India by Emperor Darius in 510 BC and the production of 'the reed that gives honey without bees' was a guarded Persian secret. Sugar was considered a luxury, which explains the abundance of sugar and sugary treats at Persian festivities."

"To what purpose cometh there to me incense from Sheba, and the sweet cane from a far country?" I said.

"Jeremiah 6:20," Sam replied. "So many parables that relate to Persia actually come from the Bible."

The Arg of Tabriz

CHAPTER 10

Summer 1887

"THIS SUMMER I WILL BE TOURING KARADAGH," SAM said, "the Black Mountain region."

"Can I go with you?" I asked.

"It is too early to bring you along. The village women will crowd around you, expecting you to speak with them and you still have trouble conversing."

"Very well. How long will you be gone?"

"Six weeks."

"But whatever will I do while you are away?"

"The Russian General Consul of Tabriz, Pierre Ponafidine, invited Mary and Will Whipple to his summer home in Nemetabad, a mountain village in Russia. They will be staying for a month with their two young boys and Emma Cochran from Urmia. I am sure you would be welcome to join them."

"Josie's sister Emma? I have not seen her since I was a child." I overcame my disappointment of not touring with Sam thinking about how enjoyable it would be to visit with Emma, a woman close to my age.

Nemetabad was three hundred miles north of Tabriz, but reachable on well-traveled roads. Sam accompanied our wagons on horseback until we reached Ahar, then continued into the village. As he waved goodbye, my heart felt empty. Our wagons proceeded north along the ridge of the Talysh Mountains to the Russian border.

"Emma, why did you return to Persia?" I asked.

"When our family friend Stephen Clement and the Westminster Church of Buffalo funded the new hospital in Urmia, I decided to return and help my brother Joe," Emma responded. "I completed an eighteen-month intensive training in surgical nursing and anesthetics, and then sailed for Persia."

"You came back alone?"

Emma laughed. "Yes, of course. I am not married."

Emma is such a beautiful, accomplished and confident woman. I feel quite humbled in her presence.

The summer home of Consul Ponafidine was an expansive estate with stables and a croquet court. Meals were a formal affair, but with limited conversation — Pierre Ponafidine spoke little English and his guests little Russian. On Fridays, Mr. Ponafidine and his secretary, both single men, joined Emma and me for horseback riding. Emma was a superb rider and often took her horse off on a gallop to the surprise of Mr. Ponafidine, who maintained a reserved trot.

Pierre Ponafidine also invited Emma and me for croquet on several occasions. "I don't know a thing about playing croquet," Emma muttered. "It seems quite boring to me."

"Yes, I agree," I responded, "but let us play along for Consul Ponafidine's sake."

When it was her turn Emma gripped the croquet mallet with both hands, a Solomon grip, and struck the ball squarely and firmly sending it off the court. Mr. Ponafidine shook his head and said in broken English, "Please, me to show you." He stood behind her and slipped his arms along her sides to place her hands on the crochet mallet. He adjusted her top hand to hold the shaft firmly and her lower hand to merely supported the shaft, placing each finger correctly. Watching, I could sense his attraction to her. Emma, however, appeared quite unmoved by Pierre Ponafidine's close proximity. *Why should she be alarmed by the man's presence? She is the one in charge.*

After the croquet match, Pierre Ponafidine sat next to Emma while we drank tea. He smiled and tried to carry on conversation in his broken English. His assiduous attention to her was remarked on by Mary Whipple as we refilled our teacups from the samovar. "I have never seen a man so taken by a woman" she whispered. "Emma is either oblivious to it or does not care to notice. The poor man."

After our month's stay at Mr. Ponafidine's summer estate, I returned with the Whipples to Tabriz and Emma returned to Urmia. Later that fall Mr. Ponafidine returned to the Russian Consulate in Tabriz and called on Will Whipple. "Pierre first asked me to give him English lessons," Will reported. "Later, after I had won his confidence, he requested that I correct his English in the love letters he wished to send to Emma."

"Those must have been interesting to read and correct," I exclaimed.

"I suppose you could have written anything, and the man would not know any better," Sam said. "I would have been tempted to make silly jokes."

Will Whipple never shared the contents of the love letters, but they were apparently effective. The next summer, Emma Cochran married Pierre Ponafidine in Middlesex, England.

After a year in transit from America, the piano, a wedding present from Sam's father, arrived in a large wooden crate. Sam and I watched anxiously as the men lowered it from the wagon and removed the wood slats with large hammers. "Be careful," I whispered and covered my eyes with my hands. "Please be careful."

"Look," Sam exclaimed. "It survived the trip." A cottage grand with black satin finish, brass feet and an ornately carved music stand sat in front of the house.

"I won't know if the soundboard cracked until I play it," I said and edged up to the keyboard to tap each key. The bass keys resonated, the tenor was rich and warm, and the treble rang out with bell-like clarity. "I cannot believe it," I exclaimed. "The piano is still in tune."

The piano became the center of entertainment at the mission and the talk of the town. Persians asked to see it, and the boys from the school begged me to play so they could watch "the hammers dance." Being able to play at social gatherings at the house was a relief at times. If I grew tired of listening to the advice of the older and wiser missionary women, I excused myself to provide entertainment.

George Washington Holmes and the *Vali Ahd*

"The Vali Ahd has appointed George Holmes as his consulting physician," Sam said. "He was called to his palace to receive a *khalat*, a robe of honor."

"Why was the honor conferred," I asked.

"When Governor-general Amir-i-Nizam was near death, Dr. Holmes was called to treat him and saved his life," Sam replied. "Later Dr. Holmes' friendship with the government officials worked in our favor. When a colporteur from the American Bible Society was robbed and beaten in a village, the Governor-general immediately sent soldiers to punish the villagers."

In 1888, Dr. Holmes was called to treat the *Vali Ahd*'s daughter, who had developed meningitis. The Persian physician was sure she would die, but after a month of special care by Dr. Holmes, the girl convalesced. Dr. Holmes received a second *khalat* for saving her life and was asked to be the Physician-in-chief of the *Vali Ahd*.

"The mission will be without a doctor if he accepts the appointment," Sam said.

A week later I asked, "What did George Holmes decide?"

"He conferred with me and although it will be a loss for the mission, I deemed it unwise to refuse the honor. After spending a day fasting and praying for divine guidance, Dr. Holmes accepted the position."

After a year as the *Vali Ahd's* physician, his wife Eliza developed a fatal disease and Dr. Holmes took her to Europe to try to prolong her life. "The *Vali Ahd* could not understand why George left after offering to find him 'a nice, new young wife,'" Sam said.

The Shah Passes through Tabriz on his way to Europe

When Sam returned from a meeting with the *beglar-begi*, the mayor of Tabriz, he was animated. "The Shah, Naser al-Din, will travel through Tabriz on his way to Europe," he exclaimed.

"The Shah is coming to Tabriz?" I replied. "What will that mean?"

"All of Tabriz will prepare the way of the 'Lord,'" Sam said. "They will 'make straight in the desert a highway for our God; every valley shall be lifted up, and every mountain and hill be made low; the uneven ground shall become level, and rough places a plain.'"

"Isaiah 40: 3-4," I replied.

Sam was partially correct. Bridges were repaired, streets cleaned and paved, walls rebuilt, shops were adorned, and thousands of kerosene streetlamps appeared for the first time. An arch was erected over Khiyaban, the roadway that enters the city from Tehran, and covered with flags and the national emblem — the Lion and the Sun.

Vali Ahd Mozaffar ad-Din and other officials traveled four days to meet the Shah on his way to Tabriz. Thousands of people gathered to see the Shah enter the city in his jewel-studded carriage. His caravan was miles in extent; his retinue comprised of four thousand soldiers and eighteen hundred horses and mules decorated in brilliant colors and wearing gold medallions. To welcome his Majesty, Armenian Christians gave an address and sang songs. At night streets were lighted by streetlamps and small pottery oil lamps twinkled along the edges of the roofs of the houses. Fireworks exploded throughout the city.

"I have never seen so much light at night in Tabriz," I exclaimed. "The sulfur from the fireworks makes my eyes sting."

"We will pretend it is winter and keep the windows closed," Sam said. "Besides there are bound to be merry revelers on the streets all night, despite the usual curfew."

The Shah enlisted an Austrian drill sergeant to train the royal soldiers to march and ride in formation. The soldiers were standing at attention as the Shah alighted from his carriage in a plain black suit, returned their salute and ascended to a platform at one end of the drill grounds. After a display of marching, mounted soldiers entered the field and the general rode with his sword drawn, giving orders in a stentorian voice.

"Aren't they splendid in their shiny boots and uniforms," Sam exclaimed.

"We are fortunate to be near the stand where the Shah is sitting," I said. "He looks much more youthful and stronger than

I imagined a man in his late fifties would. And those enormous black eyes seem to take in each individual in the crowd."

"Prominent eyes are a common trait among the Qajar dynasty," Sam replied.

"What is that enormous pale-pink gem he is wearing pinned to his jacket?" I asked.

"It is the Daria-i-Noor, the 'Sea of Light,' " Sam said. "One of the largest cut diamonds in the world."

"He certainly has all the looks and demeanor of a king," I added. "The people of Tabriz seem to worship him."

"And they should," Sam said. "He is a man of marked talent, with a strong grasp of governing and discernment in politics. He has an earnest desire for progress and his reign has been one of peace and prosperity. With forty years as Shah, he has ruled as long as Queen Victoria, and they are good friends. Some Persians complain bitterly about his concessions to the British. Discontent of the people can be a dangerous thing."

First Commencement and Two Weddings

"Grettie Holliday is returning to America on furlough, and I will take over her duties at the Girls' School," Loretta Van Hook said. "With thirty-one students, including twenty-seven boarders, I will have my hands full."

"This year the Boys' School enrollment has also significantly expanded," Sam said. "There are sixty students versus forty-four the previous year. The school is so crowded that I hold the advanced classes in my study and Annie holds the Bible Class in the parlor."

"To think that two years ago the mission Boys' School was broken up and you had to fight hard to win back your students," Loretta said.

What? "You never told me about this, Sam," I exclaimed.

"The Armenian Bishop of Tabriz, Stephanos, has opposed the missionary schools as long as I have lived here," Sam said. "He is continuously trying to undermine our missionary efforts. In 1886 when I returned to Persia, I found that during my absence Stephanos had successfully bribed and intimidated the parents of our students to send them to the Armenian school."

"No wonder you were so concerned when we returned."

"I did not want to worry you after you had only just arrived at the mission," Sam said, "but now you will understand why I am rejoicing. After seven years of labor and patience, we are graduating seven bright, handsome young men of average age of twenty-two."

Commencement consisted of four days of public oral examinations, a novelty in Tabriz. Prominent Persians, including the general of the Persian army and the principal of the government schools, attended in addition to the European Consuls. "The mission schools are no longer despised by the Persians as they once were," Sam said.

The students spoke in Armenian, Persian and English on topics such as "The Progress of Knowledge" and "Man's Object in Life," and brought enthusiastic applause from the audience. Sam had diplomas printed and embossed on the best paper available and personally conferred them.

Following Commencement, two Boys' School graduates married graduates from the mission Girls' School. We held both wedding ceremonies in the mission church, catering to the Armenian customs. Before the wedding we served tea and a platter of fruits with whole Persian cucumbers, an Armenian custom, followed by the exchange of wedding garments; the groom brought the bride's dress, and the bride provided the groom's coat. In dressing the bride for the wedding, the attending girls removed her flat cap of girlhood and replaced it with an embroidered crown, singing, "There's a crown for me, there's a crown for you."

At the groom's house the boys serenaded the groom as he donned his suit and then formed a procession, the callers in front crying, "Behold, the bridegroom cometh." The boys who followed sang and carried candelabras. Upon entering the bride's house, a large, flaring boutonniere was pinned on the groom's coat. Sam took the bride's right hand and placed it in the groom's right hand saying, "As God placed the right hand of Eve in the right hand of Adam," followed by a prayer. The procession then marched to the mission church, with the bride moving at a snail's pace feigning reluctance to go.

The mission church was decorated with flowers, and I welcomed the arrival of the bride and groom by playing the wedding march on the organ. Since a Persian Armenian couple expects a wedding to be much longer than an American-style service, Sam included three hymns, three prayers, several selections from the Old and New Testaments, and a sermon. I admit that I nearly fell asleep during the service, but tears came to my eyes as they exchanged their vows. "It is like giving away our own children," I said.

As the procession marched to the groom's house for the reception, people threw bouquets from the rooftops. Rose water was sprinkled about as guests sat down on the carpet where a festive dinner of roast lamb, *pillou* and other delicacies was served until midnight. I whispered to Sam several times, "Don't you think we should go home?" but he shook his head "No" each time I tried to persuade him.

It was my first occasion to walk the streets of Tabriz late at night. There were no streetlights, no house numbers or street signs to navigate by. Sam guided us with a large kerosene lantern, and we somehow made it home.

There on the table was a letter waiting for Sam from my mother. "Why did she address the letter to you instead of me?" I asked.

"It is written on stationery from the Women's Board of Foreign Missions in Chicago, so it must be regarding matters that affect the mission," Sam said. He slit the envelope open with a knife and unfolded a two-page letter. "It is a letter from a lawyer," he exclaimed. "Oh, my goodness." Sam sat down on a chair with a thud.

"Well, what is it?" I demanded. "I cannot take all this suspense. I am so sleepy I could faint."

"It says: 'Mary Copley Thaw, head of one of Pittsburgh's most prominent families, is donating funds to the Presbyterian Mission in Tabriz as a memorial to her late husband, William Thaw, Sr. The endowment of ten thousand dollars ($10,000) comes from shares held by Mr. Thaw, Sr., a major shareholder in the Pennsylvania Railroad. The donated funds are to be used to build and equip a new school, the Memorial Training and Theological School at the Presbyterian Mission in Tabriz.' My wonderful mother-in-law and her art of persuasion." Sam stood up and kissed me vigorously. He took my hands and proceeded to lead me in a dance around the room.

"Our crowded school will be no more," Sam shouted. "But now I need to find the land to build the school on."

CHAPTER 11

Mary Emma Jewett

"IN ADDITION TO TEACHING, ANOTHER ASPECT OF YOUR missionary work is visitation," Sam said. "Persian women will invite you to their homes and ask you to tell them stories from the Bible. I have invited Mary Jewett to dinner. She oversees 'Women's Work with Women,' as we call the visitations."

"What is the purpose of visitations with Persian women?" I asked.

"Manyfold. For the poor it is to inspire them with gospel stories and give examples of living morally and respectably. For the rich woman, it is to educate her by discussing selected Scriptures and leaving her a copy, if she happens to read. Missionary women lead prayer groups and give personal advice; how to live peacefully in the harem or how to avoid divorce. They comfort those in bereavement due to the loss of a husband, child or other member of the family."

"I did not realize that Mary Jewett has other roles in addition to being a teacher at the Girls' School," I replied.

"Mary Jewett has been so much more to the mission than a teacher. She and Rev. Peter Easton established the mission in Tabriz."

"I had no idea," I replied. "She is so unassuming."

"In 1873 she co-founded the Tabriz mission and established the first Presbyterian Girls' School in the city," Sam continued. "After the new school was built in 1882, she trained Loretta Van Hook to take charge, but the Girls' School is close to her heart, and she continues to work there when she is not on tour or on visitations." I sensed that Sam had the utmost respect for Mary Jewett and I was determined to learn as much as I could from this new mentor.

"*Salaam alakum*," Mary Jewett cried as she came through the door.

"Peace be unto you as well," Sam replied. "Come in and sit with us until Miriam calls us to dinner."

Mary Jewett was a medium-built woman in her mid-thirties and had a broad smile and a contagious sense of humor. "Are you learning the languages spoken here?" she asked me. "For each person it is a different trial."

"It is somewhat slow and confusing for me, particularly when trying to comprehend," I said. "So many words sound so much alike."

"Don't be discouraged," Mary said and patted the top of my hand. "Even after fifteen years I make mistakes."

Sam laughed. "There is a standing joke about one of Mary's mistakes. Tell the story, Mary. I would not do it justice if I tried."

"How embarrassing it was," Mary said. "I came to a house to visit an Armenian woman and was met by her husband at the door. I asked for his '*kiny*' and noticed an alarmed and bewildered look in his eyes. He nodded and turned to fetch what I had asked for. To my surprise he brought me a bottle of wine and a wine glass. I had asked for his '*kiny*,' wine, instead of his '*gini*,' his wife."

Sam hooted with laughter. "I can never grow old of this story. The man must have thought you were an alcoholic desperate for a drink. He was bewildered because it is common knowledge that missionaries abstain."

"Sam have you ever made any mistakes?" I asked with an impish smile.

"Well yes I did once," he replied. "I was at a Persian feast and a tray of meat was being passed around. After helping myself, I asked the Persian man next to me, 'Will you have some '*it*'? I thought I said '*et*,' which means 'meat' but I said '*it*,' which means 'dog.' The gentleman laughed and replied, 'Our noble host would never serve us '*it et*' (dog meat). So, I realized my mistake."

"Sam tells me that you are interested in visiting Persian women with me," Mary said.

"I am," I replied, "but my command of the language is so weak, I am afraid I would be lost in the conversation."

"You need to be seen regardless," Mary said. "It takes time to earn their trust so that they feel comfortable telling you their concerns and ask for guidance. Sitting silently in their presence with an empathic smile will go a long way."

"And it shall come to pass that before they call, I will answer, and while they are yet speaking, I will hear," Sam said.

"Isaiah 65: 24," I replied.

"Well done," Mary exclaimed.

The next day Mary came to fetch me for my first visitation. "We are visiting a *sayyida* today," Mary said, "a female descendant of Muhammad. She is considered nobility and is the highest in wealth and rank in the harem."

"Goodness, what should I wear?" I asked.

"The brown dress you are wearing is quite acceptable," Mary replied. "I wear a thin scarf over my hat and use it to veil my face when entering the house. I brought an extra scarf in case you don't have one."

We proceeded down a residential street to a stairwell leading down to a heavy wood gate guarded by Persian soldiers. One of them escorted us past a garden filled with flowers and a fountain and down a long narrow passageway that wound through the estate and emerged at an inner court. The soldier lifted a heavy curtain and left us with a young man who escorted us to a room where a lady was reclined on a pile of pink and yellow silk pillows. She wore black pantaloons and a loose-fitting red silk dress with gold embroidery.

"Wait here at the door," Mary whispered. "The maid is fastening a string of jewels to her hair."

"I was surprised that the young man was allowed into the harem," I whispered.

"He is a eunuch," Mary whispered back. "Male attendants are always emasculated."

Finally, with an affected smile the woman motioned us to come in and sit on two large blue silk pillows on the floor next to her. She showed us a piece of needlework she was working on, and Mary and I both commented, "It is beautiful." Mary was quick to inform the *sayyida* that I was still learning the language and wished to only listen to our conversation.

The woman smiled at me and bowed her head slightly in acknowledgement, then waved her maid to serve us. The maid brought a succession of sweetmeats, *sherbets*, tea and coffee. Then she offered the water-pipe, or *qalyan*. Mary politely refused, and the *sayyida* shook her head and said what I believe translated to "you deny yourself my chief amusement."

"It is not our custom," Mary responded.

"Read me a story from the Bible," she said to Mary in Azeri.

I strained my ears to understand what passage from the Bible Mary was reading. "Blessed are," she said again. *Oh, of course. Sermon on the Mount, Matthew 5:1-10.*

"Repeat slowly," the *sayyida* said. "Explain why each are blessed."

As Mary again repeated Matthew 5:1-10, I mouthed her words in Azeri. When she finished Matthew 5:8 the woman said, "Do you mean that if I am pure of heart, that I will see God?"

"Yes," Mary replied. "You will see God in your heart."

"But I don't have eyes in my heart," the woman protested.

"To see with your eyes or to feel God in your heart are the same," Mary replied.

The woman seemed to understand and, with her hand on her heart, shook her head in affirmation. "Yes, I must make my heart pure," she replied. She smiled broadly at Mary as though a revelation had come to her. "I love Jesus," the *sayyida* said to my amazement. Then she qualified her statement. "He was a good man and a prophet."

"He was more than a prophet," Mary insisted. "He is our Savior."

"He is your Savior and Muhammad is mine," the *sayyida* responded. "I am tired and bid you to go."

As we walked home, I asked, "What does she do with her time?"

"Mostly she eats, drinks and smokes. She counts the bead of her *tasbih*, the Islam rosary, while saying the many names for God in the Qur'an. Occasionally she will go out in *chuddar* and veil accompanied by many servants. She goes to the bathhouse to gossip and have her hair dyed with henna, or she goes to a friend's home for the day. Our visits are a welcome break in her monotony."

"What are the bathhouses like?" I asked. "I have seen the big domes at street level and the colored towels hanging along the walls. Steam billows out the doors each time they are opened."

"Christians are not usually permitted into a Muslim bathhouse, but I was allowed to enter a *hammam* in the guise of an attendant of a wealthy Persian woman. The rooms are hot and humid, and the sunlight that filters through the translucent alabaster dome is the only light. Women have special hours to bathe in the common hot water pool."

"Did you go into the bath?"

"Goodness no. As a Christians I did not dare to even touch the water, as it would have been considered 'polluted.' But since the bath pool water is only changed every three to four months I was not tempted."

"You said that they go there also to have their hair dyed."

"Yes. The hair dyeing process takes five to six hours. First dye from henna leaves is plastered over the hair and painted on the hands, fingernails, feet and toenails. After two hours it is washed off leaving a bright orange color. A second dye from the indigo plant is then applied on the hair for another two hours and when washed off leaves the hair shiny and black. Both men and women color their hair, so you rarely see a gray-haired Persian."

"Do only high-ranking women visit the bathhouse and have their hair dyed?"

"No. The middle-class women also come during women's hours," Mary replied. "They are the ones you see walking in plain *chuddar* and veil, unattended on the city streets. They have much more freedom than the higher-class women and a certain degree of intelligence and self-respect. Their husbands do not tend to be polygamous since they often can only afford one wife. You will be asked to visit many middle-class women in Tabriz."

"How many wives can a wealthy husband take?"

"According to the third verse of the fourth Sura of the Qur'an, a man can have up to four wives, but only if he can treat them equitably."

"I would prefer to be a middle-class Muslim woman in Persia," I said.

"Indeed," Mary responded. "A woman of a harem wears out her life enmeshed in jealousy and hatred of the husband's other wives; constantly inventing ways to secure her place as his favorite and make the other wives miserable. All of the women of the harem are in constant fear of being divorced."

"How does that happen?"

"Quite easily. The husband only has to say three times '*talaq*,' meaning 'divorced.' During the engagement the parents of the bride and groom negotiate *kabin*, how much money the husband will pay to his wife if he divorces her."

"Does a wife have any recourse?"

"Yes. If a woman is in agony over her treatment by her husband she can say, 'I make my *kabin* legitimate to you. Now let my soul free.' Divorce is feared by all wives regardless of class."

"When do Persian girls become engaged?"

"For Muslim girls, by seven to twelve years of age a marriage is arranged for her, sometimes even at or before birth. For Kurdish girls, if the engagement takes place at birth, the parents of the boy will raise her."

"When do they get married?"

"The duration of the engagement is usually six months but can last five to six years, or more. It is acceptable to marry between twelve to sixteen years of age, and it is considered a calamity if a daughter is unmarried and is twenty to twenty-five."

"Do girls have a choice who they marry?"

"Let me describe the engagement ritual. A private message is sent from the boy's parents to the girl's parents. If the girl's father sends an encouraging response, an engagement date is set. The boy's male relatives visit the girl's male relatives at her house. The boy's father brings candy and a pair of shoes."

"A pair of shoes?"

"When the topic of the engagement arises, the girl's father defers to the other male relatives saying, 'The girl does not belong to me, the grandfather must be consulted first.' The grandfather then defers to an uncle, and the uncle to a brother, etc. Ultimately the question comes back to the father who says, 'My daughter is like a pair of shoes for your son,' meaning he is willing to make the engagement."

"How does the girl find out that she is engaged?"

"An old woman carries a ring to the girl's apartment and says, 'Your father, your uncles and your brother, etc. have betrothed you to this boy, and if you are willing to obey them, you can express it by taking this ring from my hand and putting it on your finger.' "

"Is the father's decision final? Can a girl refuse to put the ring on their finger?"

"The girl is expected to take the ring. I heard of a girl who refused because she favored another boy. Her uncle came to her with the ring and a dagger and asked her to choose."

"Tell me about the Muslim girl's wedding," I said.

"Weddings last up to seven days, starting with a three-day reception at the groom's home with singers, musicians and dancers. The groom's reception is followed by a feast at the bride's home. For the ceremony, the bride rides a horse and is covered with a red veil without eye slits so she cannot see. The groom's wedding party leads the horse and escorts her, each holding a chicken, representing the 'bridegroom's bird.' "

"Chickens?" I exclaimed.

"The groom rides to meet his bride, kisses an apple and places it in her hand. He then races away, pursued by the bride's horsemen. Once they reach the groom's house the bride kisses her parents 'goodbye.' The crowd shouts and throws copper coins and raisins at the bride, symbols of prosperity and sweetness of the occasion."

"How very different from a Christian wedding held in a church," I exclaimed.

"We see Muslim weddings rarely and by chance," Mary continued. "The Christian Armenian weddings are in a church and similar to our Western weddings, but with their own unique and delightful customs. I am sure you will have an opportunity to see one."

"I have heard that only the birth of a boy is celebrated, is that true?"

"Yes, sadly it is true. When a baby boy is born, the usual greeting is 'May God bless him,' but when a baby girl is born, they greet the mother with 'May God forgive you.' I am glad you asked so you are not offended by the Persian women if your first born is a girl."

"How strange not to cherish any child, boy or girl," I replied.

CHAPTER 12

Late Spring 1888 — My First Tour

THE SNOW HAD MELTED AWAY AND THE ALMOND TREES were beginning to blossom. "I am looking forward to a long ride on my horse," I said wistfully.

Sam smiled. "By coincidence, I was thinking the same thing. I have been planning a tour in the countryside."

"Oh," I replied glumly. "Perhaps someday I can go with you."

"I am counting on you coming with me on this tour to talk to the peasant women."

"I am sufficiently fluent in the native languages to teach young children and have simple conversations with Persian women, but I am not sure I can explain the Scriptures."

"You will manage," Sam replied. "The peasant women only need simple explanations. My concern is that you will not care for the peasant fare."

Each day we traveled on horseback for many hours in the sunshine with the orchards in bloom. On one side of the dirt road farmers were plowing and sowing their fields. Three men worked together; one steered a V-shaped wooden plow as oxen pulled it through the soil creating furrows, a second man carried a sack of seeds in one hand, scattering them into the furrow with the other hand, and a third man used a long-handled hoe to cover the seed with freshly plowed earth.

"Where do the farmers live?" I asked. "We have not seen a single house nearby."

"The farmers travel a long distance to the fields from the village, where their houses are crowded together for protection," Sam replied. "The farmers do not own the land that they cultivate. They are tenants to merciless landlords, who take rent and a substantial share of the crops."

On the other side of the road, in the foothills of Mount Sahand, shepherds led sheep in search of mountain streams and newly sprouted grass. Large, muscular sable and black-haired dogs followed behind each herd. "The Persian sheep differ from those in Europe and America," Sam said. "Their offspring vary in color from cream to dark brown, regardless of the parent's coat color and they have long fatty tails, that are roasted with mutton and considered a delicacy."

"I have never seen sheep dogs like that either," I exclaimed.

"They are *Sarabi*, ancient Persian shepherd dogs," Sam replied. "They have herded sheep and protected their flocks from wolves and jackals in northern Persia for centuries."

We stopped for a herd of sheep crossing the road. The old shepherd called each sheep by a different name as it passed him. "Do you have a name for each of your sheep?" Sam asked.

"Doesn't a father have a name for each of his children," the shepherd replied.

"Like the twenty-third Psalm," I murmured, "the 'Shepherd's Psalm' — 'The Lord is my shepherd, I shall not want; he maketh me lie down in green pastures. He leads me beside still waters; he restores my soul.' "

Throughout our journey by horseback, I sat sidesaddle wearing a long skirt, with only one foot exposed in the single stirrup. As we approached a village, filthy and half-naked peasant children ran out to greet us. They giggled and pointed at me. "She only has one leg," they screamed. When I dismounted, they stood transfixed as the other foot slid out from the bottom of my skirt, as if by magic.

The men wore simple blue cotton smocks and baggy brown pants. The peasant women wore red handkerchiefs on their heads and loose-fitting knee-length dresses that exposed their limbs and barely covered their breasts. "The peasant women are so immodest compared to their counterparts in the cities," I commented.

"When they go to city to sell their rugs and produce, the women adopt the standard street clothes of Muslim women," Sam replied, "They envelop their head, face and body in white and blue checkered *chudda*rs and wear veils over their faces."

A group of women crowded around me, excited by my costume. I felt one woman touching my skirt from behind. An old woman walked directly in front of me and grimaced. "Take off your hat and cover your face like respectable Persian women do," she screamed.

"This is our custom," I responded. "We are ashamed to expose our bodies, not our faces."

The women looked at my buttoned-up bodice and long skirt, and then at their exposed breasts and limbs. I sensed that my message had been duly conveyed.

"Remember," Sam whispered. "You want them to look forward to your future visits and listen to what you say about the Scriptures. Changing their dress and appearance is not our goal; it is to bring grace to their inner being."

We rode our horses into the village. The narrow dusty streets were lined with tiny single-story, flat-roofed houses that opened directly into the adjacent stables. A fetid stench filled the air. "What is that smell?" I gasped.

"*Yapma*, or manure cakes," Sam responded. "It is the ever-present sight and smell of the villages. The women knead the manure into cakes and stick it on the walls of their houses to dry. The Persians have specific terminology for the origin of the manure; cakes made of cow manure are called *sargin*, and those from sheep or goat dung are called *peskel*."

"What do they use it for?"

"They use it for fuel, or mold it into bowls or covers for their *tandurs*, which they use for cooking. What they do not use in the village they load onto camels and sell in the cities at *caravanserais*."

"They eat from bowls made from manure?" I exclaimed. I curled my upper lip in disgust.

Sam laughed. "They bake them first in a hot oven."

At the outskirts of the village, a large vegetable garden was guarded with scarecrows and horse skulls on poles. Thirty-foot-tall mud towers dotted the field. "Why horse skulls?" I exclaimed.

"The scarecrows ward off birds," Sam said. "The horse skulls ward off the 'Evil Eye.' "

"And what are the towers used for?"

"It is a nesting tower for pigeons. The villagers use *calguz*, bird dung, for fertilizing the vegetable fields. If you were to enter the door at the base of a tower, you would be attacked by the entire flock of pigeons, who would expect you to feed them."

On the far side of the vegetable field an ox walked in circles tied to a pole. A man seated on a stool rode on a wooden platform behind the ox. "That looks like fun," I said.

"It is the village threshing floor. The man is on top of a *charkh*, a threshing sledge with sharp flintstones sticking out the bottom side. As the ox drags the *charkh* over the stalks of wheat, the straw is broken into small pieces. Later the chaff is separated from the grain by winnowing, lifting it into the breeze with paddles. The lightweight chaff blows away and the grain falls down on the threshing floor, where it is collected."

"Just as in ancient days, the agricultural process remains unchanged," I commented.

We continued riding until the late afternoon. "There are no *caravanserais* in the countryside," Sam said. "We will need to find someone in the next village who will rent us a room or stable for the night and share their evening fare. Try to forget what I said about the bowls."

Sam found a villager who offered a balcony in their livestock barn. For dinner we sat on the floor with the family in a circle around the *tandur*. A large pot of sour milk soup with herbs was lifted out of the oven and ladled into bowls. The men ate first with wooden spoons, dipping *lavash* into the soup. When they were finished, the men passed the bowls back to be filled with soup for the women. I was famished and the soup and bread satiated my appetite. "Like the bread and stew that Jacob gave to Esau when he came into the field," I murmured. "Enough to give up your birthright for."

"Genesis 25: 29," Sam replied. "I am glad you like the village fare. Otherwise, you would starve out on tour."

After dinner we maneuvered around ugly black oxen and skinny donkeys in the barn to reach the ladder to the loft. Sam and I lay down in the hay and spoke softly, listening to the animals snort and grunt.

"I enjoy sleeping in a barn with oxen," I said. "This is like a second honeymoon."

The chickens and rooster joined us in the balcony at sunrise and prevented us from oversleeping. We took bread from the farmer's wife and sat outside by the stream running next to the small yard. A woman was making *lavash* in a tall clay oven. She rolled a ball of dough on a sheepskin, tossed it into the air until it was a long sheet, and then slapped on a side of the clay oven to bake. After making twenty crisp sheets, she stacked them in a neat pile.

Another woman was working on a frame loom under a canopy attached to the side of the house. I watched her glide shuttles of colorful wool thread through the warp, plucking groups of warp threads to create her design. "How long will it take you to weave this rug?" I asked.

"It must be completed by the harvest," she replied. "The men will sell them in the city with the crops."

I wanted to stay and watch the peasant women work but Sam was anxious to move on. "In the next village you will have your first opportunity to read Scriptures to the women," Sam said.

When we reached the center of the village of Ujan, Sam led me to a wall outside of the market. "This is a good spot for you to speak with the women," he said. "I will be down the street where the men are gathered. I have asked the cobbler across the street to keep an eye on you and send for me if there is trouble. This is where *bakshish* comes in handy."

The peasant women crowded around me to examine my costume. One woman asked, "What are you doing with that old man? You look sixteen and he looks sixty."

"Old man? That is my husband," I replied in Azeri. "His beard and glasses make him look old."

"An old man like that will never give you any children," the girl retorted. "It is a disgrace not to have children."

"I leave it to God to decide if I am to have children," I replied. "Now let me read to you from the Scriptures." I took a Bible out of my saddle bag. "I will tell you the story of Ruth, whose mother-in-law, Naomi, lost her two sons and husband. Naomi told her two daughters-in-laws, Orpah and Ruth, to stay in the country of Moab and find husbands, while she traveled alone to Bethlehem, her native land. Oprah bid her mother-in-law farewell, but Ruth clung to her. I will read from Ruth 1:16. Ruth said, 'Entreat me not to leave you or to return from following you; for where you go, I will go, and where you lodge, I will lodge; your people shall be my people, and your God my God. And when Naomi saw that she was determined to go with her..."

There was such a commotion with women talking all at once that I stopped and asked, "Why are you alarmed? It is only the Lord's gospel that I am reading."

"You are the first woman that we have ever seen who can read," one woman ventured to say.

"And it is my mission to teach all women of Persia to read," I replied. The woman who spoke hugged me and then another, and another followed her example. I never finished reading the beautiful story of the strength of friendship between women in The Book of Ruth, but I felt it in my heart amongst the peasant women.

Fall 1888

Later that fall, Sam announced that a new doctor was arriving at the mission. "We received a telegram that Dr. Bradford has made it to Poti," he said. "You can join the *peshwaz* if you would like."

The day before the cavalcade left to meet Dr. Bradford I tripped and sprained my ankle. When it was obvious that I would not be able to even mount my horse, Sam consoled me. "Well, you can be Dr. Bradford's first patient then. The doctor will be staying in our guestroom until other arrangements can be made."

All day I rested in bed and read a book that British Consul Shipley lent to Sam, *A Study in Scarlet* by Conan Doyle. "Shipley says it is a detective novel," Sam said. "He wants me to read it and tell him if it is an accurate description of the Mormons in Utah. Perhaps you could read it and spare me the trouble. I have never heard of the author." The book was about the antics of the detectives Sherlock Holmes and Dr. John Watson and kept me fascinated while waiting for Sam and other members of the mission on *peshwaz* to return.

Late in the afternoon I heard the front door open, then voices and footsteps coming toward the room. To my surprise Sam came in with a tall, sturdy woman who I guessed to be in her early thirties. "This is Mary Braford," Sam said, "the new doctor at the mission." *The new doctor is a woman?*

"I understand you fell and hurt your ankle," Dr. Bradford said. "If you do not mind, I would like to check it and make sure you did not break any bones."

My mouth was still agape when Sam quietly left the room. "I take it from your awestruck face that you were not expecting a woman," Dr. Bradford said. "Rev. Wilson informed me that I am the first woman doctor in Persia."

"Yes, you are," I replied. "The women of Persia are so in need a woman doctor. They will not let men, other than their husbands, touch them."

Dr. Bradford proceeded to examine my ankle and all the bones of my foot. "It is only a bad sprain, nothing broken. Keep off it for a few days."

"Where are you from?" I asked.

"From Pleasant Hill, Illinois. I went to college at Illinois Wesleyan University, class of 1879. Then I went to Women's Medical College of Chicago."

"I am from Chicago too, from Lake Forest."

Dr. Bradford lost her strictly professional doctor's composure. "Oh, I hope we can be good friends," she said. "I will need help with the languages."

"I can act as your translator in the dispensary until you learn Azeri, the most commonly spoken language," I offered. "I would be more than happy to do so."

The women of Tabriz and the surrounding villages flocked to Mary Bradford's dispensary. For two years she stayed in our small upstairs guestroom and took her meals with Sam and me. Every morning, except Sundays, I went with her to the dispensary, where she examined Persian women and I served as her translator. In the afternoons I often accompanied her on medical visitations to women in their homes.

The first year, my service as translator was invaluable to Mary. She became invaluable to me as my first female peer at the mission. *Maybe if I become pregnant, she will help deliver my baby. How reassuring it would be to have a well-trained doctor and friend bring my first child into this foreign land.*

Shepard and Sheep

Wheat Harvest

CHAPTER 13

June 1889 — Return to Urmia, Home of My Childhood

SAM SADDLED OUR HORSES FOR OUR FOUR-DAY TRIP TO Urmia, securing our travel mattresses and saddle bags behind the cantles. He interlaced his fingers to create a basket for my foot and boosted me onto my sidesaddle. Sam smiled as I slipped my right thigh over the pommel. "I have a surprise for you," he said. "We will be spending the night at your father's former house in Ali Shah."

"What? The house where my father died of cholera?" I responded.

"Do you remember it?"

"I was only four when he died. Mother said he was stricken while the family was returning to Urmia from Tabriz. The only thing I remember is that it was very terrifying." I had a vague memory of a dimly lit room, a man lying on a bed, Mother crying hysterically and my brother Foster screaming and pulling on her skirt.

"The house has been used religiously by missionaries on tour ever since. I have stayed there several times. It is considered a sacred place since your father is a missionary legend."

"Sacred?"

"Reverend Samuel Audley Rhea is a name that missionaries speak of in awe. That he spent years in the remote outpost of

Gawar in the mountains of the Kurdistan was the epitome of self-sacrifice."

What a tribute to my father that the Persian missionaries consider his house sacred.

We traveled toward the Guneh foothills across the barren open plain, arriving in the late afternoon at my father's vacant house in Ali Shah. As I hesitantly opened the door a fluttering of wings nearly hit my face, and I jumped back knocking into Sam.

"Oh no," Sam exclaimed. "That bird must have been trapped inside. It probably came down through the open hole on the roof for the *tandur*. I hope it did not make a mess of the place."

I was too stunned to move, so Sam placed our bags next to my feet and went inside. When he returned, he slung our saddle bags in his arms, and I followed him in.

"It is not bad," Sam said. "A few dropping on the floor in the main room and a few feathers floating around, but the room in the back where we will be sleeping is clean."

When I entered the house, my breath became shallow. "I can remember," I murmured. "I can remember being here before."

When we entered the room in the back a chill ran up my spine. "Is this the room where my father died?" I asked.

"I don't know, but it likely is," Sam said. He patted my arm, "Many missionaries have used this room since then."

I swept up the feathers in the main room and we sat on our travel mattresses and ate bread and cheese. "The Urmia Mission has two separate compounds," Sam said, "the old mission in the Mount Mariam quarter and the new compound outside the walls of the city. The original mission on Mount Seir is only used for summer residences."

"Is the Fiske Seminary, the Girls' School, still located in the old compound?" I asked. "My mother taught at the school for four years after my father died."

"Yes," Sam replied. "You might recognize that part of the mission, but a new Boys' College in the new compound replaced the old one."

"Where is the new compound?" I asked.

"About two miles from the city," Sam replied. "In 1878 seventeen acres of land were acquired to expand the mission and build a hospital."

"Mother took us to America twenty years ago. I would expect things have changed."

"Yes, and I am sure you will also be surprised by what stayed the same."

Admittedly, I did not have a good memory of Urmia. I was eight years old when we left. *Would I recognize anything?*

After leaving Ali Shah we traveled through vast fields of wheat that rippled in the breeze. Then the flat road ended with an abrupt ascent up a mountain. A narrow road cut into the rock led to the summit where we were greeted with a spectacular view of Lake Urmia and the Khoi valley. "This is Seyyed Taj ol Din Pass," Sam said. "The road up to here from both directions was chiseled by the Romans."

"Are those islands in Lake Urmia?" I asked.

"Yes, I think they resemble submerged baby elephants," Sam said, "and the lake is so salty that if they were elephants they could float."

The approach to Khoi was a two-mile avenue with waterways on either side lined with gardens and willow trees. At the end loomed a double-walled battlement surrounded by a moat and towers with picket holes for cannons and musketry.

"The bridges to the gates are easily removed in case of attack," Sam said.

"Attack? Turkish or Russian cannons could knock down those walls," I said.

"The fortress still affords protection from the Kurds," Sam replied. "In 1880, when I first arrived in Persia, the Kurds had attacked Urmia and all the villages south of the lake. The roads entering Tabriz were barricaded and the missionaries anxiously talked about threats of a Kurdish raid."

In a day's travel west from Khoi we reached Salmas, a city surrounded on three sides by mountains and the fourth side by Lake Urmia. The Presbyterian Mission of Salmas was in the village of Haftdewan. "We will be spending the night with Rev. Newton Wright," Sam said. "He was a missionary in Tabriz until 1885 when he married Shushan Oshana, a Syrian-Armenian woman from Urmia. The marriage was controversial, as Newton broke an unspoken, but understood, rule that missionaries should not marry natives."

"None of the missionaries discussed the implications with him?" I asked.

"Newton was not popular with the senior members at the Tabriz mission. He was considered lazy because the primary role he performed was translating Scriptures. He left teaching, church service and missionary social work to the other missionaries. The marriage to Shushan increased his unpopularity and led to a petition to have him removed from the Tabriz station."

"Did you take part in the decision?"

"I never spoke against him. As a junior member of the station in Tabriz, my opinion did not hold much rank. I considered Shushan to be a well-educated woman; she graduated from Urmia College, where her father was a professor of ancient Syriac."

"Why didn't the Wrights go to the Urmia mission?"

"Missionaries at the other Presbyterian stations — Tehran, Mosul, Hamadan and Urmia — also refused to offer Newton a position, so he remained in Salmas. When Rev. John Mechlin became the head of the Salmas station he allowed the Wrights to stay."

"Who does the Salmas station serve?" I asked.

"The region surrounding Khoi, Salmas and Maku has one hundred thousand inhabitants, including ten thousand Armenians," Sam said. "There is also a sizable population of Kurds and Nestorians."

The Wrights were very cordial, and the guestroom was comfortable. Shushan was a beautiful woman with long thick dark hair and shining dark eyes. She tried to participate in conversation at dinner but with a two-month-old boy and a three-year old girl she was largely occupied attending to their children.

"This is a beautiful mission station," I commented, "with freshly plastered walls, pleasant and clean."

"We also have a summer residence in Gavlan with a school and chapel in a single building," Newton said. "This year with the newborn we did not want to travel there with the other missionaries."

"It will be an opportunity for Newton to take some time off from …," Shushan started, but a sharp glance from Newton kept her from continuing her sentence.

The next morning when Sam and I were on the road for Urmia I said, "It is hard for me to believe Christian missionaries could have prejudice against Shushan. I thought she was a charming woman."

"It is Newton who is out of favor with them," Sam replied. "Shushan is only an excuse."

Riding along the flat plain to Urmia one could see for miles on the horizon. "I am sorry if you are expecting a cavalcade of missionaries to greet us," Sam said. "Officially we are on a missionary tour, not guests from afar."

"What? No *peshwaz*?" I said, pouting.

"Even without a *peshwaz* your visit is a special one. The missionaries at Urmia are enthusiastically anticipating your return home."

We passed by the gates of the city of Urmia, surrounded by an ancient wall and a moat, and continued two miles further to the new mission compound. It was surrounded by fourteen-foot-high mud walls with watchtowers on each corner.

My chest was tight with anticipation as the gates opened. Standing there were my childhood friends, Fred Coan and Joe Cochran. Joe, who was six years older than me, had been like a big brother. Fred was only two years older and my playmate as a child.

"Freddie! Josie!" I cried.

"Josie?" a stern-looking woman standing next to Joe Cochran exclaimed.

"Remember my wife, Kate?" Joe said smiling from ear to ear. "She has never heard me called 'Josie.'"

Two young children clung to Kate's hands. "Clem is ten and Lily is eight," she said.

"You should give Annie a tour of the hospital you built," Sam said. "In 1880 when I arrived it was newly opened, and no one talked about anything else. It is the first hospital in Persia."

Fred Coan had a full beard and mustache, but I could still see his hallmark sinister smile. A woman carrying an infant in her arms sauntered up beside him. "This is my wife Ida and baby Elizabeth," he said.

"I was trying to remember when I saw you last. In 1878 Joe and Kate stopped in Lake Forest on their way to Persia. The last time I saw Freddie was in 1874, when the Coan family returned to America and visited us in Lake Forest; that was fifteen years ago."

"It is wonderful to see you again and have you join the ranks of second-generation missionaries," Fred said. "Please follow Ida and me to our house. You will be our guests."

As we walked up a tree-lined avenue in front of the residences, an older couple approached. "Why little Annie," the man cried. "You are a full-grown woman now. I am Ben Labaree. I preached with you father for five years before he passed away. How is Sallie, your mother?"

How embarrassing that I did not recognize Rev. Labaree. "She could not be better," I replied. "She is active promoting the missionary cause and raising money for the Presbyterian missions around the world."

"You probably do not remember me either; I am Elizabeth Labaree," the woman said. "You left when our two boys were babies. Robert and Benjamin, Jr., who we call 'B. W.,' are in America studying theology. We hope they will return to Persia as missionaries. You never met our girls, Elizabeth, Susan and Mary."

Over tea the Labarees reminisced. "In 1860 we made the long trip from America to Persia with your parents. For forty days we sailed from Boston to Smyrna on a barque, a square-rigged ship. Every day your father taught us Syriac, the tongue of the people of Urmia."

"He was relentless," Mrs. Labaree added, "even though we were all seasick."

I listened and nodded and smiled. *It has been almost twenty years and they are so enthusiastic to see me. It is like coming back to relatives.*

After tea, Fred and Joe took Sam and me on a tour of the new mission. All the buildings were constructed with sun-dried brick with red brick facings and flat mud roofs. The avenues, lined with plane trees, provided a delightful walk in the shade. "I love these shade trees," I said.

"The Persian name for the plane tree is *chenar*," Joe replied. "I chose them to line the streets of the hospital and medical school, because Hippocrates taught his students in Greece under a plane tree."

"The College, as the natives dub the compound, contains the hospital, the new Boys' School and the missionary residences," Fred explained.

"Westminster Hospital was named after the Presbyterian church in Buffalo, New York that funded it," Joe continued. "We built it in a year and opened the doors in 1879."

"It is Joe's crowning achievement," Fred added.

The Labarees and Cochrans joined us for dinner at the Coan residence.

"Why is the mission in Urmia called the Mission for the Nestorians?" I asked.

"The mission has historically served the twenty-five thousand Nestorians that live in the region around Lake Urmia and speak Syriac as their native language," Rev. Labaree said.

"Why are they called Nestorians?" I asked.

"Nestorius was a Persian who became a Christian bishop in Constantinople during the 4th century. He was considered a heretic and exiled because he believed Christ was both a man and God, and that Mary was the mother of the human Christ, but not the Mother of God. His followers fled to Persia and India."

After dinner, Fred played the Coan's piano, a Decker Brothers upright.

"I had no idea you could play piano so well," I exclaimed.

"I studied music at Wooster University," Fred answered. "I had intended on becoming a classical musician, but my mother thought missionary work suited me better. Ida is a musician too."

"It was quite a feat getting the piano here," Ida added. "The piano traveled on an ox cart in a zinc case, seven hundred miles from Trebizond. The cart tipped over twice, but when it arrived only one string was out of tune."

"My piano, a wedding gift from Sam's father, took a year to reach us," I said. "Unfortunately, I do not play as well as you and it is our only entertainment."

Kate Cochran smiled and patted my hand, "You need children, dear. They will entertain you."

"My mother would like you to visit her in Seir," Joe interjected. "She remembers you as a child."

"We have time to go to Seir tomorrow," I replied. "I would love to see Madame Cochran again."

"And a grand woman she is," Rev. Labaree said. "I would like to join you. I can point things out in the old mission compound that others would not remember."

We reached Seir in Rev. Labaree's gig, a slow six miles up a mountain road from Urmia. I was alarmed when I saw the mission compound; the walls were only fifteen feet high, and the houses appeared tiny.

"This used to be a castle and a mighty fortress in my youth," I exclaimed. "I imagined the walls surrounding the mission compound would be three times as high. The single-story adobe houses all so close together are like a miniature village."

Deborah Cochran, Joe's mother, came to the door wearing a ribbed cotton blouse with a high collar and a flowing skirt covering her ankles. "Come and sit with me, Annie dear. Your presence brings back so many fond memories of your mother and father."

"I was surprised that you are still here," I said.

"In November 1871, two years after your mother took you to America, my dear husband died," she said. "I thought of returning then but continued to find usefulness here. Now it is fifteen years later, and I am the matron of the hospital my son founded. I hold prayer meetings in the mornings and read the Scriptures to the patients the rest of the day. When we close the hospital in the summer and come here to Seir, I stay in my old home and every day I visit the church that my husband built."

Rev. Labaree showed me the small house where my parents raised me and my brother Foster. "It is empty now and no longer used," he said.

I opened the heavy wood door and the air rushing in blew up a cloud of dust. There was a main room with a fireplace and two smaller rooms. "One of these smaller rooms must have been Foster's and my bedroom," I whispered. I noticed stairs leading down to a cellar under the house. "I remember going down those steps and falling," I said. "My father picked me up and set me on his lap. He comforted me until I stopped crying. That is one of the few memories I have of my father."

"He was a loving, gentle man," Rev. Labaree said.

Our last visit was to the missionary cemetery situated in a meadow on top of Mount Seir with a view of the valley below. It was surrounded by a white picket fence, and the graves of the missionaries and some of their children were covered with rectangular boxes of snow-white gypsum. My father's grave was close to the gate and read on one side, "Rev. Samuel Audley Rhea, Missionary to the Nestorians; Born January 23, 1827; died September 2, 1865. Present with the Lord." On the reverse side it read the same in Syriac with the scripture "He was not, for God took him."

"Genesis 5:24," I murmured.

I was quiet and thoughtful on the way back to Urmia, and neither Rev. Labaree nor Sam forced conversation on me. A revelation came to me that I had come full circle in my life. *I have come back to my childhood home. Persia is my homeland.*

Seeing Joe Cochran and Fred Coan, my friends from childhood now with families of their own, made me long for my own children. *Perhaps all three of us will start another generation of missionaries.*

CHAPTER 14

1890 — Rakhsh

LEAVING URMIA, WE STOPPED IN THE VILLAGE OF SOUJ BOLAK. "I would like to buy some rugs while we are here," Sam said. "I can arrange for shipment by wagon to Tabriz."

"Are the rugs from Souj Bolak special?" I asked.

"The Kurds of Souj Bolak weave some of the most beautiful rugs in Persia," Sam responded.

As we approached the bazaar, I noticed an unusually handsome horse with a blond mane and tail and a deep golden coat dappled with rusty red. "Oh Sam, what a magnificent horse; so solid and muscular," I exclaimed. "What kind of horse is he?"

"It is a Kurdish horse," Sam replied. "Stay here while I inquire if he is for sale." He dismounted and approached a group of men wearing *jamadani* turbans and baggy pants secured around their waists with wide multicolored sashes. Sam's conversation went on for some time and I grew uneasy when Kurdish women gathered around my horse and touched my shoes. "Don't touch," I said loudly in Syriac, hoping they understood. It seemed effective as they scurried away, but it was Sam approaching with the Kurdish horse that frightened them.

"The horse is yours," Sam said as he handed me the reins. "Stay here while I barter over rugs at the bazaar."

I was surprised when Sam came back empty handed. "The rugs I fancied were too big for our house. I will return when we build a new house with more space."

"A new house?" I exclaimed. "I like the house we live in now."

"We will need more room for our children," Sam replied.

Four years ago, Grandmother Cunningham sent a layette as a wedding present and the baby clothes were still packed away in the box. *I hope I can have children and am not barren like the arid plains of Persia.*

After descending from the Seyyed Taj ol Din Pass, we again rode through waving fields of wheat. Sam rode ahead of me leading my Kurdish horse and I admired both my handsome husband and my mighty steed. *I am the luckiest woman in Persia.*

We returned to Ali Shah and my father's house, foreboding on the way to Urmia but now evoked wistful sentiments. Nothing had changed in the weeks that intervened except my perspective. *This house was the beginning of my journey to America, and I have come full circle.*

"Do you want to try to ride your new horse?" Sam asked.

"Has he been saddled before?"

"Yes, saddled and ridden, but not by sidesaddle."

Sam let the horse sniff the saddle and covered his back with a blanket. He then slowly placed the saddle and reached under his belly to cinch it. The horse blinked and turned to look at me standing by his side as though to say, "And what year were you planning on mounting me?"

Sam offered cupped hands for my foot to boost me up to the saddle, then handed me the reins. I took a deep breath in and tapped my horse lightly with a crop. He lumbered along until we had gone a quarter mile down the road. "I feel like I am riding in a rocking chair," I exclaimed. "You are so robust compared to most Persian horses."

Sam stood in the middle of the road laughing as we galloped up and he was forced to jump aside before we came to a stop.

I stroked my Kurdish horse's neck and said, "I am going to name him Rakhsh, after Rostam's horse in the *Shahnameh*."

"You read the *Shahnameh*?" Sam exclaimed.

"Yes, Rakhsh was the color of 'rose petals scattered on a saffron background.' That description perfectly fits my horse," I said. "And you are my Rostam, my Persian hero."

"I had hoped that one day Persia would win your heart," Sam said with tears of emotion in his eyes. "I am so much in love with you, Annie."

Our First Child — Samuel Rhea

"I will be taking a long journey by train to Cairo, Egypt for a conference on Christian missions that serve Muslim populations," Sam told me. "I will be gone for two months, stopping at the Presbyterian missions in Turkey and Syria on my way."

Sam wrote letters every day assuring me he was safely making progress on his journey. Despite his letters, I missed him terribly. One morning at breakfast, I confided to Dr. Mary Bradford who was still living with us. "I am unusually worried about Sam and have nightmares of a train wreck. In the morning when I rise, I feel sick, my stomach is tied in knots. After breakfast, I often vomit."

Mary raised her eyebrows, then a gentle smile spread across her lips. "Perhaps you are pregnant," she said and patted my hand.

"Oh, my goodness," I exclaimed. "Are you able to tell with certainty?"

"If menses have stopped, then there is a good chance. Once the small bump on your abdomen appears, perhaps in a month, we will know for sure."

By early September a small bump on my abdomen was beginning to bulge. Fortunately, I had some loose-fitting frocks to wear. "Fetch me six yards of blue baft and six yards of gray muslin," I instructed Ishak and sent him to the bazaar. I proceeded to cut and sew the blue baft for a warm weather maternity dress to accommodate my first four months of pregnancy and started to design my winter muslin "balloon dress," as I called it, for the later stages of pregnancy.

When Sam returned, he was enthusiastic but tired. "I am convinced education is the most effective missionary work for Muslims," he declared at dinner. "The mission schools in Turkey, Syria and Egypt put our small school to shame. I must build a new school as soon as possible or at least expand the existing school in order to take in Muslim students."

After dinner Sam read the mail that had come in his absence, and I sat in a chair opposite him knitting a baby blanket. When he took his glasses off to rub his eyes, I took the opportunity to make my announcement. "There has been a personal development while you were away," I started.

"What is it?" Sam asked.

"Well, I was sick while you were gone, so I consulted Dr. Bradford."

"What was her diagnosis?"

"It will be another six months before we know the final outcome, but she is very certain that I am going to have a baby." *How I wish I had a picture of Sam's face. He was so incredulous.*

He staggered to his feet and embraced me. "When did it happen?" he blurted out.

"Possibly in Ali Shah."

Vali Ahd Mozaffar al-Din sent his carriage to take Sam to *Bagh-i-Shamal*, his summer palace. He sought Sam's advice on the curriculum for the government schools, which were attended by the sons of Persian noblemen. When Sam returned from the palace, I asked, "What was your impression of the *Vali Ahd*?"

"His nature is humane and sympathetic," Sam replied. "He is a friend of education, and a lover of flowers and rare plants. He also enjoys music. When I told him that my wife plays piano and sings, he requested that you come to the palace and give his daughter music lessons."

"What?" I exclaimed, almost falling out of my chair. "What an incredible honor."

Throughout the fall I gave music lessons to his daughter Princess Ezzat and found her to be a considerate and adept pupil. She was married to a nobleman and after a few months of lessons it became apparent that we were both pregnant. My baby, Samuel Rhea Wilson, was born on March 6th, 1890, and named after his great-grandfathers, Samuel Rhea and Samuel Wilson. To avoid confusion with his father, we called the baby "Rhea." Princess Ezzat's baby was also born in March, and when the babies were a month old, she sent a message to me saying, "I would like our babies to meet."

I dressed baby Rhea in his white christening gown, a dress a yard long, and we were escorted in the *Vali Ahd*'s carriage to *Dar-ol-Khalafeh*, the royal compound in the city. A soldier ushered us into the palace and down a series of passageways to a large court room. I was surprised to find the room full of young Persian women dressed in colorful silk shawls; it looked like a field of butterflies. The ladies were anxious to see the babies.

Princess Ezzat's baby was wrapped tightly in swaddling clothes, like a mummy. On his chest was fastened a large gold safety pin adorned with a glass ornament containing three concentric circles

— dark blue, white, light blue and a black dot at the center. "Such a handsome baby," I said. "I have never seen such a fancy safety pin before. It is interesting how the concentric circles catch your eye."

"The pin is a *nazar*," she responded. "It protects baby Abbas from the 'Evil Eye.' Your baby Rhea should be wearing one."

"We pray to the Lord to protect our baby," I replied.

"The dress is too big for your baby," Princess Ezzat said. "Do you want us to think he is that long?"

All the ladies giggled, and I pulled the christening dress back to show them Rhea's feet. The ladies lost any remaining reticence and fluttered about between Ezzat's baby and mine, commenting on Rhea's big blue eyes and blond hair in contrast to the Princess' baby Abbas, who had dark hair and eyes. One of them asked, "Will the eyes become dark when exposed to the sun?"

They asked me many questions about American ways of caring for a baby and were surprised to hear that I breastfed the baby myself and did not have a wetnurse to feed him. The Persian women with children offered me advice. "You must feed your next baby small pieces of butter and sugar water the first three days," one woman told me.

"You must also wait until the sixth night after birth to name the baby," another said. "It is not safe to name a baby until then."

When I arrived home with Rhea, Sam wanted to hear how his son was received. "The ladies forgot our differences and were merely absorbed in a women's natural fascination with babies," I said. "They were concerned that we did not have an amulet for the baby to ward off the 'Evil Eye.' "

"I am always surprised to learn how prevalent superstitions are, even among royalty," Sam said.

"I have to admit the Persian ladies scared me a bit, warning me also against naming the baby until the sixth day after birth."

Murder of a Missionary

In mid-May news came that shocked the entire mission community. Mary Bradford rushed into the house screaming, "Shushan Wright has been stabbed by one of the teachers at the mission school in Salmas. I must leave at once to be by her side."

"I will go with you," Sam said and rushed to pack a bag. "We can take post horses and exchange them at each station to get to Salmas faster." And within an hour they were gone. Many different versions of what had transpired in Salmas circulated around the mission. For two weeks I waited for Sam and Mary to return before I learned the truth.

"Shushan was stabbed five time in the back by one of the teachers," Mary said. "We did what we could to stop the bleeding and prevent infection. She lingered for two weeks before finally succumbing. She was pregnant and the baby was lost as well."

"Why did he stab her?" I asked.

"The teacher's name is Menas, half-Armenian, half-Syrian like Shushan," Mary said. "He had improper relations with a widow named Asli, the Wright's housekeeper and nanny. One night Shushan checked on her child, who was sleeping in Asli's room, and found the nanny had left her baby alone. It turned out that she was with Menas."

"Shushan told Newton about the nanny and Menas, and he dismissed him from the mission," Sam said. "Menas blamed Shushan for his dismissal and planned her murder as revenge. On May 14th he came to the house to settle his accounts with Newton and attacked Shushan with a dagger as she sat nearby sewing."

"Did he get away with the murder?" I asked.

"Menas fled to Turkey," Sam said, "Colonel Stewart, the Consul-General, was in Salmas and captured Menas on the road to Van."

"The Persian government will bring him to justice, won't they?" I asked.

"He is in prison, but the Gregorian Armenians, including Bishop Stephanos, are taking the side of the murderer and trying to free him by circulating slanders and using their political influence and bribes."

The New Presbyterian Mission in Tabriz

A large garden and house became available next to the Boys' School and Sam was anxious to buy it. "It is perfect for the new school," he exclaimed. "The large grove of mulberry trees would provide a shady and delightful campus. The building meant for distilling *arak* from raisins could be converted into a dormitory suitable for forty boarders. The building that housed the nobleman's harem could be converted into housing for the teachers and missionary families. There is also a fine stable for the horses."

"You have the ten-thousand-dollar donation from Mrs. Thaw, so what is holding you back?" I asked.

"Only your approval," Sam said, kissing my forehead.

"Well, I am not sure I care for the apricot orchard, or the English walnut trees, or all the beautiful roses in the garden," I answered. "And I am sure my Kurdish horse, Rakhsh, would be spoiled with such a fine stable, but since you are so keen on that dreadful property, I would be selfish not to say 'yes.'"

"I love you, Annie."

A few weeks later Jeremiah Oldfather came to visit Sam on a "business matter." I waited for an hour while they talked in the parlor and then entered holding a tray with two cups of tea. "Annie don't come in here like a servant," Jeremiah said. "You must help us celebrate. A classmate of mine, John Covington from Cincinnati, Ohio wrote to tell me that his daughter Ruth died of diphtheria. Since she was interested in missions, he would like to make a memorial for her. I thought since our existing church is unattractive, and would be unsafe in an earthquake, that a new church might be fitting."

"A new church," I exclaimed. "That would be a wonderful addition."

"I thought you would agree," Jeremiah responded with a chuckle. "I offered the suggestion to my friend, and he has cordially agreed to fund its construction."

"On top of the new house and school, are you ready to help design a church?" Sam asked.

"I will be overwhelmed, but I cannot say no," I replied.

Sam and I set to work designing the new Boys' School, the new mission church and our new house. We applied to the government in Tehran for a building permit and after paying *peeshkesh*, permission was granted. We expected resistance from the Muslim community, and during Muharram, when a parade came through the grounds, we held our breath. To our surprise the procession marched through the churchyard saying to the workmen, "May it be blessed. May God give you strength."

Grettie Holliday Going on Tour

Dr. Mary Bradford Going on Tour

CHAPTER 15

Changing of the Guard

IN THE SPRING OF 1890 JEREMIAH AND FELICIA OLDFATHER left for America and were replaced by Rev. Turner Brashear and his wife Annie. We sorely needed a replacement for Dr. Holmes after he became the *Vali Ahd's* physician and then left for Europe to seek treatment for his wife. The arrival of the new medical missionaries at the Tabriz station, Dr. William Vanneman and his wife Marguerite, was celebrated by the mission and the Persian community alike.

The departure of the senior members of the mission and their replacement with younger missionaries greatly impacted the social dynamics of the station. Sam was no longer the most junior member; he was the head of the station. I was no longer the youngest woman at the mission; I became responsible for helping the new missionary women, Annie Brashear and Marguerite Vanneman, learn the Persian languages and customs.

As principal of the Boys' School and head of the station, Sam was sought out by Armenian and Persian leaders of community. In addition to teaching classes at the Boys' School, many Muslim women asked me to visit them and give them counsel. With our new roles, the expansion of the mission and the start of a family, Sam and I were busier and happier than we had been during the past four years.

At one year old, Rhea was a beautiful child with a mass of golden curls and big blue eyes. Sam held him on his lap as he watched the donkeys bring bricks to build the new school. A crowd of Persian boys crowded around him, enamored by his fair child.

In the Spring of 1891, we were visited by W. Henry Grant, the Assistant Secretary of the Board of Foreign Missions, who was on a tour of the Asian stations. He was accompanied by Luther Wishard and his wife, Eva, who were on a trip around the world. "Luther was a classmate at Princeton, and I am excited to see him," Sam said. "Mr. Grant is next in line on the Board, under Robert Speer. He will report back to the Board on his impressions, so it is important that his visit goes well."

"How long will they be staying with us?" I asked.

"A few weeks," Sam replied. "They will travel with me to Urmia to attend our Annual Meeting."

Their first day at the mission Sam gave our visitors a tour of the Boys' School. W. Henry Grant's pistol fell out of its holster and accidently went off, the bullet lodging in a wall of the hallway. The boys poured out of the classrooms into the hall.

"We did not expect someone from the Board to cause such a sensation," Sam said. "Now when I tell the boys that a visitor from the Board is here, they will expect excitement."

Sam and Luther spent hours reminiscing about Princeton. "Let us sing *Old Nassau*," Luther said to Sam. "I can manage on the piano."

"Tune every harp and every voice..." Sam and Luther sang together for four choruses of *Old Nassau*, Princeton's alma mater, and continued to entertain us with songs and music the rest of the evening.

I enjoyed talking with Eva Wishard, an 1884 graduate from Cornell College. She was a tall and amiable woman. Despite her short visit, I felt as though Eva and I had been good friends for years. Little did I know that twenty-five years later we would rekindle our relationship as next door neighbors.

As Sam and the other missionaries prepared to go with W. Henry Grant and the Wishards to the Annual Meeting in Urmia, I desperately wanted to go with them.

"What about the baby?" Sam asked.

"I will take baby Rhea with us and show him off," I replied.

"I do not advise it. The five-day journey on horseback will be strenuous trip for an infant," Sam said.

"I also want to see Joe Cochran and Fred Coan and their families." I replied. "It seems so long since I have seen them."

Eva Wishard, Marguerite Vanneman and I rode side-saddle along with the men on horseback, while Baby Rhea slept on a pillow in front of the hostler. After three days our party reached the mission in Salmas. I was alarmed when I picked up baby Rhea from the pillow and found him limp.

"Does the baby appear to be sick?" I asked Dr. Vanneman.

"The child appears to be exhausted." Will Vanneman replied. "I suggest that you stay in Salmas for at least a day so the child can get proper sleep."

"If we stay, we will miss at least a day of the meeting," Sam said.

"There is room in my carriage for Annie and the baby," John Mechlin, the head of the Salmas station, said. "My wife Ella is caring for two infants and will not be coming."

What a blessing it was. For the next two days my precious baby Rhea slept in my arms, and Sam led my horse Rakhsh as he rode beside the carriage.

"How has your work been going?" I asked John Mechlin.

"After four years I have become somewhat fluent in the languages of the region, Syriac, Armenian and Kurdish," John responded. "This year I toured thirteen Armenian villages and many villages in Turkey. Despite the persistent efforts by

Gregorian priests to prejudice the villagers against me, my audiences often numbered over ninety. I received open and courteous attention from many people in the communities I visited."

"Any converts?" I asked.

"There is no real sign of any of them turning to the Lord," John said with a sigh. "Still, I labor on, working through the strength of hope."

"How is Newton Wright doing after the death of his wife?" I asked.

"Struggling as you might expect," John replied. "Her brutal murder was only a year ago. My wife Ella found it so disturbing that she begged me to return to America right away. It took some convincing for her to agree to stay."

"Many of the missionaries were greatly disturbed by Shushan's murder. Will Newton come to the meeting?" I asked.

"Only briefly. He has two young children to care for. He intends to take them to America soon."

We arrived at the Urmia mission and were greeted by the Coans and the Cochrans. Kate and Joe Cochran's family now consisted of baby Suviah and three teenagers — Clement, Lili and Heydar. Fred and Ida Coan had two young children, Frank and Elizabeth, who kept us entertained. The center of attention was our baby Rhea. Everyone commented on his unusual fairness and beauty, and the other children took turns stroking his golden curly hair.

"Has the Gregorian church interfered with your missionary work as it has in the past?" Fred Coan asked.

"Antagonism from Armenian priests remains as strong as ever," Sam replied. "Acceptance of any interpretation of the word of God outside the tenets of their church is branded as unpatriotic and disloyal. Protestant converts are persecuted."

"Intolerance is more severe among the Armenians than we see with the Nestorian in Urmia. What about the mission's educational work?" Fred Coan asked.

"The past year has been our most successful in the history of the school," Sam replied. "We have seventy students, half of them boarders. Our current accommodations are cramped, and we look forward to our new school building. Hopefully we will complete it before the next school year begins."

"Are you teaching, Annie?" Ida Coan asked.

"I teach four hours daily in the Boys' School, kindergarten and the Bible Class," I replied.

"How has the medical work been in Urmia?" Sam asked.

"We are treating over two hundred patients a year in the hospital," Joe Cochran replied. "This year we will graduate our second class of Persian medical students. Our other achievement was building a hospital annex for the women patients. Dr. Emma Miller will be joining the mission, our first woman doctor."

"What adventures have you had touring, Fred?" I asked.

"I spent two months in the mountain villages of the Kurdistan," Fred replied. "First, I traveled through a region of prevailing spiritual darkness, then I reached Dihi, where I found a miraculous change. Several years ago, I had converted a man there, who then founded a Christian church. He told me, 'When I started preaching your religion, the priests at first told the villagers it was accursed. Now they gather an audience for me. Why? Because now they hear no swearing and see no fighting in the village.' As I rode down through the vineyards, I heard men singing hymns. When I asked a man why they sing hymns, he responded, 'The hymns they learned in the Christian church are so popular that they use them in place of the obscene songs they used to sing while working in the fields.' "

Being with our friends from Urmia filled my heart with the warm glow of comradery. On the five-day trip back to Tabriz I told Sam, "It was worth the trip to reconnect with my childhood friends."

"I only hope that the journey has not strained the health of our baby Rhea," Sam replied.

Completion of the New Tabriz Mission

While the new missionaries, the Vannemans and the Brashears, were still learning the native languages, the brunt of the missionary work fell on Sam. With the large amount of building to attend to, it was exceptionally draining on him. The new Boys' School was completed in the summer of 1891, a two-story red brick building with six classrooms, a chapel and a library. The recitation hall was equipped with desks, a globe, maps, physiological and astronomical charts, physical apparatus, and a kindergarten outfit. The library was supplied with books in Armenian, Persian and English. Classes started September 10, 1891.

The new church was completed later that fall, with three thousand dollars from J. I. Covington of Brooklyn in memory of his daughter Ruth. It was a handsome building with a session room on one end and seating for two hundred and fifty people. Sam insisted on a bell tower, even though the government would not allow us to ring a bell. "Some think I had it installed for its architectural beauty or to buttress the wall," Sam said, "but it is for a bell. And some day there will be a bell to ring in the start of church service." Years later we installed a bell from Tiflis with a timbre so beautiful the *Vali Ahd* asked Sam to strike it when he came to visit.

"For now, we need to rely on the Armenian janitor who goes door to door to announce church service," I replied. "How will the balcony in the back be used?"

"For Muslim women, of course," Sam replied.

"But Muslim women are not allowed to come to the church," I replied.

"With God all things are possible," Sam said. "Matthew 19:26. And God gives me the hope that they will come." For years, I joked about the empty balcony, but when the Muslim women later came, Sam proved my doubts were wrong.

With a new mission compound, a new Boys' School and a new church, we had such hope for the future. Sam and I had started our family and were building a new house. Our lives were full of promise and joy.

One night in November, Rhea developed a fever with a sore throat and swollen glands. Dr. Vanneman looked into his mouth and turned pale. "His throat and tonsils are covered with a thick gray membrane," he said. "It is diphtheria." I shuttered and a deep hollowness filled my chest.

All night I kept vigil by Rhea's cradle, and prayed to God to make him healthy again, but by morning he had difficulty breathing. In an attempt to help him breathe, Dr. Vanneman inserted a tube in his throat, but after struggling several more hours, baby Rhea breathed his last breath. I hid my face in my hands and sobbed. "My treasure has been snatched away. My precious baby has been taken from me."

Sam struggled too and immersed himself in his teaching to still the pain. Persian friends, hearing of Rhea's death, came to console us. "Remember that Jesus taught his disciples that God may call us to leave our earthly families," one said.

"Yes, I remember," I replied.

Another Persian Muslim woman came to comfort me saying, "I often saw the beautiful baby carried by my house, so I had to come and weep with you."

"Jesus will care for Rhea," I replied. "In Mark 10:14-16 the Bible reads: 'Let the children come to me, do not hinder them; for to such belongs the kingdom of God. And he took them in his arms and blessed them, laying his hands on them.'"

Later that winter, the woman also lost her only child. "Friends who came expected to find me frenzied in grief," she said. "Instead, they found me serene. I told them, 'The Christian lady told me that Lord Jesus takes little children in His arms and cares for them; this comforts me.'"

Over two hundred Persians and Armenians visited us to give their condolences. I found it painful when some Persians said, "It is God's will." It brought me solace to receive a letter from Joe Cochran saying, "Do not think God did it. He has more sorrow than you."

The mission did not have a cemetery, so we chose a spot by the new church for the burial. We held a private memorial with other missionaries and close friends in the new church, which was a month away from officially opening. It was a candlelight service with a solemn procession. Sam managed to deliver the sermon, although his voice failed him twice.

The dedication of church was held December 29, 1891. A festive occasion with the church filled to capacity — two hundred and fifty Armenians, Muslims and Europeans attended, the largest assembly of Protestant worshippers ever in Tabriz. In the morning, services were in Azeri and, in the afternoon, repeated in Armenian and English, and this tradition was maintained for years to come.

Sam and I spent New Year's Day alone. "I am at a loss for New Year's resolutions," Sam said holding his blank piece of paper. "We have accomplished so much this year."

I looked up from my paper and said, "Well if you want to copy my resolution I will not object."

"What is it?" Sam asked.

"To have another baby," I replied.

Persian Men's Social Gathering

Man Smoking Qalyan

CHAPTER 16

1892 – the Cholera Year

"MY BROTHER ROB IS ON SABBATICAL IN SYRIA STUDYING Aramaic languages and researching the Old Testament," Sam exclaimed. "He plans to come to Tabriz and stay with us for a month."

We held a reception for Rob to meet the other missionaries at the station. "Rob is a Professor of Hebrew and Old Testament History at Allegheny Seminary," Sam said. "He knows at least forty languages."

"Granted some are highly related," Rob said. "I needed to learn ancient languages to read the original texts that prove the veracity of the Old Testament."

"I would not be able to keep my head straight," Marguerite Vanneman said.

The next day we took Rob on a tour of the new Boys' School. "The boys' dormitory is intentionally simple," Sam said. "Most of the boys come from poor villages and the aim is to make it easy for them to return to their homes as teachers."

"Yes, I can imagine sitting on chairs and eating with knives and forks would not be good habits to teach them," Rob interjected.

"Four or five boys share a room," Sam continued. "The cement floors are covered with carpets, placed over split-cane matting to protect them from the dirt. *Takhtchas*, or niches, on the walls are provided for the boys' books."

"Do you provide any furniture?" Rob asked.

"A kerosene lamp and wood stove are provided, but there are no tables, chairs or bedsteads. The boys provide their narrow sleeping mattresses stuffed with wool, cylindrical pillows and comforters. The bed is spread on the floor at night and rolled up in a bundle in the morning and placed at the end of the room. In the summer, the boys spread their mattresses on the flat roof."

"How do they study and write without a table?"

"When a boy enters his room, he leaves his shoes in the hall and sits on his heels with his lamp on the floor. With his paper in his left hand, he writes with a reed or steel pen, left-to-right in Armenian and right-to-left in Persian."

"What about meals?" Rob asked.

"The boys take turns preparing food in a typical Persian kitchen. A fireplace built into the wall, called an *ojak*, is used for cooking with pans and kettles. Baking is performed in clay jar oven in a hole in the floor, called a *tandur*. Fuel for cooking includes twigs, grapevines and manure cakes, called *yapma*. Bread baking is performed by tradeswomen who we schedule to come in. Tomorrow happens to be bread-making day."

"That would be fascinating to watch them," Rob said.

"I love watching them too," I added. "I will join you."

The women were scheduled to bake the next day but did not come for another two days. "It is common for events to be delayed; nothing is rushed in the East," Sam explained.

I was relieved when the bread bakers arrived, as there were only a few days of bread left in the cellar of the boys' dormitory. First the women mixed and kneaded four barrels of leavened dough and let it rest.

As the women sat down around the smoking *tandur* I said, "Now the action will begin."

"One woman kneads a ball of dough," Sam said. "Another slings a roll on her arm until the dough is as thin as pie crust and two and a half feet long. A third woman casts it on the side of the oven. As the next ball of dough is cast the previous one is done and taken out."

The floor was quickly covered with thin, crisp sheets of bread as the women worked methodically through four barrels of dough.

"Now the women will pile it on a rack in the cellar five to six feet high and wide," Sam said.

"The bread, called *lavash*, is delicious, sweet and wholesome," I added, "and it will feed the boys for a month."

"Bread is the 'staff of Life,' " Sam said.

"Samuel, what Scripture is that from?" Rob asked with a sly smile. "I don't remember."

"It is from Jonathan Swift," I interjected.

"Right you are," Rob bellowed. "The Scriptures say nothing about a 'staff of Life.' It comes from a bastardization of Isaiah 3:1 which says: 'For behold, the Lord, the Lord of hosts, is taking away from Jerusalem and from Judah stay and staff, the whole stay of bread, and the whole stay of water.' The Bible says 'stay' not 'staff.' "

"Yes, Rob," Sam replied. "When it comes to the Old Testament you are admittedly the expert."

"What are dormitory meals like?" Rob asked.

"Sheets of *lavash* are placed on a width of muslin on the carpet and the boys sit on their heels around it," Sam said. "Breakfast is bread and cheese with tiny glasses of sweetened tea. Lunch is bread with cheese or yoghurt-like fermented milk, called *matzoon*, herbs and fruit, typically grapes and watermelon. At dark, dinner is served. *Shorba*, a thick stew of mutton with fragrant herbs, is their favorite. They eat it with wooden spoons or scoop it with bread."

"I have seen vegetables stuffed with ground meat and rice sold by street vendors," Rob said. "Do they eat such things?"

"You are referring to *dolmas*, highly seasoned dumplings of ground meat and rice often encased in cabbage or grape leaves. In Persia *dolmas* can also be ground meat in a hollowed-out eggplant, tomato, cucumber or fruit. *Pillou*, is boiled rice with butter. The boys typically eat *dolmas* and *pillou* with their hands rather than with bread or a spoon."

"I have wanted to try eating with my hands," Rob said. "Is there a certain technique that needs to be used?"

"I was called upon to settle a dispute between some boys at the school on that very subject," Sam replied. "One boy complained of his fellow student saying, 'He has no manners. He eats with five fingers.' So I asked, 'And how should he eat?' to which he replied, 'Why with three, of course; only a boor eats with five.'"

"And did you tell the offender to observe the rules of polite society?"

"He was duly counseled."

Sam and I had a hearty laugh when we were preparing for bed and recapped our conversation with Rob regarding the "staff of Life."

"Rob is a fanatic about the Old Testament," Sam said. "Never challenge the veracity of the Old Testament for an instance in his presence."

"Today is the Boys' School Exhibition," Sam told Rob. "Every spring, students demonstrate in a public forum the principles of New Learning. It contrasts our educational practices with the mosque schools, where boys sit on the floor and read the Qur'an in Arabic, a language they do not understand."

"We sent invitations to Persian officials, Foreign Consuls, and the students' fathers," I added.

Pupils recited lessons and sang in Persian, Azeri, Armenian, English, French, and Russian. To demonstrate their knowledge in anatomy, students identified bones on Dr. Vanneman's skeleton. Astrology students named the planets using a model of our solar system revolving around the sun. Mastery of calligraphy, an art revered in Persia, was demonstrated by boys who drew the thirty-two letters of the Persian alphabet on a blackboard. For geography class, I held up a map of the world and students pointed to the countries where imported items, such as tea, coffee, and cutlery, originated.

"The exhibition was impressive," Rob said. "I admire the boys for the number of languages they have learned."

"It is propaganda to stimulate interest in the school and draw in students," Sam said.

The next day Rob received a cable from A.V. Williams Jackson, our friend and Zoroaster expert. "We had planned on working together here," Rob said, "but Germany suddenly banned travel to Persia because of a cholera epidemic in Mashhad. Apparently, seven thousand people have died."

"How unfortunate," I said.

"How far away is Mashhad?" Rob asked. "The American government may restrict my re-entry if cholera comes to Tabriz."

"Mashhad is about a thousand miles east near the Afghan border," Sam replied.

"I pray it does not reach you in Tabriz, but I cannot afford to be quarantined, so I will arrange for my return to America tomorrow," Rob said.

I was disappointed that Rob felt he needed to leave but also alarmed that cholera was spreading in Persia. Sam decided to go with his brother as far as the Black Sea, and I feared he might contract the disease during his travels in the Caucasus. "My father died so quickly after he became ill with cholera," I said. "Please be careful and drink only boiled water."

Sam was gone for two weeks and when he returned, he said, "The trans-Caucasus train was delayed because the Russians conducted medical inspections of train passengers. They are taking precautions because cholera has erupted in Baku. While on the train I heard that the Russian government sent Persian labors home as a precaution."

"Oh no, what if they bring cholera with them?"

Within a few weeks, cholera erupted in the Persian cities of Ardabil and Rasht, near the Caspian Sea.

"In the past, cholera has spread slowly by caravan," Sam said. "Now it is traveling fast, fueled by steam, via ships and locomotives."

Quarantine was established on the road from Ardabil one hundred and fifty miles from Tabriz. "This is a laughingstock," Sam said, shaking his head. "They call it 'qirantine' because anyone can get through by paying the quarantine agents a few *qirans*."

By the Islamic month of Muharram, the cholera epidemic had reached Tabriz. The commemoration of the martyrdom of Husayn had started, the mosques were filled to capacity, and people crowded the streets to watch the processions. "The Muslims of Tabriz have turned to religion to appease God and ask Him to prevent cholera," Sam said. "Printed passages from the Qur'an hang over the street to assure those passing underneath are safe."

One evening when Sam returned from a village he said, "Thousands of prayers were posted above houses. I picked up one lying in the street to read it: 'Whoever shall post this prayer above his door, the cholera will not come to that house, and whoever shall write the prayer and put it in a cup of water and shall drink the water, the disease of cholera will not reach him.' "

Ishak overheard Sam and said, "A mullah received a telegram from Abbas Mosque in Karbala saying they received a revelation from Husayn's brother Abbas — 'on Ashura cholera in Tabriz will end.' "

"What else have you heard?" Sam asked.

"A *mujtahid*, an authority of Islamic law, said he had a vision of Imam Reza, a descendent of Muhammad, returning to his shrine in Mashhad. The *mujtahid* asked him, 'Where are you coming from?' and Imam Reza replied, 'I have gone to protect Tabriz from cholera.' "

"Cholera came to Tabriz from Mashhad by travelers other than Imam Reza," Sam said.

Ashura was August 3rd. "Religious frenzy has reached a higher pitch than usual," I commented. "Women in the streets beseech God, by his many titles, to save them from cholera and death."

Neither faith nor superstition spared the inhabitants of Tabriz from cholera. The polluted water supply, public baths, and the disbelief that infection is caused by microbes assisted in the spread. In a few days people were dying by hundreds in every quarter.

"People are fleeing the city," Sam said. "Armenians are going to Karadagh, and Muslims escaping to their native villages. Thousands have abandoned their homes, leaving their property unprotected."

"All that man has he will give for his life," I replied. "Job 2:4."

"We need to quarantine the students and missionaries," Sam declared. "You and others in the mission should flee to the village of Zinjanab below Mount Sahand. The mountain water there will be safe to drink. For those who stay at the mission, all drinking water will be boiled."

"Who will stay at the mission?" I asked.

Grettie Holliday, Mary Bradford and I," Sam replied. "I will stay with the boys in the dormitory and Grettie can stay with the students at the Girls' School. Dr. Bradford will remain in the dispensary."

"Zinjanab is sixteen miles away," I bemoaned. "I don't want to go without you. Besides I am eight months pregnant and not really in shape to go camping."

"It will be cooler on the mountain and Dr. Vanneman will be with you. I will help you pack your things," Sam said.

Those who fled with me to the mountain village of Zinjanab were the new missionaries — Dr. Will Vanneman and his wife Marguerite and Rev. Turner Brashear and his wife Annie. Rev. William Whipple and his wife Mary, the agents for the American Bible Society who lived across the street, also came with their children. Mr. Whipple kindly drove me up in his wagon as Sam rode his horse alongside.

Sam set up my tent and helped me settle in. When the sun started to set, he said, "I need to return before dark."

I started sobbing, clinging to his sides. "Let me read from Psalms 91: 1-11," he said and opened my Bible:

"My God in whom I trust.

For he will deliver you from the snare of the fowler and from the deadly pestilence;

He will cover you with his pinions, and under his wings you will find refuge; His faithfulness is a shield and a buckler.

You will not fear the terror of the night, nor the arrow that flies by day, not the pestilence that stalks in darkness, nor the destruction that wastes at noonday.

A thousand may fall at your side, ten thousand at your right hand; but it will not come near you.

No evil shall befall you, no scourge come near your tent.

For he will give his angels charge of you to guard you in all your ways."

I watched as Sam went over the mountain top against the setting sun, a silhouette of a horse and rider returning to the valley of the shadow of death. The image was embedded in my thoughts and in my dreams for nights to come.

In early September, the rains began, and my tent leaked. "You need to give up your mountain refuge and return to the mission," Dr. Vanneman advised. "Your pregnancy is too far along, and you should not risk giving birth on the mountain. Dr. Bradford will help with the birth at the mission."

Sam came to fetch me in a wagon. As we approached the city, we were greeted by a dust storm that collected and concentrated the stench of the dead and blew it down on us.

"This is a quintessence of putrefaction!" I screamed.

"Hold this bulb of garlic to your nose," Sam said. "For a month the epidemic raged, killing ten to twelve thousand people who now lie on the ground unburied in the cemeteries."

"How are the others who stayed?" I asked.

"Dr. Mary Bradford worked tirelessly from the mission dispensary and saved hundreds of lives," Sam said. "One of her patients was Armenian Bishop Stephanos, who so bitterly opposed our missionary work. It was an opportunity to minister to and win him over. His condition was improving under Mary's care, but the Russian Consul sent his physician to take over, and he died."

"We are lucky he died under someone else's care," I said. "I am sure his people greatly mourned his death, and they may have sought revenge."

"Actually, their response was curious," Sam said. "One mourner said, 'It is expedient that one man should die for the people.' They expected his death to save them."

"How are our church members?" I asked.

"I called on them once a week to pray with them and strengthen their hearts during these trying times," Sam replied. "It was also my way of checking to make sure they were boiling drinking water. The only one who perished was Hosef."

"Not Hosef," I cried.

"He helped an undertaker carry the body of a Hollander to a grave. A few days later word came that Hosef was stricken and in the morning he was dead. I was called to conduct funeral services by his daughter, also a Protestant. An altercation arose when a Gregorian priest, who was called by Hosef's wife, also arrived. A war of words was exchanged by a dozen wine-excited Armenians, and I finally stood by while the priest waved his censer and read unintelligible prayers."

"It is so sad to hear of his passing," I said. "What about life in Tabriz?"

"Sanitary conditions have gone from bad to worse," Sam said. "Funerals pass by the compound day and night, with *mullahs* reading passages from the Qur'an and mourners wailing. Some Armenians, thinking alcohol prevents cholera, sway inebriated in the streets. Others sacrifice sheep and hold religious rituals. Fear and death reign."

For the next week, I lay in bed, very pregnant and uncomfortable, and expecting to give birth any day.

Mary Agnes was born screaming early in the morning on September 10th with Dr. Bradford's assistance. Her eyes were slate gray and she only had light wisps of blond hair. Her second day, she appeared to scowl at me. "Yes, Agnes," I said. "I know this was an awful time to come out of my womb, but all the other miseries of life will now seem less so." Agnes listened and smiled, then fell asleep in my arms.

As Agnes slept, I read Psalms 116:1-9.

"For thou hast delivered my soul from death, my eyes from tears, my feet from stumbling;

I walk before the Lord in the land of the living." (Psalms 116:8-9)

With the first frost in November the cholera epidemic ceased as suddenly as it had begun. People returned to Tabriz and counted their losses. The French Consul, our neighbor, had sent his sister and little daughter to their summer home for safety. He stayed behind to care for their tutor, who had been stricken. After the tutor died, he left for his summer house, only to find that his sister and daughter were dead. So many similar stories were shared among the survivors.

"A courier brought a package from Princess Ezzat-ed-Dowleh," Sam announced as he handed me a box wrapped with a silk scarf.

"A present from Ezzat?" I exclaimed and hurried to open it. "Why these are *nazar* bracelets — one for baby Agnes and one for me."

"What is the metal box?" Sam asked.

"It is for burning *esfand*," I said. "Both the *nazar* and *esfand* are to protect us from the 'Evil Eye.' "

My thoughts were now not of my own safety, but for that of my small helpless infant girl. *I will not let anyone else touch her and infect my precious baby.*

New Wilson House, Tabriz Mission 1892

Tabriz Station from the Arg 1892: Mission church (far left), Vanneman house (left), Boys' School (center), Wilson house (right), missionary residences (low building, front center).

CHAPTER 17

1892 — Sealing of the Boys' School

BISHOP STEPHANOS DIED OF CHOLERA, BUT HIS SCHEMES against the mission were still alive. Other hostilely disposed Gregorian Armenians brought a case against us to *Vali Ahd* Mozaffar ad-Din. Despite obtaining approval from the Persian government for building the new mission school and church we now faced opposition.

In late October, Sam left to tour Hamadan, three hundred miles south of Tabriz, and Rev. Turner Brashear traveled to Urmia, leaving Dr. Vanneman as the acting head of the mission. In the early morning of October 27, I was breastfeeding Agnes when I saw Persian officials enter the mission compound from the bedroom window. With the baby in my arms, I hurried to the men's dispensary where Dr. Vanneman was busy seeing patients. When Will and I confronted the officials, we found that deputy justice minister Mirza Javat Khan and the *beglar-begi* had locked the doors of the church and school and sealed the keyholes with red sealing wax.

"*Vali Ahd* Mozaffar ad-Din gave orders to lock and seal your doors," the *beglar-begi* said.

"Why?" Dr. Vanneman asked them, exasperated.

"You will need to inquire with Mostashar al-Dowleh, the foreign agent for the Persian government," Mirza Javat Khan replied. "We just follow the orders we are given." And with that they departed.

"What shall we do?" I bewailed.

"I will try to contact agent Mostashar al-Dowleh and *Vali Ahd* Mozaffar ad-Din," Dr. Vanneman said, and assured me something would be done, but his requests for an audience were in vain.

"They only wish to speak to Sam," Will explained. "Being new to the mission station, I have not been formally introduced to the local government officials."

Why did this have to happen with Sam gone? We need to have a senior missionary present who can talk to the Persian authorities.

"With the Boys' School locked, I fear the students will flee to the Armenian schools," I said. "The boys will be asked to promise to stay as a condition for their acceptance and may not return."

"I have referred the matter to the American Consul in Tehran," Will said. "Vice Consul John Tyler agreed to pursue a resolution. Unfortunately, the Shah is on a hunting expedition, so there may be a delay."

When Sam returned several weeks later, he was agitated. "We still do not know why they sealed the school and church shut?" he exclaimed. Sam sent a telegram to Consul Tyler demanding an explanation for the closure. A few days later, he received a list of charges against the mission from the foreign agent, Mostashar al-Dowleh.

"This is what we are charged with," Sam said, his hands shaking as he read a letter from Consul Tyler. "One, lack of proper permission to build a church; two, building a church with a tower for a bell; three, writing in Persian the ten commandments on a wall of the church in the sacred Islamic color, blue; four, receiving Muslim boys into our school; five, allowing Muslim women into the church, etcetera, etcetera."

"What are you going to do?" I asked.

"I will send Consul Tyler my answers to the charges and wait for a response."

Sam was pleased by the response he received from foreign agent Mostashar al-Dowleh on official government paper. "The Persian authorities are satisfied and have ordered the seals removed."

Weeks went by and the seals were not removed, even after Sam showed the *beglar-begi* the letter that he received from Tehran.

The Persian Protestants in our congregation then sent a petition with sixty signatures requesting that *Vali Ahd* Mozaffar ad-Din allow them to send their children to our school. "We need to return to the mission church to resume our prayers for *Padishah yoshasun* (his Majesty's long life)," the petition said. The *Vali Ahd* agreed to their requests, and we again waited for the officials to remove the seals.

With the mission church locked and sealed, the congregation was meeting for service in the Girls' School. The following Sunday, the local government officials, who were angered by the petition, arrested three Armenians as they left our church service. "Will this ever end?" Sam screamed when he heard of the arrests.

A letter to Sam from foreign agent Mostashar al-Dowleh was delivered by courier. "It reads: 'The officials will remove the seals if you agree to these conditions: one, the ten commandments will be erased from the church wall; two, no religious lessons will be given to Armenians; three, doctors will not treat either men nor women; four, preaching to Muslims only in the presence of a law officer; five, you will not preach in Azeri; six, if a Protestant takes a photograph of a Muslim woman, then all Protestants must leave the country.' "

"That is a ridiculous list of demands," I cried.

"I do not know what the outcome will be," Sam said. "Man's extremity is God's opportunity. Perhaps he will teach us a lesson of truth."

"I feel cast down," I replied. "We have done everything we could."

On Friday, January 6th, Sam said. "Let us make this Saturday a day of fasting and prayer for the opening of the doors."

"I will pray from dawn until dusk," I promised.

At ten o'clock on Saturday I had skipped breakfast and was breast feeding Agnes, when I noticed the officials coming into the mission yard. "What?" I cried and ran down the hall with the baby at my breast. "Sam the Persian officials are in the compound."

The officials came to our door, and Sam went out with them into the mission yard. From the bedroom window I discreetly watched them as I nursed my baby. First, they removed the seals and unlocked the doors to the mission church, and then the Boys' School.

Sam returned smiling and said, "Annie you must have prayed up a storm."

"It was my most earnest supplication," I replied.

"Well, the fact is that it was not a miracle of God," Sam responded. "Yesterday the newly appointed American Minister to Persia, Watson Sperry, arrived in Tehran. The *Vali Ahd* was afraid that Sperry would complain to the Shah, so he ordered the seals be removed immediately."

"What did the officials say to you?" I asked.

"They read me this order: 'That we must not receive Muslim women and children to our schools or church, that we must not take photographs of Muslim women, that we must not conduct ourselves contrary to custom.'"

"What about Muslim men?" I asked.

"Apparently they can attend our Boys' School and mission church," Sam said. "We will see if the police continue to arrest and beat Muslim men who come to our church services."

"It means that after ten weeks of being locked out of our school and church, we are finally free to continue," I said.

The school opened again for classes January 9th, 1893, a joyous day.

In October 1893, on the anniversary of the sealing, the *Nadim-bashi*, the principal of the government school, with several officials, made a friendly visit to the mission Boys' School. "I bear greetings from the *Vali Ahd*," the *Nadim-bashi* said. "He requests that you furnish an English teacher and a woman teacher to teach music and embroidery for the government school."

"Do the boys in the government school wish to learn embroidery?" I asked.

"Yes, they have made that request," the *Nadim-bashi* replied. "I also ask that Dr. Vanneman give medical lessons and that Dr. Wilson visit me and give advice on the school curriculum."

"I will speak with the other missionaries and see what we can arrange," Sam replied. "For my part, I will be pleased to visit you as often as you desire."

The sealing of the doors was the last time that there was opposition to the Presbyterian mission in Tabriz by the Persian government. The Boys' School thrived and soon there were seventy students.

1893 — Death of a Missionary Matron

The following spring, Sam received a telegram from the Urmia mission station. "Deborah Cochran died March 9th," he said. "I am going to Urmia tomorrow for the memorial service."

"Oh, how I would like to go and give my condolences to Josie." I bemoaned. "But little baby Agnes is only six months old."

"Joe will understand," Sam said. "A long meaningful letter is often most appreciated in grief; it can be read again and again when all the mourners have left. I will hand deliver it."

When Sam returned two weeks later, he told me about the service and the internment on Mount Seir. "It was freezing in the small cemetery in Seir. They used an epithet: 'She hath done what she could.'"

"Mark 14:8," I replied. "So fitting for someone who served the Urmia mission station for forty-six years. I hope we can serve that long."

1893 – Week of Prayer

In May, Rev. Turner Brashear held a weeklong retreat for the students at the Boys' School he called "The Week of Prayer," after a similar retreat on the shores of Lake Urmia held by Fred Coan. After the boys spent the day with Rev. Brashear studying passages of the Scriptures, Sam led a Monday evening session on Jonah.

"When one is unaccountable, others can be damaged," Sam said. "One is mistaken if one thinks one can hide from the Lord and escape one's responsibilities. But, if one repents, the Lord will forgive you. This is the story of Jonah:

"The Lord asked Jonah to go to Nineveh to warn the people that their wickedness would be punished, but Jonah fled and boarded a ship instead. This angered the Lord and He caused a great tempest at sea that threatened the ship. The sailors cast lots to determine who had brought evil to the ship; a cup of stones was shaken, all white except one that was black. When each blindly picked a stone, Jonah held the black one, proving he was guilty. The sailors demanded that he tell them what he had done. Farzad, please read Jonah 1:10-12."

Farzad read: "Then the men were exceedingly afraid, and said to him, 'What is this that you have done!' For the men knew that he was fleeing from the presence of the Lord, because he had told them. Then they said to him, 'What shall we do to you, that the sea may quiet down for us?' For the sea grew more and more tempestuous. He said to them, 'Take me up and throw me into the sea; then the sea will quiet down for you; for I know it is because of me that the great tempest has come upon you.'"

"Jonah, realizing he had endangered others was ready to spare his own life," Sam said. "Would you be ready to make a sacrifice for your fellow brothers?"

Abgar, an Armenian Catholic stood up and said, with a trembling voice, "I have been the Jonah on the ship and resisted the truth. I have prayed only to the archangels Gabriel and Raphael. I now realize that the Lord is my only Mediator. Pray for me." He sat down with tears in his eyes.

"Thank you, Abgar," Sam continued. "The sailors saw no recourse than to throw Jonah into the sea. 'The Lord appointed a great fish to swallow up Jonah; and Jonah was in the belly of the fish three days and three nights.' Jonah's 'soul fainted' and he remembered the Lord, to whom he prayed. Bijan, please read Jonah 2:8-10."

Bijan read: "Those who pay regard to vain idols forsake their true loyalty. But I with the voice of thanksgiving will sacrifice to thee; what I have vowed I will pay. Deliverance belongs to the Lord!" And the Lord spoke to the fish, and it vomited out Jonah on dry land."

The boys' faces reflected a mixture of disgust and revelation. "The Lord accepted Jonah's repentance but still expected him to complete the task he had previously given him," Sam said.

Another boy stood up and said, "Last year I fell into temptation. I associated with evil companions and began to drink, though

I had never done so before. I quit reading my Bible. Then the thought came to me, 'If I continue this course I shall be like these men.' I abhorred their conduct and was determined to repent."

"And I am sure the Lord forgave you," Sam said.

A young boy stood up, surprising the others, and not finding the words or composure to express himself, simply interjected, "I am a great sinner, pray for me."

I was excited to hear from Urmia that two second generation missionaries had returned to reinforce their ranks – William Shedd and Benjamin Woods "B.W." Labaree. Their parents, Eliza and Benjamin Labaree Sr. and John and Jennie Shedd were in their late fifties and likely to retire or withdraw soon. "Now the Western Mission has five second generation missionaries, including me, Fred Coan and Joe Cochran," I exclaimed. "I want to go to Urmia and be part of the reunion celebration before Christmas."

"With our upcoming furlough in America, we cannot spare the time away," Sam said. "Besides Agnes is only a year old and the trip would be hard on her, particularly since it is winter."

"After furlough we will go to Urmia," I said, "that is, unless I have another baby."

Principal Wilson with Students and Teachers of the Mission Boys' School
(S.G. Wilson is in the back row standing in front of the door,
the bearded man left of center wearing glasses.)

CHAPTER 18

1894 — First Furlough

"YOU WILL NEED TO START YOUR TRIP TO AMERICA BY APRIL," Dr. Vanneman warned me. "If you wait any longer you may endanger your pregnancy."

From the Caucasus we took the ferry across the Black Sea and the train from Odessa to Europe. Agnes was nineteen months old, an active toddler, who often proved difficult to restrain from wandering. *What is the six-week return trip going to be like when I have a baby and a three-year-old child?*

On our steamer across the Atlantic I resisted my protective maternal instincts and allowed Agnes to interact with other passengers sitting near us on the deck. I discovered that their attention to Agnes gave me the freedom to read and carry-on conversations with other adults. A Russian woman doted on Agnes and took her on strolls around the ship, holding her hand and calling her "Miss Independence."

When I saw the vague outline of New York City on the horizon my chest began to swell with emotion. It was eight years prior that I, newlywed, sailed to Persia. As tears welled in my eyes, Sam took my hand. "Do you see it?" he whispered.

"See what?" I replied blinking away my tears to focus.

"The statue of 'Liberty Enlightening the World.' The bright copper statue in the middle of the harbor. The sun is shining on it through the mist. When we sailed for Persia in 1886 her face was covered by a French flag. She was dedicated a month later."

"Oh, my goodness," I exclaimed. "What a magnificent woman."

We joined a long line of passengers, including many immigrants from Europe, shuffling into a new immigration facility called Ellis Island. The air inside the immigration building was stuffy with the odor of human bodies that had not been properly washed in a week. The line moved slowly, and Agnes began to whine. When I rested my head on Sam's shoulder, he asked, "Are you feeling sick?"

"No, just weary," I replied.

Finally, it was our turn to talk to the registrar. After declaring our American citizenry, we were off to retrieve our trunks and declare customs.

A porter helped us load our trunks onto the ferry to Manhattan. "Getting through immigration and customs seems like the most arduous part of our long journey," I jested. Agnes's mood improved once we were on the ferry, and the fresh air soothed my nausea. From the ferry we sent our trunks by dray service and hired a carriage to take us to my sister Sophea's apartment. "The Hotel San Remo," I told the driver. "It is on Central Park West between 74th and 75th Streets."

The driver laughed. "You do not have to tell anyone in New York where the San Remo is."

I sighed and turned to Sam. "My sister Sophea married Will Dulles three years ago. How I regret not being at her wedding."

"He is the Treasurer for the Presbyterian Board of Foreign Missions in New York," Sam said. "How did he meet your sister?"

"Sophea worked for the Woman's Missionary Board in Chicago. She went to the annual meetings with Mother, where she was often asked to sing. Will attended one of her concerts and was quite taken by her. He arranged to visit her in Forest Lake under the pretext of visiting Mother."

Sam laughed heartily. "Your mother has always been a good excuse for men to visit her daughters."

I nudged Sam gently. "And without Mother we would have never met."

The carriage stopped in front of a ten-story stone building across the street from Central Park. Inside the marbled lobby, the receptionist rang Sophea's apartment. I was expecting Sophea to meet us, but a man wearing a uniform came instead. "I am Charles, the Dulles' butler," he said.

"Butler?" I mouthed silently to Sam. We took an elevator to the seventh floor. Sophea met us in the entry hall dressed in a flowing pink silk gown carrying her six-month-old baby, Dorothy. She reached over her baby to kiss me lightly on the cheek. "The next time you come, the girls will play together," she said. "I am five years younger than you, but now that we both have babies, we are the 'same age.'"

"Please forgive our untidy travel clothes," Sam said. "Our trunks have not arrived."

"I am afraid Will is smaller than you, so you will have to wait for your trunk," Sophea said, "but Annie I have a maternity dress that would fit you. Would you like to borrow it?"

"That would be lovely," I replied and followed her down the hall, admiring the cherry woodwork. "Your home is so elegant that I am afraid to touch anything."

"Will insisted on a maid to help me with the baby and take care of the house," Sophea said. "I do not know what I would do without her."

Sophea gave me a flowing light blue chiffon dress decorated with white and pink roses and a lace collar. "Come to the parlor when you are ready for tea," she said. "Will should be home soon."

The dress was loose fitting enough to comfortably flow over my pregnant belly. "She has so many fine things that I would never have use for at the mission," I muttered.

Entering the parlor, I was drawn to the window and gazed at people walking through Central Park below. *How lucky my sister is to have married into wealth after having nothing but necessities all her life on Mother's Secretary salary.* The arms of a man encompassing my body jolted me out of my revery and I turned around with a shriek when I realized it was not Sam.

"Oh my," the man said. "I thought you were Sophea."

"You must be Will," I said trying to regain my composure. "I am her sister Annie as you must have surmised by now."

Will smiled sheepishly. "I recognized her dress. Please forgive me."

"You must have been shocked when you felt for a moment that your wife was eight months pregnant."

We both laughed heartily. Will had trouble stopping his laughter when Sophea came through the door with a plate of pastries. Behind her Sam was carrying a silver tray with the teapot, cups and saucers.

She stopped abruptly. "And what on earth is so funny?"

Her bewildered expression only caused Will and I to convulse again in laughter. Will was doubled over, and my pregnant belly hurt. Will finally took a deep raspy breath in, and after a long exhale he said. "I mistook Annie for you, dear."

"And this will always be the most embarrassing moment of my life," I added.

"Really?" Sam said. "What on earth happened?"

"It was just a hug," I replied, "but now I will have to name my baby after Will."

Sophea did not look at all happy. "Now dear," Will said. "Don't be jealous. It was only a more affectionate greeting than I had planned." Sophea continued to appear miffed.

"This is quite a place," Sam interjected. "I have never been in a fancy residence hotel before."

"Before it opened in October 1891, I immediately gave a down payment for an apartment that overlooked Central Park," Will said. "This is one of the larger suites, with three bedrooms, a parlor, music room and a bathroom."

"No kitchen or dining room?" I exclaimed.

"There's a dining room upstairs where we take most of our meals," Sophea added. "In the basement there is a complete steam laundry."

"The maid, of course, does the laundry," Will continued. "There is a dynamo in the basement too that generates electricity. The lights on the walls are a combination of gas burning and electrical."

"Electricity is not very dependable though," Sophea bemoaned.

"Still, imagine having electric lights in your home," I exclaimed. "I am excited to see them tonight when it gets dark."

"There are other conveniences too," Sophea continued. "There is a mail chute on the wall near the door, so we do not have to find a postbox on the street, and the hall boys run the errands."

There was a knock on the door and Will left to answer it. "It is your trunks," Will announced on his return. Sam quickly rose to assist, but Will stopped him saying. "The four hall boys are carrying them to your room."

"I am glad your trunks have arrived," Sophea said. "Now you can dress for dinner."

The next day we were off to Indiana, Pennsylvania for a Wilson family gathering. Sam's brother Rob met us at the train station in Indiana and took us to the Wilson house. Andrew Wilkins Wilson, Sr., "Father Wilson," at sixty-eight had the most striking appearance — an angular chin, long white hair and beard, and untrimmed moustache. Mother Wilson was a tiny woman in her early sixties with a warm smile and a commanding presence. Sam's nine brothers and sisters had matured in the eight years since we had visited after our wedding: Harry was forty; Rob, John, and Andy in their thirties; Ella, Annie, and Dick in their mid-twenties; and Jenny and Agnes were twenty and seventeen. *Such a spread in age, over twenty years. I hope I do not spend twenty years of my life having babies.*

I sat next to Rob's wife Ellen, who was also pregnant, expecting her baby a month before mine. "I am happy to meet you finally," I said. "We heard so much about you during Rob's visit in Tabriz."

"I was happy Rob had the opportunity to visit you during his sabbatical from Allegheny Seminary, even though he missed the birth of his second child," Ellen said. "The cholera epidemic was the only thing that brought him home."

I smiled sympathetically. "At first I admired his zeal for studying the Old Testament in the original languages, but then I realized that it was the same passion that drives Sam to go on tour for months in the villages and leave me alone."

"We certainly married two zealots, didn't we?" Ellen replied.

Ellen's four-year-old boy Howard and two-year-old Eleanor welcomed Agnes as their new playmate without hesitation. "How freely children accept others into their circle," Ellen said.

"It is a good time to teach them cultural and religious tolerance," I commented. "We try to take advantage of the innocence of youth and encourage Christian and Muslim students to play together."

"Yes, you must," Ellen replied. "If children had the opportunity to play with all races and religions, they could change the world."

"I look forward to spending time with you after we have our babies," I said. *Ellen will be a good friend; we think alike.*

Sam's younger brother Andy arrived with his wife Bessie. "You should come to Saltsburg and see my Boys' School," Andy said. "In 1888 I bought a resort on the Kiskiminetas River and transformed it into a first-class school. We have graduated forty-six boys so far and twenty-six have gone on to Princeton."

"We also added to the family," Bessie interjected. "This is Sarah, our four-year-old and Anna, our two-year-old."

"How old are Harry's children?" I asked.

"Five and seven," Bessie replied. "Lad is the older one. Margaret was only six months old when her mother died from appendicitis."

"It was such a shock," I said. "So sweet for sister Jenny to take care of Harry's children."

"The year 1889 was very eventful for the family," Andy said. "Robert and Ellen were married and sailed to Europe with Ella and Annie. Bessie and I were married in August. On September 28th we were coming by train for an evening reception to greet the European travelers back home. We found Mother gone, attending to Maggie who had become ill. Then Father was called to see her before she died."

"The reception was a very unhappy one," Bessie added.

"The last time I saw Ella, she was a recent Vassar graduate," I said.

"Now she has a two-year-old son, named Andrew," Andy said.

"She married George Stewart, a man eighteen years her senior. Can you imagine?" Bessie whispered.

"Now Bessie," Andy said. "Let us not be judgmental. I think it is a good match. Ella is very strong and independent, and he appreciates that in a wife."

Harry told Lad to take the four older children outside to play in the yard. Bessie corralled the two-year-old cousins in the parlor where we could watch them. Sam's parents were highly amused watching their grandchildren. "Imagine," Mother Wilson said, "I will have ten grandchildren by the end of summer. Ten is a good number."

At the end of June, Sam and I took the train from Pittsburgh to Chicago. "In Persia it is custom for the bride to return home after eight days and kiss her mother's hand," I said. "For me it has been eight years."

My brother Foster met us at the train station in Chicago. I covered his sweet gentle face with kisses until he pushed me away. "We need to hurry to the next platform," he said, "or we won't catch the next train to Lake Forest."

"What is the hurry?" I replied. "If I remember correctly, there is a train every half hour."

"There is a rail workers' strike in Chicago," he said. "It is interrupting trains all the way to the West coast. There have been days when I took the train to Chicago with no guarantee of returning home."

"Annie should not be standing on a train platform for hours in her condition," Sam said.

A well-dressed gray-haired man wearing a top hat grabbed my arm. "Why aren't you Annie Rhea?"

"Mr. Durand?" I replied in astonishment.

"Yes, Calvin Durand. I am the Mayor of Lake Forest now, elected three years ago by only twenty-eight votes. I favored cedar blocks to pave the roads versus bricks, because they were quieter for horse carriage traffic — quiet won over durability."

"Mother and I were two of those votes," Foster interjected.

"Sallie and Foster Rhea admit to helping me get elected, do they?" Mayor Durand said. "Well then, come sit with me at the front of the train." He led us out of the crowd to a compartment behind the locomotive. "Only the US mail and dignitaries are permitted in this space," he added.

"Where are you working these days, Foster?"

"I have a draying business in Chicago," Foster replied. "We deliver loads by wagon east of the Chicago River. It is a thriving business. I live with Mother in Lake Forest and take the train to Chicago every day, except Sunday."

"When on earth do you have time to paint?" Mayor Durand asked.

How did he know that Foster was a painter?

Foster flushed, as he had when he was younger, and people teased him about his love for painting. "In the evenings and Sunday afternoons I go to the art studio at Lake Forest College," Foster replied. "My true passion is painting, not business. Draying, however, earns me the money I need for canvas and paint."

"We all have a true passion that is not our work of employ, but Foster's is a productive one. My wife Sarah collects his paintings and pays him handsomely for them. I also find they reflect your positive spirit."

The train screeched to a halt at the Lake Forest station. "Mayor Durand, you have truly done my homecoming a great honor," I said.

After eight years' absence coming to the door of Mother's house and my childhood home, brought a rush of nostalgia.

"You are here at last," Mother said. "God bless you." She took me in her arms and held me, a big hearty hug that took my breath away. She was nearly sixty and her hair was whiter than before, but she was still the solid energetic Mother I left eight years ago.

"The bride has returned to kiss her mother's hand," I said and took her hand to my lips.

"I have everything ready for the baby," Mother said.

The next day my dear childhood friend Anna Holt Wheeler came from Chicago to visit me with her mother, who lived across the street in the Holt mansion.

"I wanted to see you as soon as I got here," I said. "How is dear Arthur?"

"He is a partner with the Williams & Thompson law firm," Anna said. "If he has a chance before the baby is born, he will come calling, but as you know the trains are unpredictable. I will be staying in Lake Forest for a month."

"Oh, wonderful," I gasped as a contraction took me by surprise.

"The baby may be coming sooner than you think," Mrs. Holt said. "When your mother gives me the word, I will be the 'street caller' who spreads the news to your old friends and neighbors. They are all looking forward to seeing you."

"We plan to have a baby party for you," Anna interjected.

After Anna and Mrs. Holt left the contractions ceased. *It was likely the excitement of seeing Anna again.*

On Independence Day the Holt's held a picnic in their garden. Mayor Durand attended with his wife Sarah. "Goodness you are large," Mrs. Durand commented. "You must be having the baby any day."

"I am afraid that the baby is quite content to stay where it is," I replied. "The doctor says I am overdue."

"We keep anticipating," Mother added.

"It is like waiting for a train with the railroad strike," Foster said.

"Tomorrow President Cleveland is sending troops from Fort Sheridan to confront the protesters," Mayor Durand said. "The strike may be over soon."

"Won't that be interpreted as anti-labor?" Sam asked.

"Undoubtedly," Mayor Durand responded. "Our state governor, J.P. Altgeld, is a radical and took sides with Eugene Debs. They will condemn the President's actions as unconstitutional interference with the State's rights."

The Pullman strike ended July 20th and a few days later my contractions began to come at regular intervals. Mother held my hand, while Sam kept Agnes busy at play. Foster graciously took the role of "house maid" and supplied all of us with food and drink.

Rose Dulles Wilson was born in Mother's house July 25, 1894.

"She is a beautiful baby, a perfect rose," Mother said.

I was surprised how fascinated Foster was with the baby and requested to hold her frequently. "He is so much like your father," Mother said. "When you and Foster were born your father wanted to hold you as often as he could, even while preparing a sermon. As toddlers you struggled away, and he followed you. He was so gentle, just like Foster is now."

"Does Foster look like Father?" I asked.

"Yes, he does, very much so." Foster was a handsome man, and I tried to envision my father in him.

My sister Sophea came from New York with eight-month-old Dorothy to attend Rose's baptism and they stayed the rest of the summer.

In October, Mother received a telegram from Tennessee that made her drop back into an armchair. "It is from my mother's stepson, Samuel Cunningham. He says: 'Mother very ill with pneumonia. Come quickly to Jonesborough.' I must go at once," Mother exclaimed.

"I will go with you," Foster said without hesitation. "I want to see Grandmother Cunningham one more time."

I was distraught. "I want to see Grandmother Cunningham too," I said, "but traveling with baby Rose is out of the question."

Mother and Foster returned the first week of November. "She tried her best, but at eighty-three she was too weak to fight off pneumonia. On October 21ˢᵗ she breathed her last breath, and the good Lord took her to His eternal home," Mother said. "How I will miss her." Tears rolled down Mother's cheeks.

"Her headstone is beautiful; white marble with a bouquet of flowers carved as an inlay on top," Foster added. "Her name and dates of birth and death are followed by the Scripture Job 5:26."

"You shall come to your grave in ripe old age, as a shock of grain comes up to the threshing floor in its season," I said. "How that Scripture brings memories of the Persian countryside."

The year's furlough was soon over. On Rose's first birthday, we started our trip back to Persia, sailing through the Mediterranean Sea to Genoa, Italy. Sophea and Will were taking a trip through Italy, and we met them in Venice. A photograph Will sent us of Sophea and me helping Agnes feed doves in St. Michaels's Plaza reminds me of those splendid four days together.

On September 10ᵗʰ we celebrated Agnes's third birthday. She sat on a high stool in a frilly white dress and Sophea treated her to pink ice cream. I watched anxiously, hoping Agnes would not drip melting ice cream on her new dress. *So much attention from her relatives has likely spoiled her.*

When we crossed the Aras River into Persia, I exclaimed, "We are almost home."

"It was good to see our families," Sam said, "but I missed our work here."

To my dismay Agnes said, "Why did we come here? It isn't as nice as Grandpa's country."

"That is just the reason," I responded curtly. "We are here in Persia to help those who are less fortunate than Americans."

CHAPTER 19

1895 — Tabriz Mission

SEVEN MILES FROM TABRIZ, MY EYES WELLED WITH TEARS AS a party of friends and missionaries rode to greet us. "A *peshwaz* to welcome us home," I cried.

Nearing the city, boys on foot and on donkeys raced toward us. "There are my boys," Sam exclaimed. "My boys have come to greet us." Of all our greeters none were more appreciated than the students from the mission Boys' School. They had organized their own *peshwaz* for their beloved "Principal *Sahib*."

Our first day back in Tabriz, Rev. Turner Brashear and his wife Annie held a reception dinner for us with the other missionaries of the station. In our absence the Brashears had taken on most of our usual mission duties. "Before you left, I had no idea how much work Sam is required to do," Turner said. "I am more pleased to see your safe return than anyone else."

"How is school attendance?" Sam asked.

"I am afraid the Gregorian bishops have been actively opposing our schools and threatening the parents of our students again," Turner replied. "From eighty students in the Boys' School last year we are down to forty-three. But do not worry, our family-like atmosphere is lacking in the Armenian schools. The boys will miss the congenial interactions they are used to, and it will bring them back."

"What about the Girls' School?" I asked.

"Grettie Holliday left for Constantinople to see if the Turkish doctors could save her eyesight," Turner said. "Despite the breakdown in her health, the Girls' School has maintained enrollment of about fifty."

"With Mary Jewett touring who is teaching the students?" I asked.

"Baron Vahan Tamzarian and his wife Anna."

"Bringing that Turk from Harput to the mission was one of the best decisions we have made," Sam said.

Will and Marguerite Vanneman joined the group to welcome us back. "I missed you, Annie," Marguerite said, "as did the Persian women you visit."

"How many patients were seen at the medical dispensaries this year?" Sam asked.

"About the same as last year," Will replied, "over five thousand men and three thousand women. Mary Bradford and I made some fourteen hundred home visits. My most interesting house visit was to *Vali Ahd* Mozaffar ad-Din."

"The *Vali Ahd*?" Sam exclaimed. "That is quite an honor."

"Yes, his Highness's physician was in Europe this summer. In addition to helping him with a minor medical issue, he wants me to be a consultant to for the medical care of his harem."

"It is certainly good to have the *Vali Ahd*'s favor on our side," I added. "That will help prevent the local government from locking the doors of our school again."

Dr. Mary Bradford joined our conversation. "The woman's dispensary waiting room has become a real melting pot with Persians of different religions and social status mingling freely — Christians, Muslims, Nestorians, Jews; wives of common laborers and princesses," she said. "With Grettie gone, her cook Yagoot became our Bible reader in the waiting room. She made it quite comfortable and attractive with flowers and a samovar for serving tea. Sometimes patients are so engrossed in conversation that they let their turn with the doctor go to someone else."

"Do you need me anymore to evangelize with the ladies while they are waiting?" I asked.

Dr. Bradford smiled. "The women miss your kind words, and we will always need your help."

"Were your two hospital rooms used much?" Sam asked.

"Yes, more than any previous year," Dr. Bradford answered. "The women's hospital rooms were occupied half the year, primarily by Muslim women, one was a princess with her friends. They managed to overcome their prejudice against Christian lodging and food and expressed sincere gratitude for my care."

"What progress," I exclaimed.

As we walked across the room to speak with Mary Jewett, Sam whispered, "I am relieved. Except for the Boys' School, things went well while we were away on furlough."

"Did news reach you that we lost two of our missionaries in Urmia while you were on furlough?" Mary Jewett asked.

Sam and I exchanged alarmed looks. "No, who?" Sam asked.

"Rev. John Shedd passed away April 12th," Mary replied.

"Although only sixty-two, he was very feeble," Sam said. "I assume his son William has taken over."

"Yes, he has," Mary replied. "But his father was a strong and noble leader of the station and profoundly trusted by the Nestorians. It will take some time for his son to succeed him."

"You said there were two deaths," I interjected.

"Yes, the second death took us all by surprise," Mary said, looking down at the floor as her eyes welled with tears. "Kate Cochran died in March."

"How can that be?" I asked in astonishment. "She was only forty-two."

"She had a bad case of grippe in January and never recovered her strength. In March she developed pneumonia and complications set in rapidly." Mary hid her face in her hands and sobbed.

I shuddered as a cold wave of disbelief passed through my body. Sam put his arm around my shoulder. "Annie, remember, your father was only thirty-eight when he succumbed to cholera. Diseases that might stand a chance of being cured in America are more often fatal here. It is a risk we accept as missionaries."

"Joe lost his mother only two years ago," I cried. "He must be devastated. What about the children?"

"Ida Coan, bless her heart, has become their 'mother in residence,'" Mary said. "She has taken on the Cochran children as well as her own."

"Ida Coan is a saint," I said. "She is a real saint."

"There is such a spread of age in the Cochran children," Sam said. "Clement is sixteen and Andrew is three. Joe planned to take the older children to America to live with his in-laws and go to school."

I wrote letters of sympathy to Joe Cochran and William Shedd. Joe wrote back that Kate died on March 21st, the first day of Spring, and that the chapel was decorated with pussy willows, the Nestorian symbol for resurrection.

As we prepared for bed, I said, "I wish I had help with the children. Then I could continue to teach at the Boys' School."

"I agree. It is time for us to hire a nanny," Sam replied and kissed me on the forehead. "We can ask Miriam if she feels comfortable adding that responsibility to her work."

During our furlough, Ishak and Miriam had worked at the Vanneman's house and preferred to stay there rather than return. "Whatever shall we do?" I cried.

"It is never difficult to find native men and women to work at the mission," Sam replied. "They are well-treated and highly paid here."

After interviewing four women to be our nanny and cook, we hired Teltel, a young Armenian woman who graduated from our Girls' School. "You should speak your native tongue around Agnes and Rose so they can learn it," I instructed her.

"I will speak both Azeri and Armenian," Teltel replied, "never English."

She proved to be good at cooking and taking care of the children, and a source of amusement since her name was a standing joke. When I instructed Agnes to communicate a message to her, I said, "Tell Teltel," and Agnes always ran away singing, "Tell, Teltel, tell Teltel."

It proved harder to replace Ishak, our general factotum. "Since we need to hire someone new, I suggest that we also add being the door-keeper to his duties," Sam said. "We need a butler to keep up with the Dulleses."

Weeks went by without applications for our general factotum position, and I began to despair. "Who will fill our water jars from the *kariz*? Who will go to the bazaar and buy food?" I asked.

"Ishak offered to help our family until we replace him," Sam assured me, "but I am sure someone will soon take the position."

A few weeks later a medium-built Persian man named Mousa came to our door. On first impression, he appeared too "rough" for the position. "He will be escorting women to the house, serving tea at social gatherings, and chatting with the guests," Sam said. "We cannot have someone uncouth in that role."

"I happen to like him, even if he is illiterate," I said. "He boasts that he was a bandit in his youth but has changed his ways. Now he says, 'I would rather be a doorkeeper in the house of my God than dwell in the tents of wickedness.'"

"He quoted Psalm 84:10?" Sam exclaimed.

"Yes, and when I asked him if he could quote another Bible verse he said, 'You shall not muzzle an ox when it treads out the grain.' Deuteronomy 25:4."

"Did you ask him if he knew what it meant?"

"Yes, and he responded that it means *mudakhil.*"

Sam laughed and said, "*Mudakhil* means corruption or graft, taking something as your presumptive right to do so. It is a cherished national institution in Persia; the wood chopper takes home wood under his coat, the miller takes some flour that he grinds for a customer, etcetera."

"Well? Can we hire him?"

"Of course," Sam replied. "He may be of great entertainment value."

Mousa took the position of doorkeeper and general factotum; he shopped at the bazaar, filled our water jugs, escorted women guests to our home, announced the arrival of male guests and served tea. He was a faithful servant and friend for many years, and the children loved him.

1895 — Wedding of Mohammad-Ali Mirza E'tezad es-Saltaneh

A courier from *Bagh-i-Shomal,* the *Vali Ahd's* summer palace, came to the door. He handed Sam a paper sealed with golden wax with the insignia of Mozaffar ad-Din. Sam hastily tore it open as the servant waited for a response. "Please tell his Majesty that we will be honored to attend his son's wedding. Please send my sincere greetings."

"Did I hear correctly?" I asked. "Are you invited to a royal wedding?"

"Yes, the Crown Prince's eldest son, E'tezad es-Saltaneh, 'Glory of the Kingdom,' is marrying his cousin, Princess Zahra Malekeh Jahan, 'Queen of the World,' " Sam replied.

"I wish I could go with you," I bemoaned.

"You are also an honored guest, not only as my wife, but for giving piano lessons to the *Vali Ahd's* daughter Princess Ezzat."

"How exciting it will be to see a royal wedding."

"Princess Zahra is coming from Tehran with a huge caravan loaded with her dowry," Sam said. "The bazaars will close, and Prince E'tezad and his retinue will journey seven kilometers outside the city to meet her, a grand *peshwaz*."

Covered with a silk shawl, Princess Zahra sat upon a *takhtarevan*, a traveling throne. Military guards and a caravan of one hundred and forty donkeys and camels carried her dowry. As Prince E'tezad road his decorated steed toward the Princess's *takhtarevan*, he burst into an angry rebuke when he saw another prince standing near to the Princess, engaged in conversation. "How dare you approach the Princess," he cried. "He must be beaten immediately."

Blood gushed from the other prince's nose after a soldier knocked his face with the blunt side of his sword.

"Oh, my goodness," I exclaimed.

"Turn away and say nothing more," Sam whispered. The procession continued toward Tabriz, initially subdued, then, after half a kilometer, became restored to its initial gaiety. Nearing Tabriz, a crowd of foreign consuls, government officials and the entire city thronged the cavalcade.

A week of festivities followed for all the residents of Tabriz. The garden at *Bagh-i-Shomal*, a one-hundred-and-seventy-acre park, was opened to the general public and tea was served. On separate days feasts were held for different categories of guests

— the princes and governors, the *mullahs*, the foreign consuls and officials, and missionaries and other prominent foreigners.

The wedding feast that Sam and I attended was held in the palace, a circular building, open in the center with a marble fountain and six tiers of galleries with balconies surrounding it. Servants scurried about serving coffee and tea and passing silver platters of chicken, lamb, *pillou*, fruits, *lavash* and cheese to guests seated on the floor.

The streets of Tabriz were decorated for the wedding procession with lanterns hanging from arches that displayed mottos from Persian poets. Princess Zahra, completely covered in a red silk veil, was escorted by the *Vali Ahd* in his carriage and accompanied by a regiment of soldiers on horses. Fireworks burst into the air from every corner of the city.

No vows were exchanged, no prayers were said. When Princess Zahra reached the *Vali Ahd*'s city palace in *Dar-ol-Khalafeh*, she was simply presented to Prince E'tezad.

CHAPTER 20

May 1, 1896

"A COURIER FROM THE VALI AHD HAS ARRIVED," MOUSA announced. "He says he has an urgent message for Dr. Wilson." Sam took the courier into his study and closed the door.

I paced, wringing my hands as I waited in the parlor with Agnes and Rose. *What could it be?* I heard the front door close, and Sam charged into the parlor, startling me. "Naser al-Din Shah has been assassinated," he exclaimed.

"Who would assassinate such a noble man?" I asked.

"A follower of the political activist Al-Afghani, the former advisor to the Shah on foreign affairs," Sam replied. "He fell out of favor with the Shah and was expelled from Persia."

"That would be a good way to make enemies," I said.

"Al-Afghani also publicly stated that he reserves his strongest hatred for the Shah and criticized him for making too many concessions to foreign powers. He has a large following in Persia. The assassin, Mirza Reza Kermani, was one of his followers. He dressed as a woman and shot the Shah while he was praying in the Shah Abdol Azim Shrine."

"What will happen?" I asked.

"*Vali Ahd* Mozaffar ad-Din will become Shah of Persia," Sam replied. "He has never had any great responsibilities in government, so his capacity is largely unknown. He is devoutly religious and has a humane and sympathetic nature. A mother of a con-demned man can appeal to him with likely assurance of mercy."

"What about the assassin?" I asked.

"He escaped to the Ottoman Empire. Mozaffar ad-Din sent troops on camels to capture him. I am sure he will be tried and executed."

"How will this affect the mission? Are you concerned?"

"I think not. The *Vali Ahd* is a friend of education and had European tutors for his sons. He asked us to provide an English teacher to the government school in Tabriz. I would suspect he will also look kindly on the people of Tabriz, having lived among them."

"I hope you are right. Sometimes when people are given power, they become corrupt. Persia's autocracy would lend itself to an abuse of power."

Will Vanneman visited *Vali Ahd* Muzaffar ad-Din to congrat-ulate him. The new Shah in return requested that he care for his harem and accompany them to Tehran. Will spent a month trav-eling with the harem in a royal caravan of fifteen hundred persons. After the harem reached Tehran safely, the new Shah ordered that Will be transported back to Tabriz in the king's carriage.

Princess Ezzat sent word that her husband would transfer to Tehran with the new Shah. "He hopes to become Prime Minister," she said. I was sorry to hear she was leaving Tabriz but understood and rejoiced that her status had risen as daughter of the Shah.

The Global Financial Crisis Reaches the Mission

In the spring of 1896 two announcements came from the Presbyterian Board of Foreign Missions. First, given the finan-cial conditions in America, the Board decided to close the station in Salmas. The second announcement was that the Secretary of the Board, Robert Speer, was coming to tour the missions in Asia with his wife.

"The economic depression in America has affected every sector," Sam said. "Mines in the West have glutted the market with silver, the wealthy who invested in unprofitable railroads lost thousands of dollars, industrial workers face high levels of unemployment, and wheat farmers are suffering from low crop prices. With fewer contributions to the Presbyterian Church, the Board needs to retrench funding of the missions."

"What will the closing of the Salmas station mean?" I asked.

"Newton Wright and his wife Mattie will join the Tabriz mission," Sam replied. "John and Ella Mechlin, the other missionary family in Salmas, have decided to withdraw from missionary work and return to America."

"What will the Wrights do here?"

"Unfortunately, it will not change our workload; Newton is engaged in translating Scriptures and his wife has three young children and is not fluent in Azeri or Armenian."

"What about the visit by the Speers?" I asked.

"Robert Speer will be touring the Presbyterian missions in Persia, China, Japan and Korea," Sam said. "This is an important opportunity for us to demonstrate the progress and achievements of the Tabriz mission. With the recent decision to close the Salmas station, we do not want reductions to occur at our station."

"Where will the Speers stay while they are in Tabriz?" I asked, dreading the answer.

"They will be staying with us, of course," Sam replied with a wry smile. "We are the only residence with an adequate guest room. We will be responsible for ensuring the Speers are comfortable and entertained during their visit. It will go a long way to portray the mission in a positive light."

"Are the Persian missions in good standing with Dr. Speer?" I asked.

"Robert and I disagree on the role of education at missions," Sam replied. "He is adamant that the primary aim of missionary work is evangelistic, whereas I see education as my primary goal and spreading the gospel as secondary. He is not pleased with the little progress we have made in converting Muslims to Christianity."

"Does he not realize that a Muslim who openly professes their conversion is putting their life at stake?"

"He knows but disregards it. We should highlight our evangelistic work. In your discussions with him emphasize your Bible Class and visitations with Persian women to discuss the Scriptures."

Preparing the house and planning social activities for such important guests made my head spin. In the morning I started to wake up queasy. *How can I make sure they are comfortable? How am I to make the children behave while they are here?*

At first, I was so distracted that I failed to recognize the reason for my nausea. Mary Braford visited me one morning for coffee. "I am so anxious about preparations for Robert Speer's visit that I feel ill every morning when I rise," I complained. "Everything must be perfect. I am just a bag of raw nerves."

Mary smiled and said, "Annie, dear. Maybe you are pregnant again."

Dr. Speer and his wife visited Urmia for sixteen days before coming to Tabriz. Fred Coan accompanied them, and his sense of humor put me at ease. While the Speers toured the mission compound with Sam, I asked Fred, "How did the visit with the Speers in Urmia go?"

"Quite well, I thought," Fred replied. "We took Speer to the outstations to see the native Christian preachers who graduated from our school and returned to their villages. A good-sized congregation greeted him at the ten places we visited."

"That was ingenious. Sam told me that Dr. Speer emphasizes the necessity of developing local churches with native pastors. What did he think of Joe Cochran's Westminster Hospital?"

"When Joe took him to the mission hospital it was full of typhoid patients, so he did not stay there long. I sensed that both our medical and educational programs are of little interest to him."

On Fred Coan's suggestion, Sam planned a four-day tour for Robert Speer to the Tabriz mission outstations. "The problem is that compared to the Urmia station I can hardly impress him. Urmia has over one hundred outstations, and we have only ten," Sam said.

"You can easily take him to all of our outstations then and have time for a visit to the leper colony," I retorted.

"Take Robert Speer to a leper colony? What if one of the lepers touched him?"

"Fred told me Joe Cochran took him to a hospital ward full of typhoid patients," I said.

"This is a man who works in an office on Fifth Avenue in New York City," Sam retorted. "I do not think visiting a leper colony would be palatable to him."

"Will his wife Emma be touring the outstations?" I asked.

"No, when I mentioned that in some villages we would sleep in tents, she asked to have a break from traveling."

"How should I entertain her?"

"How you entertain other women who visit."

After Sam and Robert Speer left for the outstations, Emma and I sat in the parlor and suffered through several moments of uncomfortable silence. *I need to make my best effort to converse with the wife of Sam's boss.* "How long have you and Robert been married?" I asked.

"Three years."

"Any children?"

"No children yet."

"Do you have any hobbies to keep you busy?"

"I work for the Young Women's Christian Association, the Y.W.C.A., and for women's suffrage organizations," Emma replied.

"When did you become associated with the Y.W.C.A.?"

"I became involved when I was at Bryn Mawr. Did you go to college?"

"Yes, I graduated from Lake Forest College and went to Wellesley for a year."

"I have never heard of Lake Forest College."

"It is in Lake Forest, Illinois."

"I see. What books do you read?"

"We do not have many books in English here," I replied, "and with visitations and teaching I do not have time."

"I enjoy reading poetry. I brought a book of poetry with me by a new poet who you likely have not heard of; her name is Emily Dickinson. She died ten years ago, and her poems were published in 1890." Emma looked at me smugly.

"I do know of Emily Dickinson," I said, and laughed. "My uncle Perez Dickinson Cowan was her favorite cousin. He sent me a copy of her poems."

"I am impressed that you have a connection with her," Emma replied, clearly surprised. "In the evenings we can read her poems together. I find her spirituality intriguing."

After the Speers left for Hamadan, I breathed a sigh of relief. "I enjoyed reading poetry with Emma, but otherwise she was quite exhausting," I told Sam. "What did Dr. Speer say at the end of his visit?"

"Regarding our evangelization efforts he commented that 'visible results are unsatisfactory.' He was impressed that the Boys'

School enrollment was over one hundred but was less impressed that none of the students were Muslim. He suggested separate classes for Muslims and starting a night school. These recommendations I will strongly consider."

"What about Emma Speer?" I asked.

Sam smiled and patted my shoulder lovingly. "She thought you were the most charming hostess. She enjoyed reading poetry with you and hearing you play the piano and sing with the children each evening."

A few weeks later we heard from the mission in Hamadan that Dr. Speer had contracted typhoid and was severely ill. It was a relief when word came that Robert Speer was weak but recovering. Then on October 30, 1897, we received a telegram informing the mission that the Speers arrived safely back in America. "I hope his bout of typhoid did not affect his overall impression of the Persian missions," I said.

"I hope the same," Sam replied.

In June, Sam received a telegram and I found him sobbing in his study. "What is it, dear?" I asked.

"My father," he managed to say. "My father died."

"When?"

"June sixteenth. After a brief illness he unexpectedly died of pneumonia."

"Oh, Sam, I know you wish you were there, but he was most certainly surrounded by your brothers and sisters."

Sam was deeply affected by the loss of his father. He had suffered the loss of his first son, Rhea, but this time his grief was more profound. He spent hours looking aimlessly at the same page in a book, or out the window. "We will name the baby after my father," he said one evening.

"But Sam, I cannot guarantee the baby will be a boy," I replied.

"Of course," he replied. "Yes, of course. But we will have a son and name him after my father."

Dr. Bradford helped me deliver our baby girl, and I chose the name Esther, after Esther Thompson the principal of Ferry Hall.

"Esther in the Bible asked the Persian king to spare the Jews," Sam said. "Perhaps our Esther will help persecuted people, like the Armenians in Turkey. In the last two years Sultan Abdul Hamid II ordered the massacre of three hundred thousand Armenians, and the rest of the world did nothing."

"Does God have to do all the work?"

CHAPTER 21

1898 Failing Crops in Northern Persia

"WITH WHEAT SO SCARCE, THE WOMEN WHO MAKE BREAD for the school could not secure flour," I said.

"In northwest Persia the crops are failing," Sam said. "The drought ruined the hay crop and prevented villagers from planting rice, the vineyard harvest was destroyed by cold, and locust devoured wheat and other crops. The landlords raised the price of flour to exoboridant levels."

"We will need to say in earnest the Lord's Prayer from Matthew 6: 9-13," I said, "particularly the verse 'Give us this day our daily bread.'"

One morning following a special prayer session, a converted Muslim, named Abas Cooley Agha, offered to buy wheat for the school at a reduced rate. He had the wheat ground at the mill with servants watching that none of the grain or flour was taken by the miller. Then he rode with his servants to the school to deliver the flour, standing by as they filled our bins to make sure his servants did not steal any as *mudakil* or demand *bakshish*.

"It is a blessing," I said, "an answer to our prayers."

"Now that we ask for some support, instead of offering free tuition, attendence at the Boys' School is down from one hundred and twenty to eighty-five," Sam said. "Lack of monetary support from the Board for our schools is hurting our progress."

"Due to the retrenchment by the Board, we started charging students at the Girls' School three tomans for the academic year, equivalent to three dollars," Mary Jewett said. "We expected a decrease in enrollment, but instead we saw an increase from fifty-five to one hundred pupils. The girls' mothers tell me, 'Yes we are members of the Armenian church, but we send our girls to your school because they learn so many bad things in the Armenian school. We trust you with their education.' The boarders now perform all the work of upkeep of the dormitory — cooking, washing, cleaning, keeping house, and making their clothes. In addition, they sold their needlework to buy new carpets."

"A Kurdish chieftain visited me last week and said he heard about our 'educated girls' and expressed interest in seeing them," Sam said. "Could you arrange his visit to the Girls' School?"

When the Kurdish chief came, Sam and I accompanied him and his retinue to the Girls' School. "I am interested what his reaction will be," Sam said.

The girls spoke and sang in four different languages. Then the chieftain examined the girls in Azeri and Persian. Afterward he threw his book down and exclaimed, "The half was never told!"

"That is what the Queen of Sheba said when she tested Solomon," I replied. " 'Half the greatness of your wisdom was not told to me.' 2 Chronicles 9:6."

The chief started ranting, "Who would think that girls could learn to do these things? Compared to your girls, our Kurdish girls are mere donkeys. I pray for the day when our children might go to school too."

"You obviously made an impression," I told Mary Jewett. "I am so proud of what your school has accomplished. There is hope that the Kurdish girls will also be educated now."

"It is such a contrast to the Kurds south of Lake Urmia," Sam said. "They descended on the villages, robbed and carried away

hundreds of sheep. One man's wife was taken by a Kurd for a debt
of ten dollars. He and the poor children are heartbroken, knowing
her probable fate of sexual servitude."

Sam held a station meeting to prepare for our Annual Report
to the Board. With the Vannemans in America on furlough, Dr.
Bradford cared for all those seeking medical attention at the mission. "Since the Whipple Woman's Hospital opened, I have seen
over five thousand patients," Mary Bradford said. "I also made
close to seven hundred home visits."

"What have been your primary difficulties?" Sam asked. "I
will ask the Board for funding for your medical work, if needed."

"Since receipts from medical treatment sustains our medical
missionary work, we do not need to ask the Board for funds,"
Mary Bradford replied. "The problem is that the poor worry that I
will not come because they have nothing to pay me. When I arrive
their squalid homes have barely a basin for washing. On the other
hand, wealthy Muslims allow patients to suffer for days due to
their belief that my presence in their house would render 'everything unclean.' When they finally call me as a last resort, I often
treat them in the nick of time."

"Any stories from the new hospital that we can share with the
Board?" Sam asked.

"The Board will appreciate this one," Mary Bradford said. "Last
June a seriously ill Muslim woman in the hospital was visited by
members of her family. While they sat in the waitng room I spoke
about her condition and led a prayer for the patient. The mother
cried and said, 'This is good. I shall gather some of my neighbors
and come every week to hear these words,' and I replied, 'Yes,
please come.' And thus the prayer meeting for Muslim women

began. We continue to meet every week with an average attendance of twenty-five."

"Let me help you with the next prayer meeting," I said. "Perhaps I could eventually arrange an afternoon at our house for a women's gathering, kicking any men out of the house, of course." I winked at Sam.

"Tell us about your most interesting patients," Sam said.

"The most difficult patient was a beggar boy, Fat Ullah, who was run over by a carriage," Mary Bradford replied. "His mother brought him to the hospital with a gangrenous foot. He rebelled at every effort to care for him, scowling when I visited his bedside, and spitting out medicine. At night he aroused the house with groans and cries. Despite his stubborn and churlish behavior, his leg became better. One day he surprised me by returning my greeting of '*Salaam alakum*,' although in a timid voice, and a week later he sang this greeting whenever he saw me."

"Any other stories?" I asked.

"I have many," Mary Bradford replied. "One Muslim woman was in the hospital for several weeks. Each day Khawa, our nurse, came by her bedside and read from the Bible. One day I was there when Khawa read from 1 John 4:10: 'Not that we loved God but that he loved us and sent his Son to be expiation for our sins.' The Muslim patient replied, 'When my husband died and I was left with a blind daughter, I often blamed God. No one told me he was a loving Father. I see now that blaming Him was sinful.' 'We love, because he first loved us,' Khawa replied."

"1 John 4:19," I said. "How touching."

1898 – Sam's Eight Month Tour with Grettie Holliday

Agnes was six, Rose four and Esther was a one-year-old. My nanny and cook Teltel helped take care of the children while I taught classes at the Boys' School, but I enjoyed being a mother to my little girls and took over their care whenever I could. After school was out for the summer, I spent many days on the veranda with the children. While baby Esther slept in her cradle, and Agnes and Rose played with dolls or picked flowers in my garden, I read or sewed clothes for them. When it rained, I gathered the girls around me and read to them from James Atkinson's English translation of Ferdowsi's *Shahnameh*, the Persian Book of Kings. The story of Prince Zal and the *Simurgh* was one of their favorite stories:

"The *Simurgh* is a gigantic bird with the head of a dog, claws of a lion and feathers the color of copper. She lives on top of a peak in the Alborz mountains, the snow-capped mountains we see far to the East. Prince Zal, the son of Saam, was born an albino, with pure white hair and pure white skin, and his father abandoned him in the Alborz mountains. Hearing the baby's cry, benevolent *Simurgh* took mercy on Prince Zal and took him to her nest where she raised him as her own. When Prince Zal became older, he decided to live with other men. Before he left, *Simurgh* gave Prince Zal three golden feathers to burn if he ever needed her help in the world of man.

"Prince Zal fell in love with beautiful Rudaba. They were married and Rudaba became pregnant, but the childbirth was difficult and threatened the lives of both mother and baby. What did Prince Zal do?"

"He burnt the golden feathers to call the giant bird for help," Agnes said.

"Yes, that is what Prince Zal did. *Simurgh* came and assisted with the birth of their baby boy. They named the baby *Rostam*, who becomes the greatest hero of Persia. *Rostam*'s horse was named *Rakhsh*, the name I gave my horse."

"Can we go to the mountains and see the bird?" Rose cried.

"No, if women set their eyes on *Simurgh*, their pregnancies will not go easily," I replied.

When Sam returned from a tour, he was enthusiastic about his encounters with the Persians on the Salmas plain. "I have never experienced such openness to religious discussion before," Sam exclaimed. "On multiple occasions the *kanda kuda*, the village chief, organized a gathering for me to talk to the villagers. The villagers listened attentively to our Christian stories and asked many questions."

"What was the most interesting part of your tour?" I asked.

"Visiting the Yarsanis in the Kermanshah province," Sam replied. "They have a fascinating religion that mingles Islamic, Zoroastrian and Christian components. They are also called the *Ali Illahis*, because like Shia Muslims they revere Ali, the son-in-law of Muhammad, but their holy book is the *Saranjam*, not the Qur'an. Like the Zoroastrian fire-worshippers, they believe the sun and fire are holy. Their beliefs in transmigration of the soul and that God can manifest in human form, like Jesus, are similar to some Christian religions."

"Mary Jewett visits a town ninety miles southwest of Tabriz called Ilkhichi, where all of the inhabitants are Yarsani," I said. "The men have prominent moustaches and play the *tambur*."

"The *tambur* is a sacred symbol of the Yarsanis," Sam said.

"How did the religion originate?" I asked.

"Some speculate that during the Islamic conquest of Persia some Christians formed a secret sect, accepting Islam outwardly, but keeping their Christian faith. Without Christian Scriptures within several generations they lost much of their Christian religion. As a group, they are very accepting of our Christian teachings, which comes as a surprise. They particularly enjoy the story of the Virgin Mary."

"Really?"

"Yes, it is because the religion's founder was Sultan Sahak who was said to be born to a Kurdish virgin."

"Now I understand the possible connection with former Christians."

"It is a beautiful story. Sultan Sahak's mother, Dayerak Rezbar, was sleeping under a pomegranate tree when a bird pecked on a fruit above her. A pomegranate seed fell into her mouth and impregnated her."

"Goodness," I exclaimed. "I will have to pay more attention when walking under pomegranate trees."

Mary Jewett's Eight Month Stay in Miandoab

Mary Jewett visited me on Sunday after church. "I wanted to say goodbye," she said. "For the next eight months to a year I will be living in the village of Miandoab, a four-day journey southwest of Tabriz."

"Why are you going to Miandoab?" I asked.

"On a previous visit, I rented a house for one month and found both the Armenians and Muslims receptive and friendly," Mary Jewett replied. "They invited me to their homes, listened as I taught the Scriptures, asked intelligent questions, and were apparently eager and willing to learn. While there, I felt that I would like to spend the remainder of my life with them."

After Mary left, I thought about her from time to time and imagined her surrounded by villagers, either outside or crowded into her small room.

One day after an eight-month absence Mary returned. "I came back because of the cramped quarters," she explained. "My one-room served as sitting room, dining room, bedroom, meeting room, and school room. On my last day Muslim and Armenian men filled my yard, and women and children crowded into my room. As the horses were loaded, I spoke to them of the love of Christ and our coming separation. Their hearts were touched, and the room was filled with weeping. As we rode out of the village, a crowd of men, women and children followed my wagon as far as the Zarrine River."

"Such a special relationship you built with them," I said. "And how sweet that the pure moral wisdom of the Scriptures draws the people of different faiths to you."

Dr. Mary Bradford and Marguerite Vanneman made two trips to Payon, the leper colony situated six miles from Tabriz. "Payon means 'Village of the Sick,'" Dr. Bradford explained. "The village was created by the Governor of Tabriz forty years ago, and the lepers are essentially the wards of the state. They maintain the village and cultivate their own farms."

"Before the children were born, Sam and I came back from a tour of the outstations and saw scores of lepers sitting along the roadside," I said. "They were dressed in rags and begging piteously, saying '*Ya Yaradan Allah*' over and over."

"Yes, we have all heard them crying 'O Creator God,'" Dr. Bradford replied. "They pray continually for hope, and of course for *bakshish*, or alms."

"Doesn't the government support them?" I asked.

"They used to give them charity, but now they tax them for use of the land. This year with the failing crops, the lepers sneak into the city and demand bread."

"But you cannot cure leprosy, so what medical help do you give them?" I asked.

"The bumps and blisters all over their faces, and their disfigured fingers and toes are not something I can cure," Mary Bradford replied. "As a doctor I can approach them and ignore their disfigurement unlike others. In that way they are no longer ashamed of the way they look and feel humanized."

"The Bible has many references to leprosy," I said. "Do you read them those Scriptures?"

"They enjoy hearing Matthew 8:2-4, the story of the leper that Jesus cured," Marguerite Vanneman replied. "A leper came to him and knelt before him saying, 'Lord, if you will, you can make me clean.' And he stretched out his hand and touched him, saying, 'I will; be clean.' And immediately his leprosy was cleansed."

"The lepers also enjoy hearing of Jesus's healing powers for other ailments in Matthew 8 and 9," Mary Bradford continued. "With the lepers, Jesus is my best medicine. It gives them hope."

"I had no idea that you brought evangelization into your medical practice," I said.

"With the retrenchment, I try to do my part and spread 'the Word of Life,' when I see patients in the hospital and the dispensary, and as I visit the lepers in their colony. Medicine cost money, but the spoken word is free."

1898 – Mary Jewett and the Maragha brothers

Mary Jewett made a brief visit to Maragha in the fall. "I met the most interesting Muslim man from a village near Maragha," she said. "His entire family, including all seven brothers, can read, something very unusual in Persia. Our conversation turned spiritual, and we spent three hours reading the Scriptures together. Afterwards he was overjoyed when I handed him a Persian translation of the New Testament as a gift."

"Do you think other members of his family read it?" I asked. "Or did they burn it as fuel for their fire?"

"At least two other brothers read it because they recently visited me in Tabriz," Mary Jewett replied. "When they claimed to have read the book that I gave to their brother, I wanted to be convinced so I asked what story they remembered. To my amazement, they told me the story of Jesus giving sight to a blind man from the ninth chapter of John. They remembered details; how Jesus spat on the ground, made clay and anointed the blind man's eyes, how after washing his eyes they opened, and that the man whose sight had been restored was questioned over and over by the Jews how it happened, not believing Jesus was capable."

"Why did they come to visit?" I asked.

"They were in Tabriz on business and wanted to read the Scriptures with me, as I had done with their brother. They came almost every day, and when it was time for them to return to their village I gave them the entire Bible in Persian, a hymn book and *Pilgrim's Progress*."

"Even if they are not converted to Christianity, their unbiased curiosity indicates that they seek spiritual enlightenment," I said. "Let us pray that their reading leads to their salvation."

"My sheep hear my voice, and I know them, and they follow me; and I give them eternal life, and they shall never perish," Mary Jewett replied.

"John 10:27," I said.

Princess Ezzat sent word that when her husband proclaimed himself Prime Minister, a coalition formed against him and convinced her father, the Shah, to dismiss and exile him. "I am going to Egypt with him. I don't know if I will ever see you again," she wrote.

She is brave to follow him. A father would not break bonds with his daughter, would he?

CHAPTER 22

1899 — Mother Visits Persia

"AFTER TWENTY-SIX YEARS OF SERVICE AS FIELD SECRETARY for the Women's Presbyterian Board of Missions in the Northwest, I am retiring," Mother wrote. "The first thing I want to do is come to Persia for a year or two and help care for my grandchildren. During his furlough Joe Cochran visited me in Lake Forest and agreed to let me travel with his party. We are scheduled to sail on the *SS Mesaba* in July."

"Oh, what a help it will be," I exclaimed. "I can barely wait for her to arrive. Maybe she will come before I have my baby and care for the girls."

The baby did not wait for Mother to arrive. On September 2nd, after three girls, I gave birth to a baby boy. We named him after Sam's late father, Andrew Wilkins Wilson. Mother arrived September 9th, a week after the baby and the day before Agnes' seventh birthday.

Sam took Agnes and Rose in the wagon to meet Mother, a two days' journey from Tabriz. "The rest of her traveling party will be headed for Urmia, so we need to meet Grandma at the junction," Sam said told them.

The day of their expected return I impatiently watched out the bedroom window for the first sight of the wagon. Before sunset Sam drove through the mission gate with Rose and Agnes sitting on either side of Mother. When they entered, Esther and I were in the parlor with baby Andrew on my lap, wrapped in an afghan Mother had crocheted. I blanched when I saw that he had burped up on it. "This your Grandmother Rhea," I said.

"Isn't Esther precious with her golden curls and big blue eyes," Mother exclaimed. "Rose and Agnes almost look like twins, both with long brown hair and gray eyes. You can tell them apart only because Rose inherited your dimple."

"I had hoped that one of the children would inherit it," I said.

"As we passed through Tabriz we dodged camels and donkeys loaded with baskets of fruit and netted piles of hay, showering us with loose bits as we passed. It was a real homecoming," Mother said.

As she spoke our new cook and nanny came in. "Dinner is served, Mrs. Wilson."

"This is Tarlan," I said.

"*Tarlan* means 'hawk' in Persian," Mother said. "She must be bright."

Tarlan took Andrew from my lap and placed him in a bassinette next to the dining room table.

"Tarlan helps me care for Andrew," I said. "In the early morning if she hears him crying, she cradles the baby in her arms and sings softly in the garden to quiet him."

"I am sure she will be happy to have me here to help," Mother said. "I will start a school for the mission children and call it the Rhea Academy."

The next day, Sam and I took Mother on a tour of the Boys' School. "After twenty years of missionary work, I gained the conviction that education rather than proselytizing was the best approach," Sam said.

"Did you abandon teaching the gospel?" Mother asked, with a tone of disapproval.

"Quite the contrary," Sam answered. "My time outside of the Boys' School is occupied giving private religious counsel and touring the villages reading Scriptures. One of the *mullahs* comes to visit me every week to debate verses in the Bible. Last week he asked me, 'And at the wedding of Cana, when Jesus turned the water to wine, what type of wine was it?' and I answered, 'I suppose the same as the wine Muhammed says flows like a river through the streets of Paradise.' He was quite amused."

"Do you also deliver church sermons?" Mother asked.

"On some occasions, I give the Sunday afternoon service in Armenian," Sam answered.

"Instead of attending the Armenian service at the mission, I read Scriptures to Armenian women and their children gathered at one of our students' homes," I said.

"Persian women ask Annie to teach the gospel and give spiritual counsel," Sam added.

"You are welcome to accompany me on my visits," I said.

Sam unlocked the door to the Boys' School, and we stepped inside. The air was cool and musty, and the sound of our footsteps echoed down the hall.

"There are six classrooms, one for each grade, a chapel and a library on the bottom floor," Sam explained. "Upstairs is the large assembly room that we use for meetings, student plays, and physical exercises in the winter."

"Do you require the students to attend chapel?" Mother asked.

"Yes, it is a requirement since this is a mission school," Sam said, "I explain the significance of passages in the Bible for their ethical worth primarily. The goal is teaching the boys universal religious values and moral behavior at a young age. With so much immoral behavior surrounding them, anything to promote the internalization of religious values is a benefit to their society."

"You have lofty goals," Mother said.

"The effect of exposure to Christian values has already been demonstrated," Sam replied. "Merchants have told me that our graduates are 'fine lads, honest, hard-working, and trustworthy.' Our students easily find work with such a favorable reputation."

"Do you have social gatherings with Persians at the mission?" Mother asked.

"Tomorrow we invited twenty-five Muslim women to our house for a luncheon," I added. "The men will be excluded from the house for the day, so the Muslim women can take off their street veils and feel at home."

The next morning Sam and Mousa moved the dining room table and chairs to the wall. Tarlan placed a round tablecloth in the center of the floor and the samovar on the table for tea. The menu for the luncheon was *lavash* served with native dishes.

When the women arrived, they removed their shoes at the door and knelt on cushions around the tablecloth. First a basin, ewer and towel were passed around the circle so everyone could wash their hands before eating with their fingers. After lunch we played games, in a circle, such as *Who has the button?* and *Musical Chairs* using pillows on the floor in a circle. The ladies enjoyed the games like little children, especially Mother. Then we adjourned to the parlor and sang songs as I played the piano. The house party ended with the usual drinking of tea, the third glass being the signal for leaving.

As promised, Mother began a little school, she called the Rhea Academy and taught Rose and Agnes to read. This allowed me to devote more of my time to teaching at the Boys' School. Mother was also instrumental in arranging many social gatherings at the mission, such as the children's plays and music recitals, convincing any of the missionaries with musical talent to participate. For Thanksgiving she was hostess to a large communal dinner at the mission station with a whole roast lamb, instead of turkey,

as the latter is not to be found in Persia. After dinner she had a
Spelling Bee, suiting the words to each person, such as 'dog' for
Esther, a word she had just learned to spell.

"You have become an integral part of the mission," I told
Mother. "Now you can never leave."

1900 — Mother's Return to Urmia

"I want to spend the summer in Urmia," Mother declared. "I
left my home thirty years ago and it is my goal to return. Should
I go alone, or do you want to come with me?"

"We would not think of letting you go alone," Sam replied.

"This will be the first four-day journey with the children,"
I replied. "Andrew will sleep in his bassinette next to me in
the wagon."

Sam hired two *charvadars* with mules and wagons for the
family's journey to Urmia; one to transport Mother, Esther, baby
Andrew and me, and another for our cook Tarlan, Mousa, our bags
and provisions.

"I will ride my horse and lead Rakhsh, who will carry Rose
and Agnes in *cajavahs*," Sam said.

"They enjoy traveling in the large baskets," I added.

The first day's journey was across barren plain to Ali Shah to
the house where my father died of cholera in 1865. Mother stood
outside the house, at first refusing to go in with the others. "What
is it?" I asked.

"I need to take this in," she said. "Thirty-five years ago, my
husband died here. It was the worst moment of my life. I am
remembering it now as though it was yesterday. I never loved any
man other than your father. Let me sit down and cry."

I felt helpless, trying to convince Mother to go inside the house, then the children came to my aid.

"Does Grandfather Rhea's ghost haunt the house?" Rose asked.

"No, my dear," Mother replied, "but his spirit is always here. Returning to this house brings back poignantly sad memories. The sense of closure I feel now mends my broken heart."

On the third day while descending from the Seyyed Taj ol Din Pass our wagon lurched over a rock and the jolt sent Mother flying out. Sam dismounted and rushed to her aid.

"Oh, my knee," Mother moaned, still sitting on the ground.

"Your knee is badly cut and bruised," Sam said and wrapped a handkerchief around it. "We have a day until we can get medical attention for that. How will you do?"

"This old Persian will live to see better days," Mother answered breathlessly, grimacing in pain. "The wind was only knocked out of me."

We set up camp outside the walls of Khoi near the Aland River and I applied a cold compress to Mother's knee. "To think that my child is taking care of me," she muttered.

"Now be a good patient," I replied.

The next morning, we arrived at the Urmia mission and were met by Rev. Benjamin Labaree, who joined the mission in 1860, the same year as Mother. "Sallie Jane, you have not aged a day," Rev. Labaree exclaimed and hugged Mother.

"We are the last of the old missionaries," Mother replied.

"Mother's knee was injured during our trip," I said. "She needs medical attention."

"After taking your baggage to the house, tell the driver to bring her to the Westminster Hospital," Rev. Labaree said. "Joe Cochran is seeing patients there."

Joe examined Mother's knee and shook his head. "I will put your knee in a cast, Mrs. Rhea. I am afraid you won't be able to play soccer this summer."

The house we rented near the mission was a roomy Persian-style adobe with apricot trees and a delightful garden with pink, white, and yellow roses. Sam also rented a carriage so the family could go on trips around Urmia. There were fourteen missionary children at the Urmia station that summer, eleven between three and nine years old, and our yard and the mission grounds were their playgrounds. The teenagers, Elizabeth and Frank Coan and Harry Cochran, looked after the younger children, which allowed the adults to enjoy each other's company.

The Coan house was the gathering spot for the missionary families. Fred enjoyed telling stories of his traveling adventures, with Esther and his son Howard sitting on his knees.

"Isn't the Kurdistan a dangerous place to travel?" I asked. "I have heard the Kurds rob and kill travelers."

"I always ask the *Vali*, the governor of the province, for a *zaptieh*, a Turkish soldier who serves as escort on my journey," Fred said. "They know every road and short cut, and which villages offer food and accommodations."

"When one meets a Kurd, who has been treated in our hospital, they are always lenient," Joe Cochran said.

"What Joe says is true," Fred added. "On another trip a Kurd, who was a former patient, guarded my tent all night and told me, 'I will not let a brother of Dr. Cochran be robbed and murdered.' They always call me that, 'a brother of Dr. Cochran.' "

"A little medicine goes a long way, but you never want to become a personal enemy of a Kurd," Joe added. "It is a death sentence."

On Sundays, Mother toured the outlying villages with Benjamin Labaree, Sr. and the pastors remembered her, saying,

"Mrs. Rhea, you are our mother. Won't you speak to us?" Walking with crutches, she visited many of her old pupils from the Fiske Girl's Seminary and spoke to them in Syriac.

After two months in Urmia, we were on the way back Tabriz, staying again in Ali Shah. Mother took my arm and asked me to accompany her on a short walk. "Annie, dear," she started. "I have enjoyed being with you and the children in Persia, but the altitude and the water in Tabriz do not agree with me. I am afraid that I will be ill all year if I stay."

"You are leaving us?" I exclaimed.

"I will leave and go back to America with the first party that can accompany me and live with Sophea's family when I return."

Mother's decision was hard for me to accept but I agreed that it was best for her health. Agnes, Rose and Esther were also sad to see their grandmother leave as she added so much entertainment to their lives. "Grandma, I will miss you," Esther said.

"It will not be too long before you see me again, dear," Mother replied. "Four years from now you are due for your next furlough in America. When you come, you will stay with me at Rosenvik, and we will pick flowers in the garden."

Just as they had met Mother coming to Tabriz, Sam, Rose and Agnes rode out to see her go. I heaved a deep sigh, watching Mother's wagon disappear on the horizon. *How will I now cope with the children without Mother's help?*

Sarah Jane Foster Rhea, 1899

CHAPTER 23

Fall 1900

LILLIE BEABER JOINED THE TABRIZ MISSION IN 1899 AS a teacher at the Girls' School. She was a natural learner of foreign languages and to my astonishment quickly became functional in Armenian, Azeri and Persian. She enthusiastically began teaching, uninhibited initially by her language deficet. "I forge ahead at all times," she said, "knowing that the things that must get done, will get done as long as you have courage."

Until Lillie was fluent I helped her teach Bible classes to the young students. We gave a lesson from Song of Solomon 2:15: "Catch the foxes, the little foxes, that spoil the vineyards, for our vineyards are in blossom." On a picture of a vineyard Lillie pinned up paper cut-out drawings of small foxes and the children gave the foxes names. Then I picked up a cut-out of a larger fox and asked, "What shall we name this one?"

"Disobedience," they suggested, which made me laugh.

We talked about what obedience is and what the Bible says in Colossians 3:20: "Children, obey your parents in everything, for this pleases the Lord."

When I turned to pin up the large fox, a little Armenian boy in the front row cried out with a sob, "Don't let the fox eat the grapes."

"This is just the effect we had hoped for," Lillie said.

In December the Tabriz mission held an annual meeting to discuss the yearly progress of the station in preparation for our Annual Report to the Board.

"I am seeing a record number of patients in the men's dispensary," Will Vannemen said, "over eight thousand since returning from furlough. I see fewer conditions related to malnutrition and starvation, which is promising."

"We have seen over six thousand patients in the Whipple Women's Hospital dispensary," Mary Bradford said, "and I have made over two thousand home visits."

"Were any of the home visits interesting?" I asked.

"A *sayyid* called on me saying, '*Hakim Khanum*' (Madame Doctor), I ask you as a last resort to save my daughter,' " Mary Bradford said. "When I came to his house, her mother vehemently protested my presence, but the *sayyid* insisted that I be allowed to treat her. When the daughter survived, the old woman thanked me. Since then, she has visited me at the mission several times and frequently invites me to her house and garden. On Sunday, six women from the *sayyid*'s harem appeared at my door and announced that they had come to spend the day. They went with me to church, and I realized afterwards that it was the longest they had gone without smoking their *qalyan*."

"Many Muslims attend the mission church service in Azeri," Charles Pittman said, "but they remain as cold as ever when the topic of joining the Presbyterian church is brought up. Frankly it does not concern me if they ever join, but I know that is not the view of the Board."

"I have had so many requests from Muslim parents to admit their boys to the mission school that I have decided to open a separate department for them," Sam announced. "I thought it best to gradually introduce them to the Armenian boys once I am certain that they will get along."

"How many students will you have with the new department?" Will Vanneman asked.

"We currrently have ninety boys, and with the addition of a new Muslim department, there could be as many as one hundred and fifty," Sam replied.

The following year, the Boys' School enrollment was one hundred and forty-five students, with twenty boarders. Sam was busier than ever serving as principal of the school, teaching advanced classes and filling in as pastor of the mission church with Charles Pittman. After Mary Jewett left for furlough in America, Sam made up for her absence by touring on weekends during the school year and for two months during summer school recess, visiting seventy villages on horseback.

June 15, 1901 — The Birth of my Sixth Child

"Oh, this dreadful heat," I moaned when Sam came to visit me in bed. He took a washcloth from a basin of water, wrung it out and placed it gently over my forehead. "Have the children had lunch?" I asked.

"Not yet," Sam replied stroking the top of my head. "Tarlan has lunch ready, but we are waiting for Esther to come back from the Girls' School. Miss Holliday took her there this morning."

"Esther shouldn't be playing outside in this heat. Tell her to stay inside the rest of the day."

"Are you interested in eating something?" Sam asked.

"I do not think I could eat anything. The contractions are starting."

"I will let Dr. Bradford know after lunch to come and check on you."

Sam was headed downstairs when I heard Esther's shrill screams. "My head, My head!"

What on earth? I desperately wanted to get up and run downstairs to see what was wrong with my child. With much effort I managed to lift myself out of bed and stagger down the hallway. A strong contraction bent me over and I leaned against the wall for support.

Sam rushed up the stairs holding Esther in his arms. He lay her on a towel in the washroom and poured a pitcher of water over her head and body. Her face was bright red. I got to my knees to touch her forehead; her skin was dry and burning.

"Esther stumbled through the door and held her hands to her head and screamed," Sam said. "Then she collapsed in the hallway. I sent Agnes to run to the dispensary and fetch Dr. Bradford."

"Oh, my dear child. My beautiful Esther," I bemoaned.

Sam took her limp little body to the bedroom she shared with Andrew and set her on her bed, placing wet towels on her body. The pang of a contraction buckled me over and I gasped for air. Sam took my arm. "Let me help you back to bed."

"No, let me kiss her cheek first," I stammered. The tears pouring down my face wetted little Esther's cheek. "Oh, my dear, please get better. Rest and get better."

I could hear the steps of a solid woman coming up the stairs. *It must be Mary Bradford. She has come at last to take care of my Esther.*

Mary's footsteps were coming towards my bedroom door when I heard Sam say, "No, Mary. Annie is fine. Esther is unconscious. Please tend to her first."

"Oh, I assumed the emergency summons meant Annie was in labor," Mary said.

"Just periodic contractions, but she will need you and Dr. Vanneman soon enough."

It was excruciating, hearing muffled conversation down the hall in Esther's room and trying to decipher what Mary and Sam were saying. When they emerged from Esther's bedroom, I heard Dr. Braford say. "It is a severe case of sunstroke. I took her temperature twice, not believing it was one hundred and eight the first time."

"How is she doing?" I asked.

"Her breathing is unlabored but shallow, and her heartbeat is rapid but still strong."

"What should we do?" Sam asked.

"You are doing the right thing," Mary replied. "Keep using wet compresses to cool her down. If she wakes, try to get her to drink some water, but she may not be able to hold it down at first."

The rest of the day Sam divided his time between visiting my bedside to hold my hand and applying wet cloths to Esther's head and body. My contractions were now coming more frequently, every three minutes. When I started screaming in pain, Sam sent Tarlan for Dr. Bradford and Dr. Vanneman.

"Esther?" I whispered.

"Still sleeping," Sam replied. "Nothing has changed. Agnes and Rose are praying by her bedside."

It was dark outside when Dr. Vanneman announced, "The baby is crowning." The burning was unbearable. Sam squeezed my hand and I pushed and let my breath follow the contractions. "Almost there, almost there," he said with a compassionate smile on his face.

"This is one big baby," Dr. Braford announced with a chuckle. "Look at the size of that shoulder."

"And big baby wants out," Will Vanneman added.

Then like a slimy seal, the baby slipped out. I sank into the bed with exhaustion, my body covered with sweat, and my vision blurred. "What is it?" I whispered.

"A big sturdy baby girl," Sam said. "I promised that if the baby was a girl, you could name her."

"She will be named Annie Rhea Wilson, Jr," I said.

Dr. Bradford cleaned up after the birth and placed our baby girl in my arms. A wave of gratitude spread through me. "Annie Rhea Wilson, my namesake," I whispered. "Some day when I am old, you will care for me. I do not know how I know this, but my heart tells me it will come true."

Sam and I stayed awake with our new baby and stared at her face. "She is named for me, but she looks like you," I said. "I hope that it was not a mistake to name her after me."

"Why would it be a mistake?" Sam asked.

"We named our first child after our grandfathers, but Sam was also your name. We thought it was bad luck when he died."

"Nonsense," Sam replied. "We named Andrew after my father, and he is a sturdy little fellow."

"And Esther? How is she?" I asked.

"Her temperature has come down, but Dr. Bradford is still concerned. Her breath is shallow, and her pulse is weak. Perhaps she will open her eyes tomorrow."

The next morning Esther did not wake as we had hoped and prayed. She continued to breathe softly throughout the day. I was too weak to go to her bedside, and each time I asked if her eyes had opened, Sam shook his head "no."

Sometime that night, Esther took her last breath. *Sunstroke took her, from light into darkness.*

Andrew was only two years old and did not understand death, but Agnes, who was eight, and Rose, who was seven, understood that their sweet little sister had died. Rose counted it this way: "We were five one night and the next night we were only four again."

Agnes and Rose came into the bedroom sobbing. Exhausted from labor I sat up, with the new baby at my breast. "Amongst sorrow, there is also joy," I said. As I cried for little Esther, the family surrounded the bed and touched the hands of the new baby, Annie Rhea Wilson, Jr.

"Sam, bring me my Bible," I said.

I opened the Bible to 2 Kings 4:18 and read of the son of the Shunammite who went with his father reaping in the fields. "And the son of the Shunammite said to his father, 'Oh, my head! My head!' and died of sunstroke that day. The prophet Elisha came and lay upon the child, 'putting his head to his head, his mouth to his mouth and his eyes to his eyes.' And upon Elisha's rising the child sneezed seven times and opened his eyes."

"But there is no prophet Elisha here in Tabriz to save beautiful Esther," Sam said. And we wept together, holding hands.

Sam had a carpenter make Esther's small coffin. We held a funeral service with the other missionaries of the station in our small Presbyterian mission cemetery. We buried the coffin next to Samuel Rhea Wilson, her older brother. I placed yellow roses, the color of her hair, on the mound and planted white lilies around it.

"No more appropriate words could be found to put on Esther's grave than 'Of such is the Kingdom of Heaven,'" Sam said. "She was a heavenly child in appearance and character."

Rose and Agnes were shaken by the death of their dear little sister Esther and found it hard to grasp her absence. Andrew continued to ask for her by name, particularly when he crawled into bed, with her empty bed next to his. "Pray to Esther," I responded. "For she is now an angel in heaven and can help you."

Some weeks after the baby was born, I wrote a poem in memory of Esther:

ESTHER
1896-1900

My Beloved came down to my garden
To look at the lilies one day,
As they stood with the dew of the morning
On the whiteness of their array,
And the one He stooped to gather
And bore in His bosom away
Of them all was the sweetest and fairest,
But how could I say Him nay?
The garden and all that was in it
Belonged to Him alone,
So how could I refuse Him
What was His very own?
There's a gap in my row of lilies,
As they stand in my garden today
With the glory of the sunshine
On the whiteness of their array,
But the one that will never wither
And will never fade away
Is the one my Beloved transplanted
To Paradise that day.

Chapter 24

Winter 1902 — Scarlet Fever

IN THE EARLY WINTER, THE NEXT CRISIS CAME. THERE WAS AN epidemic of scarlet fever and many children died. First Agnes, then Rose, came down with a severe sore throat followed by the rash all over their bodies and a high fever. For six weeks Dr. Bradford kept them in quarantine in the Whipple Women's Hospital isolation room. During the day, Dr. Bradford and the missionary nurses monitored them, and at night Sam slept in their hospital room. Each morning before leaving he bathed and changed his clothes in the hospital basement, which prevented further spread to the children in the school and the mission.

Rose and Agnes survived, and their homecoming was a red-letter day. Andrew was so excited to see his sisters again that he ran around the house with his hobby horse RoRo screaming, "The Princesses are coming! The Princesses are coming!"

May 15th, 1902 — Sam's Appendicitis

During Easter with the students on vacation Sam took the opportunity to tour in Karadagh. When he was a day late returning, I grew anxious, and by the second night past his expected arrival, I became distraught. Agnes and Rose implored me. "When is Daddy coming home?" and I could only say, "It should be soon."

On the third day, I sat in our bedroom by the window sewing and waiting. A horse appeared at the mission gate and Sam sat in the saddle slumped forward. I dropped my sewing and ran to greet him. Sam dismounted slowly and hobbled toward me, his face grimacing. "I need to see Vanneman right away. I have had severe abdominal pain for three days and could barely ride."

Dr. Vanneman came at once and examined Sam. "It is an appendicitis," he said. "You need it removed before it bursts and causes peritonitis. Unfortunately, I am not a skilled surgeon and will need to telegraph Dr. Cochran to perform the operation."

Sam lay in a hospital bed so he could be observed until Joe Cochran came from in Urmia. "When will he get here," I asked Will.

"He is traveling chapper," Will replied, "exchanging fresh horses at each station. He should arrive late the second night."

I kept vigil by Sam's bed, praying that Joe would arrive before peritonitis set in. "My brother Harry lost his wife to appendicitis," Sam said in a weak voice. "Perhaps Joe will not arrive in time."

"Do not think of that," I said.

"In case I am taken, I know my brothers will take care of you and the children," he said, "just as they took care of Harry's children. With my trust in Wilson family loyalty, I will not worry about you."

As Will predicted, Joe arrived at ten o'clock the second night and the next morning performed the operation. Mary Bradford sterilized the surgical instruments and assisted with the operation while Marguerite Vanneman gave the anesthetic. I waited impatiently in the waiting room, until Joe emerged with a smile. "We got it out in the nick of time," he said. "Now the tough job will be making Sam stay in bed to recover."

During Sam's convalescence, little Andrew stood by his bed and took tidbits from the tray of food. "That is your Daddy's food," I scolded him.

"Nonsense," Sam replied. "He is only learning the communal way of eating in Persia. I am pleased that he eats with three fingers, as opposed to five; only boors do that."

Sam and I held a welcome reception for Lucille Drake, a new teacher at the Girls' School, and Loretta Van Hook, who returned to the mission after an eleven-year absence. It was also a send-off for Mary Jewett, who on her return from furlough decided to transfer to the new station in Qazvin.

Mary Bradford approached us. "Sam, I have been worried about how tired you look. Is everything all right with your health?"

"With other missionaries on furlough, I am responsible for mission church sermons, as well as teaching classes and administration of the Boys' School," Sam replied. "Have you been busy at the women's hospital?"

"We have seen eighteen in-patients and about seven thousand out-patients," Mary Bradford replied. "The in-patients often are accompanied by curious superstitious rituals."

"Like what?" I asked.

"After a patient is put in bed, to ensure protection from the 'Evil Eye,' a man unsheathes his sword and uses the point to scratch a circle on the surrounding walls," Mary Bradford said. "Then they pass the sword around the patient, and sometimes, if they feel generous enough to protect me, they rub the sword along the bottom of my skirt."

"I would be scared to death if a man encircled my skirt with a sword," I said. "What else?"

"To scare away the *jinns*, the bad spirits, three onions are pierced on a spit and placed near the patient's pillow and three eggs are placed in a bowl of water. Prayers written on small pieces of paper are left soaking in her drinking water and inserted into her bed clothes and under the mattress."

"Having raw onions near one's nose all day would make anyone feel ill," I said. "How interesting to observe these rituals."

"How many home visits this year?" Sam asked.

"A thousand so far," Mary replied. "At least one hundred were long challenging cases, some requiring operations. The other members of the household often make treating them difficult. If I suggest an anesthetic, a woman will say assertively 'If that is given, she will die.' If I try to give a patient a pill for fever with a glass of water, I will be told, 'We have not given her water for three days. It will make her worse.' Usually, the patient pleads for more water after wetting their throat."

"Goodness, they make it hard for you to help the patient," I exclaimed.

"During an evening house visit to a Muslim woman, the husband said angrily to his wife, 'Why do you get sick at night. You keep the *Hakim Khanum* (Madame Doctor) out too late," Mary Bradford said. "As I was leaving one of the other women whispered, 'He wants you to go so he can smoke *teriak*' (opium)."

In late August, I reminded Andrew that his third birthday was approaching. "Am I going to have a birthday?" he asked, meaning a party. Sam bought a wooden top painted with rings of different colors for a birthday present, and I asked Tarlan to bake a cake and invited the mission children to attend a party at our house. Andrew was excited the morning before the party and galloped his hobby horse RoRo around the house yelling, "Giddy-up, we're going to a birthday. We're going to a birthday."

A few weeks after the party, Andrew developed swollen lymph nodes and a sore throat. Dr. Bradford examined him and gasped when he opened his mouth. "It is diphtheria," she said. "I will send for immune horse serum from Tehran."

"After ten years, the tragedy of Rhea's death cannot be repeated," I cried. "You must cure him."

Two days later Andrew could barely breath and when Mary Bradford listened to his heart, she shook her head. "His heartbeat is irregular," she said. "I hope the injections come soon."

I prayed next to Andrew's bed. "Please let the injections come today. Please save my boy."

Despite my prayers, the injections came two days too late. People asked, "Does lighting strike twice in the same place?"

A few days later Agnes, Rose and I developed the same symptoms — sore throat, fever, swollen glands. Dr. Bradford gave us the injections meant for Andrew and we lay in bed too ill to go downstairs to Andrew's funeral service.

"Muslim women are here to give their condolences to you. Are you able to come downstairs?" Sam asked. "It is the first time they have attended a Protestant funeral service."

"Oh goodness no," I cried, "I would not risk infecting those beautiful women and their families. Please tell them I know that they are here."

Afterward, Sam came to my bedside. "The dining room was filled with Muslim women, Europeans and Armenians," he said. "One Muslim woman said, 'He was our own little brother, born in our country.' " Many more came after the service and the following days to show their sympathy.

For Sam, Andrew's death was a staggering blow. School had just started, and I wondered if he could continue to teach as usual. As I watched Sam go to the school one morning I said, "Sam's strong faith and self-control sustain him. I too will try to fill my days too full for memories of my lost boy."

At night we gave way to grief. After dinner Sam went to his study and shut the door, and when he finally came to the parlor to read Scriptures to the children, his eyes were puffy and red. As he read his lower lip quivered and his voice cracked with emotion. When it became clear that he could not go on, I patted his hand and said, "Your voice is giving out from teaching all day. I will continue reading for you."

I also felt the deep throbbing pain of loss. At least once a day I walked to the mission cemetery where my three babies lay under little mounds of earth with white lilies growing beside them.

It was three months before I could play the piano again.

Rose asked me to play and sing songs with her. "Mother, let's sing, it has been so long."

"Oh, Rose," I replied. "I just don't think I have finished mourning your little brother's death. We will sing again soon, I promise."

By November, the rains had come and my daily visits to Andrew's grave had ceased. The gloom cast over the family started to lift, and I began to prepare for the holidays. Sam again took visitors in his study, and we could hear his loud laughter in the parlor even with his door closed. Agnes took my hand and squeezed it, with tears welling in her eyes. "We have suffered too," she said.

"Yes, I know," I replied. "We have all suffered the loss of your brother, but we will suffer no more. 'He heals the brokenhearted and binds up their wounds.' Psalms 147:3."

Winter 1903

During the winter of 1903 A. V. Williams Jackson from Columbia University stayed with us. He had written several books on Zoroastrianism, including the *Avesta, the Bible of* Zoroaster, published in 1893, and *Zoroaster, the Prophet of Ancient Iran*, published in 1898. When the missionaries heard of his imminent arrival, they honored him with a formal *peshwaz*. A party of men rode out to greet Professor Jackson but returned to the mission after dark without him.

At nine o'clock, three hours later, A. V. Williams Jackson arrived alone shivering. "The only thing I want is a fire," he said.

"You must be a fire-worshipper, like the Zoroastrians," I replied.

"Yes, I am," he said, "but for warmth only."

He was a tiny energetic man about my age with flashing blue eyes. He had no interest in the typical tourist attractions, such as the Arg, the Blue Mosque and Persian rugs in the Bazaar. He only wanted to see and read everything associated with Zoroaster.

In April he arranged for a guided trip to see the cuneiform inscription of Darius on a cliff on Mount Behistun. It was a four-day journey from Hamadan by horse and a steep ascent up the snow-covered mountain. In order to photograph the inscription, he was suspended by ropes above an abyss. He came back saying, "I verified one saying of Zoroaster; that in Persia winter lasts for thirteen months."

"What is your interest in the Behistun Inscription?" I asked.

"The inscription is written in Old Persian, Elamite and Babylonian by Darius the Great," Dr. Jackson said. "It played a crucial part in deciphering the cuneiform script used for ancient languages of the Persian Empire, much like the Egyptian Rosette Stone."

A. V. Williams Jackson came again to Persia in 1907 and in 1911 and became a life-long friend of the family.

Spring 1903

"We finally have a pastor for the mission church," Sam exclaimed. "Rev. Frederick Jessup has arrived. He is the youngest son of Henry Jessup, a pastor and educator at the mission in Syria. We will hold a small reception for him on Sunday."

Fred Jessup was a handsome man in his late twenties with a broad forehead and an aristocratic nose. His gaze and voice communicated an earnest sincerity. "My father asked me to deliver his well wishes," Fred said. "He remembers you from your visit on your way to a conference in Cairo."

"Your arrival is sincerely rejoiced," Sam said. "I have been delivering sermons, poorly at best. I am much better suited for teaching and administering the Boys' School."

"How are the mission schools doing?" Fred asked.

"Ten years ago, there were seventy students, of whom twenty-six were boarders," Sam responded. "We had no regular Muslim students, as their attendance was prohibited. The Boys' School has now grown beyond the capacity of the building. We have the same number of boarders, but the total number of pupils is two hundred and eleven. Thirty-five of the students are Muslim boys, the sons of the *Kalabegi*, the *Kalantar*, *mullahs* and *sayyids*. As many as half will inherit the title Khan."

"What about the Girls' School?" Fred asked.

"Ten years ago, there were only forty girls. In the past five years we have seen a steady enrollment of one hundred girls with ten to twenty boarders," Lillie Beaber replied. "This year we have one hundred and sixty-five girls, the majority under twelve years of age."

"Our medical missionary work has also expanded," Mary Bradford said. "Will Vanneman and I have constructed new buildings with recent donations and receipts from our patients."

"Both the men's and women's dispensaries treat seven thousand patients each this year," Will Vanneman added.

"That is over one hundred men and one hundred women each week," Mary Bradford said. "And we are only open in the mornings. In the afternoon we make house visits; I have visited seven hundred women this year."

"With such a productive year for the mission, I am regretting going on furlough next year," Sam said.

"Sam, you should not worry while you are away," Newton Wright chimed in. "I will oversee the continued success of the Boys' School."

Sam swallowed hard and did not respond. I knew he was apprehensive about Newton overseeing the Boys' School in his absence.

On July 26th our son, Robert Graham was born; a frail baby due to difficulties suckling. When I asked why he was not gaining weight, Dr. Bradford replied, "He has tongue tie."

Each day I held him to my breast for hours trying to get him to feed. I became tired and frustrated and developed painful engorgement and infection from clogged milk ducts. Sam found me crying in the bedroom one day trying to feed little Bobby. "I am afraid he will die from starvation," I wailed. Sam silently stroked my hair.

In the winter baby Bobby contracted a cold and I feared it would settle in his lungs. The constant coughing wore him out and made it even more difficult to feed him. "I beg to have the elders come in and pray," I told Sam in despair.

Sam recited James 5:14 in response. "Let him call for the elders of the church and let them pray over him, anointing him with oil in the name of the Lord. The prayer of faith will save the sick man, and the Lord will raise him up."

"I will continue to pray for dear Bobby," I said. "I will not give up hope. 'The Lord sustains him on his sickbed, in his illness thou restore him to full health.' Psalms 41:3."

When Sam went on tour, I felt helpless and searched through my jewelry box for the *nazars*, the amulet bracelets Princess Ezzat gave me over ten years ago. "Baby Bobby and I will wear these as a last resort, to protect us from the 'Evil Eye,'" I cried. "I will try anything to save my child."

Annie Rhea Wilson, 1904   Samuel Graham Wilson, 1904

CHAPTER 25

March 1904 — B. W. Labaree's Murder

ON MARCH 10ᵀᴴ, 1904, WE WERE MAKING ARRANGEMENTS FOR our furlough in America when a cable from the Urmia mission arrived for Sam. He stood at the door of the parlor where I was sewing with his pupils dilated and his lower lip quivering; the shock on his face sent chills down my spine.

"B. W. Labaree has been murdered," Sam said in a hushed voice.

"Murdered?" I cried. "Who would do such a thing?"

"His father's telegram did not say," Sam replied.

"He had the heart of a lamb, so self-sacrificing," I said. "His wife Mary and children must be devastated; Leonard is seven and Clara nine, old enough to dearly miss their father."

"I will leave tomorrow for Urmia to see if I can be of any help and should have more details when I return," Sam said.

"Send me a telegram so I know you have arrived safely," I said.

After Sam departed, I was anxious for news. Usually, my friend Fred Coan would write me a long letter explaining what happened, but he and his family were in America on furlough.

Will Vanneman came to the house two days later. "Sam is unaware of how unusually perilous his journey to Urmia is," he said. "A letter from Joe Cochran arrived yesterday saying it was Kurds who ambushed and killed B. W. on the main rode from Khoi to Urmia."

The blood drained from my body, and I was dizzy with panic. "Sam will take that same road," I said trying to stay calm. *I am anything but calm.*

Waiting the next three days for news from Sam was torture. On the fourth day a telegram came: "In Urmia, Love, Sam." I wanted Sam to turn around and come home, but I knew I was only being selfish.

The day that Sam was to return I watched impatiently by the window. Late in the afternoon when he appeared on his horse, I dashed out the door. "I was so worried that you would be attacked too," I said.

"It was the same band of Kurds led by Sayyid Jaffar, who in June attacked the Christians in the villages of Targawar. They slaughtered men and women, burnt their villages and stole their sheep. Those who fled were protected by the Urmia mission."

"But those were Christian Persians," I said. "Why did the Kurds kill a foreign missionary?"

"Last year at the end of June there was another incident involving a graduate of the Urmia mission school who became one of their teachers," Sam said. "His name was M. G. Daniel. While supervising farmworkers in his family's vineyard, Sayyid Jaffar shot him because he refused to give him his watch."

"I cannot see the connection," I said.

"Joe Cochran brought the murder of M.G. Daniel to the attention of the Persian government," Sam replied. "Apparently, this angered Sayyid Jaffar, and he made it well known that he intended revenge."

"How did the Kurds mistake B. W. for Joe?"

"It is unclear. The teacher of the Urmia mission children, Margaret Dean, required an escort to her caravan back to America, a days' journey from the mission. B. W. and his servant Israel volunteered and, on their way back to Urmia, Sayyid Jaffar and three other Kurds were waiting for them. They shot Israel in the back, then carried B. W. a *farsag* or more before killing him. Sayyid Jaffar cut his mouth to his ear, then another Kurd stabbed him twice in the chest."

I covered my face with my hands and wept. "Oh, what a painful and undeserving way to die. How is his wife?"

"When people offered condolences, cursing the murderers of her husband, she responded, 'Your words hurt my broken heart like daggers. I pray as our Master did for His enemies,'" Sam said.

"And Jesus said, 'Father forgive them for they know not what they do,'" I said. "Luke 23:34."

"Benjamin Labaree, B. W.'s father, is taking it much worse than B. W.'s wife," Sam said. "His health is failing, and the loss of his son was a severe blow. His other son, Robert, plans to come to Persia and take B. W.'s place."

"He was so proud that his son became a second-generation missionary," I added. "How admirable of Robert to replace him."

"Joe is taking the burden of trying to bring punishment to the Kurds who murdered B. W. Labaree, M. G. Daniel and the Christians slaughtered in Targawar. He is consumed by this. I fear for his health and sanity."

"Joe has always been a pillar of strength."

"But this may be too much for him."

1904 — Our Second Furlough

In May 1904 we left Tabriz for our furlough in America. Our family was accompanied on our journey by Mary Bradford, who was going home to care for her sick mother, and widow Mary Labaree and her two children. Agnes and Rose read books, while I held baby Bobby, and Sam took charge of three-year-old Annie.

I was lucky to have Dr. Bradford with us as the baby was sick the entire trip and developed pneumonia.

In London, prior to taking a steamer to America, Dr. Bradford insisted we seek medical attention for Bobby. "The child is too sick to be on the ship for a week. You need a doctor to administer a type-specific serum injection. I recall that Mrs. Shedd has a brother studying medicine here. I will try to contact him."

Mary went to the University College London that afternoon and returned to the hotel smiling. "Bobby has an appointment to be serotyped tomorrow morning. It will take a few days, but once they determine which pneumococcal strain he has, they will inject him with strain-specific horse serum."

"I wished type-specific serum was available when my father contracted pneumonia," Sam said. "It is amazing how much medicine has advanced in seven years. Thank you for your help."

"I have only done what I could to help your poor baby," Mary said. "Tomorrow I will be on the boat to America with the Labarees."

Just as Mary promised, Bobby was called back to get his shot of horse serum and the doctor bid us a safe trip to America. "Make sure to keep the baby warm," he said.

For the first three days, the weather was cold and foggy. I stayed in our cabin with the baby, while Sam took care of the girls, and had meals brought to our room. By the fourth day, I was stir-crazy and ventured out on the deck to have some fresh air while the baby slept. A thick fog had engulfed the ship and I could barely make out the faces of people fifteen feet in front of me. I heard Sam laughing and followed the sound of his voice through the mist.

The face of a small girl with golden curls emerged through the fog. "Esther?" I cried. The girl recoiled and buried her face in a woman's skirt. Across from her was Sam with a shocked expression. "Annie," he said. "This is Charles and Hattie Stewart. Hattie is a Wilson relative from Pennsylvania. They have four girls that have been playing with ours."

Six young girls appeared through the mist. "Such a coincidence," I marveled. "Your little one looks just like my sweet little Esther who we lost to sunstroke. I thought she was a ghost."

"Her name is Ursula, but we call her Sue," Hattie said.

When we arrived in Philadelphia, my brother Foster and Will Dulles met us with a carriage and escorted us onboard the train to New York. My dear brother Foster insisted on holding the sick baby the rest of the trip.

The Dulles' new home in Englewood, New Jersey was a three-story stone house with an extensive garden, a carriage house and separate servants' quarters. "We call it 'Rosenvik,' " Will said.

Mother moved to Rosenvik after returning from Persia and greeted us at the door. Sophea joined her carrying baby Winslow.

My nieces, Edith and Dorothy, and nephew Rhea were excited to meet their cousins from Persia. "The children can play in the garden while we have tea in the parlor," Sophea said.

"We waited to build the house until Englewood could supply electricity to homes," Will said. "When the Hackensack Power Plant caught fire in 1903, we decided to install combined gas and electrical lighting in the house in case electricity is not dependable."

"For three months, Englewood was without streetlights," Sophea said. "Can you imagine not having streetlights?"

"One would think that Thomas Edison would do something about it since he lives twenty-five miles from here," Will retorted.

"In Tabriz, we do not have streetlights; one carries a lantern at night," Sam said. "It will likely be a decade before we have electric lights at the mission, so I am afraid we cannot commiserate with you."

Every morning Sophea made twelve bottles of milk for the babies, and within a month, Bobby was well and of normal weight. It was such a relief to me. *To think that I feared losing my baby to pneumonia only six weeks before.*

Each morning, Mother took a walk with Winslow and Bobby in a baby carriage. As the neighbors passed, they peeked in and said, "Goodness, I did not know the Dulleses had twins."

Mother's standard reply was, "Yes, they have twins from different mothers and fathers." Then she continued on her way leaving the neighbor dumbfounded.

At the end of September, we rushed to Indiana, Pennsylvania. Sam's youngest sister, Agnes, was marrying Stacy Smith, the assistant postmaster. The wedding was held in the Presbyterian Church assisted by Sam's brother Rob. Mother Wilson had a reception at her house.

"Everything is the same, Mother. Except you replaced all the gas lighting fixtures with electric ones," Sam exclaimed. "I am pleasantly surprised."

"When Harry's family moved in and Jenny came to take care of his two motherless children, they insisted on improvements," Mother Wilson replied. "It is much brighter and better for my tired old eyes. After you were here on your last furlough, Indiana remodeled the town's electric plant. We now have electricity from dusk to dawn. They are talking about supplying continuous day and night electricity in a couple of years. I may be an old lady, but I like change."

"We simply cannot complain," Jenny added. "We feel sorry for the farmers who cannot be supplied with electricity."

There were eleven of us staying with Mother Wilson, who was a frail woman in her seventies. "We will be staying in Indiana for six months," I said. "As I mentioned in my letters, we can rent a house nearby."

"No, I would not hear of such a thing," Mother Wilson replied. "I insist that you stay with us. I feel lonely when there are fewer than twelve at the table."

For Thanksgiving, there were over twenty people for dinner with Sam's single brothers John and Dick and his sisters Agnes and Ella, their husbands and children. Alarmed by a loud sputtering noise outside, Sam and I ran to the window. "What on earth," I exclaimed.

"It is Dick with his new automobile," Sam said. "He is the first person in the city of Indiana to own a horseless carriage."

Our girls rushed to the window too and little Bobby tried to toddle after them but fell and burst into crying screams. I was bent over my toddler and wiping his tears, when Dick came in with a pleasant-looking fellow who I guessed was about thirty. "Dicky, you see, you have frightened the child with your noisy machine," the man said.

"Sorry we have not met," I said as I stood up. "Are you family?"

Dick and the young man laughed. "This is Blair Sutton," Dick said. "His stepmother was Father's half-sister. Somehow that relationship earned him a clerk's position in Father's store."

"Blair Sutton has been part of the family for years," John, Sam's younger brother, said. "If we fail to invite him, he will somehow invite himself; he is a lonely bachelor."

"I am interested in your automobile," Sam interjected. "What kind is it, not that I know the difference."

"It is a Pope-Hartford Modal B," Dick said. "Come outside and see it."

Even though it was brisk outside Sam and I followed Dick to see the bright red automobile with shiny black leather seats. Except for a canopy the passengers were exposed to the elements. "It has two drive ranges," Dick explained. "The foot pedal is the low range and the lever on the right-hand side is the high range. It takes some practice."

When we returned inside the girls were at the window with Bobby, who was screaming, "Bubble."

"What?" I exclaimed.

"Bobby named the horseless carriage 'Bubble,'" Agnes replied.

"Well Bobby, let's go for a ride around the block in 'Bubble,'" Dick said.

"I will need to hold him, so he does not fall out," I said.

"You and Bobby can sit in back and I will sit in front with Dick," Sam said.

It was a chilly, bumpy ride around the block on the cobble stone street. "Can you drive it in the snow?" I asked.

"This will be my first winter with 'Bubble,'" Dick replied. "I have been told that if the horse drawn carriages pack the snow down it is possible to drive. In the spring when all but the main roads are muddy, the wheels could get stuck."

Bobby squealed for joy for the entire ride and whenever Bobby heard Dick drive up to the house, he screamed, "Bubble. Bubble."

To my surprise, Mother Wilson was equally enthusiastic, asking for her turn in the automobile. "I feel so safe with Dick driving," she added.

For the first time Rose and Agnes were attending regular classes with their cousins George and Andrew Stewart. During our six months in Indiana, Ella Stewart was closest to me of Sam's sisters. She had graduated from college, Vassar class of 1887, and, like me, taught high school students before marrying.

After the school year ended, we said a tearful goodbye to Sam's family. "You owe it to me to come back before I die," Mother Wilson said, her jaw quivering.

"I will, Mother," Sam replied. "I will."

On the train to New York, Sam looked silently out the window, deep in thought. Then he covered his face with his hands and sobbed. "I don't know if I will make it back in time," he gasped. I took his hand and whispered, "She will hold on until you return. Your promise will keep her alive."

My own mother was a robust seventy-year-old woman, but Sam's concerns about his mother elicited my own fears. *Would Mother die before I returned on our next furlough?*

"Children," I said in a solemn voice. "You must cherish every moment you have had with your grandmothers on this stay in America. They may not be here the next time we come."

"Where will they go?" Annie asked in bewilderment.

"To the house of the Lord," Sam said.

CHAPTER 26

Tabriz 1905

SEVEN MILES OUTSIDE OF TABRIZ WE WERE MET BY THE missionaries, members of the mission church and throngs of students from the Boys' School. Since Tarlan was now the Vanneman's cook, Marguerite and Will Vanneman brought dinner to our house. "You must be famished," Marguerite said.

"Yes," I responded. "We are hungry, tired and happy to be home."

"We can catch up later on events that occurred while you were traveling back to Persia," Marguerite said, "except there is some sad news that cannot wait."

"What is it?" Samuel asked. "Tell us at once."

"Joe Cochran died August 18th at his home," Marguerite said in almost a whisper.

"How?" Sam exclaimed.

"It was typhoid," Will Vanneman said. "He died after only three days of illness."

"No," I exclaimed as a chill ran through my body. "Not Josie."

"The past year was very difficult for him," Will continued. "The American Minister in Tehran demanded punishment of the Kurds that murdered B. W. Labaree, but the Persian government failed to act. As a result, the lives of the missionaries in Urmia were almost in constant danger, especially Joe Cochran's."

"Were there attempts on his life?" I asked.

"Kurds prowled the gardens between the city and the mission looking for an opportunity to shoot him," Will continued. "One Kurd gained access to the mission compound by crawling through a water course, and, on another occasion, a band of Kurds attempted to scale the wall with a ladder."

"Did the British Consul in Urmia offer protection?" Sam asked.

"Yes, when Joe rode between the new mission compound and the city the British Consul's lancers escorted him," Will said. "It was a desperate situation. At night in his house Joe never dared to appear in front of a window in a lighted room. Overworked and sleepless with anxiety, he was enervated and when he contracted typhoid, he did not have the strength to fight it."

"Joe was a captive in a maze of suffering, danger and anxiety," Marguerite added. "I am convinced that death was absolutely the only way out."

"God in His love and mercy did not try His servant beyond his strength," Sam said. "He gently released him."

Tears spilled from my eyes. "Not Josie."

"Such incredibly sad news," Sam said. "I am sure his funeral was attended by thousands of mourners — Muslims, Nestorians, Christians and Jews. I would have liked to have been there to honor his life and achievements, having built the first hospital in Persia. He will be difficult to replace."

"We were *en route* to Persia when he passed away," I added. "There was no way of knowing until we arrived at the mission."

"The other sad news is that Mary Bradford is still in America because of her mother's health," Will said. "We do not know when and if she will return. As a result, the Western Persia Mission is without two of its primary medical missionaries."

"How has Persia reacted to the victory of Japan over Russia this year?" Sam asked. "Hopefully it means the end to Russia's aggression in Asia."

"They are afraid that Russia, having failed in the Far East, will now turn to the South and exert more power over Persia," Will replied.

"Have there been any unusual disturbances in Persia this year?" Sam asked.

"There is growing discontent about the Shah's extravagant lifestyle and foreign travel," Will replied. "The *Sadrazam,* Prime Minister Ayn al-Dawla, is exacting arbitrary taxes on the bakeries and slaughterhouses. He *bastinadoed* merchants for increasing the price of sugar. There is a growing movement to have him dismissed."

"*Bastinadoed*?" I exclaimed.

"He tortured them my caning the soles of their feet," Will replied. "The feeble sometimes die from it."

"So many changes, yet things stay the same," Sam said. "We are sad about the loss of our missionary brethren, but happy that the mission has thrived in our absence."

"And we are happy that you have returned," Will said. "There is much work to do."

Sam returned from his first day at the Boys' School with wild excitement in his eyes. "The total number enrolled this year is one hundred and eighty-eight; one hundred and eighteen Armenians, ten Nestorians and sixty Muslims. The desire for education is becoming more widespread. There is much restlessness, a spirit of inquiry, a desire for improvement, a yearning for liberty, education and enlightenment."

"This is what we had been hoping for," I replied and wiped tears of joy from my eyes. "The Persians have put down their bigotry towards us and realize we are here to give their children a solid intellectual and moral education."

"It has been twenty-five years of hard unrelenting work," Sam said as he sank into a chair. "At the same time, it worries me too."

"Why so?"

"The restlessness of the people. They are dissatisfied with a government that gives concessions to foreign powers, namely to Russia and England. They want a government that listens to the people. They want a representative parliament."

"What is wrong with that?"

"The Shah does not govern Persia as a democracy, and he will not support it. Surely there will be conflict."

I received news that Princess Ezzat had returned to Persia from exile. Her father Mozaffar ad-Din Shah not only allowed her family's return to Tehran, but appointed her husband, Prince Abdol Hossein, Minister of Justice. I rejoiced in my friend's return to her homeland.

Before Christmas we held a holiday party at our house for the missionaries. Lillie Beaber was excited to tell me about the new students attending the Girls' School. "One winter day a blind Armenian man and his wife, a frail little woman with a baby in her arms, came to the school. They asked if their two daughters, who were ten and twelve years old, could be admitted as boarders. The father had worked in Turkey with four brothers in soap and silk factories. Turkish soldiers raided their Christian village and destroyed the factories and homes, killing his brothers and their families.

"The helpless man and his family escaped and begged their way to Tabriz. They were referred to us by a reliable Armenian man, so we said we would accept them. The next day the entire family arrived — the two older girls, an eight-year-old boy, a sweet little girl of four and the baby, all in ragged calico clothes and no underwear. We admitted the three girls and gave the mother work at the school. After baths, new clothes and plenty of food, the children were miraculously transformed. The two older girls are bright and studious and perform at the top of their classes."

"Stories of what the Turkish soldiers did to the Christian Armenians give me nightmares," I said. "I am glad your story has a happy ending."

"On another cheery note," Will Vanneman said. "I have news that the Board has found a replacement for Dr. Cochran's position."

"How can you even think of referring to anyone as Joe's replacement?" I retorted.

Will winced. "What I mean is that another doctor has been selected to run Dr. Cochran's hospital in Urmia. His name is Harry Phineas Packard, a physician in his thirties practicing in Denver. He is married and has a two-year old son."

"It will be such a relief to have a physician at the hospital in Urmia," Sam said.

"How I wish we could find someone to fill in for Mary Bradford." Will added. "With the women's hospital closed, the Persian women of Tabriz are in great need of expert medical care."

When we returned from furlough Mousa returned as our butler and general factotum, but since Tarlan wished to continue to work at the Vannemans we needed to hire a new cook and nanny. After interviewing ten women we settled on Kizbus, an Armenian woman. "What does Kizbus mean?" I asked her. "I have never heard that name before."

"*Kizbus* means 'girls enough,'" she replied. "My father gave me the name after my mother had six girls."

Kizbus proved to be a competent nanny and looked after five-year-old Annie and two-year-old Bobby, leaving me time to teach classes and visit Persian women.

Before leaving on furlough, I had petitioned the Board for a teacher for the eight school-age children at the mission. The petition was granted, and Edith Lamme came from America to organize a school for our missionary children. Our large bedroom became the school room, and I hurried after breakfast each morning to make it ready for the children. "I can set my watch by the sound of Miss Lamme's feet coming up the steps," Sam said.

Mrs. Brunton, an English lady living across the street from the mission, gave piano lessons to the six older missionary children, including Agnes and Rose. At first all six children took turns practicing on my piano in the parlor, but eventually the Vannemans and the Wrights were able to secure pianos for their children, much to my relief.

As usual Sam had visitors almost every day. One visit was from the Governor Mukhbir-al-Sultana accompanied by his retinue. As was customary, they left their shoes outside Sam's study door, and I counted the shoes to tell Kizbus how many cups of coffee to serve.

When the Governor was taking his leave, he found his shoes were missing. "My shoes!" I heard him bellow from down the hall. "Someone has taken my shoes!"

Sam ran into the parlor. "See if one the children has taken the Governor's shoes."

A wave of consternation made my head spin. *What could have happened to his shoes?* The girls were outside in the garden, but I remembered hearing Bobby run up and down the hallway squealing.

Halfway up the stairs to the bedrooms, I heard Sam laughing loudly in the hallway. "Annie, you must see what the baby has done," he called to me. When I peeked down the hall, I saw Bobby shuffling along in the Governor's shoes. One of his servants was trying to catch Bobby and the Governor was bent over laughing. The servant took Bobby by his hand and led him up to the Governor, who brushed the top of the toddler's head and asked, "Could you return my shoes?" pointing at his feet. Fortunately, Bobby understood and relinquished them.

After Governor Mukhbir-al-Sultana and his retinue departed, I asked, "What did the Governor have to say?"

"The disturbances by the merchants and *mullahs* in Tehran are growing," Sam said. "The Shah employed Belgians to direct financial reform. A photograph published in the newspaper of a Belgian official dressed as a *mullah* at a costume party has outraged the Muslim clergymen. They are demanding that the Belgians be dismissed, along with Ayn al-Dawla, the Prime Minster. Some go so far as to propose a democratic form of government with a popular assembly."

"I understand the outrage about the *mullah* costume," I exclaimed, "but what does the Governor want you to do?"

"The Governor is concerned that disturbances will spread to Tabriz," Sam said. "He asks that, as a neutral party, I promote peaceful solutions to issues that might arise. With the growing discontent he is not sure conflict can be avoided."

Kizbus, the Wilson's Nanny and Cook

Mousa, the Wilson's Factotum

CHAPTER 27

Tabriz 1906

"UNCLE FRED!" THE GIRLS SCREAMED WHEN FRED COAN and his ten-year-old son Howard arrived.

"I am always pleased to have you stay with us," I said. "Our children love hearing your stories and listening to you play the piano. Sam enjoys hearing your first-hand accounts on the Urmia station and your perceptive commentary on the political situation in Persia."

"Are you still having problems with the Kurds?" Sam asked.

"Assaults, murders and robberies by the Kurds are a common occurrence," Fred replied. "The Urmia mission is inundated by refugees from the Christian villages. God has kept the missionaries safe. For that we have deep gratitude, but our nerves are frayed."

"The foreign newspapers say the governments of Persia and the Ottoman Empire are quarreling about the border again," Sam said.

"Traveling near the border and in the Kurdistan is risky due to the dispute," Fred said. "We fear that the Ottoman army might at any time invade western Persia. The weakness of the Persian government is painfully evident from their lack of response to the Kurdish raids."

"For some time, there has been grumbling against the government for giving concessions to foreigners," Sam said. "Anger reached a higher level when Belgians were put in charge of the customs and postal systems. There is talk that the Shah is considering turning over the country's internal revenue to foreigners to manage as well."

"The Islamic clergymen, who have such power in the criminal and judiciary courts, see this as a dangerous trend," Fred said. "They fear losing their religious influence in the courts. In many cities they have stirred up open demonstrations against the Shah and his administration."

"In Tabriz, there was a demonstration that compelled the *Vali Ahd* to take refuge in another town," Sam said. "Other than that, the year was relatively uneventful. There were no disruptions other than the death of the pastor of the mission church and the loss of two teachers at the Boys' School. Their loss will increase my teaching load."

"We were fortunate to have Rev. Paul Vauthier join the Boys' School," I interjected. "He will teach French to both the school's students and the missionary children."

In March we received a letter from Rev. Robert Labaree at the Urmia station. To our surprise it was a wedding invitation. "Robert Labaree and Mary Fleming are to be married July 27th," Sam exclaimed. "We are cordially invited to come to the wedding in Urmia."

"What happy news," I exclaimed. "Imagine, a wedding at the mission, but will it be safe to travel?"

"With the American government seeking punishment for B. W. Labaree's murder, the Kurds are careful to leave missionaries alone."

"What about the children?" I asked.

"We will leave Annie and Bobby here with Kizbus and take Agnes and Rose with us to Urmia," Sam replied.

At the end of May, we received a letter from Fred Coan: "I have sad news to relay to the Tabriz station. On May 14th, Rev. Benjamin Labaree, Sr. died at sea, two days out of Hamburg. He had been quite ill with cancer and hoped to reach America to see his daughters."

"Mother will be sad to hear of his death," I said, "and he will be missed at his son's wedding."

"He was seventy-two and the oldest missionary in the Persian missions," Sam said.

"Do you think we will still be here at seventy?" I asked.

"Undoubtedly," Sam replied.

July 1906

There were three wagons in our procession to Urmia for the Labaree-Fleming wedding. The lead wagon was Newton and Mattie Wright with Lillie Beaber and Mary Jewett. Dr. Vanneman chose to stay in Tabriz and see patients, so Marguerite Vanneman rode in Fred Jessup's wagon with Lucille Drake and Charles Pittman. Our wagon pulled up the rear, with Sam and I riding in front and Agnes and Rose in back.

"I have been watching Charles and Lucille in back of the Jessup's wagon," I whispered. "They are sitting rather close to each other and seem, well, intimate."

Sam laughed so vigorously that he shook the wagon. "Is this the first time you have noticed that Lucille and Charles are in love? The rest of us are expecting an announcement any day."

"Will there be another wedding?" Agnes asked from the back seat.

I cringed. *What if Agnes or Rose say something inappropriate?* "Now girls," I replied. "Promise not to say a thing about your father's speculation about another engagement."

When we reached Khoi, Loretta Van Hook, who was returning to Urmia after an itinerating tour, met us at the *caravanserai*. We were eager to hear about her experience during a seven-week stay in Maragha and Miandoab.

"On the way down, I met a Muslim woman in Goilgon, who wanted to be 'my sister,' so we went through the ceremony of locking fingers. 'I know God as my Father,' I told her, 'and if you want to be my sister, you too must become a child of God.' On my return I stopped at the same *caravanserai*, and the woman, hearing of my arrival, hurried to see me. When I mentioned, 'Our Father in Heaven,' her face lit up and she said, 'Yes, I remember you said God was our Father.' It brought me great joy to hear that she had grasped the concept of God."

"How satisfying to know that you reached someone," I said.

"In Maragha," Loretta continued, "My most interesting work was with the intelligent high-class Muslim women. One Muslim woman heard I was in Maragha and at first sent her servant to 'spy out the land.' After receiving a favorable report, she invited me to an elaborate breakfast, requesting I bring 'my book' along. After our visit she requested a Bible and invited me to come and explain it. After my last visit, she warmly grasped my hand in parting and said, 'Thank you for opening my eyes to a book that gives me so much comfort.' I felt gaining the interest of an intelligent Muslim woman was a major achievement."

"Yes, it is," I said. "I visited twenty Muslim homes this year with different opportunities to speak of the Lord. Some are believers, and to these I can talk freely; our hearts burn within us together as I reveal Christ in the Scriptures. Some are receptive but fear displaying interest in the presence of other Muslims. Others are indifferent but like to have our social visits and we cultivate friendships. At the homes of the boys in our school, we are always cordially received, and at festival seasons they are in the street in front of their houses to waylay us and compel us to come in."

"Let me tell you about my last visit at a village near Khoi," Loretta said. "We showed pictures of Bible stories outside on a large screen fastened to the court wall. The crowd sat on the ground as we explained each of forty Bible stories. When I finished going through the pictures, no one in the crowd moved a muscle to leave, so I asked, 'Are you not satisfied?' A village Khan, replied emphatically, 'No,' to which I responded, 'Very well. We will go through the stories again.' The crowd of peasants sat intrigued as I once again explained the Bible stories illustrated in the pictures. I did not realize evangelical stories were so captivating."

"We bring them *tamasha*," Sam said. "A spectacle of Christian entertainment."

"It is the treat of their lives," Loretta said. "We are not just missionaries, we are entertainers."

Fred Coan approached with an eager expression on his face. "Have you heard about the incredible developments in Tehran this past week?"

"Before we left Tabriz, I heard that *mullahs* and merchants in Tehran advised the *Sadrazam*, the Prime Minister, that unless financial and political reforms occurred there would be disturbances," Sam said. "Did something happen?"

"The Shah's troops were summoned to a disturbance at a bazaar where a large crowd was clamoring for a representative assembly," Fred replied. "The soldiers fired on the crowd killing sixty to seventy. The next day eighteen thousand took *bast* in the gardens of the British Legation."

"The British intervened and gave them refuge?" Sam exclaimed.

"The senior British Minister, Sir Grant Duff, showed the *bastis* unprecedented hospitality and went to Mozaffar ad-Din Shah on their behalf," Fred said. "After conferring with His Highness about their demands, the Shah said he would grant their requests."

"What?" Sam cried. "The Shah is going to allow a Parliament? Next it will be a constitution."

"Yes, you guessed it," Fred said. "He agreed to allow a constitution as well."

"I cannot believe my ears," I added.

"The changes will extend beyond Tehran," Fred said. "In other cities people are demanding 'liberty, justice,' and local representative assemblies that they call *Anjumans*."

"Will the *Anjuman* replace the existing local government?" I asked.

"No, they say they will cooperate with the existing government."

"The people of Tabriz will surely insist on an *Anjuman*," Sam said. "The city is full of revolutionary types, some our former students."

"Enough of politics," Ida Coan said. "You are boring the children."

The wedding of Robert Labaree and Mary Fleming was held in the Urmia mission church, adorned with native Persian flowers. Fred Coan presided over the ceremony, assisted by William Shedd. It was a simple wedding with the bride, groom and attendants dressed in their best church clothes. Mary Van Duzee, a teacher at the Fiske Girls' School, was the bride's maid and eleven-year-old

Katharine Coan was the flower girl. The ceremony was followed by a feast of lamb and *pillou* in the school's Assembly Hall. After cake was served, individuals stood up and made speeches of congratulations. Toward the end, Lillie Beaber stood up and said, "I have been asked to make happy announcement; Rev. Charles Pittman and Lucille Drake are engaged to be married." A roar of applause and laughter exploded.

"Do you have any plans for the wedding?" I asked Charles and Lucille.

"We plan on having the wedding in September before the school year starts," Charles replied. "And we were hoping that Sam would perform the ceremony."

"Why of course," Sam replied. "I would be honored."

"I have another request of the Wilsons," Lucille said. "I would like Agnes, Rose and Annie to be my bridesmaids."

Our girls were thrilled. When the day came, we woke early and picked fresh flowers from my garden for their wreaths and bouquets.

On August 19th the *Baharestan*, the new House of Parliament, was officially opened in Tehran. Sixty of the two hundred elected *Majlis*, the members of Parliament, began drafting the Constitution. With Mozaffar ad-Din Shah's health deteriorating, the *Majlis* desperately wanted to secure his approval of the Constitution before he either changed his mind or died. Although the Constitution would only affect the missionaries indirectly, we often discussed the topic and speculated on its ramifications. We were eager to hear any news from Tehran on the progress of *Masruta*, Constitutionalism.

"*Vali Ahd* Mohammad Ali is hourly expecting to be called to occupy the throne," Sam said. "Daily his horses ostentatiously exercise in *Dar-ol-Khalafeh*, his palace grounds, in readiness to march in the parade of his coronation."

"When the Shah granted a Constitution and a National Assembly, other cities of Persia were placarded and illuminated as a sign of rejoicing," Will Vanneman said. "In Tabriz no notice was taken of the Shah's decrees. *Vali Ahd* Mohammad Ali prohibited all demonstrations of rejoicing in the entire Province of Azerbaijan. Even the *Hadid*, the solitary newspaper, was interdicted from discussing the subject."

"This is a direct challenge to the Reform Party and the *Majlis*," Charles Pittman said. "*Vali Ahd* Mohammad Ali is giving the revolutionaries plain notice that as the new Shah, he would not be bound by the decrees of Mozaffar ad-Din Shah."

"The *Vali Ahd* is a man of resolute will and stern disposition," Sam said. "Quite a contrast to the present Shah."

"This is ominous," Will said. "The *Vali Ahd* is also blamed for maintaining famine prices for a bushel of wheat. All over the province landlords are holding wheat in granaries three years or more, preferring to let the grain mildew rather than lower the price. Even though the harvest is abundant, many people are reduced to living on bread mixed with barley and sand. I am treating adults and children with diseases from starvation and malnutrition, some dying from dysentery."

"The Persians call it 'man-made scarcity — not from God,'" I said.

"The Bolshevik uprisings in Russia are discussed over tea in the *chai-khanas*," Sam said. "The Persian people, downtrodden for so long, are now rising up to right their wrongs. The worm has turned."

Some weeks after the crisis in Tehran, the leading merchants, bankers, *sayyids* and *mullahs* of Tabriz took *bast* at the British Consulate, mimicking the actions of the protestors in the capital. The yard of the British Consulate became a forum, where orators harangued several thousand people by day and at night hundreds lodged there. For ten days the bazaars and all businesses were closed; trade and manufacturing stopped. The protestors demanded the right to an *Anjuman*, a local popular assembly, and British Consul General, Sir Albert Charles Wratislaw, acted as mediator between the protestors and the *Vali Ahd* Mohammad Ali.

While the *Vali Ahd* prolonged negotiations and endeavored to find ways to refuse compliance, the number of protesters increased, and demonstrations became more vociferous. When the local government soldiers joined the demonstrators, the *Vali Ahd* was left without military support. Fearing for the safety of his family, he sent them to an undisclosed location and then agreed to yield to popular demand and allow an *Anjuman*.

The bazaars opened and business resumed. The *Anjuman* of Tabriz began implementing reform measures and overseeing the election of eight *Majlis* delegates. They brought wheat from the villages into Tabriz by camel and reduced the price of bread by twenty per cent. Then they closed the opium dens, restricted wine production, and developed plans for building roads and schools. "They are swiftly implementing progressive reforms," Sam said. "When the East is motivated, it can hustle."

Vali Ahd Mohammad Ali bribed Mir Hashim, a member of the *Anjuman*, to work against the reforms and instructed the *Anjuman* to cease deliberations. The *Anjuman* threatened to riot if refused their right to assembly. They also discovered that Mir Hashim was a traitor, removed him from the assembly and expelled him from the city.

"Mir Hashim is a powerful man," Sam said. "He controls *Davachi*, the northern district of Tabriz known as 'camel men's quarter.' He will exact revenge on the reformists of Tabriz."

At the end of October, the Constitution was presented to Mozaffar ad-Din Shah for his signature. Two months later, the Shah, who was close to death, ratified the Constitution. *Vali Ahd* Mohammad Ali, the heir to the throne, also signed the Constitution and in a separate document promised not to dissolve the *Majlis* for the next two years. Both the Shah and the *Vali Ahd* swore their ratifications on the Qur'an.

"The outlook is hopeful for greater political and religious liberty," I said.

"Perhaps," Sam replied. "We will wait and see if *Vali Ahd* Mohammad Ali keeps his promise after he is crowned as Shah."

On January 3rd, 1907, Mozaffar ad-Din Shah died of cancer.

CHAPTER 28

Tabriz 1907

ON JANUARY 19ᵀᴴ, MOHAMMAD ALI WAS CROWNED
Shah and his second son, nine-year-old Sultan Ahmad Mirza,
became the *Vali Ahd*. The new Shah angered the *Majlis* by not
inviting them to his coronation. Then he arranged for new loans
from Russia and England to fund his regime. To his surprise, the
Majlis refused to sanction the transactions, denouncing the loans
as the final sale of Persia's independence. The *Majlis* instituted
reforms and became bolder in their demands. Soon it became
apparent that it was not the Shah who ruled Persia, but the *Majlis*.

Rahim Khan, a tribal chief from Karadagh, who was imprisoned for robbery, was contracted by the Shah to arrange for his son
to lead an attack on members of the *Anjuman* in Tabriz. When the
telegram from Rahim Khan to his son with instructions from the
Shah was intercepted, Tabriz was in an uproar. The unsuccessful
plot resulted in death of one of the assassins and the confession
of the others.

The Shah sent representatives to the *Baharestan* to convince
the *Majlis* that he had no connection with the attack. They were
greeted with angry cries of "He lies." It happened to be May 26ᵗʰ,
the Shah's birthday, with decorations and illuminations prepared
for an evening celebration; all were taken down by six o'clock
that evening to avoid a clash with an imminent demonstration
against the Shah.

In May and June general strikes occurred in Tabriz and throughout the province of Azerbaijan. One issue the new Constitution did not address was land reform. Under the Qajar *tuyul* land allotment system, landlords had virtually unlimited power — taxing peasants for their livestock and fields, punishing them, forcing women to comply with sexual demands. Now through rent strikes villagers were able to expel their landlords.

June 1907

"Rev. James Hawkes sent word from the mission in Hamadan that they are surrounded by a miniature civil war," Sam said. "The Shah's younger brother, Salar od-Dowleh, is prancing around Hamadan with an army of Lurs. He threatened to march on Tehran and depose his brother. The Shah sent his army to fight them. After three days and two hundred casualties Salar od-Dowleh withdrew."

"I am relieved that here in Tabriz it is relatively calm," I said. "There is so much unrest in Tehran, Hamadan and the other mission stations. The missionaries in Urmia are threatened by the border dispute, and the Ottomans continue to march toward Khoi."

"John Wishard at the Tehran mission wrote that a new missionary, Rev. Frank Moore, arrived and a few weeks later suffered a nervous breakdown," Sam said. "The Wishards are taking furlough to help him back to America."

"The unrest does take a strain on one's nerves," I replied.

"July 25th was the anniversary of the Constitution, and *Jashn-e Melli*, the National Celebration, took place at the *Baharestan*," Sam said. "Missionaries from the Tehran station attended the reception, and reported that children marched around the *maydan*, the square outside the *Baharestan,* singing glorifications of the *Majlis* and the Constitution. At night people chanted, 'Long live the *Majlis*,' 'Long live Freedom.'"

"I would have liked to have witnessed the historic occasion," I said. "In spite of the tyranny and opposition, I hope the *Majlis* triumph. It is the only way Persians will achieve progress."

On August 31st Russia and England signed an agreement to divide Persia into "spheres of influence," with Russia taking northern Persia and Britain taking the southern provinces. A cartoon in the October issue of *Punch, The London Charivari* satirizing it depicted a British lion and a Russian bear playing with the tail and head of a terrified Persian cat. The cat was saying, "I don't remember being consulted about this." The Shah was not consulted about the "spheres of influence" either.

In the summer of 1907 Mary Jewett retired from the mission after thirty-six years of service. "She was indefatigable," Sam said. "She traveled far and wide and stayed alone for months in far-off villages to spread the gospel. The mission will never have another like her."

"The Tabriz mission was my baby," Mary said. "After all these years it is also hard for me to leave the Girls' School I founded. I remember steaming out of New York harbor, August 9th, 1871, with Deborah Cochran and her two girls. Finally on October 18th we arrived in Urmia, and what a joyous arrival it was."

"What do you plan on doing in America?" I asked.

"My friends and family tell me that I must write a book about my experiences in Persia," Mary replied.

"Will you be including us in your book?" I asked.

"I believe I will."

Oh dear. What will she say?

Sam belayed my fears saying, "Maybe a book about you will make you famous."

August 1907

Princess Ezzat's husband was appointed Governor-general of the Azerbaijan province and the family returned to Tabriz. The Princess sent her carriage for me so we could meet. "I had two more babies in exile," she said, "and now I have six boys. My husband is marrying the daughter of a Kurdish chieftain to form an alliance. I told him that his new wife can have the babies now; I want to continue my piano lessons."

For the next four years, when it was safe to travel through the streets, I visited Princess Ezzat at the Governor's mansion. After her piano lessons, we chatted and drank tea. Sometimes she confided in me, and I counseled her. She was disturbed that her husband took another wife even though it served to form an alliance. "You are the only woman I can confide in," she said.

Amidst the political upheaval a new temporary teacher for the Boys' School arrived — Howard Conklin Baskerville. He recently graduated from Princeton University and received an eighteen-month missionary assignment from the Board. Sam took a special fondness to Howard since he graduated from Princeton, his alma mater. At first Howard lived with us and we tried to teach him Azeri, Armenian and Persian. Agnes and Rose made a concerted effort to only speak in Azeri around Howard, which seemed to frustrate and embarrass him.

"As a pastor's son from Nebraska, Howard could not be more awkward and naïve," I said to Sam in private. "He blushes when our thirteen- and fifteen-year-old girls make fun of him, and he is almost a decade older than them."

"Unfortunately, the boy does not have a natural talent for learning languages," Sam muttered. "He will not be of much use to me if he cannot teach classes in the Boys' School."

"Maybe you should ask one of the other teachers to be his translator," I suggested.

"Yes, that would probably be best," Sam replied. "We need him to start teaching this spring to make the most of his short teaching assignment with us. I will ask Sayyid Hasan Sharifzadeh, our teacher of Persian and Arabic. As one of my most promising graduates of the Boys' School, he would also be an excellent role model."

"Five years ago, Sharifzadeh begged to be admitted to the Boys' School and concealed his coming from his father, a prominent *mullah*. Now he is proud of his son, one of the most accomplished intellectuals of Tabriz — a writer, an editor and an eloquent speaker for the Constitutional movement."

"Considering Sharifzadeh's involvement with the Constitutional movement I need to warn Howard that as a member of the mission, he needs to avoid any association with Persia's political affairs."

Shortly before Thanksgiving I received a letter from Mother: "Sophea contracted typhoid and is taking bed rest. She instructed me to tell you that she sent three boxes of presents to Tabriz that should be opened before Christmas."

"Sophea has typhoid?" I exclaimed as I put down the letter. "I will be worried sick until I hear she is better."

"She has the best medical care in the world at her disposal and a husband who can afford to pay for excellent physicians," Sam said. "She is also a healthy forty-year-old woman."

I wept and prayed for my beautiful sister Sophea, and then with less than a week before Christmas a second telegram came. "It is for you," Sam announced solemnly as he handed it to me. My hands fumbled as I opened it holding my breath. The scream I let out must have been heard throughout the mission compound. "Sophea is dead," I wailed. "How can it be?"

Sam took my hands and helped me from the chair. He held me in his arms and stroked my hair as I sobbed uncontrollably. "As for man, his days are like grass," he said, "he flourishes like a flower of the field; for the wind passes over it, and it is gone, and its place knows it no more. Psalms 103: 15-16."

"Like a flower," I murmured, "the wind passes over it."

The next day the three boxes arrived that Sophea had sent almost two months before. I wept as I slowly opened the boxes and unpacked presents for each member of the family. They were carefully wrapped in embossed red and green paper and tied with cloth ribbons. *My dear Sophea wrapped these with her delicate hands.*

At of bottom of one box was an artificial Christmas tree — a trunk with branches made from green-colored goose feathers that could easily be assembled. It was complete with blown glass ornaments, all the colors of the rainbow. The children squealed with joy when they saw it. "We're going to have a Christmas tree," Rose exclaimed, "just like in America."

"What a special heart-felt gift," I said. "The Christmas tree will serve as a remembrance of Aunt Sophea each holiday season."

Mother wrote a long letter about Sophea's death: "Pneumonia settled into her lungs, and the doctors were in her room day and night, despairing as to how to save her. The children are of course distraught beyond belief. Having helped Sophea care for them for the past six years, I hope it will be a bit easier for them to see me now as both their grandmother and a substitute for their mother. Will is devastated. She meant everything to him. He was so much in love with Sophea, and still is."

I smiled when Mother told me what Will insisted that her gravestone be inscribed with: "Till the day breaks and the shadows flee away."

"It is the parting of true love," I told Sam. "Song of Solomon 2:16-17: 'My beloved is mine and I am his, he pastures his flock among the lilies. Until the day breaks and the shadows flee, turn, my beloved, be like a gazelle, or a young stag upon rugged mountains.' Sophea's spirit left earth like a gazelle."

News on the progress of the Persian Parliament in Tehran reached us through some of the many newspapers that sprang up after the Constitution was signed: *Majlis* (Assembly), *Neda-ye Vatan* (Voice of Nation), *Tamaddan* (Civilization), *Mosavat* (Equality), and *Sur-i-Israfil* (Archangel Israfil). At our annual station meeting we discussed the new newspapers, the political developments and the progress of the mission.

"The newspaper *Sur-i-Israfil* is named after one of the four Islamic archangels," Sam said. "Israfil blows the trumpet to announce the Day of Judgment. On the front page is a picture of the archangel flying over a cemetery carrying the trumpet and a scroll with the words 'Liberty, Equality, Fraternity.' "

"Here is a recent sympathetic article about the Christians attacked by Ottoman troops near Urmia," Charles Pittman said. "It claims that 'Persians are free of religious bigotry, ascribed to some Muslim nations.' It goes on to say: 'In the dreadful calamity at Urmia, and barbarous conduct of the Ottoman troops toward our Christian fellow-countrymen, we, in harmony with you, are pained and affected.' "

"The constant ideological discussions and debate seem to have increased religious tolerance," Will Vanneman interjected.

"It is only what the newspapers profess," Sam said.

"The newspapers are crude, but they are outspoken for the people," Charles Pittman added. "As yet no one dares to stop them."

"The young Persians are also buying books and asking to be taught," Will Vanneman said. "They want to be educated in modern science which they believe has given the West preeminence. When the conflict between faith and science inevitably comes, many will reject faith."

"One of the leaders, a man wearing a *mullah*'s turban said to me, 'The people will cast off Islam, but do not imagine that they will accept Christianity in its stead,' " Charles Pittman said.

"Irreligion is a dangerous thing," I added, "a world without moral principles."

"In spite of all the agitations, patriotic processions, demonstrations, closing of bazaars and businesses, riots, mobs and murders, rumors of war and Kurdish raids, the Memorial School has gone on quietly and regularly," Sam said. "Attendance of Muslims remains at eighty along with one hundred and thirty Armenians. Many of our students are from the families of *sayyids*, *mullahs* and Persian nobles. It is curious to call a roll in which half have the title of Khan, followed by their father's title, such as 'Regulator of the State, 'The Glory of the Court,' 'The Prosperity of the Kingdom,' 'The Splendor of the Country,' 'The Pride of the Army,' 'The Sword of the Physician,' etcetera, etcetera. The fact that we are training the sons of the ruling class has a marked significance in this new era of Persia's development. Besides leaders of the people, we are training teachers for their schools."

"The Girls' School started out with one hundred and sixty-eight students but opposition by the Armenian community to our school reduced it by half," Lillie Beaber said. "Armenian bishops made a house-to-house canvas and collected taxes for their own schools. Some of the students' parents were badly frightened and their girls left immediately, while others refused to withdraw their children."

"So much for religious tolerance," I muttered.

"Attendance at the men's dispensary has been greater than any previous year, almost eleven thousand patients and primarily Muslims," Will said. "Rev. Jessup came every morning and spoke with the patients. In the afternoon I visited patients at their homes, over fourteen hundred patient visits."

"What type of medical visits have you been seeing?" I asked.

"These are difficult cases, with patients confined to their beds, and are really hospital cases," Will said. "The native physicians request my help, and I merely give my directions, as I do not have time to see each patient every day. In no other way would it be possible to meet the demands made upon us, and it allows us to cover the whole city. We treat everyone from the *Vali Ahd* and his family down to the poorest person. The patronage of the rich enables us to give free medical treatment to the poor."

"Your success speaks both to your expertise and your charity," I said.

The second week of December, Sam was reading an article from *Neda-ye Vatan* (Voice of Nation).

"The continual struggle between the Shah and the *Majlis*, each to limit the authority of the other, has come to a crisis," Sam said. "On Sunday, December 15th the Shah staged a demonstration by hiring some *mullahs* and rogues to parade about the square near the palace and scream, 'May the Shah live; may the *Majlis* die.' Meanwhile a number of *Majlis* were summoned to the palace and arrested."

"Arrested?" I exclaimed. "On what grounds?"

"The Shah accuses the *Majlis* of 'trampling the Qur'an under foot,'" Sam said. "He declared a *jihad*, or holy war, saying, 'All good Muslims are urged to march against the *Majlis*.' The newspaper says, 'The turnout of good Muslims was weak; four hundred came from the Shah's village and put tents up in the square. By Tuesday afternoon the Shah's attempt at an uprising was a ludicrous failure. He was forced to concede to the *Majlis*, who won through inaction and conscious strength.'"

"For God did not give us a spirit of timidity but a spirit of power and love and self-control," I said. "2 Timothy 1:7."

The Persian Constitutional Revolution 1905-1909

The two opposing sides in the Persian Revolution are called by various names:

1) Nationalists, Constitutionalists or Reformists — supporters of the Constitution, the *Majlis* (the National Assembly or Parliament) and the *Anjumans* (local assemblies).

2) Royalists, Anti-Constitutionalists or Reactionaries — supporters of Mohammad Ali Shah.

In Tabriz the attacking forces are led by:

1) Satter Khan and Baqir Khan — leaders of the Nationalist Volunteer Army, whose soldiers are called the *fidais* ("the devoted").

2) Mir Hashim, Rahim Khan and Samad Khan — leaders of the Royalist forces.

CHAPTER 29

January 1908, Tabriz

"WHAT IS THAT NOISE COMING FROM THE NORTHERN DISTRICTS?" I asked. "It sounds like fireworks."

"It is gunfire," Sam replied. "I will go to the American Consulate to ask William Doty who is fighting." After returning Sam explained, "Mir Hashim, the traitor who was expelled from Tabriz by the *Anjuman*, managed to secretly return to the *Davachi* district. He assembled a troop of Anti-Constitutionalist soldiers supporting the Shah. They are fighting the Nationalists in the *Amir Khiz* district."

Men on each side concealed themselves on the flat roofs of houses and kept up straggling gunfire for days. There were few causalities except a few innocent bystanders who were hit by stray bullets. Then one day the firing stopped as unexpectedly as it had started.

After the Shah's failed *coup d'état* in December 1907, the National Assembly made earnest efforts to improve relations between the *Majlis* and the Shah, forming a Conciliation Committee. Many of the Nationalists, however, remained leery of the Shah and his apparent willingness to negotiate with the *Majlis*.

February 1908

Sam rushed in holding a newspaper. "A bomb exploded in Tehran wrecking the Shah's automobile and killing a passenger," he said. "Someone threw it from a window as it drove by."

"Was the Shah hurt?" I asked.

"The Shah was riding in a carriage and uninjured, but I am sure the attempt on his life scared him to death," Sam replied.

In subsequent reports, the Royalists blamed the Nationalists, and the Nationalists accused the Royalists saying they did it to prevent reconciliation between the Shah and the *Majlis*. It later surfaced that the bomb-throwers had communicated with the Shah's aide and confidant, Shapshal Khan, his former Russian tutor and evil genius.

"Was the bombing staged by the Shah to discredit the *Majlis*?" Sam asked.

May 1908

The Shah demanded that the newspapers and popular orators stop speaking against him. The *Majlis* acted on behalf of the Shah and negotiated with orators and newspaper editors to adopt a more respectful tone towards the Shah. In exchange the *Majlis* demanded dismissal of six the Shah's courtiers who were attempting to undermine the Constitution. The Shah consented to dismiss the courtiers but stalled in performing his part of the bargain until June.

We learned from the American Consul, William Doty, that during the intervening time the Shah enlisted the help of the Russian Colonel Vladimir Liakhoff, who was stationed in Tehran. "The Shah implied that after the bombing of his automobile, he thought his life was in jeopardy and feared the Nationalists were going to get rid of him by whatever measures were necessary," Doty said. "The Russian Minister threatened that if the Nationalists deposed of the Shah, Russia would intervene."

"Were the *Majlis* warned of this?" Sam asked.

"Yes. When the *Majlis* heard of Russia's sinister threat, they abandoned the option of armed opposition to the Shah," Doty replied. "A former student of your Boys' School, Sayyid Hasan Taqizadeh, led the discussion. He told the *Majlis*, 'The dread of foreign intervention exceeds the expediency of an armed solution. A sick nation is better than a dead nation.'"

"Hasan Taqizadeh was a student here from 1899 to 1900," Sam added. "We are proud that he has made such a name for himself in Persian politics."

On June 3rd William Doty came again to update us on the situation in Tehran. "The Shah staged an uprising and ordered two thousand soldiers to surround the bazaars and had three hundred Russian Cossacks march past the *Baharestan*."

"Why did he do that?" I asked.

"The Shah used it as a diversion to escape from the Palace in Tehran," Consul Doty said. "He slipped through the barracks where Colonel Liakhoff escorted him to *Bagh-i Shah*, the King's Gardens in Behshahr near the Caspian Sea. Once safe in his refuge, the Shah established martial law under Colonel Liakhoff and his army of Cossacks. He then demanded the expulsion of the leaders of the Nationalist party, control of the press and disarmament of the people of Tehran."

That afternoon Mousa returned from the bazaar saying, "There are riots in the *Bazaar* district. Satter Khan and Baqir Khan are assembling a volunteer Nationalist army to ride to Tehran to support the Constitution and the rights of the people. Many are former students from the mission Boys' School. They called themselves *fidais*, the devotees, and march through the city shrouded in white."

We held our annual mission station meeting after Commencement. "Has school attendance been affected by the agitations in Tabriz this year?" Will Vanneman asked.

"Despite the street fighting between the Nationalists and the Royalists in Tabriz, the Boys' School has gone on quietly and regularly," Sam replied. "We had two hundred and thirteen students, eighty of them Muslim. We plainly state in the Persian advertisement of the school that religious instruction is emphasized, and Bible classes are part of the curriculum. Still Muslim parents see the value in having their children educated at our mission school."

"Enrollment in the Girls' School was much the same as last year," Lillie Beaber said. "Responding to demand we started a separate Muslim class of twelve students. On June 18th, Nusrat-al-Dawla, cousin of the Shah, visited the Girl's School with a company of Muslim women. The program included reading Scriptures in Azeri and other selections in Persian, songs in Armenian, followed by a calisthenic drill. At the close of the exercises, one of the ladies made an address, saying: 'From our earliest time until now, the women of Persia have longed for a door of emancipation for our daughters, through the light of knowledge and training. Thanks to God, this wish has been realized. We are proud and honored to witness today this accomplishment and the results of educating our Persian girls at this great assembly.' "

"How has the medical missionary work gone?" Sam asked.

"The men's dispensary was visited by eleven thousand patients this year, busier than ever," Will Vanneman said. "Fred Jessup attends the waiting room, reading Scriptures and talking to patients. I also have a native doctor, Dr. Eshoo, who helps me in the dispensary. Most my afternoons are spent on home visits as usual, over fourteen hundred this year."

After the meeting Sam left for Urmia with Howard Baskerville. "Be careful," I warned them. "With the Shah's actions threatening the people's rights there is bound to be unrest."

On the morning of Tuesday, June 23rd Russian Colonel Liakhoff and a thousand Cossacks surrounded the *Baharestan* in Tehran and fired cannons, bombarding the Parliament building until it was reduced to ruins. Most of the Nationalist leaders were either killed by the Cossacks as they tried to escape or were arrested and taken to *Bagh-i Shah* in chains. Thirty to forty reached the British Consulate and sought *bast*, including our former student, Hasan Taqizadeh.

During the following week the aftershock of the bombardment of the *Baharestan* rippled throughout Persia. In Tabriz gunfire rattled from rooftops and bullets flew through the streets. The Nationalists dragged a cannon on top of the Arg and fired at the *Davachi* district to the north, where the Royalists were headquartered. The blasts continued night and day, echoing in the foothills surrounding the city. The children were terrified, and I was haggard from lack of sleep and anxious for Sam to return from Urmia.

The Russian and French Consuls told their subjects to protect their houses by displaying their national flags. Paul Vauthier, the Boys' School French teacher, tried desperately to seek permission to fly the American flag over the mission. The American Consul in Tabriz, William Doty, could not be reached. As a last resort, he telegraphed the American Consulate in Tehran, but received no response. I asked him to telegraph Sam and let him know that fighting had broken out, but the lines from Salmas to Urmia were cut so he forwarded a letter by post horse.

On July 15, Sam returned from Urmia. I ran down the hall when I heard his voice and threw my arms around his shoulders. "I cannot tell you how relieved I am to have you here," I said. "Paul Vauthier could not reach Consul Doty or get a reply from the consulate in Tehran. We need to raise the American flag to protect the mission."

"We started back as soon as the message came about the fighting," Sam replied. "I will send a cable to the Board of Foreign Missions asking them to contact the State Department." Sam wrote a note to give to the telegraph operator: "Communicate the following message to Washington in the quickest manner possible: 'Serious disturbances in Tabriz. Presbyterian Mission is very anxious to have flag hoisted.'"

The US State Department Assistant Secretary of State, Robert Bacon replied: "The American Consul at Tabriz has been instructed by telegraph today, that flag may be shown on dwellings, *bona fide* owned property of native Americans for protection."

"Thank God," I said.

On June 28th when news reached Tabriz of the bombardment of the *Baharestan* and dispersal of *Majlis*, it was a signal for Royalists to attack the *Anjuman*, the local assembly. Mir Hashim, the leader of the Royalists in the *Davachi* district, began firing on Satter Khan and the Nationalists in the *Amir Khiz* district. Heavy firing continued, with over ten thousand shots fired from house roof tops. At first, due to the surprise of the attack, Mir Hashim's troops pushed forward, but Baqir Khan, head of the Nationalists in the *Khiaban* district, soon reinforced Satter Khan's troops and

pushed the Royalists back. The Nationalists retained the predom-
inant support of the people of Tabriz and maintained control of
the government armory in the *Khiaban* district, giving them an
advantage.

When the Royalists ran low on ammunition, the Russian
Consul and forty Cossacks, carrying machine guns and ammunition, attempted to cross over the firing line to the *Davachi* district. "We are going there to protect Russian subjects," the Russian
Consul said.

The Nationalist leaders, realizing the Russians' mission was to
deliver ammunition to their enemy, vehemently argued that they
had no right to interfere in internal politics. They stood resolutely,
and the Russian Consul and his Cossacks gave in and turned back.

It was clear, however, that the Russians supported the Royalists,
and this discouraged the Nationalist volunteer army. In despair,
some *fidais* sought refuge in the British Consulate but were turned
away. "Even the British have forsaken us," they said.

On Wednesday, July 1st the son of Rahim Khan, the robber
chief of Karadagh who supported the Shah, rode with five hundred
bandits to the south of the city to implement a vicious campaign
of rape and robbery. They invaded a *hammam*, a public bathhouse,
on women's day and followed women into mosques, stripping
off their clothes and jewelry, and carrying off girls and young
women. This caused the Nationalist troop led by Baqir Khan to
divert efforts from their attack on *Davachi*, allowing the Royalists
to cross the *Ala Gapi* bridge and take the telegraph office and
government buildings unhindered. Reaching the *Khiaban* district
Royalist, soldiers looted the bazaars and destroyed houses.

By that afternoon, it appeared imminent that the whole city
would fall to the Shah's forces. The Russian Consul instructed
Baqir Khan to surrender and have the inhabitants of Tabriz hang
out white flags. Satter Khan and his Nationalist troops were

fighting in the far north side of the *Davachi* district. Hearing of the surrenders to the south, he charged in, blowing trumpets and knocking down the white flags of truce. With Satter Khan's arrival, Baqir Khan reversed his surrender and ordered his troops to rally. They joined Satter Khan's forces, seized the arsenal stored at the Arg, and repulsed the Royalists with cannonballs from the top.

In mid-August the Shah released Rahim Khan from prison and ordered him to lead a regiment of fierce tribesmen, known as the *Shahsevan*, protectors of the Shah, against the Nationalists. The *Shahsevan* pressed hard upon Satter Khan's entrenchments in the *Amir Khiz* district. By digging through the walls of houses, they surprised Satter Khan and nearly killed him. After a hard fight resulting in fifty Nationalists casualties, Satter Khan's troops drove back the *Shahsevan*.

After nightfall throughout the city, we heard voices calling out, "*Allah askar, Allah askar*, (God is great, God is great.) There is no God but God. Mohammad is the prophet of God. Ali is the vice-gerent of God." For several hours the creed of the Shia Muslims rang out, repeated times without number.

"What does it mean?" I asked.

"It is to convince the *Shahsevan* that the Nationalists are devout Muslims," Sam said. "It is a confession by the Nationalists to the opposing army of their shared faith. The Shah led the *Shahsevan* to believe that this is a *jihad*, or holy war. The Royalists slander the Nationalists saying they trample on the Qur'an."

"It is a very moving demonstration," I said. "One I shall never forget."

The *Shahsevan*, realizing that the Rahim Khan and the Shah misled them, mounted their horses and returned to their mountains.

"After an exhausting fight, I am sure they are vexed," Sam said. "They had expected their efforts to be repaid by a wealth of plundered booty. On their way out of town they snatched what they could, including velvet and brocade from a fine fabric shop. The wild mountain dames of the *Shahsevan* will be in gorgeous apparel hereafter."

On August 18th fierce firing of musketry broke out in the *Baron Avak* district, the Armenian quarter next to *Lawala*, where the mission is located. Bullets and parts of shells flew over the *Baron Avak*, landing in the mission yard. Sam and I were attending a meeting with the other teachers in the Boys' School assembly room. "Our children are outside playing," I shrieked in panic, as a bullet came through an open window.

We ran across the yard in front of the school toward the house and heard Mattie Wright screaming. "I will go and see what happened," Sam said. "Take the children into the house, away from the windows."

I feared that Sam might be struck running across the compound and was relieved when he returned unharmed. "A bullet flew through a window in the Wright's parlor," he said. "It lodged in the back of a chair once occupied this time of day by the former mission children's teacher, Edith Lamme. Mattie Wright is terrified."

"But Edith Lamme transferred to Urmia a year ago," I said.

"Yes, we should tell her someday that her move saved her life," Sam responded.

After the firing ceased, William Doty ventured to the mission. "No Americans appear to have been harmed," he said, "but I cannot say the same for Old Glory. The flag on the American Consulate is riddled with stray bullets."

Prince Ayn al-Dawla, the notorious former Prime Minister, came from Tehran to take over the command of the Shah's troops and resume negotiations. "Lay down your arms, you are acting in rebellion against the Shah," he said.

The Nationalists answered, "Let the Shah restore the Constitution and we will submit to him."

Sattar Khan replied, "Unless the Prince is prepared to swear allegiance to the Constitution, he enters Tabriz at the peril of his life."

"Negotiations are futile," Sam said. "How could people trust the Shah when he promised to uphold the Constitution, pledging his oath four times on the Qur'an, and then broke his promise."

The *Anjuman* elected peace-delegates, among them Sayyid Hasan Sharifzadeh, a teacher in our mission Boys' School. He was on the proscribed list of the Shah as a prominent Constitutionalist leader and had taken refuge at the French Consulate. On August 25th he spoke at the *Anjuman* advocating a truce so that peace could be negotiated. Some of the *fidais* at the meeting disagreed and argued for battle without delay. As Sharifzadeh was returning, two *fidais* shot him at the door of the French Consulate.

Sam and I were shocked by the death of our beloved teacher. "Why would other Nationalists shoot him down in cold blood?" I asked. "It makes no sense."

"I am as incredulous and appalled as you are," Sam replied. "Possibly Sharifzadeh offended them, or maybe they were incited by bribes from Royalists."

"He was our finest and most promising Persian teacher," I bemoaned.

"Outside of school hours he developed a strength and power in the new politics of Persia which was truly remarkable," Sam said.

"Sharifzadeh had an ambition to learn which was rarely equaled here," I said. "He was a forceful and persuasive speaker, an equal cannot be found in Tabriz. He will be deeply mourned."

"The new era in Persia needed him sorely," Sam added.

Our temporary teacher at the Boys' School, Howard Baskerville, was very disturbed by the death of Sayyid Hasan Sharifzadeh. He was his translator and became Howard's mentor and friend. When I broke the news to him, he shouted, "I shall avenge his death."

Fortunately, before Howard acted on his impulsive promise of revenge, the murderers were dragged in front of the French Consulate and shot down by a squad of *fidais*.

September passed with alternate fighting and negotiations. The death of an Armenian Georgian Christian who assisted the Nationalists was the occasion of a remarkable demonstration. The body of this man, though a Christian, was borne to the Armenian cemetery with a guard of five hundred Muslim soldiers carrying wreaths and candles according to Armenian custom. Some of the Muslim *fidais* even helped carry the bier.

"It is a remarkable exhibition of how the new principles of liberty and justice are abolishing religious prejudice and bigotry," Sam said. "Tabriz has never seen the likes of this."

On Tuesday September 22nd, Prince Ayn al-Dawla, the commander of the Royalist troops, sent formal notice to the foreign consuls from his camp at the outskirts of Tabriz. Consul William Doty hurried to the mission to warn us. "They gave forty-eight hours warning of a general attack. They will bombard Tabriz with shells and throw off all responsibility for the lives and property of foreigners."

"What did Satter Khan say?" Sam asked.

"He ordered that no foreigners or native Christians should leave the city," Doty replied. "His volunteer army will fight to protect them."

"I must tell the other missionaries to prepare their cellars for refuge," Sam replied.

"It is the best you can do," William Doty said, "but hurry."

The day of the attack by the Shah's army was awaited with much anxiety by the missionaries and the rest of the city. The bombardment was a concerted attack, and despite considerable noise, the damages from the shells were minor. Satter Khan repulsed the Royalist attacks on every side of the city with significant loss by the Shah's troops.

When we emerged from our cellars the missionaries assembled in our church.

"I heard that Russia and England urged the Shah to reinstate the Parliament." Newton Wright said. "However, representation of Tabriz and Azerbaijan will be excluded due to rebelliousness."

"A guaranty of the reinstatement of the Constitutional government and the *Majlis* would ensure peace in a day," Charles Pittman said, "even if they exclude representation by Tabriz."

"The city was attacked by the reactionary cleric Mir Hashim from the north, the *Shahsevan* and bandits of Rahim Khan from the south, and the Shah's troops lead by Ayn al-Dawla from the east," Sam said. "After three months of fighting the people of Tabriz maintained the cause of liberty against the strongest forces the Shah could send against them."

"Nothing except hunger can conquer them now," Will Vanneman added.

"Distress has been great in this formerly industrious and now idle city," Sam said. "We have distributed relief to the poor from funds that the Board sent us, but the winter before us will be one of great poverty and suffering. I hope Tabriz will survive."

The first siege of Tabriz ended on October 12th when the Shah's cavalry scattered.

CHAPTER 30

Tabriz 1909 – The Second Siege of Tabriz

AFTER LOSING THE BATTLE WITH SATTER KHAN'S NATIONALIST forces, the Shah implemented another strategy to squelch *Masruta*, the constitutional movement in Tabriz. He ordered the Royalist army to cut off the roads to Tabriz and block the transport of provisions into the city. The roads to the east and northeast of Tabriz, the chief routes supplying grain, were held by the Royalist commander Ayn al-Dawla and a small regiment encamped ten miles from the city.

Despite the blockade of the main roads, the *Anjuman* found alternative routes to lay in a store of wheat and other provisions at the Arg for the winter. The missionaries and private families hoarded what they could in their cellars. The position of the poor was more precarious since they could not afford to stockpile supplies for the winter and lived day-to-day.

At the end of January Royalist Rahim Khan returned with his Karadagh bandits and occupied the remaining south and west sides of the city. With Tabriz completely besieged, all incoming provisions were immediately and completely cut off, including fuel for heat and cooking. By mid-winter many trees in the orchards of the city were cut down to supply firewood.

The mail was interrupted, destroyed, or robbed by Rahim Khan's bandits. Registered parcels, checks, cash for the foreign banks were seized, and our personal letters, containing nothing political, were torn up. Then the telegraph lines were cut, and the city of Tabriz was completely isolated from the outside world.

"We cannot receive or send messages to the Board, to relatives or to our fellow missionaries at other stations," Sam said. "It is like being on another planet."

By February bread became scarce. Crowds thronged bakeries, women filled the streets screaming and quarreling to get a turn at the window. The *Anjuman* intervened and confiscated the land-owners' wheat reserves and supplied bakers with a daily allotment of wheat at a cheap price. Nationalist soldiers stood at each bakery to keep order and ensure the bakers sold rations of bread fairly and equally. One Muslim baker was caught selling bread to Armenians at a higher price and was summarily shot by Satter Khan.

One day four women came to the mission gate begging. When I came out to speak with them, one woman screamed, "*Khanum.* Please give us bread for our children."

"Wait here," I replied and ran to the cellar to retrieve a few sheets of *lavash.*

When I returned there were ten women crying, "Khanum, please give us bread." I broke the sheets in half and started to hand them to the women when they pushed open the gate, toppling me over, *lavash* flying out of my hands.

Sam raced out of the house and shooed the women away as he helped me up. "There will be a riot if you try to hand out bread again," he said. "We need to save what we have for the children under our protection — the missionary children and those attending our schools."

Meat became scarce and nuts, peas, and dried fruit were consumed instead. The poorer class of people, who lived day-to-day for food, were forced to eat clover and roots. This unusual kind of food produced stomach and intestinal diseases from which many died.

As weeks grew into months the persistent dull pains of hunger, the gnawing of starvation on their bodies and minds, began to take a toll on the people. They voiced resentment toward the Nationalist soldiers who obtained daily rations. "We want food, not *Anjuman*," some said.

"With the city's morale weakened, the danger of capture by storm by the enemy is increased," Sam said.

In February we held a station meeting to compile our Annual Report for the Board.

"Malnutrition has made the epidemics of typhoid, cholera and scarlet fever worse this year," Will Vanneman said. "Scarlet fever raged through the city, killing eight thousand children, including some of our pupils."

"The total enrollment at the Boys' School was two hundred and thirty-four of which about half were Christian Armenians, and the other half were Persian Muslims," Sam said. "Of the eighteen boarders, five were Muslims, including the Governor's son and those of several prominent Nationalist leaders."

"The significance of this is great," I added. "Eating Christian food is thought to prevent Muslims from reaching Paradise."

"Apparently, they are willing to accept this potential sacrifice to guarantee their sons are well educated," Sam said.

"With scarlet fever and whooping cough, the kindergarten and primary school rooms of the Girl's School were at times almost empty," Loretta Van Hook said. "Otherwise, enrollment was unaffected by the fighting. One hundred and twenty-seven pupils were enrolled, including twenty-one Muslim girls. Among the twenty boarders, there was a very bright Muslim girl named Rubaba. I told her father, 'Rubaba, is the brightest pupil in the school. There is not another little girl in Tabriz so far along in her studies.' Her father replied, 'Nor in the Shah's palace.' "

"Though routine duties of the mission schools continue, anxiety prevails not knowing when the Shah's lawless troops will rush into the city," Lillie Beaber said. "Rumors have spread that the Kurds plan to plunder the Armenian quarter where the Girls' School is situated. We will need a safe refuge for the girls, or they will be carried off by bandits."

"Even during these dark days, we have seen good attendance at the Sunday morning church service," Fred Jessup said. "There are so many Muslim men attending that it may be advisable to restore the old screen that separated the women's side from the men's side."

"Hearing that God will not forsake them strengthens the courage of the people of Tabriz," Newton Wright added, "regardless of their religious identity."

"God may not forsake them, but what about the Nationalists from Salmas and other regions of Persia?" Will Vanneman retorted. "People have been led to believe they are coming to help Tabriz."

"What do the Royalists stand to achieve by starving the city of Tabriz?" Mattie Wright asked.

"The Shah is bent on punishing the Nationalists of Tabriz as rebels," Sam replied. "The unpaid Royalist troops have endured the cold of winter. They are unwilling to give up their hopes of looting the city."

In early February there was fighting reported at the *Aji Chai* bridge west of *Amir Khiz* with casualties on both sides. Then on February 25th the Royalist leader Samad Khan initiated an aggressive two-day battle. Three *anjumans* were killed and fifteen

Nationalist soldiers wounded, but the Royalists were pushed back by the Nationalists and suffered heavy losses.

The children were saddened when I told them Mashadi Shafee, the candy man, was killed. He loved children and gave the them pieces of candy when they visited his shop in the bazaar.

"Why would anyone kill the candy man?" nine-year-old Annie asked.

"He was one of the *fidais*," I replied, "devoted to the cause until death."

March 5th, 1909

Amid all our concerns for the starving people and fear of an attack by the Royalists an unusual thing happened; Howard Baskerville, a temporary teacher at the Boys' School, asked Sam for permission to marry our daughter Agnes.

"What?" I exclaimed when Sam told me.

"I said 'No,' of course," Sam replied. "I told Howard that Agnes needs to finish her education. Besides there is the difference in age, he is seven years older."

"Something must have happened between them that we are not aware of," I said. "They read, they sang and rode horses together, and apparently he fell in love with Agnes."

"This would not have materialized without Agnes's encouragement," Sam said. "We will need to discuss this with her."

"After what has transpired, it will likely be uncomfortable for Howard to take meals here and spend the evenings with us," I said.

"I full-heartedly agree," Sam replied. "Perhaps I can arrange for Howard to board with the Wrights for the remaining three months of his appointment at the mission."

The following morning, Sam and I spoke with Agnes in the study.

"Howard asked for my permission to marry you," Sam said. "I told him, 'No.' "

"It was a decision for your best interests," I interjected. "You need to complete your education, see the world. Women have their own careers these days and get married later."

"Instead of waiting to send you to America next year with Rose and the Vannemans," Sam continued, "we have decided it would be better for you to accompany the Pittmans. If the roads are open, they plan to leave May 15th, less than two months from now."

"You are ready to go to college, and there are no colleges for you to attend here in Persia," I said. "You will go to Vassar, where Sam's sisters went to college."

"I'm not ready," Agnes protested. "I'm only sixteen."

"I was only fourteen when I went to Princeton," Sam responded.

"Your cousin Anna is going to be a freshman at Vassar next fall, and you will be together with someone you know," I said. "You won't be alone. Tomorrow, we will start to pack your trunk so that you will be able to leave as soon as the roads are open."

Afterward Agnes ran upstairs, and I cried in Sam's arms. "It is so hard for me to have my first child go off to America," I said.

"But it is best for her," Sam replied.

On March 6th, the mission woke to the sound of cannons, bombs and gunfire. Later we heard from Newton Wright that Samad Khan and his Royalist troops attacked the city, and Satter Khan and his Nationalist troops drove them back, killing forty Royalist soldiers.

"Only a few Nationalists were wounded," Newton said. "Howard Baskerville and I met Satter Khan on the street, and Howard congratulated him on his victory. Being a pro-Royalist, I, of course, did not congratulate him. Satter Khan responded, 'God is on our side.' Howard was amused by his theatrics and rode off with Satter Khan to tour his army camp."

"This is likely the beginning of a dangerous relationship," Sam said.

"A fatal attraction, I would call it," Newton said. "Satter Khan is to blame for prolonging this conflict. If the Nationalists had surrendered in July, we would be better off."

"Newton, you are the only missionary who supports the Shah," Sam said. "The rest of us admire the principles of democracy that the Nationalists are fighting for."

Notices were posted on every street in the *Khiaban* and *Bazaar* districts requesting volunteers for the Nationalist army and inviting the public to a military display on March 10th. The Nationalist troops performed military drills in the armory courtyard. Baqir Khan and Satter Khan sat on a raised platform on one end, and Howard Baskerville and a European gentleman sat directly behind them. *What is Howard doing with the leaders of the Nationalist troops?*

On Monday, March 29th I was coming down the stairs and overheard Sam and Howard Baskerville talking. "William Moore, an Irish correspondent for the London *Times*, volunteered to drill

Nationalist volunteer soldiers, and I decided to join him," Howard said. "Satter Khan asked me to take charge of a regiment."

"Howard, you cannot be associated with the Nationalists," Sam retorted. "As foreigners we cannot participate in Persian politics. You came here as a teacher, not as a revolutionary."

Howard responded, "I cannot watch calmly from a classroom window the starving inhabitants of the city fighting for their rights. I am an American citizen and proud of it, but I am also a human being and cannot help feeling deep sympathy with the people of this city. The only difference between me and these people is my place of birth, and this is not a big difference."

"How can you lead a regiment?" Sam retorted. "You do not even have a command of their language."

The next day, Sam was surprised when he received a note from Howard delivered by Khachador, one of his students. "Howard is resigning?" Sam exclaimed. "Have Howard come here at once to discuss this."

Shortly afterward Howard came to the house and Sam took him directly into his study and shut the door. Later Sam told me, "I tried to dissuade him the best I could. Since the Board will need to document my disagreement with his actions, I will write him a note to reiterate what I said and keep a copy. Maybe as he reads it over it will sink in."

"I hope he responds to your logic," I said. "Neither Howard nor William Moore have military skills. I am surprised that the Persian soldiers accept them as their leaders and do not balk, finding it arrogant and presumptuous for them to be their superiors."

The next morning Howard came to see Sam in his study again. When the door opened, I heard Howard say, "All right, I will go and tell Satter Khan that it is best for me not to come."

"Good, Lad," Sam replied. "Glad you have come to your senses."

The next day Sam received another note from Howard. "Howard changed his mind and is bent on joining the *fidais*," Sam exclaimed in exasperation. "He will not talk to me."

"It is William Moore, the Irish correspondent for the London *Times*," I said, "He convinced Howard to volunteer with him, and now Howard thinks it is his duty not to desert him. If anything happens to Howard, I will always hold Mr. Moore responsible."

"I must now respond and accept Howard's resignation," Sam said. "This is not my happiest moment. I am quite attached to the boy, almost as if he were my own son." Sam was clearly distressed as he wrote, tearing up two versions prior to finishing his brief response.

"Sam, you did what you could," I said. "He is in God's hands now."

After Sam sent word of Howard's resignation to the American Consulate, William Doty asked us to join him to confront Howard. We rushed over to the courtyard where Howard was drilling his troops. "You need to reconsider," Consul Doty shouted, "I regard your resignation and enlistment with the Nationalists to be a rash decision and irrational. Your actions may put other Americans in jeopardy. I am also compelled to remind you that as an American citizen, you have no right to interfere with the internal politics of this country."

"As an American citizen, I am free to do what I wish," Howard replied.

Mr. Doty bristled and continued, "If you join Satter Khan's forces then you will no longer be protected by the American government. You will need to relinquish your passport to me and declare yourself a man without a country."

"I will not give you my passport," Howard replied. "I fully intend to return to America after I perform what my duty as a human and a Christian calls me to do, to help these starving people."

"This is foolish, Howard. Please reconsider," Doty pleaded. "You have no military training. You are risking your life for a cause that does not serve you or the other missionaries in Persia."

"This is my duty," Howard replied, "I have made up my mind."

Howard Baskerville later wrote to Consul Doty saying, "William Moore and I do this in hopes of helping the government to defend innocent citizens from lawless pillage, rape and murder."

In the course of a few weeks, Howard Baskerville and William Moore drilled the troops and planned attacks to surprise the Royalists. On the night of April 16th, Moore, Baskerville and their soldiers spent the night waiting for Satter Khan to bring a cannon. Finally, when Satter Khan failed to come they returned home in dismay.

The next day in the meeting of the *Anjuman*, Baskerville and Moore were informed that only two days' supply of wheat remained in the city. The *Anjuman* spoke in favor of requesting that the English and Russian Consuls ask their governments to mediate peace negotiations with the Shah. Sattar Khan was skeptical of the peace negotiations and was determined on battle. Baskerville and Moore advised him to wait but pledged to lead their forces if an attack was declared.

Late in the evening Howard came to the mission. "We plan to attack *Sham Gazan*, one of the suburbs occupied by the Royalist troops," he said. As we prayed with each other with sad hearts we were interrupted by a messenger from William Doty. Howard wrote to us after he left and at early dawn, the message reached us by soldier:

April 19, 1908.

My Dear Dr. Wilson, There is a dangerous rumor that Europeans will be attacked so as to secure immediate interference by England and Russia. Please warn all Americans not to be seen on the streets any more than necessary. Baskerville.

At half past four I woke to the sound of quick, sharp firing. *The attack on Sham Gazan has begun.*

As we later learned from Khachador, one was the fatal shot. "Howard led his soldiers with great courage," Khachador said. "He continued to advance even though most of his men fell back, leaving only eleven soldiers. The enemy was nearby preparing their morning tea, and Howard motioned for his dwindled regiment to jump into a ditch. When one of his soldiers jumped, his gun struck a rock and shot a stray bullet that alarmed the enemy, ruining their surprise attack. After a little while Howard raised himself to look about and was shot. We laid him in a garden, and he was conscious only a short time."

Consul Doty sent for Howard's body, and it was brought to our house. Marguerite Vanneman and I washed away the blood before Will Vanneman examined it. "The bullet cut through a major artery above the heart," Will said. "He died almost instantly."

At the grave various Nationalists spoke, among them Sayyed Hasan Taqizadeh, the leader of the Liberals in the defunct *Majlis*. There was universal sorrow over Howard Baskerville's untimely death, some bewailing his mistake with grief in their hearts, others applauding his courage and self-sacrifice. The wreath from the *Anjuman* had a ribbon with the inscription in Persian:

"Oh, Martyr for the world of humanity!

Oh, Sacrifice for the liberty of Persians! Mr. Baskerville, Zealot!

We commit your body to the bosom of our dear Father Land!"

One of the eleven soldiers who stayed with him to the end said to Sam, "Would to God we all had died instead of him."

"Many will love and honor his memory as one who gave himself in sacrifice for Persia." Sam said. "No thought of self-seeking or vain glory impelled him. His motives were the purest and loftiest. We shall cherish his memory devotedly as one who was willing to give his life for the safety of the people of Tabriz."

The Foreign Ministers in Tehran communicated that the Shah granted an armistice of six days to arrange terms of peace, during which food would be allowed to enter the city. Prince Ayn al-Dawla, the commander of the Shah's troops, however, insisted he received no such orders from the Shah. After several days the order was sent directly to the foreign consuls from the Shah. Ayn al-Dawla relented and gave orders for flour to be allowed into the city, but the soldiers refused to obey, swearing that the city had been defeated by starvation and was now their lawful prey.

Negotiations with the Shah produced no effect. Famine was increasing, people were dying in the streets. "The people of Tabriz will either die from hunger or suffer pillage, murder and rapine, from the lawless horsemen of the Shah," Will Vanneman said.

"The remaining, perhaps equally undesirable solution is intervention by a foreign army," Sam replied.

On April 26th, William Doty came to the house with an urgent message: "A report arrived saying that a brigade of four thousand Russian Cossacks crossed the Aras River and is coming to open the roads to Tabriz."

Afraid of Russian intervention, the *Anjuman* sent telegrams to the Shah, asking him to save their land from the hands of the foreigner, but the Shah did nothing. Four days later the Shah's troops withdrew to one side of the city, and two hundred Russian soldiers marched into Tabriz without firing a shot. The Czar's troops paraded in the streets as if they had come for a civic celebration. Seeing that resistance was useless, the *fidais* of the National Volunteer Army stacked up their guns.

The roads were opened, and provisions poured in. The starving inhabitants of Tabriz rejoiced.

"The people of Tabriz think the Russians are saviors," I said. "What does occupation by the Russian soldiers mean in the long term?"

"The Russian Czar communicated that his troops would only remain as long as necessary to guarantee the security and lives of the Russian and foreign consulates and their subjects," Sam replied. "I am suspicious of the complete lack of resistance by the Shah's troops to their occupation."

CHAPTER 31

Tabriz, May 3rd, 1909

"THE NATIONALIST ARMIES ARE MARCHING TOWARD Tehran," Sam cried. "From the south, the *Bakhtiari* troops are coming from Isfahan, and from the north the troops from Rasht have mobilized."

"Who are the *Bakhtiari*?" I asked.

"They are an ancient Lur tribe from the west central mountains of Persia," Sam replied. "They are tough, resilient and resolute warriors, and devout Muslims. They fight on the side of justice for the underdog, in this case for the Constitution."

"How did you hear about the march on the capital?" I asked.

"Consul William Doty," Sam replied. "The leaders of the Isfahan army, brothers Sardar Assad and Samsam al-Saltana, tele-graphed the foreign legations expressing their gratitude for saving Tabriz but asking them to no longer interfere with the internal affairs of Persia. Then they told them that all the Nationalists were marching to Tehran to force the Shah to fulfill his pledges to the people."

"And the army from Rasht?" I asked.

"This is interesting, because the *Sipahdar*, or Field Marshal, of the Shah's army, joined the Nationalists. The Shah sent him to fight against the rebels in Tabriz and he refused. His name is Muhammad Wali Khan Nasurs Saltana, but all refer to him as '*Sipahdar*.' After he left the Shah's forces, he returned to the Gilan province on the Caspian Sea and organized his own Nationalist army."

"How admirable. Do you think the Russians will interfere?" I asked.

"I am sure both the Russians and the British will interfere," Sam replied.

Sam's speculation turned out to be correct; the Russian and British Legations convinced the Shah to say he would reinstate the Constitution and the *Majlis* in order to stall the Nationalist's attack on Tehran.

May 15th, Agnes and Pittmans leave for America

"Oh, I cannot bear it," I lamented as I watched the wagon disappear on the horizon, tears streaming down my face. "We will not see Agnes for three years."

"I knew this would be hard for you," Sam said as he put his arm around my shoulders, "but your children will one by one take the next step in their lives."

"This has been such a traumatic year for all of us, but especially for Agnes; first Howard Baskerville proposed marriage to her, then he was shot."

"Agnes is only sixteen," Sam replied. "She had a schoolgirl crush on Howard and will quickly forget him. The Pittmans plan to take her to Italy and France. The excitement of seeing Europe will take her mind off the events of this past year."

"We could all use two weeks in Florence and Paris," I retorted.

"She will also need to study in order to pass the entrance exams for Vassar," Sam said.

"Yes, I certainly hope she passes. She will be so discouraged if she does not."

The first report I received of the progress of their journey came from Lucille Pittman. "They made it to Rome," I cried. "With Lucille's help, Agnes is now wearing a corset."

Sam erupted in laughter. "It had not occurred to me that learning to wear a corset would be news to write home about."

When they arrived in Paris, Agnes finally wrote to us. "Agnes says she was so busy sight-seeing in Italy that she did not have time to write," I said. "In Paris she received our first letter and cried in the hotel lobby as she read it."

"She sent the letter over two weeks ago," Sam said, when he looked at the date stamped on the envelope. "She is probably now on the steamer to America."

Several weeks after the Russians troops marched into Tabriz, Muslim friends came to visit us. "The Russians soldiers are molesting Muslim women in the street," Darya said. "A group of them surrounded a woman, who was walking alone, and lifted her veil. I have heard of an instance where one of the soldiers tore off a woman's veil and laughed at her when she screamed and covered her face with her hands."

"They go to the bazaars and take handfuls of nuts and fruits, refusing to pay," Bijan said.

"Imagine their dirty hands in our food," Darya added, wrinkling her nose.

"Without permission they strung telephone wire from their camp on the *Ajai Chai* Bridge to the Russian Consulate," Bijan said.

"Did they cause any damage?" I asked, not completely understanding the issue.

"In doing so, they climbed on the roofs of people's houses, looking down into the courtyards of the harems and scaring women and children," Darya replied.

"The soldiers have also been instructed to disarm the citizens of Tabriz," Bijan said. "They take guns and rifles from any man they meet walking on the street, even the *nazmiyya* (policeman). Is there anything that you can do?"

"I will report this abominable behavior to the American Consul, William Doty. If necessary, I will also complain directly to the Russian Consul," Sam said.

William Doty told Sam that he was aware of the matter. "Sattar Khan, Baqir Khan and Taqizadeh have registered complaints against General Znarsky and his Russian troops. They telegraphed a protest letter, describing the treatment by the Russian military of the inhabitants of Tabriz. It was published in the British *Daily News* and the *Manchester Guardian*. Several hundred Nationalists took *bast* at the Turkish Consulate in protest. Tehran has been forced to act on this."

"The poor inhabitants of Tabriz, a few weeks ago they thought the Russian soldiers were their 'saviors,' and now they have true animosity for them."

"I know," Doty replied. "I am afraid there will be trouble."

By June 23rd Sardar Assad's and Samsam al-Saltana's Nationalist army from Isfahan had traveled north to Qom, ninety miles south of Tehran, and *Sipahdar*'s army from Rasht occupied Qazvin, ninety miles to the north of the capital. The Russian government assembled an army in Baku on the Caspian Sea, ready to proceed to Persia and intervene if the Shah was threatened. The British Legation from Tehran sent representatives to both Nationalist armies to exercise their powers of persuasion, saying, "The Shah will reinstate the Constitution. Do not complicate things."

"We do not trust the Shah," was the Nationalists' response.

On July 10th the two Nationalist armies joined forces at Badamak, fifteen miles west of Tehran. The Royalist army, advancing in a menacing semi-circle ten miles long, reached the banks of the Karaj River and engaged with the Nationalists in gunfire. At 5 o'clock the Royalists ceased fighting and retired for the evening. In the night, the bulk of the Nationalist forces crept around the hills to the north of Tehran, leaving a regiment to continue desultory engagement as a feint to distract the Royalists the next day. *Sipahdar* and three hundred men slipped through the unguarded north gate of Tehran without firing a shot and, in the morning, stood guard to allow several thousand Nationalist forces join them. A bomb explosion announced their capture of the city and they shouted, "Long live the Constitution."

In the ruins of the former Parliament building, the *Baharestan*, the Nationalists leaders and members of the former *Majlis* deposed Muhammad Ali Shah, who took refuge in the Russian Consulate. The Shah's eleven-year-old son, *Vali Ahd* Sultan Ahmad Mirza, was chosen as his successor, and Azod al-Molk, an older member of the Qajar family and an honest politician, was appointed as his Regent. The Constitution was reinstated and the Second *Majlis* was convocated. The Nationalist army leaders were proclaimed "Saviors of the Revolution;" *Sipahdar* was appointed Minister of War and Samsam al-Saltana became Prime Minister.

Ajudan-bashi, who commanded the bombardment of the *Baharestan* was executed. Mir Hashim, the traitor to the *Anjuman*, who fought the Nationalists in Tabriz, was hanged. Colonel Vladimir Liakhoff was recalled to Saint Petersburg, and the ex-Shah and his harem left Persia to reside in Odessa on a pension paid by the Persian government.

Rahim Khan escaped to the Karadagh and revolted against the new regime. In October he attacked Ardabil, near the Caspian Sea and threatened to march to Tehran, overthrow the Constitutional Government and restore the ex-Shah. In December the new Persian government army marched to Ardabil and surrounded Rahim Khan's troops and forced him to escape to Russia. Rahim Khan remained in Russia until 1911 when he ventured back to Tabriz, where he was imprisoned and executed.

"Thus ends the Persian Revolution," Sam said. "The future of Persia now lies in the hands of the Persian people. Fortunately, some of their leaders were educated in our schools, like Sayyid Taqizadeh."

"How many Persians died in order to reinstate the Constitution and the *Majlis*?" I asked.

"The number killed and wounded during the five days of fighting is estimated to be five hundred," Sam replied, "but the exact number will never be known as many were likely thrown into pits or eaten by the dogs in the streets."

Tabriz Mission 1910

With the opening of the roads, three new members of the station arrived — Helen Grove, a new teacher for the mission children, George Pierce, a teacher for the Boys' School with a three-year assignment, and Dr. Edna Orcutt, a new woman physician.

"We and the women of Tabriz rejoice at your arrival," I told Dr. Orcutt. "The Whipple Women's Hospital has been without a doctor for five years."

The last day of June, prior to Dr. Vanneman's and Newton Wright's departures for America on furlough, the missionaries met at our house to recount our year's activities for our Annual Report to the Board. "This year was one of relative peace and repair from emotional and physical damage to the city and people of Tabriz," Sam said. "We had three hundred and ten pupils enrolled in the Boys' School. Our lower grades were comprised of primarily Armenians, whereas the higher grades were primarily Muslim boys."

"Our graduates are highly sought after for employment in Tabriz and other cities," I added.

"I am often made proud by compliments regarding our pupils," Sam said. "A few days ago, a Catholic European said to me, 'I like the young men from your school. They are of a superior stamp.' Our graduates are intelligent, well-educated and of high moral character. Many do not accept Christ as a Savior, but they learn His moral teachings from the Scriptures."

"How did the Girls' School fare this year?" Marguerite Vanneman asked.

"Thirty-three Muslim girls attended this year, twenty-two of these were boarders," Lillie Beaber said.

"Did the parents protest against teaching religious classes to their daughters?" Mattie Wright asked.

"Of course," Lillie responded. "For example, a well-to-do Muslim family applied for admission of their bright little girl with the stipulation that she not be required to attend chapel and that all religious instruction be omitted. We boldly replied that our school was established for religious purposes and all pupils are required to attend prayer sessions and Bible Class. After some demur, the family sent two girls to us, who became fascinated with prayers and hymns and treasured their New Testaments. When they shared the stories of Christ at home, their mothers and relatives became frequent visitors to our devotional exercises."

"How do the young girls at the school learn to read?" Marguerite Vanneman asked.

"The girls start by learning to read Azeri," Lillie replied. "First, we give them a slip of paper with the Azeri alphabet and an Azeri primer, which they finish in a few weeks. Then they read *That Sweet Story of Old*, by Mary Angeline Hallock, first published in 1857. It is a delightful short story of the life of Christ, and we translated it into Azeri. Finally, the girls are given a copy of the New Testament in Azeri."

"What shall I report for the medical department?" Sam asked.

"From the fall of 1909 to the summer of 1910, my medical work has been the heaviest of the twenty years I have been in Persia," Will Vanneman said. "Fourteen thousand patients visited the dispensary and I made fourteen hundred home visits. The men's medical department collected three thousand dollars in receipts, making us self-sustaining again this year."

"You will have a well-deserved furlough in America," I said.

On June 15th we celebrated Annie's ninth birthday and coupled it with a going away party for Rose, who was leaving with the Vannemans two days later. For the past six years we had celebrated Rose's and Bobby's birthdays on two consecutive days, July 25th and 26th, and this year Bobby would be the only one at home.

"Where will you be on our birthday?" Bobby asked.

"We will be traveling through Europe," Rose replied. "We have a month's sightseeing trip planned."

When the wagon stopped in front of the house with Will and Marguerite and their three girls, Rose hopped in next to Dorothy

Vanneman with a smile stretching across her face. *How different it is for Rose to leave home compared to Agnes, a cheerful goodbye versus a tearful farewell. How can my Rose look so happy when my heart is breaking?*

Sam and I followed in our wagon to the edge of the city with Annie and Bobby riding in the back seat. "When will we see Rose again?" Bobby asked.

"In two years, when we go to America on furlough," I replied. "It will just be the two of you." My voice cracked as tearful emotions seized me.

Sam put his arm around me. "Now Annie, the chicks have not all left the nest yet."

I tried not to cry as I kissed Rose goodbye, but it was impossible to hold back the tears. "Take care of my Rose," I said to Marguerite.

"Like one of my own," she replied with a sympathetic smile. "Like one of my own."

When we returned to the mission, Sam said, "Rose will be fine. The Vannemans will show her Europe and she will spend a year with my sister Annie Barr in Detroit and her family. She will be fully Americanized when you see her next."

"That is what worries me," I replied. "I worry that she will change."

"Annie, all of our children will change," Sam said.

"But will they throw away all that they learned at the mission, the joy of helping others?" I asked. "Will any of my children become missionaries?"

From behind me Annie put her arms around my waist and said, "Mother, I promise to become a missionary."

CHAPTER 32

Tabriz 1911

"AFTER COMMENCEMENT AT THE BOYS' SCHOOL WE WILL go to Urmia for the Annual Meeting of the Western Persia Mission," Sam said.

"This will be our last visit to Urmia before our furlough," I said. "I would like to go a few weeks earlier with the children and extend our stay through August."

"It is not safe for you to go alone with the children," Sam said.

"Charles and Lucille Pittman plan to go early and offered to take me in their wagon."

"What about the children?" Sam asked.

"They can travel by *cajavahs*," I replied. "Charles Pittman offered to lead an extra horse to carry the baskets for them to ride in."

"If I am not mistaken you planned this several weeks ago," Sam said.

Fred and Ida Coan welcomed us as guests in their house at the Urmia mission. We reminisced about the summer we spent there ten years ago when ten children were running about the house. "It seems too quiet with only four children," I said, "Particularly only two little ones."

"I do not think I am strong enough to have Annie and Howard sitting on both knees as they did then either," Fred added.

"We will be taking our teenagers Katharine and Howard to America next year and staying for three years," Ida Coan said. "Otherwise, we would now be in America for the college graduations, Frank from Williams and Elizabeth from Wellesley."

"We will be going on furlough next year as well," Mary Labaree added. "Hopefully we can arrange to travel together."

"We could meet you in Julfa and continue together from there, one grand party of traveling missionaries," I said.

"It should be a gay time," Fred said.

"How was the school year at the Tabriz mission?" Robert Labaree asked.

"The total enrollment of the Boys' School was two hundred and forty-one, of which one hundred were Persian Muslims and the remaining Christian Armenians," I replied. "Two of the boys are the sons of the new Governor, Ijlal-il-Mulk. He, like his predecessor Mukhbir-al-Sultana, is a warm friend of the mission. The Girls' School run by Lillie Beaber enrolled one hundred and seventy-seven girls; one hundred and twenty-three Christian Armenians and fifty-four Persian Muslims."

"It warms my heart to see the Christian Armenian and Persian Muslim girls sitting side by side," Lucille Pittman added. "They walk arm in arm in the yard and join indiscriminately in games."

"Another development was the resignation of Rev. Newton Wright and his wife Mattie," Charles Pittman said. "They announced their resignation while on furlough in America. We are rather ambivalent about his loss; over the years he had contributed less and less. He openly criticized the other missionaries for voicing support for the Nationalists and submitted a formal written complaint to Robert Speer. It was very damaging to the other missionaries at the station and the rift it created was such a contrast to our close family atmosphere. Shortly after that, he announced that the Wright family was taking an early furlough."

"He called the Memorial Boys' School a 'hotbed for revolutionary activity,' " I said. "The most painful thing he wrote was the accusation that our support of the Nationalists was to blame for Howard Baskerville's death."

"Mattie Wright also rarely participated in teaching at the Girls' School or visitations to the homes of Persian women," Lucille Pittman added. "The Board expected her to perform missionary work, not just raise their family."

"How is the political climate here in Urmia these days?" I asked, trying to change the topic.

"In Urmia *Masruta*, or Constitutionalism, has been allowed to proceed without plots and counterplots to disturb it," Fred replied. "The Turkish government has replaced the local officials and is now responsible for controlling the Kurds. Certainly, the leopard has not changed his spots nor the Kurd his character, but something has happened to prevent them from having a free hand."

"Is it safe to take horseback rides on Mount Seir?" I asked.

"Yes, of course. The riding on Mount Seir this spring was beautiful with wildflowers all the colors of the rainbow carpeting the hills," Mary Labaree said, "like an impressionist painting."

"I especially love the wild lavender irises," Ida Coan added.

"Could we have a picnic in a vineyard too?" I asked.

"All that can be arranged," Fred replied. "But you sound as though you are asking for last wishes. You are planning on returning after your furlough next year, aren't you?"

"Yes, of course," I replied. "It is only that I have not done these things for so long."

"I hope you are right, my dear Annie," Fred said. "It is just that things are changing in this world that are beyond our control."

"The most unexpected thing has happened," Robert Labaree interjected as he charged in with the London *Times*. "The Persian government appealed to President Taft to provide someone to reorganize Persia's finances. They appointed an American, William Morgan Shuster, as Treasurer-General to set Persia's finances straight."

"Most remarkable," Fred exclaimed. "I hope Shuster solicits an international loan to pay off Persia's debt to England and Russia and eliminate their exploitive imperialism."

"They should collect taxes to pay for the loan from the Persian landowners and noblemen," Robert Labaree said, "and from the Russian and British subjects who have benefited from all the concessions from the Shah."

"That would ruffle some feathers," Fred remarked.

On July 18, 1911, shortly after Sam joined us in Urmia, he received a telegram from the American Consul in Tabriz: "Ex-Shah returned to Persia."

"What does that mean?" I asked.

"He is trying to retake the throne," Sam replied.

A few days later Fred Coan received a full account in a Persian newspaper. "Mohammad Ali came from Russia by steamer to Astrarabad on the Caspian coast," he said. "He is marching towards Tehran with Russian Cossack troops. At the same time his brother Salar od-Dowleh crossed the border from Turkey with an army of Lurs. They attacked Kermanshah, three hundred miles south of Urmia."

"Are we safe here?" I asked.

"Fighting will be far south and east of Urmia," Fred replied. "The mission in Hamadan is likely in the thick of the skirmish."

"It is Tabriz that concerns me," Sam said. "Samad Khan is one of the ex-Shah's loyal generals. As chief of the *Shahsevan* tribe, he may descend from the north and attack Tabriz if the ex-Shah is successful."

My fiftieth birthday was August 24th and my friends at the Urmia mission held a waffle supper in my honor. People made speeches and I responded with an impromptu acrostic for Urmia: "U, Unrivaled in beauty and verdure; R, Renowned for its gardens and trees; M, Mourned for by its sons beyond seas; I, I hail thee as home of my childhood; A, And name thee to God on my knees." Everyone applauded loudly, and Bobby pleaded for me to repeat it until Sam said gently, "Enough."

Grettie Holliday joined us in Urmia for the birthday party from her itinerating tour on the Salmas plain. "I was on tour with the Armenian pastor Garabed," Grettie said. "We visited a Kurdish encampment by the road where we had expected to stay on Sunday, but our reception was a little peculiar and made us suspicious. When Garabed spoke to them of Sin and the Ten Commandments, one of the Kurds slyly whispered, 'Don't mention stealing in this place.' They were noted robbers and I was relieved when after two to three hours we were able to safely leave without incident."

"Did you find a safe place to spend the night?" Sam asked.

"Yes," Grettie replied. "We stopped at a village and were kindly entertained by a *mullah*. His little girl took great fancy in us, touching our clothes and holding our hands. Her father said, 'If Tabriz were only a little nearer, she should come to your school.' The villagers were very sad over their harvest being eaten by great flocks of quail."

"Not locust, but quail?" Charles Pittman exclaimed. "Quail are not one of the plagues in the Bible."

"Did you meet any Kurdish women?" Lucille Pittman asked.

"Yes," Grettie answered. "For the first time I became acquainted with high-ranking Kurdish women. How I admired their modest and graceful dress and their relative freedom compared to most Muslim women in Persia. They exhibit genuine affection for their children. For example, when we stayed at a Kurdish home, with only a curtain separating us from the family, we heard considerable kissing in the dark, which we attributed a greater part going to a fat little toddling boy who was the family idol."

"Did you run into any bands of marauding Kurds?" Fred Coan asked.

"After arriving in one village we heard that a band of Kurds were heading in our direction," Grettie said. "We decided to leave at once, but we had already become a *tamasha* and a crowd gathered around our wagon and began to ask questions. Half in fun and half in earnest, one of the villagers asked, 'Then you want us all to give up Islam and become Christians?' to which I replied 'Yes, that is exactly what we want.' The man looked at us earnestly and said, 'Well it is a great pity that you cannot stay to tell us more about it.' We looked at each other in surprise, but I replied, 'We are fleeing from a band of Kurds and must go at once.' The same village was attacked by Kurds that night."

"Did you consider your evangelizing successful?" Sam asked.

"The village people displayed a very different attitude towards us than what we have been used to," Grettie replied. "They no longer shun us but are instead interested in talking to us about spiritual enlightenment."

"Regardless, we can only give the message as faithfully as it lies in our power," Fred Coan said. "The results we leave to God."

"Yes," Grettie replied, "We cannot make Lazarus arise from the dead and walk out of the tomb, but we can roll away the stone that blocks the entrance."

"John 11: 38-44," I said.

On September 5th the Persian government troops defeated the ex-Shah's forces and Mohammad Ali fled back to Russia. A few weeks later, as we were preparing to return to Tabriz, we were relieved to hear that the ex-Shah's brother, Salar od-Dowleh, was also defeated, and that he had fled to Europe.

"We have averted another civil war in Persia," I said with a sigh. "I would not want to relive the last upheaval."

As we neared Tabriz, the driver of a caravan going in the opposite direction waved at us frantically with outstretched arms. "Stay here while I see what he wants," Sam said and approached the caravan.

Sam returned shaking his head in bewilderment. "The ex-Shah is gone but Samad Khan, who is sympathetic to the ex-Shah, remains a threat," he said. "He has ambitions to command Tabriz and formed an alliance with the Russians camped there. He has the *Shahsevan* tribesmen blocking all the roads to Tabriz, except the road from Julfa. We will have to take that route into the city."

When we returned to the mission, Mousa told us, "Samad Khan started the road blockade in August. It produced an artificial famine by preventing food and fuel from entering the city. The prices of necessities rose four-times above normal. Many could not afford to buy food, and destitution soon prevailed."

"We knew nothing of this in Urmia," Sam said. "What are the conditions now?"

"Suffering is still widespread," Mousa replied.

"We will provide what relief we can," I said.

The next day was Saturday, September 16th, our twenty-fifth wedding anniversary. Sam and I planned on a quiet evening together with the children, but it was not meant to be; while we were in Urmia, Mousa arranged for a party that Lucille Pittman had planned months prior. First, a man from the bazaar came to the door balancing a *khoncha* on his head, a wooden tray two feet wide and four feet long filled with cookies, pastries and candies. While Sam and I were distracted by the *khoncha* man, Mousa let the missionaries enter from the veranda. When Sam and I brought the *khoncha* to the dining room, they cried in unison, "Happy silver wedding anniversary!"

"You did not plan on eating all the sweets by yourselves, did you?" Charles Pittman said.

The teachers from the Boys' School gave us Armenian silver filagree spoons from Zanjan. Esther, our new cook, brought in the samovar, a tray of glasses for tea and two three-layer cakes. After singing songs, Charles and Lucille Pittman started dancing and the rest of us joined in.

"In Persia, I thought men and women were not permitted to dance together," Annie said.

"In our own homes sometimes missionaries break the rules," Sam said. "Besides, we have practically forgotten how the dance and when we go back to America on furlough next year, some of your cousins will be getting married."

At the end of the party, as the other missionaries prepared to leave," I exclaimed, "You are such wonderful friends. I hope we are still together in fifteen years for our fortieth anniversary."

"That might also be our retirement party," Sam added.

"Oh Sam, what are you saying," Charles said. "You know you will never retire from missionary work."

Princess Ezzat sent word that her husband had relocated to Kermanshah, where he led the army forces that defeated the ex-Shah's brother, Salar od-Dowleh. "I am sad to tell you that we will not be returning to Tabriz," she said. "Our family is moving to Tehran. I will sincerely miss my piano lessons and our conversations."

And I will also miss our delightful visits together.

On November 29th the Russian and British Legations in Tehran revolted against Treasure-General Shuster's anti-imperialist policies and issued an ultimatum demanding his dismissal. When the *Majlis* refused to comply, Russia troops marched toward Tehran and British troops came from India and occupied the southern Persian provinces. Even in the face of foreign occupation, the *Majlis* refused to concede. In a desperate act, the Cabinet and Regent Naser al-Molk, acting on behalf of the young Ahmad Shah, capitulated to the imperialists' demands, ousting Shuster and dismissing the *Majlis*.

To avoid widespread outbursts of indignation in the other provinces, news of the dissolution of the *Majlis* and the Constitutional government in Tehran was strenuously controlled. Russia acted quickly to invade several northern cities including Tabriz, where seven hundred Russian troops from Ardabil arrived on December 18th. The *Anjuman*, suspicious of their intentions, instructed the Nationalist Volunteer Army to move cannons and ammunition to the Arg and keep troops continuously on guard.

On the morning of December 21st, the *Anjuman* were informed that during the night the Russian troops stormed and now occupied the Police Headquarters, the Government House and the High Court of Justice. Without hesitation the Nationalist Volunteers, the *fidais*, defended the city. Some surrounded the *caravanserais* where the Russians were quartered, and others armed themselves on roofs and shot down any Russian passing through the street.

Within hours the Russians suffered severe casualties and ran in fright to their main camp at *Bagh-i-Shamal*, the North Garden. From there the Russians continued to fire on Nationalist troops at the Arg, but with little effect. Instead, they resorted to dynamiting houses, killing over five hundred innocent women and children.

The merchants and notable citizens of Tabriz fearing the Russians would lay the entire city in ruins, sought out Seqat-ol-Eslam, an influential Muslim cleric and intellectual. He agreed to negotiate a cease fire with the British and Russian Consuls, dodging bullets and cannonballs as he made trips between the consulates. On the night of December 22nd, the Russian Consul declared an armistice.

The Russians, unfaithful to their promises, resumed bombarding Tabriz from dawn to dusk on December 25th. Again Seqat-ol-Eslam went to the British and Russian Consulates. Firing ceased until the next day, when new regiment of eight hundred Russian soldiers arrived from Julfa. Without a map of the city and a plan of attack, and not knowing there was a truce in effect, they began firing throughout the city, endangering the lives of Europeans and the Consulates. Fortunately, the Russian Consul sent a peremptory message to the colonel of the new brigade to stop firing. Otherwise, severe damage to the city and innocent inhabitants would have occurred.

On December 27th, after five days of fighting, the Nationalists were defeated, and the Russians took command of the city. The Nationalist Volunteer Army disbanded, and their leaders fled. The Persian flag flying on the top of the Arg was hauled down and the

Russian flag hoisted in its place. Russian soldiers indiscriminately entered houses, shot the men inside and then destroyed the buildings with dynamite. Swarms of women and children ran to the mission for refuge, one woman carried a two-day old baby.

The Governor, Ijlal-il-Mulk, sent his two sons to us for protection. Soon other Muslim notables and merchants supporting the Nationalists also sent their boys to us. Overnight we filled our dormitory with Persian Muslim boys.

"It was one thing for Muslim parents to send their children to the mission schools for an education," Sam said, "but now they are entrusting us with their lives."

The Russians were not finished punishing the city of Tabriz. On December 31st, the holy Day of Ashura, the Russian Consul sent a carriage for Seqat-ol-Eslam, the Muslim cleric who had negotiated the cease fire. He was taken to the Russian Consulate where he was hanged, along with eight other Nationalists. The gallows were brightly painted like a barber's pole, white, blue and red, the colors of the Russian flag, and grinning soldiers stood to have their photograph taken beside the corpses.

On January 6th, Armenian Christmas, Pedros Andreasian, the most prominent Armenian in Tabriz, was seized and dragged to the gallows. Being a heavy man, on two attempts to hang him the noose broke. A young Russian soldier protested the third attempt saying, "He has suffered enough. In any civilized country he would be released." The young soldier was severely reprimanded, and later committed suicide. The third execution attempt of Pedros Andreasian was successful. That night the Russian soldiers paraded in the Armenian quarter and sang songs to intimidate the people living there.

After the Russians installed the Royalist general Samad Khan as Governor, the "Reign of Terror" began with greater barbarity. Samad Khan arrested, extorted and imprisoned Nationalist leaders, their relatives and other prominent citizens of Tabriz *en masse*, about twelve hundred in total.

Some of the barbarous acts instituted by Samad Khan on his prisoners included sewing their mouths shut, nailing horseshoes to their feet and leading them through the bazaar by a rope through their nose, submerging them in a vat of water and beating their head when they tried to surface to breathe until they drowned. Before hanging, the eyes and tongues were often cut out. One man was beheaded and cut in half. The corpses were strung up on ladders in the street and at the bazaar like slaughtered sheep. The sight and smell of the executed were so grotesque that we dared not venture out of the mission compound.

When the Russian soldiers were not hanging Nationalists, they tormented the people of Tabriz. Soldiers walked down the streets with whips, striking any Persian within reach. They looted houses, lifted Muslim women's veils, and pilfered in the bazaars.

Russian soldiers handling explosives in the Arg blew up a magazine, killing forty-two men. By coincidence, the explosion happened when a total of forty-two Tabrizis had been hanged. The superstitions of the Russian soldiers and Persian alike were enlivened by the ominous cloud of smoke that arose from the Arg, the symbolic citadel of the city of Tabriz.

Many Nationalists leaders went into hiding or fled the country. Disappearances led to false rumors of people being arrested and imprisoned. Among those rumored to be executed were staff members of the newspaper *Shafaq*, meaning 'Light' or 'Dawn'. The founder of the paper, Sadeq Rezazadeh Shafaq was only nineteen and a former student at the mission Boys' School. We were deeply grieved until a month later we learned that he fled to Constantinople.

The people of Tabriz questioned why the Persian Government and the foreign consuls did nothing to intervene and stop the torture and executions by the Russians. Before the British Consul Shipley left in early February, Sam confronted him. "How can you stand by and watch this barbaric behavior by the Russians, especially considering that Samad Khan's appointment to Governor was never recognized by the Persian government?"

"Tabriz is within the Russian sphere of influence so there is nothing England can do," Shipley replied. "I have personally asked Sir Walter Townley, the British Minister to Persia in Tehran, to demand action by the Persian government. They have communicated that *Sipahdar* will replace Samad Khan. Hopefully that will end this terrible chapter for Tabriz."

"In June we will leave the mission on furlough," I said. "I hope *Sipahdar* arrives by then and ends this massacre."

The takeover by the Russians in 1911 was followed by one with the longest, coldest winters within memory.

CHAPTER 33

Tabriz 1912

"THE RUSSIANS HAVE PUT STICKS OF DYNAMITE AROUND the Girls' School," Lille Beaber screamed as she barged through the door. "I evacuated all the girls to the mission church."

"Why would they want to blow up the Girls' School?" I exclaimed. "We must speak at once with Gordon Paddock at the American Consulate."

Lillie and I dodged Russian soldiers as we ran through the streets arriving breathless at the American Consulate. "We must see Consul Paddock immediately," I stated firmly to the receptionist. "The Russians are about to blow up the mission Girls' School."

The receptionist paled and ran off, bringing Gordon Paddock back with him to speak with us.

"Yes, that is a matter of utmost urgency," he said. "I will call the Russian Consul at once."

Later that evening, we heaved a sigh of relief when Gordon Paddock came by to deliver the message personally that the dynamite had been removed. "They thought it was an Armenian school, being in the *Gala* quarter. The students are safe to return tomorrow."

Throughout the spring of 1912, torture and execution of Nationalists and other prominent citizens of Tabriz continued. Just as the people of Tabriz recovered to some degree from the shock and horror, Samad Khan arrested a new group on his proscribed list to be extorted, tortured and hanged. Persia's people were subdued by the destruction of their dream for independence; the nerve of their ambition for a Constitutional government was numbed.

The wife of the late Seqat-ol-Eslam came to visit me with her daughter, Masruta. "I am afraid to call my daughter by her name," she bemoaned. "She was named for *Masruta*, Constitutionalism, because she was born on July 25th, 1907, the anniversary of the ratification."

"Call her 'Masra,' " I suggested. "It means 'joy' or 'pleasure' in Arabic."

Seqat-ol-Eslam's wife smiled. "She is one of the few joys I have left. I take her with me when I go out so she does not worry herself sick that I too, like her father, have been hanged and will never return."

Unlike the Persians, the Russians did not mistreat the Europeans or the missionaries. Russian soldiers attended mission church service and Sunday School on a regular basis. One positive outcome of Russian occupation was the installation of a bell in the mission church tower. The local Persian government had opposed installation of a bell for many years, but now that the Russians were in favor of one, Sam hastily ordered one from Tiflis.

We rang the bell for the first time on Sunday, April 7th to call the congregation to Easter service.

"Twelve years after I built it, the church tower finally has a bell," Sam said. "I never lost faith that the day would come."

"I never understood the objection of having a bell ring on Sunday," I said. "The Muslim *muezzins* call *anan* five times each day from the minarets of the mosques."

Following Easter service, the missionary families gathered for a celebration lunch at our house.

"After these past dreadful four months, both Muslims and Christians are celebrating a resurgence of hope," I said.

"The new spirit of intellectual inquiry and religious tolerance is exceptional," Fred Jessup said.

"Whatever form of government rules Persia, the young men and women are realizing that they must become useful in this society and become educated," Sam said. "They are thronging our mission schools."

"The majority of the students in the mission schools are now Muslims," I added. "Twelve years ago, there were none enrolled. What is most remarkable is the friendships that have developed between the Christian Armenian and the Persian Muslim students. Sam fostered those relationships."

"With the mission school running so smoothly I can safely leave on furlough," Sam said.

"What will happen to your house while you are gone?" Lucille Pittman asked.

"Fred Jessup will be staying in our house and taking on my duties as acting-principal of the Boys' School," Sam said. "We will move our things into one of the rooms, so they are out of the way."

"How considerate of you," Lucille responded. "Most people going on furlough pack and leave hastily, expecting the temporary residents to make their way around their things for a year."

"Our house belongs to the mission." Sam said.

"The most generous thing that Annie did was to sell her piano to the Girls' School," Lillie Beaber said. "The girls will be able to take piano lessons this coming school year."

"And those who are not taking lessons will simply be amused by watching the hammers dance," I replied. "I remember how when it first arrived in 1887, it was the talk of the town. Eight missionary girls, including our own, practiced on it over the years."

In June at the Boys' School Commencement one of the seniors in his valedictory speech referred to me as *"Mayrig,"* which means "little mother" in Armenian. "I am so touched," I murmured. "I wish that I could have mothered the boys."

"We had a great influence on these ambitious, eager young men," Sam replied. "One boy told me, 'Learning English opens to me a great window on the universe.'"

"I remember going to a student's house to speak to his mother," I replied. "She told me his father asked him, 'Whom do you love best?' and he replied, 'You, Dadda.' Then the father asked him 'Whom do you love next to me?' To his surprise the boy replied, 'The *Sahib*, Rev. Wilson.' 'Why? He is a foreigner,' the father exclaimed. 'Because *Sahib* will make a man of me,' the boy responded."

Sam's eyes welled with tears. "In many ways I would prefer to stay here rather than go to America on furlough," he said. "We have reached a pinnacle of success with the Boys' School."

"Our fine school will be here and full of eager and ambitious young men when we return," I replied.

On June 25th before we left the mission compound, our dearest Muslim friends, the Kalantars, came to visit and say goodbye.

Since we had already stored our clothes, china, silverware and personal items in Bobby's bedroom for our year in America, I brought a tray upstairs in search of cups and saucers to serve coffee. The cups were stacked high on an upper shelf and as I fumbled to grab a fourth cup it slipped from my hand. Something inside me let go as I heard it crash on the floor; dread seized me as though it was a bad omen. The handle had broken off and split in two pieces. I sat on the floor and picked up the pieces sobbing like a child.

Bobby's big blue eyes peaked around the corner of the door. "Mommy why are you crying?' he asked.

"Because I am a silly sentimental old woman," I replied. "This set of china was a wedding present."

"Can you glue it back together?"

"Yes, dear, I can try to repair it when we return."

"Then why are you crying?"

"Because I will miss our home," I replied, the words of truth slipping from my tongue. "I will miss Persia." Bobby put his arms around me and pecked my cheek.

"You are a sweetheart," I said. I carefully placed the broken handle into the bowl of the cup and placed it with the other cups, dried my tears and took the cups and saucers downstairs to serve coffee.

As we left the house, Esther, our cook, threw water from a pitcher on the ground and the spray wetted my heels. "Why did you do that?" I exclaimed.

"Spilling water for your journey," she replied. "It will ensure your safe travels. *Khoda hafez* (God be with you)."

"Did you bring your amulet to ward off the 'Evil Eye?' " Sam asked.

"Not intentionally," I replied, "but it is likely in my jewelry box, which I packed."

"To be protected you need to wear it," Sam added.

As a result of the Russian occupation a well-graded road was constructed from Tabriz to Julfa that did not exist four years prior. We made the eighty-mile trip to Julfa via automobile in two hours. "It used to take four days by wagon," I exclaimed. "This is miraculous."

"The Russians want to extend the railroad to Tabriz as well," Sam said. "That would make the trip even faster."

In Julfa we met Mary and Robert Labaree, and Fred and Ida Coan, who had traveled there from Urmia. Our three families traveled together for the remainder of the trip, stopping in Vienna, Berlin, Warsaw and Paris before taking a ship across the English Channel to London.

We were a gay party of eleven, six adults and five children.

Our steamer from Southampton to New York was the *RMS Olympic* of the White Star Line, a large ship with four stacks and three thousand passengers. "This is the sister ship of the *Titanic* that sunk two months ago," Fred said.

"Sister ship of the *Titanic*?" I exclaimed, with a hollowness in my stomach.

"Annie don't let Fred scare you," Ida Coan said.

"But she is the *Titanic's* sister," Fred insisted.

"I am pleased that the children are old enough to amuse themselves," Ida said, changing the subject. "While they spend the week playing games in the salon or running around the deck, the adults will be free to read and converse."

On the second day at sea Bobby began coughing and developed a fever, so I brought him to the ship's infirmary. The ship doctor asked Bobby to open his mouth and let out a gasp of horror when he looked inside. "It is diphtheria," he said in a hushed voice.

"I will need to keep him here in quarantine or we will have an epidemic on the ship. I do not have many beds."

"Two of my boys died from diphtheria," I said. "Do you have anti-toxin?"

"Unfortunately, I do not have the diphtheria anti-toxin to give your boy nor a respirator if he starts to struggle to breathe," the doctor replied. "I am only prepared to treat minor illnesses."

"You are less equipped than our dispensary in Tabriz," I exclaimed.

The next day Bobby was having trouble breathing and the doctor said his heart was beating irregularly. "It is a bad sign," he said. "It means the diphtheria toxin has entered the blood stream and is starting to cause organ damage."

"We should prepare for the worst," Sam said. "I will ask about a coffin and burial at sea."

"Burial at sea?" I exclaimed. "Bobby is still alive."

"Annie, we have been through this before," Sam said solemnly. "If we hang onto slivers of hope, we will be crushed when our hopes are shattered."

It is the curse of three, the Persian superstition that bad events happen in threes. "*Khoda be kheyr kone sevomisho,*" I whispered. "God have mercy on the third one."

When I ran into Ida Coan on the deck with tears in my eyes, she took my hand and said, "Let's walk together and find a place where you can cry on my shoulder." We walked in silence, and I sobbed until my eyes could no longer produce tears.

Two agonizing days passed. On the third day, after a long walk on the deck with Ida, I found Sam talking to the doctor in the infirmary. "Where did you go to school?" I heard Sam asking the doctor.

What? Sam is smiling.

"Bobby asked about his coffin this morning," Sam said when he saw me enter.

"What?" I replied.

"He heard the carpenter in the back of the infirmary nailing boards on his coffin and asked what the noise was," Sam replied.

"How morbid," I retorted. "Couldn't the carpenter work on it elsewhere?"

"The carpenter brought the coffin in and showed it to Bobby and said, 'Hey son, why did you waste my time making this thing. You look fit as a fiddle.'"

"And is Bobby fit as a fiddle?" I asked.

"He is still feverish and weak," the doctor said, "but breathing quite well."

"Will we need the coffin?" I asked.

"Bobby wants to put wheels on it and use it as a race cart," Sam said. "He wants to call it 'Bubble.'"

For the next day we were lulled by the expansive empty ocean, chatting happily about this and that.

"Look, on the horizon," Fred said. "The looming buildings of New York City are ahead of us."

The passengers crowded the deck, gripped by anticipation as we slowly came closer to the port. As the ship docked, I scanned the crowd below for familiar faces. "There they are, Sam," I screamed. "There below; it's Agnes and Rose. Oh, I want to leap down and hug them."

The *RMS Olympic* shuddered as the anchor was lowered. It seemed an eternity while we waited in queue to walk down the plank to the dock. Annie and Bobby waved to Rose and Agnes, screaming and jumping up and down as we slowly proceeded. Finally, I held my two older girls in my arms. *My precious ones.*

We stayed at Rosenvik, the Dulles estate in Englewood, for six weeks. Will had remarried to a charming woman, Helen Rollins, the daughter of a newspaper editor and publisher. She was twenty-three years younger than Will, spunky and intelligent, a graduate of Wellesley College.

In the afternoon, Will and Sam retired to the study to discuss politics, and Mother took the children to the garden to pick flowers. I sat with Helen on the veranda, and we reminisced about Wellesley College, where I had lived a year with my Aunt Maggie and Uncle Perez.

When she left to bring us glasses of lemonade, I sighed thinking about my sister Sophea. *Everything here is just the same, but she is gone.* "As for man," I murmured, "his days are like grass; he flourishes like a flower of the field; for the wind passes over it, and it is gone, and its place knows it no more."

"*Psalm of David*," Helen said. She had silently approached and stood at the porch door holding a tray with two glasses of lemonade and a plate of sugar cookies.

"Psalms 103:15-16," I said.

"You must miss your sister fearfully," she said.

"I do," I replied as a tear rolled down my cheek.

"Mrs. Rhea takes the children to Brookside Cemetery every Sunday. You should go with them."

I was relieved when Mother brought the children in from the garden so we could drop the subject. My twelve-year-old nephew Rhea handed me a large bouquet of pink and purple sweet peas. Helen produced a vase and set the flowers in water, and they perfumed the guest bedroom where Sam and I stayed until Sunday when I left them on my sister's grave.

The slab was inscribed: "Sophea Rhea, wife of William Dulles, 1866-1907. Till the day breaks and the shadows flee away."

"Will loved her very much," I said. "Song of Solomon 4:6 is the loss one feels when a lover departs."

After a week together in New Jersey, the Dulleses drove to West Hampton Beach while Sam and I took the children there by train. Will rented two adjacent houses on the beach with long porches facing the ocean. The children enjoyed frolicking in the water every afternoon as the adults watched them.

"Where is the furnished house that you rented in Indiana?" I asked Sam.

"The address is 36 South 6th street, on the corner of 6th and Gompers," Sam replied. "Three blocks from the Wilson homestead."

"I hope I can remember how to cook," I said. "In Tabriz, Kizbus and Esther cooked all the meals for the past eight years. I am quite out of practice."

"I promise not to complain," Sam replied, trying to conceal a grin under his mustache. "And it would not hurt for me to lose some weight."

"Mother asked me if she could live with us while we are here," I said. "I think she could help with the cooking. What do you think?"

"How long have you been planning this?" Sam asked.

"About nine months," I replied with an affectionate smile and patted the top of Sam's hand.

"Very well, two cooks are better than one."

On Labor Day, we received a telegram from Sam's brother Harry: "Mother very frail. Come soon."

"We need to hurry to Indiana," Sam told me. "I would not be able to console myself if she passed before I reached her bedside."

We packed up and bade farewell to Mother and the Dulleses. Agnes and Rose took the train with the rest of the family to see Grandmother Wilson and to help us settle into our rented house. As soon as we reached Indiana, we rushed over to the Wilson homestead. Sam's brothers Harry, Andy, John and Rob were there with sisters Jenny, Agnes, and Annie. "Dick and Ella will arrive on Friday from California," Harry said. "I hope they get here in time."

"Sam, you and Annie go up first," Jenny said. "I will bring the children up after you have had a chance to be with her alone."

Mother Wilson lay in bed with her eyes closed, her breathing shallow. Sam pulled a chair next to her bed and gently cradled her hand in his. "Mother, it is Samuel," he said. "Mother I am here." I held back a gasp and the flow of tears as her eyelids fluttered and her signature smile spread across her face. "My Samuel," she whispered. "You have been gone so long."

"I am here with you now. I am here with Annie and the children."

"Come close. Let me hold you." Her thin emaciated arms struggled to wrap around him, then she let go with a gasp. She fixed her eyes on me standing at the end of the bed. "Your wife looks like an angel. She will take me to heaven."

"Dick and Ella are coming from California," Sam said.

"Yes," Mother Wilson responded. "They should come soon."

"The children are here," Sam said.

"Let them come. Then I will sleep." By the time the children came upstairs, Mother Wilson had closed her eyes again. Rose, Agnes, Annie and Bobby took turns kissing her cheek, and then we left to settle into our rented house three blocks away.

Every day Sam came to the Wilson house to read Scriptures to his mother and sat by her side as she slept.

On October 12th at six thirty in the morning, Sam's mother, Anna Dick Wilson, died. On Friday afternoon Sam held a service at her home with all of her children present. They sang the same hymns that were sung at Sam's father's service – "Jesus, The Very Thought of You" and "Heaven is My Home." The internment was in the Wilson family plot in Oakland Cemetery.

"As we are already emotionally exhausted from our furlough, I think we should return home to Persia," Sam said.

"You need a break from your mission duties," I replied, "but I only hope our stay in America will not see any other tragedies."

CHAPTER 34

Furlough 1912 – 36 South 6th Street, Indiana, Pennsylvania

"HAVE YOU HEARD IF *SIPAHDOR* ARRIVED IN TABRIZ TO take over as Governor?" I asked.

"Fred Jessup wrote that with the arrival of *Sipahdor* the arrests and hangings of Nationalists abruptly stopped," Sam replied.

"That is a relief," I said. "Nightmares of the torture and hangings continue to haunt me."

"I will get more updates on the mission when I visit the Board in New York," Sam added. "At the end of October, I speak at Western Theological Seminary in Pittsburgh. The following week I give a lecture at Princeton Theological Seminary and will stay with my brother Rob. On my way home for Thanksgiving, I stop in New York at the Board of Foreign Missions to give a report on the Tabriz station. I will be traveling for the next six weeks."

"You should visit Agnes and Rose at Vassar," I said. "They would be disappointed to learn that you were in New York and did not travel to Poughkeepsie to see them."

"I can only squeeze in a short visit," Sam said.

"Daddy, we never have time to play together," Bobby whined.

"Soon you will have friends from school to play with and will not miss me when I am gone," Sam said.

"Annie is outgoing and a show-off," I said. "The schoolgirls ask her to speak 'heathen,' and she happily speaks to them in

Azeri. On the other hand, Bobby runs away, embarrassed to be different."

"Bobby will win friends with his sense of humor," Sam replied.

With Bobby and Annie attending Normal School, and Sam traveling to give lectures, I did not know how to occupy my time. Sam's sister Ella Stewart, with whom I developed a close friendship on our last furlough, now lived in California with her family. "I miss my work at the mission, teaching Bible class and visiting Persian women," I muttered.

"You should be enjoying a leisurely sabbatical," Sam said. "Aren't there books you would like to read? Maybe *The Lost World* by Arthur Conan Doyle or *Tarzan of the Apes* by Edgar Burroughs."

"I will go mad if I do not find other activities," I replied.

A week later, a letter from Mother arrived: "Foster and I plan to come for Christmas and would like to stay through the winter." *So much for my leisurely sabbatical.*

Agnes, Sam's youngest sister called on me. "Every year we had Thanksgiving at Mother Wilson's house," she said. "Jenny feels it would be too sad to have it there without Mother, so I have offered to host Thanksgiving at our house. Will you be coming?"

"We would not refuse your offer for an instant," I exclaimed. "I have never roasted a turkey and was dreading my first attempt, having not touched a stove in years."

Agnes laughed. "You can come to my house any time and I will teach you to cook my recipes."

"I should take advantage of your offer so that my husband and children do not starve," I replied.

Sam took the *Cleveland, Cincinnati and Chicago Express* No. 19, the 10:48 o'clock sleeper, from Philadelphia. It was due to arrive Thanksgiving morning at the Blairsville junction, where Sam would take the local train to Indiana.

"We will meet your father at the train station about eleven o'clock in the morning," I told Annie, Bobby and Rose, who was home from Vassar for the holiday. "Then we will join the rest of the Wilson family at Aunt Agnes' house for Thanksgiving dinner."

The regional train from Blairsville to Indiana arrived on schedule at eleven o'clock, but Sam was not on board. "Where is Daddy?" Bobby asked.

"Let's go into the station," I said. "I will ask if they know if the train from Philadelphia was delayed."

The station attendant told us that there was a train wreck about midnight outside of Philadelphia. "The *Cleveland, Cincinnati and Chicago Express* No. 19 derailed at Glen Loch and is blocking the tracks," he said. "They brought in another train to take the uninjured passengers west from there about three hours later."

I sighed looking at the expectant faces of my children. "Let's go to Thanksgiving dinner at Aunt Agnes' house. Your father will probably join us later this afternoon."

Not wanting to burden others with my concerns about Sam, I conversed with the Wilson family wearing a cheerful façade. That evening Sam still had not returned and there was no word as to his whereabouts. After putting the children to bed, Rose sat up with me. At eleven at night, Sam's brother Dick drove up to the house with a telegram.

"Sam was injured and taken to a hospital in West Chester," Dick said.

My heart sunk into my shoes. "I must go to the hospital," I cried.

"The last train from Indiana has already departed," Dick said. "We can call the hospital tomorrow morning."

I did not sleep all night, worrying about Sam. The memory of Sam's appendicitis haunted me. Joe Cochran saved him in the nick of time riding "chapper" from Urmia. *At least there are good doctors here who do not live two days by horse away.*

In the morning, I informed the children that their father was in the hospital.

"Will Daddy be okay?" Annie wailed.

"We need to talk to the doctor," I replied. I called the hospital in West Chester and fretted as I waited for the doctor to come to the phone, wringing my hands.

"Your husband injured his back," the doctor said. "It may only be a sprain, but we need to perform a more extensive evaluation."

"Is he in pain?" I asked.

"He appears to be, but he refuses opium," the doctor said. "He mentioned something about Persian opium addicts."

"Is he able to speak to me?" I asked.

"No, he cannot be reached by phone. He told me to tell you not to come to the hospital."

"What?" I exclaimed.

"We expect he will be ready to go home in two weeks."

I tried my best to relieve the children's consternations. "Your father will be home before Christmas."

Friday evening Sam's brother Rob called. "The *Evening Star* listed Rev. S. G. Wilson as among the injured in the Glen Loch train wreck. How is he?"

"I apologize for not sending you a telegram," I said. "I am still waiting to learn how serious his injuries are."

"The paper says that the coach and seven Pullman cars were whiplashed twenty feet down an embankment and then rolled off a coal freight train traveling on a parallel track below," Rob said. "Hopefully he was not in the wooden coach car when it was crushed below the steel Pullmans. Four died in the wreck and over fifty were injured."

"Rob, I do not know what car he was in," I replied. "I assume he was in a Pullman sleeper when it derailed about midnight."

"When are you going to the hospital?"

"Sam asked me not to come." I gasped, as tears tumbled down my cheeks.

There was silence on the other end. Then Rob said, "Sam is afraid."

Two weeks later Sam was delivered by train in the care of an orderly. Dick and Blair Sutton drove them to the house and carried Sam upstairs. "What is his condition?" I asked the orderly.

"The x-rays show that two vertebrae between his shoulders were fractured and ligaments torn," he said.

"Will he be able to sit up and walk again?" I asked.

"It will take time. We will have a better idea regarding his prognosis when the inflammation resolves."

It was hard to see Sam, a man of strong physique, crippled by pain and barely able to sit up in bed. At night his groans kept me awake. The lack of sleep and angst about Sam's uncertain prognosis wore on me. *What will our lives be like from now on? Will we be able to return to Persia?*

Rose and Agnes returned from Vassar for Christmas and pitched in with holiday preparations, and Mother and Foster arrived a week later. Sam's sister Jenny invited Mother, Foster and our children to Christmas dinner at the old Wilson house. Sam and I had soup and spent a quiet Christmas together; I read Charles Dicken's *Christmas Carol* aloud while he lay in bed.

When I finished reading, Sam said, "God bless us, every one. I hope I do not end up like Tiny Tim Cratchit."

On Sam's birthday, February 11th, I proudly baked a cake with Mother's oversight. I invited Dick and Blair Sutton to the birthday party to help carry Sam downstairs. After they arrived, Blair was telling jokes and we were distracted. A figure appeared in my peripheral vision, and I turned to see that Sam had managed to get out of bed, dress and come down the stairs. He heaved himself into a chair in the parlor with a groan.

"Sam?" we said in unison.

"It was a feat of strength and determination," he replied with a sigh. He was smiling, but his arms were quivering. *Oh please, let this mean that he is getting better.*

It was the first step, and Sam was weak from being bedridden for three months. Although a strain, he insisted on sitting at least four hours a day with a typewriter. "I need to work on the lectures I promised Allegheny Theological Seminary on the migration of Muslims," he said.

It was a blessing that he could now sit up, type and occupy his mind. Each day when the children returned from school, he asked them how lessons went. He seemed happy, but I knew he was concerned about what would happen when our year's furlough in America ended this summer.

In June Sam insisted on going to Agnes' graduation ceremony at Vassar. She was one of the speakers and read a story she wrote about a Persian peasant bringing melons to a bazaar and incorporated a section on the dire situation in Persia. Sam, a man devoted to education, was proud and elated to see his first child graduate from college.

After graduation Sam returned to Indiana on the train with Mother and Foster. As a graduation present, I rented rooms on Rye's Beach for Agnes and her friend Marcia. I was embarrassed when Marcia's father, a banker, gave his daughter a Model T Ford as a graduation present. *We could never afford to give the children automobiles on a missionary salary.* "You will not need a car while you are living in New York City and going to Teachers College at Columbia," I told Agnes.

When we returned, Dick picked us up from the train station. "I stopped by to see if Foster needed any help with Sam, and he told me that Sam insists on climbing the stairs by himself now," Dick said. "He is making good progress, isn't he?"

"He is doing better," I replied, "but I insist that someone be there when he goes up and down the stairs in case he slips and falls."

I found Sam in his study reading letters when I returned. "Some letters from the Western Mission arrived in your absence," he said. "Louise Shedd sent us her annual report with several interesting stories about patients at the hospital in Urmia. Apparently, the hospital was closed for two months after Dr. Packard contracted typhoid. Everyone was frightened that they would lose another doctor, but he is healthy and strong and was able to shake it off."

"Read me some of her stories," I said and settled down next to Sam.

"Louise says this spring when the hospital reopened, she made rounds every day reading Scriptures in Syriac and Azeri to the patients. One patient woke the entire ward one night exclaiming that he had a vision of Christ standing next to his bed, waiting to receive him in heaven. He lingered for a day, all the time in a transport of joyful anticipation of his release and then passed away. She said that an expression of perfect peace and happiness lingered on his face."

"I am sure he affected the other patients around him," I said.

"She writes: 'His death cast a radiance over the whole hospital and others longed to know what faith could make death a joy instead of a terror.' "

"What else does she say?"

"Her other story is about the wife of a Kurdish sheikh," Sam said. " 'She came enveloped in a pink veil with silver threads and wearing a necklace and turban richly adorned with gold pieces. Six maids dressed in colorful silk were at her bidding, and six warriors armed to the teeth protected them. Despite all her accessories, she was friendly and open, even requesting that I read to her from my Bible.' The other letter is a report from Fred Jessup on the schools in Tabriz."

"Goodness, I hope all is well."

"He writes: 'The Boys' School has two hundred and seventy-two boys enrolled. Two are the sons of Princess Ezzat, the daughter of Mozaffar ad-Din.' "

"Ezzat's boys are at our school?" I exclaimed. "I can hardly wait to see them."

"The Girls' School has also fared well with a separate department with fifty-eight Persian Muslims girls," Sam continued. "The most substantial change to the mission was the arrival of Dr. Charles Lamme and his wife and the transfer of Robert and Mary Labaree from Urmia to Tabriz. It is good to hear that the missionary force is expanding."

"Do they need us anymore?" I asked.

"Well, of course, they do," Sam said. "Jessup says that eleven boys joined the church. He writes: 'Nearly every boy when asked what had first led him to desire to follow Christ replied that it was talks with Mrs. Wilson, her prayers that we would give our hearts to God. She is greatly needed for her personal work with the boys, mothering and caring for them.'"

"I wonder if the Persian women who came to my prayer meetings miss me," I said.

"The Persian women at the dispensary and those that Lucille Pittman visits in your absence ask when you will be returning."

I wish I knew the answer.

At the end of June, the family, including Mother, took the train to Chautauqua, New York, while Foster stayed in Indiana. Sam had agreed to be the resident chaplain at Presbyterian House on the Chautauqua Institute campus for the summer. A special podium was built so he could preach while sitting. Sam was enthusiastic about leading church services in their quaint chapel.

"It will be a small congregation, sixty or seventy people," he said, "not too challenging."

I seated guests and served food in the dining room, and Agnes and Rose helped with laundry. The children were enrolled in classes and activities at the Chautauqua Institute and spent time swimming, sailing and canoeing in the lake. Mother enjoyed the comradery of the older guests and reading on the second story porch each day in a rocking chair.

On June 29th, a telegram arrived from Sam's brother Rob: "Howard died yesterday. Funeral July 2nd — Indiana."

"Howard was only twenty-three," I exclaimed. "Rob and Ellen must be devastated."

"I can't possibly leave with daily services to give," Sam said. "Could you and Foster represent our family at the funeral?"

Although I hated to leave, I could not refuse. The funeral was held in the Wilson homestead, and sister Annie's husband, Rev. Alfred Barr, came from Baltimore to lead the service. Rob and his wife Ellen and their other children were distraught. "He was our only son," Rob said. "He will be sorely missed."

"We had no idea that he had a heart condition," Ellen added, "but with heart disease there nothing that can be done."

It was strange to be with the Wilson family without Sam, yet when we stood around the grave in a circle holding hands, I felt I belonged there with them. "Let us pass a hand squeeze around the circle to bind us together," Rev. Alfred Barr said. When Ellen, who stood next to me, squeezed my hand, tears came to my eyes.

This is my family. If anything ever happens to Sam, I know I can depend on their family loyalty.

"A thick letter arrived from the mission in Tabriz," I told Sam.

"It is likely a draft of the Annual Report to the Board that they want me to review," Sam said. He shuffled through the pages of a fifteen-to-twenty-page letter and shook his head. "The Russian soldiers are still causing problems. This is what Loretta Van Hook wrote: 'With Russian soldiers in Tabriz, two evils have developed: widespread intoxication of the troops and the establishment of houses of prostitution in the Armenian quarters. The latter are conducted with such noisy revelry that they draw the attention of young male Persians. These bordellos have the attraction of novelty to the Persians in addition to the usual attractions of such places.

"Not having previous experience contending with this issue, we asked our Y.M.C.A. to take up the matter. At the end of February, the Y.M.C.A. scheduled meetings in the mission church to protest the opening of houses for prostitution — three meetings for men and three for women. The speakers were prominent Armenians including physicians, teachers, and the Armenian Bishop.

"At the women's meetings, I gave an address on the responsibility of motherhood, presenting the highest ideals. The response from the Armenian women was so gratifying that I consider it one of my most successful efforts to uplift Persian women. We are glad to report that the Russian Consul closed some of the brothels and conditions have improved in some respect."

"Brothels," I exclaimed. "What a nuisance. Any news from Will Vanneman?"

"He has sad news — Dr. Edna Orcutt died on March 8th from pneumonia," Sam said.

"Oh dear, she only started missionary work the year before we left," I bemoaned. "Her death is a great loss to the women's medical effort at the mission."

"Despite her death, the new medical buildings are coming along," Sam said. "In March ground was broken on the edge of the city for the Kirkwood-Whipple Hospital for women and a new hospital for men, both under one roof. This year Will Vanneman and Charles Lamme saw twelve thousand patients in the dispensary and made over a thousand home visits."

"When the hospital is in running order, it will allow our medical work to reach more distant villages," I added. "Any news on the schools?"

"Yes, we have a brief report from Fred Jessup on the Boys' School: 233 students were enrolled this year, 136 Christian Armenians and 97 Persian Muslims," Sam said. "Fred is trying to get the boys interested in athletics. He held a Field Day, the first in the school's history. There were fourteen track and field events, followed by a football match. He split the boys into Red and Blue teams, and apparently there was keen rivalry, much to the enjoyment of the large crowd of spectators."

"What a wonderful addition to the school's traditions," I exclaimed.

"The Girls' School report section is from Helen Grove, since Lillie Beaber is managing the building of the new dormitory," Sam said. "Enrollment is similar to last year. They now have a weekly Bible meeting with Muslim women in the *Charandab* quarter south of *Lawala*."

"What about the Wednesday afternoon meeting with the Muslim women that Mary Bradford and I started?"

"It has been continued by Grettie Holliday and Mary Labaree. Grettie adds that the women ask, 'When will Mrs. Wilson return? We love her passionate stories.' And I only reply, 'I wish I could answer.'"

I wish I could answer too.

During Sam's convalescence he spent his time researching and writing two books: *Bahaism and Its Claims; a Study of the Religion promulgated by Baha Ullah and Abdul Baha* and *Modern Movements Among Muslims*. The Board and Robert Speer were astounded that he was able to be so productive and encouraged him to continue until he was ready to return to the field. I was also glad the Sam gained a sense of accomplishment and had a diversion from his frustration about his physical condition.

At the end of June, the newspapers reported that the heir to the Austrian throne, Archduke Franz Ferdinand, and his wife were shot in Sarajevo by a nationalist Serbian, Gavrilo Princip.

"Why did a Serbian nationalist shoot him?" I asked.

"They want to end Austria's rule of Serbia," Sam replied. "I wonder how Austria will respond?"

A month later Austria, backed by Germany's Kaiser Wilhelm II, declared war on Serbia. Russia's Tsar Nicholas II, who supported Serbia, mobilized troops, and asked its allies France and Great Britain to side with Russia if war broke out. Within days Germany declared war on Russia and France, then sent troops across Belgium to invade France. The German advance into France was halted and held at bay through prolonged trench warfare.

Agnes who was home for the summer from Columbia Teachers College was hoping to complete her master's degree in the spring of 1915 and spend six months studying at the Sorbonne in Paris. She was crestfallen when Sam told her the war would likely prevent her from traveling to Europe.

"When will the war be over?" Agnes cried.

"It is hard to tell," Sam said. "We would also like to return to Persia next year, but the war may make it difficult."

After the children were out of earshot I said to Sam, "We have not talked about returning to Persia next summer. I now have the responsibility of taking care of Mother. She will be eighty next year and has nowhere else to go."

"My brothers and sisters admire and love your mother," Sam said. "They affectionately call her 'Grandma Rhea.' Surely they would help to look after her."

I shook my head and sighed.

Sam was quiet for several minutes, looking vacantly out the window. "We can discuss this again after a few months when we have a better idea how long the war will last."

Sam is determined to continue his work at the mission but going back would mean leaving Mother alone. The war at least gives us some time to think about the future.

CHAPTER 35

Furlough 1915

"ANY NEWS ON HOW THE WAR IS AFFECTING THE MISSIONS?"
I asked.

"Although Persia is a neutral country, the missionaries of
both Urmia and Tabriz are experiencing serious consequences of
the war," Sam said. "The armies of the Central Powers and the
Allies use the northwestern corner of Persia as a passage to the
battlefields."

Sam read from a letter he received from Rev. Fred Jessup in
Tabriz. He wrote:

"On November 1st, 1914, the Ottoman Turks declared a *jihad*,
or Holy War, in support of the Central Powers and against the
Allies. In December a small force of Turkish troops crossed into
Persia south of Urmia, but we thought nothing of it, knowing
that the Russian forces here would be able to suppress them. On
the last day of December, the Russians began to withdraw from
Tabriz, and there was general panic among the Armenians and
other native Christians fearing massacre by the Muslim Turks.
The Armenians fled toward the Russian border, and out of 750 or
more families only about 250 remained.

"We were barraged by people asking to take refuge in the mission compound. The Board only granted us permission to admit
Europeans and any Persians connected with the mission. Then
it was decided that the missionaries of all other denominations

should come to our compound. You can imagine the rushed work during the first days of January — clearing the schoolrooms for the crowds of anxious people, setting rules for who could be admitted, making our own houses ready for the advent of the missionary families. For example, your house, in which I had been living alone on Friday, by Saturday night contained five families, consisting of ten adults and seven children; and whereas up to that time Dr. Vanneman and I had been having our meals alone, now in my dining room all the Americans ate together, nineteen adults and several children.

"By this time almost all the Europeans had left the city, including the Consuls of the Allied Powers; the banks were closed, and the Indo-European telegraph office was shuttered. The Europeans who remained sought refuge at the mission, along with several prominent Muslims. Four hundred refugees of all nationalities and religions came to us. All lived together with goodwill and lack of friction.

"By Tuesday, January 5th, the Russian troops had left Tabriz and on Friday, the 8th, the Turkish army and the Kurds entered. For the next four weeks of the Turkish occupation, we were given a great opportunity for evangelistic work; instead of having to seek a congregation, we had a large one within our gates. Our night church services, which were typically attended by fifty to sixty people, had one hundred and fifty in attendance, and we held religious services in the assembly hall of the Boys' School. The congregation was composed of those whose hearts were softened by our common danger and life together, and all listened with the most earnest attention.

"January 30th was indeed a welcome day when the sound of cannons and machine guns to the north signaled that the Russian soldiers were returning. In God's providence we and the many lives entrusted to us were kept safe from harm. When the roads were once again open and word reached us from other places, we began to hear of the terrible plight of the Christians elsewhere, especially Urmia and Salmas."

"Did the Turkish army also invade Urmia?" I asked.

"My guess is that the situation is worse in Urmia, being closer to the Turkish border," Sam said. "We have not received any letters from the Urmia mission for some months. I expected to hear from Fred Coan and William Shed. It is a bad sign."

"Perhaps mail from Urmia has stopped," I said.

In June, I was relieved to receive a letter from Fred Coan. He wrote:

"On New Year's Day, we received one hundred and forty of our Muslim and Christian friends 'to bless our New Year.' Then, like a thunderbolt from a clear sky, we were informed the next day at ten o'clock at night that the Russian army was withdrawing. The departure of the Russians left the Assyrian and Armenian Christians defenseless from the Turks and Kurds camped a few miles away. By midnight there was a mass exodus from the Christian villages. People left cattle in the stables and their household belongings and hurried away to save their lives. About twenty-five thousand stayed.

"On Sunday morning we put American flags over the entrances to the mission and thousands of Assyrian and Armenian Christians poured into the gates until every room and storeroom was full, not lying down but sitting or standing. By the end of the week there were over fifteen thousand refugees in our yards.

"On Monday, January 4th, Henry Packard rode to Geogtapa carrying American and Turkish flags. His mission was to speak with the Kurdish chieftains to prevent the massacre of Persian villagers.

Some of the Kurds had spent weeks in our hospital and had been operated upon by Dr. Packard, so he was in a good position to negotiate. When Dr. Packard first tried to signal to them, they did not recognize him and kept shooting, but then one of them shouted, 'It is the *Hakim Sahib*. Stop firing.'

"Dr. Packard pleaded for the lives of the people and after several hours' entreaty, they agreed to let the people go with him. Dr. Packard brought fifteen hundred more refugees to the Urmia mission. The number totaled seventeen thousand by the end of the month. The Osmanli officers promised safety for all within the mission gates, but there was no certainty this would occur.

"Lucy, the daughter of Assyrian priest Kasha David, came to the Urmia mission with her baby from the village of Gulpashan. She told us that when Kurds surrounded the village, the people fled in terror to their roofs. Kurds surrounded her house and commanded her to come down. When she reached the ground, she saw a Kurd looking intently at her younger sister, Sherin. 'Pull your veil over your face,' she called to her. 'Do not look into his face.' Sherin daubed her face with mud and tried to conceal it with her veil, but her beautiful dark eyes and rosy cheeks were difficult to hide. As the Kurd dragged Sherin away, she implored Lucy to save her. 'Every night, when I try to sleep, I hear her entreaties,' Lucy sobbed.

"A Jew brought us word from Usknuk that Kasha David's daughter, Sherin, was there in the house of a Kurd. He was trying to force her to convert to Islam, he told us, but she replied to his threats saying, 'You may kill me, but I will never deny my faith.' Her stubbornness helped us to get her back.

"I was alerted that our letters could not be sent, so I stopped writing and now continue five months later.

"As I made the rounds of our mission yards and visited refugees herded together in dark storerooms and classrooms in the

Girls' School, I was struck by a change — the absence of small children; hundreds died during these last months. An epidemic of dysentery, due largely to lack of proper food, killed many young children. Thousands of people were without fuel and with very little clothing. The conditions were about as miserable as they could be — a combination of cold, hunger, filth and sickness.

"The verse from Romans 8:32 helped to keep my faith steady: 'He that spared not His own Son. If He gave his Son to die for us, it is impossible that He should refuse us anything that will help or bless us. He has nothing he values more than his Son.'

"Urmia missionaries also became sick with typhoid in February, twelve adults and two children. On February 27th, the teacher of the missionary children, Mlle. Perrochet, a Swiss girl, passed away, and Louise Shedd died on May 17th. Since we could not take them to the missionary cemetery in Seir, we buried them in my garden. Harry Packard and my daughter Elizabeth were also sick but recovered. In those weeks we were not only walking in the valley of the shadow of death, but we were dwelling there.

"At the end of May we watched from our roof as six thousand Russian troops marched through Urmia. It was a blessed sight for the besieged people, and we are emptying our yards of refugees. The stench of the mission grounds is almost unbearable as that yard has been used as a latrine for thousands of people for more than five months. The property damage from the refugees in the Urmia station is large, and the summer residences in Seir are in utter ruins from the plundering of the Kurds. We have been trying to contact the other missions for weeks but were unable to send or receive messages until the Russian army opened the roads. One of the hard things during these five long months was our isolation from the outside world.

"Amid all the disorder the mission stood firm. 'The storms beat, and the rain descended and the floods came and the winds blew and beat upon the house, and it fell not, for it was founded upon rock.' Matthew 7:25."

"William Shedd lost too wives in Persia, Adela and now Louise," I said. "How sad. I feel for him."

"I cannot imagine what it was like with seventeen thousand refugees for five months," Sam said.

Another letter came from Rev. Robert Labaree describing the exodus of Christians from Persia to the Caucasus, where he followed them. He wrote:

"The people of the Urmia plain who fled from Persia walked seven days through the slush and mud to the Russian border. As they grew more tired, they discarded quilts, extra clothing and even bread; it was a choice of whether to carry their bedding or their babies. Many of the weaker ones never made it to Julfa but lay down by the roadside and died. At night many could not find shelter, and those who could found standing room only.

"The story I heard from many was the same, with only a few different details. Here is an example: One old man with two daughters-in-law and six grandchildren fled from the village of Karagoz. The women took turns carrying the children. The old man stumbled along, but at last he gave out, lay down by the roadside and died. The two women and their children pressed on for two days longer. When one of them gave birth to a baby by the roadside, the mother tore off her dress, wrapped the baby in the pieces and resumed the weary tramp. While giving birth, two of the other children were separated from the party and lost.

"Crossing the border from Persia, the two women found their husbands waiting for them in Julfa. Two days later, a kind-hearted Russian soldier brought a wagonful of lost children and the parents found their two little ones among them. Unfortunately, the children were so emaciated by their hardships that they died shortly afterward. People dying and children being born by the way were commonplace on this journey, but not everyone had a combination of such misfortunes.

"Time and time again I have wondered whether the panic-stricken exodus of the Christian Assyrians and Armenians was not a terrible mistake; whether the people would have fared better if they stayed at home. As the stories of the sufferings of those who remained behind and were subjected to the cruelties by the Kurds began to reach us — stories of bloodshed and forced apostacy, of women and girls being carried off to a life worse than death — I revised my judgment. At the end of their journey the villagers in the Caucasus responded to the needs of the refugees and provided shelter and food in an out-poring of compassion. Being in a strange land is better than the fate of those who remained at home."

"I wish I could help with the relief effort for the poor Christian Armenians and Assyrians," Sam said. "I am very stirred by the sense of needing to act. No longer being a total invalid, if there is something I can do then I will do it."

"And you know that I will support you," I said.

The first week of October a letter for Sam arrived from Columbia University. "It is from a Professor Samuel Dutton," he said. "Maybe it has something to do with Agnes' position as Secretary of Religious Organizations, or a request for a contribution; the latter most likely."

Sam let the letter in his hands fall to his lap and stared blankly at the wall.

"What is it, dear?" I asked.

"Professor Dutton is the Secretary of the Armenian Relief Committee," Sam replied. "It is a joint request from Cleveland Dodge, president of the Relief Committee, and Henry Morgenthau, the American Ambassador to the Ottoman Empire. They have raised sixty thousand dollars and are splitting the funds amongst various relief efforts. They are asking if I would be willing to help distribute relief aid to refugees in the Caucasus."

"How did they locate you?" I asked.

"Another member of their committee, James Barton, the head of the American Board of Foreign Missions, is well familiar with my success in running the finances of the mission in Tabriz. He contacted Robert Speer for my address. He says, 'You can make a dollar go farther than any other man.' I must admit that his comment has some validity."

"Since they are located in New York City you could see Agnes on your trips to their office," I said cheerily, hoping this was what was being asked of Sam.

"They are not asking me to go to New York," Sam said. "They are asking me to travel to the Russian Caucasus."

"What?"

"They are asking me to work with the American Consul in Tiflis and travel around the Caucasus delivering relief aid. What do you think?"

I was speechless.

"Annie, what do you think?"

"How long would you be gone?" I asked.

"It is hard to say, perhaps until the Armenians can safely return to their native lands. I wish you could come with me, but with the war, women and children are forbidden from traveling through Europe."

"When do you need to give them an answer?" I asked. "We should discuss the consequences."

"By the end of the week," Sam said. "I will need to leave by mid-November."

I could barely see straight I was so shocked and confused. *How can he even think of going?*

It was a momentous decision.

Seeing how elated Sam was that he was going to contribute to a worthy cause, I tried hard to hide my feelings of dismay. Sam wrote many letters to the missionaries in Persia, which I took to the post office to mail for him. I wondered what he was telling them, but I respected his privacy and never thought of trying to use the steam from the tea kettle to secretly open them. *Well perhaps I wanted to, but never tried.*

Some days it angered me when he spoke proudly to his brothers and sisters about his upcoming adventure — riding on horseback to deliver aid in distant mountain villages, preaching the gospel of hope to the helpless distressed people.

I will also be helpless and distressed being responsible for this family alone. At times when I found myself resenting his leaving, I prayed for strength to continue while he was gone, I believed that God would help me. *'God is our refuge and strength, a well proved help in our trouble.' Psalms 46:1.*

The Presbyterian Church in Indiana held a farewell meeting for Sam and he asked them to sing *Guide Me, O Thou Great Jehovah*: "Guide me, O my great Redeemer, pilgrim through this barren land; I am weak, but you are mighty; hold me with your powerful hand."

Hold him tight God, hold him to Your breast.

The words were not spoken, but we both knew there was a chance that we would never see each other again. We embraced and I held my head to his chest to listen to his heart beating. *This is the husband I have loved for thirty years and he is leaving me, perhaps to never return.*

I wiped away my tears, smiled and said, "Dear soldier, be on your way."

CHAPTER 36

Letters from Sam 1915-1916

ON NOVEMBER 18ᵀᴴ SAM'S STEAMER LEFT NEW YORK for Bergen, Norway. Although Norway was a neutral country and Sam was sailing on a Norwegian-American Line, I was anxious about his safe passage. In July a Norwegian ship, the *SS Tronhjemsfjord*, was torpedoed by a German U-41 submarine.

Sam promised he would send letters as soon as he reached Bergen. After Thanksgiving when I received his first letter I breathed a sigh of relief, but his journey was not over. He would take another ship through the Norwegian Sea to Archangel. I prayed for his safety and was overjoyed when I received his letter from Russia.

Sam was delayed a few days in Petrograd waiting for certification from the Russian government to be allowed to travel and conduct relief work in the Caucasus. A series of letters were postmarked from train stops traveling south through Russia, the last being from Nalchik on Christmas Day. A few days later he arrived at Tiflis by troika.

"December 28ᵗʰ, Tiflis

"I have arrived at the American embassy in Tiflis. Richard Hill and Consul Felix Willoughby-Smith are overjoyed to see me. I am going out on an expedition with Mr. Hill tomorrow to see first-hand the extent of the refugee situation. They told me that the first wave of the Armenian exodus from the Ottoman Empire arrived between January and April, about one hundred thousand. This was followed in July and August by a second wave of two hundred thousand Armenians who fled after the Russians withdrew from Van.

"Richard Hill gave me an account of the exodus observed by a man he dined with from Persia who was by traveling by train to Tiflis. 'When he reached the plain of Erivan, it was black with a slow-moving mass of humanity on the horizon as far as the eye could see. It must have numbered two hundred and fifty thousand, moving listlessly in the sweltering heat. Children dying by the hundreds, old men and women falling by the roadside. He found the wails of woe and misery so unbearable to hear that he closed his window and wept.' They had been marching for weeks. I cannot imagine what I will see tomorrow, but we will have to make careful decisions how to distribute the twenty-five thousand dollars of relief funds we presently have secured."

I must try to help to do my part and secure relief funds from members of the church and community.

"Erivan, December 30th

"On the train to Erivan, Richard Hill told me some heart-warming stories of how the Russian soldiers helped lost Armenian children, picking them up from the roadside in their wagons and sharing their rations. One story was particularly touching, of a soldier who had built a small fire and a little Armenian girl stiff with cold snuggled up next to him and fell asleep in the folds of his army coat. For several hours he apparently suffered sitting in a cramped position to let her sleep.

"When we reached Erivan, we were told there were twenty thousand refugees gathered in large buildings, orphanages and homes of local Armenians. In the villages some were given shelter in bakehouses, stables and barns, heated by smoky ovens or the bodies of oxen and buffalo. The cold winter winds from the Caucasus range and Mount Ararat blow down on the Erivan plain, and most of the refugees have insufficient clothes and bedding. Some wear shredded rags or are half-naked. In the rooms of a barracks four people lay under a single coverlet, head to foot.

"We heard many pitiful stories. A woman from Ardjish near Lake Van told us, 'All our men were collected from the bazaar and taken before the government. After dark we heard gunshots; they killed them, and we fled in the night.' Another woman told us, 'There were four hundred and fifty households in our village, and only twenty men escaped the massacre, some surviving by lying under dead bodies. A boy survived by hiding under his mother's skirts. Our pretty girls were carried off, and we were stripped naked.' The woman hid her face in her hands, silent to the rest of their suffering and outrage.

"The refugees are living in wretched conditions, crowded together in filthy shelters with at most bread and water as food for the past months. In the field, we also have only bread and water, supplemented with hard-boiled eggs. However, yesterday we attended a reception with Grand Duke Nicholas Nikolaevich, the commander-in-chief of Russian forces in the Caucasus. He assigned us to the Erivan province for relief work. We were entertained in the evening by the Catholicos, the supreme head of the Armenian church in Etchmiadzin, a town near Erivan. He thanked the American people for their sympathy and aid to his distressed people.

"The American Far East Relief effort works independently, but collaboratively with the other relief efforts by the Russians. *The Bezhenets* (Refugees) weekly newspaper, interviewed us and has agreed to publicize our aid work to the Armenian community. All wish us 'Godspeed.'

"We will be returning to Tiflis for supplies of clothes and bedding to distribute to the refugees, where I will write again."

"Tiflis, January 15th

"General Tamamshev, the head of the Russian Department of Refugees on the Caucasus Front, advised us that the greatest need of the refugees is for bedding and clothing. Their relief efforts have focused on supplying food stations, establishing orphanages, and arranging occupation of empty buildings by the refugees. The Russian troops have picked up four thousand stranded children from the roads in wagons and transferred them to the orphanages.

"After some discussion with the other relief organizations, we have decided to focus our efforts on the districts in the mountains — NorBayazid (Gavar), on the east shore of beautiful Lake *Gokcha* (Lake Sevan), Gagakh (Tavush), and Vayots Dzor, to the south. There are twenty thousand refugees in the mountain villages who have been sleeping for months on the bare ground, and warm clothes and bedding do not exist. Besides the mountain districts, we also plan to distribute in Samaghar, on the plain directly below Mount Ararat. Being familiar with the roads that we have taken many times traveling through the Caucasus to and from furlough, you should be able to imagine my picturesque surroundings.

"Richard Hill and I have secured seven thousand ready-made garments in Tiflis and large quantities of bedding. Consul Willoughby-Smith's efforts have helped us to overcome the difficulties of transportation. The Russians will grant us freight cars to Erivan, which we greatly appreciate considering their army transport demands as great as they are.

"General Tamamshev surprised us by providing a list of all the refugees in the districts that we will be serving; each head of the family is listed with their place of residence, the number in the household, and the sex and age of each member. We have been instructed to write next to each name whatever is given; for example, what garment or article of bedding was supplied and the amount of bread allowance, typically fifteen kopeks, or five cents, per mouth per day. The Russian Department of Refugees is more organized and efficient that we had expected.

"We will now return to Erivan and begin distribution."

"February 21st, Erivan

"I have returned from distributing our first load of clothing and bedding in the mountain villages. Our load arrived from Tiflis by train and was taken to the villages three to four days journey from the railroad in covered wagons and oxcarts. The tales of distress that the refugees have poured into our ears are heart rendering, and their grateful thanks and prayers repay our efforts manyfold. On receipt of an article of clothing, happy tears flow from their eyes and gratitude bursts from their hearts. It is hard to keep them from kissing our hands, as is their custom. It is surely a privilege to minister to their needs and provide clothes that warm their bodies and their hearts to God and man.

"Before leaving Erivan I established a workshop for making additional clothing and bedding. Many refugees asked to help make clothes and I have enlisted any who can use a sewing machine. These downtrodden people are rising up to help others like themselves. Richard Hill supervised them in my absence, and I returned to find ten thousand garments waiting to be distributed.

"Giving the refugees in Erivan an opportunity to be industrious gives them courage and hope. Seeing this I have obtained tools for our workshop to allow refugees to learn or apply their skills at various trades.

"In a day's time I will be off again to the mountain villages."

"March 2ⁿᵈ, Dilijan

"I now travel with Armenian assistants from Erivan who help me distribute clothing and bedding. A few days ago, I arrived in Dilijan, a beautiful mountain village and a summer resort for the wealthy in Tiflis. Many vacant rooms are available for the refugees here amid winter. There is also a hospital set up for relief work with over one hundred patients.

"Yesterday was our distribution in Dilijan and today in Jarkhech (Haghartsin), eight miles east. The refugee families are given notice of our distribution and crowd around the storeroom we set up. We have a system where numbered coupons are handed to each family, and one of us lays a comforter on the floor and throws the garments specified for that family onto it, then gathers the four corners together and they carry the bundle away on their back. We often hear young girls squealing at the sight of a bright colored dress, or a little boy chuckling when he realizes the red shirt is meant for him. The mother or father give thanks, saying 'God bless you,' or 'May God keep you in his heavenly kingdom.'

"Tomorrow we go to Karakilisa (Vanadzar), also called 'Black Church,' where I will meet up with Rev. Frederick MacCallum and George Gracey who volunteered for relief work, coming from a mission in Turkey. Richard Hill has returned to Tiflis to purchase and ship additional clothing and bedding to Erivan."

"March 6th, Karakilisa

"We have been waiting for our goods for distribution in Karakilisa and the surrounding twenty-six villages to arrive by train. Consul Willoughby-Smith arranged for a freight car, but due to military necessity our car was taken for a Russian army shipment to the Front. After some days Richard Hill was suddenly alerted that the train would come at 1:30 that afternoon, so he hustled about and had the one hundred and forty-six bales loaded on a transfer wagon. After some hours waiting for the train, the men who drove the transfer wagon dumped the bales on the platform and left. Hill waited with our goods until two o'clock in the morning when the train finally arrived. The soldiers gave him a stretcher to sleep on in the hospital car and the train proceeded slowly down the tracks an hour later, arriving in Karakilisa after ten o'clock at night. The ninety-mile trip took nineteen hours.

"With no workers available to unload the bales, the soldiers dumped them out of the car, most of them landing on the second track. Then a train came from the other direction and the cowcatcher of the engine scattered them right and left. Mr. Hill roused some refugees to help move the bales to our stockroom with the reward of a coat that night rather than waiting until distribution the next morning. Mr. Hill took a room in a rickety hotel at three in the morning.

"At noon the next day, Hill took a *phaeton*, an open carriage, to Dilijan to meet me. I was just leaving for Karakilisa, so we returned together arriving at ten at night. Poor Hill had been riding over the mountain ridge back and forth for ten hours and chilled to the bone, so I was happy that I could offer him a short rest in my room heated by a Russian stove. He took the train back to Tiflis at one in the morning. Tomorrow he goes to Akstafa and then back to Dilijan to meet Rev. MacCallum and me. He keeps busy.

"We distribute to six hundred refugees tomorrow in Karakilisa and six surrounding villages. Then we take a lot to Nalband and five other villages, twenty miles west."

"March 10th, Nalband

"One of the difficulties with working in the mountain villages is finding a posthouse to take my letters. Worse though is receiving mail; since my address is c/o American Consul, in Tiflis, I must wait for Richard Hill to bring letters to me. I received a large packet of letters from his recent visit: several from my lovely wife, a birthday letter from daughter Agnes, and letters from missionaries in Urmia and Tabriz.

"Henry Packard wrote from the Urmia mission that the Boys' School building was in bad condition after allowing refugees to live there last year. It took one hundred tomans to clean up the filth left behind. The Fiske Girls' School was open, but the dormitory also needs work to restore it to good condition. The hospital and medical school began again in the fall. A few of the outstations' churches that were set on fire by the Kurds were reroofed and refitted with doors and windows.

"Life of the missionaries at the Urmia station is being restored, but they are alert to any rumors of an attack on the station. He mentioned that on three separate instances the missionary women, fearing they would need to take flight, stayed up all night baking bread to take with them.

"Robert Labaree wrote me from the Tabriz station, where he transferred after we left. A cholera epidemic caused them to start the academic year a month late, but the Boys' School enrolled two hundred students and for the first time had four class grades in High School. The Girls' School had the largest enrollment in the history of the school, 229 pupils. The new men's hospital is almost completed.

"All seems to be recovering at the Tabriz station since the invasion of the Turkish army last year."

"March 18th, Erivan

"On returning to Erivan, I visited our workshop to find it filled with industrious Armenian refugees. In one area they were sewing refugee clothing and bedding. On another side of the room artisans were performing their trades with tools we had provided — carpenters, cobblers, silversmiths, tailors, and an artist produced paintings of Mount Ararat for sale with paints we gave him. I was excited by the din of lively voices, and people laughing. Yes, laughing. Their spirits are recovering.

"In the intervening month, much has happened on the Turkish Front. The Russian army has made splendid progress and driven the Turks back many miles beyond Van. The return of the refugees by the Russians is officially authorized. Men are returning to the fatherland in large numbers even though there is still snow on the ground; already twelve thousand have returned and soon there will be thirty thousand. Besides these, those who have been concealed or protected by friendly Kurds are returning to their villages.

"The repatriation of Armenians to their homeland requires a different effort. Large amounts of funds are now needed to put roofs over their heads, to supply seed corn, ploughs, oxen and carts. They will need relief until the harvest in the fall. Fortunately, spring sowing has not begun. We will buy what is necessary to support the planting of their crops for an abundant harvest, but we must move quickly. Every day is precious."

I hope Sam's mission is coming to completion so he will return home.

"April 4th, Erivan

"Twenty to thirty thousand Armenians have returned to Van via the district of Igdir. Some Armenians wish to stay and farm in the Caucasus, and we are supplying the means to be successful. This second phase of our relief work is much harder logistically than the first since it means transporting large farm animals, such as oxen, cows, and buffaloes. I have just returned from the Vayots Dzor region, south of Lake Sevan, where we distributed four hundred oxen, one hundred cows, fifty buffalo and ten thousand rubles' worth of seed in thirty-five villages. The cows primarily went to widows.

"Charles Pittman and other members of the Tabriz and Urmia missions are in Salmas providing relief work to forty thousand Assyrian Christian refugees from the mountains of Turkey. I plan to travel to Khoi and join them briefly and then on to Turkey where I hope to see firsthand what relief is needed for the returning Armenians."

"May 4th, Khoi

"I arrived in Khoi. What a joy it was to visit with Charles and Lucille Pittman who are in Salmas, living in the village of Dilman near the Assyrian Christian refugee camp. With the crowded conditions epidemics of cholera and typhoid are taking their toll. In March the Western Persia Mission received $150,000 for relief work. I stayed briefly and did what I could before going to the Turkish border.

"Despite American neutrality the Turkish officials refused me permission to cross over, so I am back in Khoi. To my surprise, when I arrived Will Vanneman was here treating a doctor for the Red Cross. I have decided to travel with him on his return to Tabriz and see if American Consul Gordon Paddock can help me obtain permission to go to Turkey. The Pittmans will also join us and have telegraphed ahead that I will be coming.

"I had hoped to return to Tabriz to visit much earlier, but on my arrival in the Caucasus I was inundated with the tasks for the relief effort there. I could not think of leaving even for a brief visit. Apparently at the Tabriz mission, there was much anticipation of my return several months ago, and Fred Jessup had the teachers and pupils compose and learn songs in Armenian, Persian and Azeri, and speeches were prepared for my arrival. My delay in returning was a horrible disappointment for them. I must do something special for them while I am there."

"May 10th, Tabriz

"Will Vanneman, the Pittmans and I traveled by wagon to Julfa and then took the new railroad to Tabriz, the train taking only two hours to travel the eighty miles to reach our destination. The downside of the new train is, of course, that a formal *peshwaz*, where friends ride seven miles to greet you, is not possible. Instead, they filled the train platform with almost the entire Boys' School, from the oldest teacher to the smallest kindergarten boy — over two hundred. There were songs and speeches, many referring to you as their 'Mayrig,' their little mother.

"Tomorrow there is a dinner reception for me at the Pittmans. There were also many other invitations extended. I was immediately invited to speak before the Armenian Club on my relief efforts in the Caucasus, and to be the guest of honor at a banquet held by the Armenians. The Armenian bishop also asked to meet with me, which I find gratifying. Our European and Muslim friends have invited me to their homes, as you would expect. The Kalantars have asked that I spend the weekend with them. From everywhere, I am flooded with invitations.

"Fred Jessup is now the principal of the Boys' School and still occupies our house. I am there now in the guest room, where I will stay while in Tabriz. Having never slept in this room, it feels unfamiliar although it is a room in a house where I lived twenty years of my life. I realized for the first time that, except for our last summer here, when you traveled early to the Annual Meeting in Urmia, you have always been in this house with me. After being gone for six months, I cannot say that I have ever missed you as much as I do right now. I am close to tears with longing for you.

"All the memories of our life together come rushing back. The joys and sorrows that we shared together with the births and deaths of our children, my pride in your success with meetings for the Muslim women at the house, my pride in your devotion to the Persian women of Tabriz. Although in coming to Persia I was content at first to pursue my work alone, I knew not then what extraordinary happiness that you would bring to my life. I feel empty now without you."

And I am empty without you.

CHAPTER 37

1916 — Indiana, Pennsylvania

"OUR LANDLORD INFORMED ME THAT OUR RENTAL LEASE
expires next month," I told Sam's brother Harry. "What should I do?"

After hearing that the air in Southern California could cure
tuberculosis, my brother Foster moved to a sanitarium in Pasadena,
California. The four of us still living in Indiana — Mother, Annie,
Bobby and I — needed a four-bedroom house with a guest room
for Agnes and Rose when they visited.

"I know the owner of the house at 553 Church Street a few
blocks away," Harry said. "He told me that it will be available to rent in the spring. It is a bigger house than this one, but
unfurnished."

"Furnishing a house could be expensive," I said, "but I might
be able to pick up secondhand furniture. I could also write to
Fred Jessup in Tabriz and ask him to send two of our rugs from
the house at the mission. It would lift my spirits to have something Persian."

The move from 36 South 6th Street to 533 Church Street was
only a distance of two blocks but seemed like miles. Dick drove
us back and forth with a fully packed automobile. From the old
Wilson homestead where he and his children lived Harry brought
a set of dishes and pictures for the walls. He then surprised us by
ordering a new set of dark-stained wood furniture for the living
room in the popular mission style. When the wagon arrived at the

house I told the driver, "It must be a mistake, we did not order any furniture."

"Mr. Harry Wilson sent it," the man replied with a wide grin. "He will be pleased when I tell him how surprised you were."

Over ten years ago when Sam had his appendicitis and I feared that Dr. Cochran would not arrive in time to save him from peritonitis, he told me not to worry, that the Wilson brothers would take care of me if he died. Sam had only left us for the Caucasus, but the promise of their family loyalty was true. Every evening one Sam's brothers who lived in Indiana, either Harry, John or Dick, stopped by to make sure Mother and I were doing well and asked Annie and Bobby about school or how they spent their day, just as Sam would have done. It helped the children stay connected to the Wilson family, although they still missed their father.

The newspaper headline "Persian Prime Minister Resigns after Two Months in Office" caught my eye. After reading a few lines of the article, I exclaimed, "Why it is Princess Ezzat's husband." Abdol Hossein Farman Farmaian, her husband, had become Prime Minister and refused to sign an agreement allowing Russia and Britain to supervise the military and financial affairs of Persia. He resigned saying, "I cannot consent to the slavery of Persia by signing such a document." *I am sure Princess Ezzat is proud of him.*

Saturday, July 1ˢᵗ I was returning home from an afternoon party with the rest of the family and found Sam's brother John waiting for me on the stoop. "A telegram arrived at the old Wilson house," he said. "It is from Robert Speer."

"The Secretary of the Board," I exclaimed as I took the telegram and opened it. "Oh no, how can that be?"

"What is it?" Mother asked.

"It says, 'Dr. Wilson in hospital — typhoid,' " I replied, "but Sam was inoculated before he left." Tears were welling in my eyes, but I refused to let myself break down in front of the children.

"I will take the children inside while you talk to John," Mother said and herded Annie and Bobby into the house.

"Perhaps it is only a mild case, since Sam was inoculated," John said.

"We need to pray that he has the strength to overcome his sickness," I bemoaned. "I wish I was there to care for him."

I could barely concentrate on anything else, and Mother seeing how distracted I was, took it upon herself to cook and feed the children. I sat at the table with them and tried to eat, tried to carry on conversation as usual, but it was too forced. I excused myself and went to my room.

At night I tossed and turned. Unable to sleep, I knelt by the side of my bed and prayed for Sam to recover. "The prayer of faith will save the sick man, and the Lord will raise him up." I whispered. "James 5:15."

When I dosed in the middle of the night, I had the strange sensation that Sam was lying next to me and touched my shoulder. When I rolled over and placed my hand on the bed where I imagined he was lying, the bed was empty, and the sheets were cold to the touch. I shuddered with fear at this bleak omen.

The next day both Harry and John appeared at the door after church service. "A cablegram for you from the Board came to the house," Harry said.

My heart was a hollow cave as I fumbled to open the telegram with others standing around expectingly. "No," I screamed. "No."

"Mommy?" Bobby asked, pulling on my arm.

"Children, the Lord has taken your father to His house in heaven," I managed to say.

Will Vanneman's letter was the first that I received and hundreds more would follow. Will wrote that after Sam become sick with typhoid, he cared for him in the mission hospital for three weeks. At first his fever was very high but began to wane in the third week. When his temperature was near normal, Sam unexpectedly collapsed. Will determined that it was likely from the rupture of an enlarged aorta.

A letter came from Lucille Pittman describing how Sam was honored in Tabriz after his death:

"The funeral service was held in the mission church, where he had so often preached in Armenian. The missionaries of the station, teachers and former pupils of the Boys' School, and a few prominent Armenians gave addresses in the small cemetery next to the graves of your three children. We had his stone inscribed, 'He that loseth his life for my sake shall find it,' Matthew 10:39. After the service we sang *The Task*. He was laid to rest at sunset on a cloudless day."

"How appropriate to sing *The Task*." I said and sang:

"Now the laborer's task is over,
Now the battle day is past;
Now upon the farther shore
Lands the voyager at last.
"Earth to earth and dust to dust.
Calmly now the words we say;
Leaving him to sleep, in trust,
Till the resurrection day.

"Father, in thy gracious keeping
Leave we now Thy servant sleeping."
— John Ellerton (1870)

My happy marriage of thirty years had ended, and I was in mourning for months to come. I lost not just my husband, but my prospects of returning to Persia to the missionary work that I loved. I was doubly grieved.

The older children sent word that they were coming to be with the family. Rose came from Watertown, New York, where she was teaching high school, and Agnes came from Columbia University in New York City, where she was the Secretary of Religious Organizations. It was an unusually hot summer making it difficult for us to sleep. Agnes and Rose, who slept in a small room on the third floor, were particularly irritable and argued with each other over trivial differences in opinion.

Annie Barr, Sam's sister who lived in Baltimore, sent a *Thermatic* Fireless Cooker, which came with an eighty-page instruction manual, *A Treatise on the Management of the Thermatic Fireless Cooker*, with recipes for meats, vegetables, cakes, puddings and soups. The fireless cooker was a large, insulated metal box where one placed radiators and food you heated up on the stove and completed cooking for several hours or overnight. "They use fireless cookers to feed the soldiers on the Western Front," Annie Barr wrote, "not that I want you to feel as though you are at war."

With Agnes and Rose throwing barbs at each other, this "war gift" is quite appropriate.

"What is it?" Rose asked when I set the fireless cooker box on the floor of the kitchen.

"They call it a fireless cooker," I replied. "It reduces the time that the stove is on, saving fuel and keeping the house cool. *Thermatic* claims it is destined to be 'a greater benefactor to humanity than any other modern invention.'"

To my surprise, Rose and Agnes were fascinated by the fireless cooker and insisted on taking over the cooking. Later they helped with housekeeping, which I greatly appreciated. The loss of Sam and subsequent depression impacted my level of energy no matter how I forced myself to recover from grief and be cheerful.

We delayed the family memorial service for Sam until August. His relatives in California needed time to arrange for travel, and the new pastor of the Presbyterian Church, Rev. Jesse Zeigler, was arriving August 18th. I especially wanted Rev. Zeigler to perform the memorial service since he knew Sam from attending his lectures at Princeton Theological Seminary during our furloughs. Robert Labaree and his wife Mary, who had recently resigned from the mission, accepted my invitation to speak about Sam's missionary service and their presence was a great comfort to me.

"I have sadly lost another 'brother' to the missionary cause," Robert Labaree said.

All Sam's brothers and sisters came to the memorial, and we celebrated Sam's accomplishments and shared the sorrow of our loss. Letters from around the world continued to pour in all summer with condolences and praise for Sam. The Armenians considered him to be a martyr; foreign missionaries considered his educational accomplishments and the building of the new mission and Boys' School in Tabriz to be his crowning achievements. Robert Speer said, "His five books and numerous writings were his best memorial." Of all the letters, the one from his student, Haritune, was the most touching, saying, "He died for me."

The outpouring of support from Sam's brothers and sisters and other relatives in Indiana continued to make the town an appropriate place to call home. Mother felt differently and wanted to move to Pasadena where she could be closer to my brother Foster. "In the spring, the lease will need to be renewed if we plan to stay longer," she said. "It is a good time to move."

I waited until Rose and Agnes came home for Christmas to breach the subject of the family's move to Pasadena. "How will you get there?" Agnes asked.

"By train, of course," I replied.

"What I mean is, how are you going to move your things?" Agnes asked.

"We will have the furniture shipped to us," I said.

"I will go with you," Rose interjected. "I could not bear having you so far away and can find a teaching job in California."

"Rose, you have always been such a considerate child," Mother said. "God bless you."

"For me this is very sad news," Agnes bemoaned. "I will only be able to see you during summer vacation."

"I know, dear," I replied. "We will miss you but your job in New York City is too important for your career to give up."

Agnes was concerned where she would go on short holidays when there was not time to travel to California. "There are always the Dulleses and Uncle Rob who are close by," Rose said as though reading my mind.

"When we have Christmas dinner with the Wilson relatives our move will be a delicate subject," I said. "Please let me initiate that conversation." To my surprise brother Dick and his wife Clara, and sister Agnes and her husband Stacy were planning to move to Southern California as well. "Clara's sister Irene lives in Santa Ana and invited us to stay with her until we are settled," Dick said.

"Our family is moving to Pasadena," sister Agnes Smith said. "Stacy will be treated for his tuberculosis at the same sanatorium as Foster."

"There will be just as many Wilson relatives in or near Pasadena as there are here," Harry said. "It will be a good excuse to visit a warmer climate during the winter."

"I will look forward to seeing your sister Ella," I said.

The next day I wrote to Ella, feeling that our family's move to Pasadena was blessed by the Wilsons. I was pleased by her immediate invitation to stay with them while we looked for a house. *This will be a happy move, a good change for the family.*

In packing my things for the move, I found my old jewelry box sitting on the bottom of a trunk. *I thought I had lost it somehow during the previous move, and there it is.* The little box was a treasure trove —there were Persian bracelets and necklaces that Sam had given me on various birthdays and Christmases in Tabriz. As I tried them on it brought back vivid memories of those occasions during our years together. *Those were the happiest days of my life.*

One special piece that I held in my cupped hands and kissed was the *nazar*, the amulet to ward off the "Evil Eye" that Princess Ezzat gave me. *Oh, beautiful Princess Ezzat, how I would love to know how you are. I will keep the nazar somewhere that I can always find it.* That place was my nightstand as my deepest fears always came at night.

1918 Pasadena, California

Ella's husband, George Stewart, offered to drive Mother and I around to look for a house in Pasadena. We stopped at a house for rent at 177 South Mentor Street. As we were approaching the door, out of the house on the adjoining property burst Eva Wishard, the woman who visited us in Tabriz in 1891 and with whom I felt a kindred spirit. It was settled on the spot — this was the house where we would live.

Annie became best friends with the Wishard girls, Winifred and Margaret, and she and Bobby went to high school with them nearby. Rose took education classes at Occidental College to qualify to teach in California.

Every morning Mother walked two-and-a-half miles to the Las Encinas Sanitorium to visit Foster. In the afternoon she sat on the porch swing and read stories to the neighborhood children. "At eighty-two, I am too old to make new friends," Mother declared, but soon the children called her "Grandma Rhea" and brought her flowers.

And so began our new life.

CHAPTER 38

Western Persia Mission 1918

GRETTIE HOLLIDAY SENT ME A LETTER FROM QAZVIN IN August:

"On May 30th we heard the Turks and Kurds would invade Tabriz. The European Consuls evacuated their women and children and disapproved of the missionaries staying. 'At the very least, you'll be interned in the mission property as prisoners of war for an indefinite period of time,' they told us. 'Besides you are actually giving the people that you help a false sense of security by staying.' We decided to leave and split up between the Eastern Mission stations in Qazvin, Tehran and Hamadan. Rev. Jessup and Dr. Vanneman decided to stay and protect the Tabriz station from looting.

"Before leaving we held the Boys' and Girls' Schools Commencements as planned despite meeting over one hundred Turkish soldiers on our way to the ceremonies. The last four days were a terrible rush, arranging transportation, packing up and preparing at least twenty days of food for our large party's journey. Each person was allowed 120 pounds of personal effects including bed and bedding.

"On June 10th at 10:30am the long caravan left Tabriz. There were 20 large *kibitkas* each drawn by four horses and resembling old Prairie Schooners, 16 *droshkys* or Russian open carriages each drawn by one horse, several vehicles of nondescript nature, a number of men on horseback, more on donkeys, 20 camels, 10 pack horses, an escort of 110 Persian Cossack officers led by a Russian, including 40 mounted men and two machine guns. Twenty days later we arrived in Qazvin."

Charles and Lucille Pittman were on furlough in America and wrote to me with news they received about Tabriz:

"We received a letter from Fred Jessup who gave us an account of the invasion. After the Turks invaded Tabriz, they occupied the English and American Consulates and the mission hospital. The Spanish Minister, one of the remaining foreign consular officials, granted the Turks permission to use our mission residences, the Boys' School and hospital buildings for a couple of weeks. Fred Jessup and Will Vanneman protested but the Minister assured them it was best to cooperate with the Turkish soldiers or they might molest them.

"Sunday morning, Sept. 9th, as Fred was heading for church to give the service, word came that the Turkish commandant was coming to see them. Instead of a visit, Dr. Vanneman and Rev. Jessup were placed under house arrest; they were taken to the large upstairs bedroom in your former house with an armed sentinel outside the door. The Turks demanded Dr. Vanneman, the treasurer of the Relief Fund, to tell them where the funds were. Unable to get the money from the Persian banks, the Turks left them captive for six weeks. Will and Fred settled into a routine of reading all day and playing dominoes at night, and Mr. Rieben, a Swiss neutral, brought them food, without which they would have starved to death.

"The other reason Fred Jessup wrote us was to let us know that the Turks looted the mission hospital, our house and another vacant missionary's house. Our house was gutted, and we lost all our earthly possessions."

How sad. Charles and Lucille had collected so many beautiful Persian rugs.

In 1916 Fred and Ida Coan had returned to America due to a breakdown in Ida's health. Their daughter, Elizabeth, returned to Urmia after graduating from Wellesley and became a third-generation missionary, a proud accomplishment for the Coan family. When Fred received her letters, he sent updates to me on the conditions in Persia. In August, he wrote:

"The Bolshevik Revolution resulted in the disintegration of the Russian forces in Persia. Without Russian protection, the Christian populations became at peril of attack by the Turks and Kurds. Many took refuge in the mission compound, which became both a refuge and a prison, surrounded by Turkish soldiers. The missionaries and refugees were captive for almost six months (February to July), without mail or other means to communicate with the outside world.

"On July 8th while eating breakfast, Elizabeth heard a strange noise and ran outside to find a British plane circling the mission compound, the pilot waving the Union Jack. The British aviator, Lieutenant Kenneth Pennington, was able to land near a camp of Assyrian refugees, and the women went wild, smothering him with hugs and kisses. He had flown from Qazvin, at the request of the American Consul to secure word on the missionaries' well-being. He brought the first letters that they had received in months and took their letters, such as the one I received. He also let them know that a British contingent, called "Dunsterforce" was coming from the South to relieve them.

"The leader of the Assyrian forces, Agha Petros, moved with his army to meet the British army and obtain needed ammunition. This caused widespread panic among the people who relied on them for protection. On July 30th eighty thousand Assyrians fled after them toward the British lines in Hamadan, four hundred miles south. Turks and Kurds followed, killing thousands and carrying off hundreds of girls into captivity. William and Mary Shedd volunteered to take the rearguard of their unorganized march. On August 6th they reached a small British regiment in Sain Qaleh. There William Shedd, stricken with cholera, died."

I dropped the letter in my lap and sobbed, "Another martyr of whom the world is not worthy."

Fred wrote me again in late November:

"On October 8th the missionaries of the Urmia station. were given three hours-notice that the Turks were evacuating them to Tabriz. They were packed into auto trucks and taken to Lake Urmia. Fifty people — Americans, Turks and Persians — were packed into a room 20 by 10 feet that night. The next morning, they were crammed between the decks of a barge and taken across Lake Urmia, and then loaded into train box cars and taken to Tabriz. The missionaries were told to stay in Tabriz for the winter in the Russian Bank Garden until the Armistice. Likely their houses in Urmia were looted, and they may not have any furniture or possessions left, if and when they return."

August 1918 — Pasadena

Annie practiced Mendelsohn's Wedding March on the piano every day, and the neighbors, even the postman, asked, "Who is getting married?"

"My eldest daughter Agnes is getting married to a man from the telephone company," I replied.

"Not a reverend or doctor pursuing missionary work?" Eva Wishard exclaimed.

"She had plans to become the principal of the Girls' School at the Tehran mission after the war was over. In the meantime, she fell in love."

"I know of a dressmaker from New York who is visiting her sister here this summer," Eva said. "Perhaps she would be willing to make the wedding dress."

The woman kindly offered to make Agnes' wedding dress and another for Mother. While fitting Mother's dress, she said, "We'll make you beautiful, Mrs. Rhea."

"I dare you to," Mother retorted.

September 1918

In August, Mother had looked radiant at Agnes' wedding sitting in the front row next to her missionary friend Jennie Shedd. Foster had commented, "They are the most beautiful women here. They have the radiance of Heaven in their faces."

It was a shock to us when four weeks later, Mother became ill with influenza and passed away the next day, September 11th. Rose, Annie, and Bobby were so distraught they could not eat. Everything in my being was rattled, and I felt helpless not knowing what to do. The Wilson relatives offered to help, but my sickly brother Foster took charge of the arrangements. He purchased a plot in Mountain View Cemetery in Altadena with a view of Mount Wilson and the San Gabriel mountains and had a large stone erected with the name "Rhea."

The Lake Forest Presbyterian Church held a special service in Mother's honor and sent me a program. The Women's Board for Foreign Missions published a pamphlet on her life. Sympathy letters filled my mailbox from those who knew and admired her work for the missionary cause. A coworker from the Women's Board office in Chicago wrote: "No one could elicit monetary support for the foreign missions like your mother."

November 11th, 1918

"The war is over," Rose screamed as she raced into the house. "There are people running through the streets in Los Angeles, jumping up on top of anything they can find. People are hugging and kissing strangers that pass by."

"Dear peace at last," I cried. "I hope the Armistice will also bring peace to war-stricken Persia."

CHAPTER 39

Pasadena 1919-1920

AFTER PUTTING ASIDE MY GRIEF, I REGAINED MY POSITIVE outlook and decided to buy our rented house for six thousand dollars. One of my favorite things about the house was the climbing rose bush next to the front porch. It was the source of the fresh flowers I kept in a vase under a life size photograph of Sam in the parlor. I imagined I would always be happy in Pasadena as a part of the tight-knit community formed by my neighbors, particularly the Wishards.

Although I committed to giving two Bible Classes each week at Occidental College, I had time to visit my brother Foster every day in Las Encinas Sanitarium. He was deeply depressed by Mother's death and emaciated from "consumption." He was so thin that the bones in his face protruded like a skeleton. Now lacking strength, he needed to hold my arm as we walked.

He enjoyed sitting in the sun with me in a detached porch in the sanitarium yard. In the sunlight, he appeared to have aged thirty years in the two years since we moved to Pasadena. We had hoped and prayed that the air in Southern California would cure Foster's tuberculosis, but it was not to be. *It will be too much to bear when I lose you too, dear Foster.*

In the fall several visitors came to Pasadena and brought cheer to our household. The visit by niece Dorothy Dulles Bourne and her husband, James, delighted Foster. He had the opportunity to know the Dulles children while living at Rosenvik, and Dorothy was his favorite niece. "She reminds me so much of Sophea," he said.

Before returning to Persia, Fred and Ida Coan stayed with me for several weeks.

"Sadly, Grettie Holliday passed away in Indianapolis during her third furlough," Ida said.

"She was one of the most courageous and interesting missionary women I have ever had the privilege of knowing," I remarked.

"Ida and I will transfer to the Hamadan station and continue missionary work," Fred said.

"It won't be the same," Ida added, "but we are needed in Hamadan. Thousands of Assyrian refugees went there, and we are the only missionaries left who are fluent in Syriac."

"Will you go to Urmia?" I asked.

"The station is not open, but I want to see the ruins for myself," Fred said.

"In May, Harry Packard, his wife Julia and his children traveled to Urmia with two representatives of the French Consul and their families to survey the damage to the mission stations. Approaching Urmia, they passed three hundred villages, the houses were abandoned and plundered. The villagers, out of fear for the Kurds took refuge in the city; forty thousand were in desperate need of food.

"The Packards found that almost all the mission buildings had suffered pillage and abuse by the Turks and Kurds. All the furniture and decorations were taken from the residences, hospital, dispensary, and school buildings. Most of the windows and doors of the buildings were missing. Bricks were loosened and removed. Woodwork, flooring and staircases were stripped for wood. The magnificent ninety-foot-tall *chenar* trees, that had arched over the avenues and provided shade to the compound, were chopped down, except for one tree that was saved because a stork was nesting in it, which is considered an omen of good luck.

"On May 24th, Dr. Packard and the French representatives visited the Urmia mission yard in the city, where nine hundred Christian Assyrian refugees remained. As Dr. Packard spoke to them, an army of Muslims descended on the compound, with swords, sickles, hatchets and clubs and proceeded to hack the refugees in the mission compound to pieces. About twenty children were trampled underfoot and young men were separated and murdered. The Muslim mob killed two hundred Christian men and children. The women were stripped naked, outraged and thrown into the mission wells until they were filled to the top.

"When Harry Packard's life was threatened, Mirza Mohammad Agha, a *mullah* whose sight Dr. Packard restored with cataract surgery, came to his rescue. He warded off Harry's attackers with a sword and dragged Harry to the Governor's house. Dr. Packard's family, unaware of the attack, was escorted by soldiers there, along with six hundred Christian Assyrian women from the mission. They waited twenty-four days for American Consul Gordon Paddock to negotiate their rescue.

"On June 7th Gordon Paddock's rescue team, including Dr. Edward Dodd and the Governor in Tabriz, arrived in Urmia and quietly carried out their rescue mission. They returned to Tabriz with the Packard family and six hundred Christian Assyrian women."

"Dr. Edward Dodd is now head of the men's medical hospital in Tabriz," Ida said. "It was looted by Persians and Turks when the missionaries previously evacuated. The hospital building was intact, but it was damaged and filthy, so he directed the cleaning, repairing and white washing of the hospital and dispensary, and sourced bedsteads and bedding."

"Any word on the Boys' School?" I asked.

"Fred Jessup reports that enrollment in the Boys' School is four hundred, the largest in the history of the school, and the

Girls' School also saw good enrollment. They also started refugee schools for the Christian Assyrian families."

"I am so glad that the Boys' School continues to do well," I said. "Sam would be proud."

In June Rose received a letter from the Near East Relief Commission. "That can't be," she exclaimed, her hands trembling as she held the letter. "They want me to sail on July 1st, less than a month from now."

"Where are they assigning you?" I asked.

"Constantinople," Rose cried.

One week later, Rose was on a train from Los Angeles to New York. She stopped for a week in Montclair, New Jersey to visit her sister Agnes, who was madly sewing clothes for her to take on her trip. Saying goodbye to Rose was as hard as it had been ten years ago, when I stood in Tabriz watching her wagon disappear on the horizon with the Vannemans. *I am becoming a sentimental old lady.*

After Christmas a brief letter came from Lucille Pittman in Tabriz:

"I wanted you to know that Rev. Fred Jessup died of pneumonia on December 1st. Being imprisoned by the Turks for six months took a toll on him physically and mentally. When the rest of us returned both Fred and Will Vanneman looked as if they had aged ten years. I wish now that we had been more persuasive about insisting that all the missionaries abandon the station, for their captivity meant they could not protect the property of the mission, although that was their goal in staying there.

"In his honor his wife Helen took over as principal of the Boys' School and will continue her work for the leper colony at Arpa Dara, visiting them by donkey in their remote mountain colony ten miles north of Tabriz."

"Helen Jessup was an inspiration to me," I said. "I accompanied her to the leper colony several times."

Charles Pittman wrote to me in December 1920:

"Attendance at the Sunday mission church services challenge our capacity. We now give four services — in Azeri, English, Armenian, and Syriac, the latter to serve the Assyrian refugees. The church needed repairs so in the summer months we held services in a large tent next to the Boys' School. One of the improvements to the church was the installation of electrical lighting. I knew that you would be pleased to hear of this modernization.

"In November, Turkish and Bolshevik invasions were menacing Tabriz, and the European Consuls planned for all their citizens to leave the city. The Relief Committee also decided to move 1,200 Assyrian Christians from Tabriz to Hamadan. In December, the American Consul urged the missionaries to also leave. Rev. Crothers and I are the only missionaries who stayed.

"After a few months, conditions in Tabriz improved, and I telegraphed that in my opinion it was safe for them to return. They came back in groups over the spring and summer and medical work by Dr. Vanneman resumed in July."

Wednesday, December 15th I was about to leave for Occidental College with Annie and Robert when the phone rang. Rose answered the call before I had a chance to get to the receiver. "It's Foster's doctor at Las Encinas Sanitarium," Rose said. "He wants to speak to you."

My heart sunk into my stomach as I took the receiver. "Foster has taken a turn for the worse and developed pneumonia from a respiratory infection. Breathing has become very labored," the doctor said.

"Do I need to come to see him right away?" I asked.

"I would advise that you come as soon as you can."

"Foster has pneumonia," I cried after I hung up the receiver.

"I can stay with him at La Encinas this morning," Rose offered. "I will wait for you to return from teaching your Bible class."

My mind was on Foster as I tried to engage my class on the teachings of the Apostle Paul, and I watched the clock on the wall on the back of the room, thinking each minute that passed felt like an hour. When I reached Foster's room at Las Encinas, Rose turned to me with a grim expression. Foster's face was ashen gray, and he wheezed as he tried to breath. There was blood on the corners of his mouth.

"Uncle Foster, your sister Annie is here," Rose said. "I will be going now."

Foster opened his eyes and whispered, "Annie." He was too weak and out of breath to say much more.

My little brother Foster Audley Rhea died early in the morning the next day. I had not anticipated the wave of loneliness that overcame me. Besides my in-laws, the only close relatives that remained were my children and my Dulles nieces and nephews. Although they too mourned the loss of their Uncle Foster, my loss ran deeper; I had lost the boy who was my first playmate in Persia and the spit and image of a father I could not remember.

Chapter 40

Pasadena 1920

Bobby cornered me while I was preparing dinner. "Now that I am seventeen, I want to be called Robert," he said. "Bobby is not a proper name for a grown man."

"Very well," I said, "Robert."

"I have also decided to go to Princeton for college, like Father."

"But you have never taken a train across country alone," I exclaimed. The idea of Robert traveling alone scared me. Perhaps it was because on our journeys to America for furlough he almost died from pneumonia and diphtheria. I worried about Robert for two weeks while he traveled to New Jersey and was relieved when Agnes wrote that he arrived safely.

With only Annie and I living in our house in Pasadena, I decided to rent the spare rooms. When Annie joined a sorority, I was glad I had. Otherwise, I would have been living in my "empty nest" alone.

A letter arrived from Rose in Constantinople: "Ned and I are engaged," she wrote.

Dr. Edward Dodd from the Tabriz mission met Rose in a Near East Relief shop where she sold embroidery made by refugee women. When he learned of her connection to the Tabriz mission, he invited her to dinner. After accepting, Rose realized that she did not know his name, as they had forgotten to introduce themselves.

In the letters that followed, Rose made frequent mention of things she was doing with Dr. Dodd, and a few months later "Dr. Dodd" became "Ned." I had my hunches that Rose had found her match but never expected such a sudden announcement. "He helped rescue Harry Packard so he must be a worthy man," I wrote. I had the opportunity to meet Dr. Dodd when he came through California on his way to America on furlough. I knew instantly that he would be a beloved son-in-law.

"When and where will the wedding be?" I asked Rose.

"The wedding will be July 28th in Montclair," Rose wrote. "It is Ned's 'American home' and, with Agnes there and Robert close by at Princeton, we thought Montclair would be the most convenient."

Most convenient? What about your poor old mother? Very well a trip to the East Coast is well overdue. I planned to visit with my best friend Anna Holt Wheeler, Wilson relatives and other retired missionaries. My dear daughter and namesake, Annie was excited to go on a trip East, and I enjoyed our conversations on the train. She was now a spirited and charming woman, who was interested in many social causes.

We stopped in Chicago to visit Anna Wheeler and were about to leave the train station when a porter ran up with a telegram. "I hope the wedding has not been called off," I said jokingly as I opened it. "What on earth? Our tenant wants to buy our house in Pasadena."

"Tell them you are not interested," Annie said. "I like our house."

"But they want to pay me $6,500," I said. "That is five hundred dollars more than I paid for it. I do not know how to respond."

"Call Aunt Ella and Uncle George and see what they advise," Annie said.

"Uncle George thought I should take their offer," I told Annie when I hung up the phone. "I need a day or two to think it over."

When I mentioned the telegram to Anna Wheeler her eyes twinkled, indicating an idea had exploded into her wise little head. "You could move in with me," she exclaimed. "I have been a lonely widow for a decade now living in 'Thalfried' by myself. There is nothing to hold you back."

"What about me?" Annie cried.

"You could attend Lake Forest College and live with us," Anna Wheeler said.

Annie scowled. "I enjoy my sorority friends at Occidental."

"My head is spinning," I said. "I need to think about the ramifications."

There were many logistical issues to consider, but the idea of living with my best friend, two widows in a huge mansion with servants to wait on our every need, was inviting. *At sixty, I deserve to be selfish.*

I accepted the offer for the house but decided to wait and tell Annie after the wedding considering how distressed she was about the potential of losing her sorority friends in Pasadena. In private, Agnes and I discussed where it would be best for Annie to complete college. "I think Annie would be better off finishing two years at Teachers College at Columbia University," Agnes said. "I can pull some strings to have her accepted."

After the wedding, Agnes and I presented the plan to Annie. At first, she cried. "I will miss my sorority friends." Later, realizing she would be close to Rose, Agnes and Robert in New Jersey she warmed up to the idea. "You will receive an excellent education at Columbia," I told her. After Annie was accepted to Columbia University, I moved to Lake Forest to live with Anna Wheeler. Annie never regretted going to Columbia University after she met the love of her life in a class at Union Theological Seminary

— Stephen Peabody. They married in 1924 and spent five years in China as missionaries. Annie kept her promise to become a missionary.

In the meantime, living in Lake Forest with Anna Wheeler was the most comforting part of my life — returning full-circle to my best friend and surrounded with neighbors who remembered me and my family. *This is where my memories of Mother, Sophea and Foster live.*

Anna Wheeler found a position for me in Chicago giving English language classes to Persian Assyrian refugees. I also played piano at an Armenian church, and at times I was transported in my mind back to Tabriz singing Armenian hymns. I attended church service with Anna, and a soprano in the chore sent us a note saying, "I love to look down on you two ladies sitting together, you look so happy."

I was happy with my childhood friend Anna by my side; I felt whole.

Fred and Ida Coan stopped to visit while traveling through Chicago. "Have you heard about the latest coup d'état in Persia?" Fred asked. "In February 1921 Helen Jessup was on her way to Tehran when the Persian Cossack Brigade marched past her into the capital and overthrew the government. It was an almost bloodless coup that seemingly did nothing, leaving inept Ahmad Shah in place. The new Minister of War, Reza Khan, took control."

Agnes and Rose each had two girls and wanted me to live with them in Montclair. My parting with Anna Wheeler after three years together was sad, but I felt obliged to perform my grandmother duties. My first seven years passed happily in Montclair with my headquarters in Agnes' house. Rose lived nearby and

Ned Dodd's connection with missionary service meant frequent visitors at their house by missionaries particularly the Vannemans and the Packards. I discovered that Charlotte Skinner Thurston, my classmate from Lake Forest College, lived in Montclair and she frequently invited me to their home for Sunday dinner. I also began yearly "Rhea luncheons" with my sister Sophea's children, Dorothy Bourne, Edith Snare, and Rhea and Winslow Dulles.

In October 1925, the *Majlis* deposed and exiled Ahmad Shah and declared Reza Khan the new Shah, ending the Qajar dynasty. Reza Khan's title became Reza Pahlavi Shah, when he selected a surname.

During the coup of 1921, Princess Ezzat's son Nosrat was the Minister of Foreign Affairs and in line for accession to the Qajar throne. He was among the four hundred noblemen arrested by Reza Khan, including Princess Ezzat's husband and her son Abbas. After their release, her husband remained under house arrest, and her son Nosrat was again imprisoned and assassinated.

The goals of the new Persian government were to modernize Persia and to remove foreign control. Railroads and communication networks were constructed, a modern educational system established, and European dress codes implemented. Reza Pahlavi Shah eventually banned the *chuddar*, veil and all *hijabs*.

Reza Khan is trying to change Persian culture too fast. Will his epitaph be: "A fool lies here who tried to hustle the East?"

Annie Rhea Wilson's Children with their Spouses, 1924: (back row, left to right) Ned (Rose's husband), Robert, Stephen (Annie Jr.'s husband), Annie Jr., and Hal (Agnes' husband); (front row, left to right) Rose, Annie Sr. holding Rose's baby Nellie, Agnes holding her baby Margaret.

CHAPTER 41

1930 — Montclair, New Jersey

FRED AND IDA COAN VISITED ME AFTER RETURNING FROM India, where their son Frank worked for the Y.M.C.A. "When we arrived in 1929, we only planned on stopping briefly in Urmia," Fred said, "but the remaining members of the mission church congregation prevailed on me to stay and train a class of Assyrians to be preachers."

"We stayed fifteen months, instead of fifteen days," Ida Coan added.

"It was heartbreaking seeing the desolation that the Great War brought to our beloved childhood home," Fred said. "It clashed with the happy and precious memories of my boyhood."

"It was hard to believe the gutted and destroyed buildings of the Urmia mission station was once the crown jewel of the Presbyterian Mission Board, with avenues lined with *chenar* trees," Ida said. "It was where we raised our family."

"Although the mission buildings were damaged or destroyed, surely they can be rebuilt and trees replanted," I said.

"It is the precious loss of life that cannot be replaced," Fred said. "Of the eighteen missionaries who were in Urmia during the War, seven have died and the others scattered, not one remains in the station; only a few native teachers. The mission compound will likely remain closed indefinitely I fear."

"The effort of one hundred years of missionary work seems to be largely wasted and lost," Ida said.

"But we know that God rules," Fred interjected. "It must be His purpose to bring some great blessing out of the suffering and tragedy in Persia."

We held hands and cried together. "Our grief for the demise of the Urmia mission is the same as for a dear relative who we have known for many years," I said.

"There are other changes affecting the missions," Fred said. "Reza Pahlavi Shah has nationalized the schools and instituted measures to limit foreign control of education. In 1928 the Ministry of Education, seeking conformity of all educational institutions, ruled that the first four years of elementary school must be taught in Persian. The next measure was to ban teaching the Bible to Muslim students."

"At least the Persian government is allowing the schools to continue," I said.

"Another curious change is the requirement for Persians to have surnames," Fred said.

"Sam so enjoyed calling roll and noting half his boys had the last name Khan," I said. "What if they pick the same surname, like Mohammadi or Hosseini?"

Fred smiled. "It will be interesting to return in a few years and find out if that happened."

1930 — Ripon, Wisconsin

After Annie and her husband Stephen Peabody returned from China they moved to Ripon, Wisconsin, and I spent the summer with them. In September when I was about to return to Montclair, word came that my best friend, Anna Holt Wheeler died in Lake

Forest. Annie drove me to the train station to attend the funeral service in Chicago.

"The days are becoming shorter, and the cold of fall is settling in," I said. "This is the most depressing time of year."

My five-hour journey was in drizzling rain through forests of maple trees with leaves colored yellow, orange and red. *What is death? It is our ultimate goal. How can I feel angry about the loss of my dear friend, Anna? Throughout life we all have losses — friends move on, children leave home, we all lose our youth. Anna has lived a full happy life, all in the lap of luxury. She was loved by her family, her friends, and above all, by me.*

In October 1930 I traveled to Indiana, Pennsylvania, my last reunion with the Wilson family. The occasion was the funeral service of Sam's brother Rob. I stayed with Harry and Jenny in Indiana at the old Wilson homestead. Brother Andy died in March the same year, so I was there to give my condolences to two widows, Ellen and Bessie.

Dick Wilson, Ella Stewart and Agnes Smith came from California, and sister Annie and her husband Rev. Alfred Barr came from Vermont, where they had retired. Once again, we stood in a circle around the Wilson family plot holding hands. Rev. Alfred Barr gave a blessing, and a hand squeeze traveled around the circle. Tears filled my eyes. *My dear Wilson family. How would I ever have made it through these past fifteen years without your family loyalty?*

In February 1931, Annie and Stephen announced that they were adopting a baby boy from The Cradle in Evanston, Illinois. "His name is Larry," Annie wrote. "A very active baby."

Having just written Annie that I was looking forward to my summer in Ripon to see my new grandson, Agnes announced at dinner, "In June Hal and I are taking a trip to Europe. Will you be able to look after the girls while we are away?"

"Why of course, dear," I replied. *How could she spring this on me? Agnes knows I planned to go to my 50th Class Reunion at Lake Forest College in June. I also hoped to see my new grandson in Ripon.* Secretly I cajoled Nellie, Agnes' cook, to cover for me while I went on my planned trips to Wisconsin and Illinois.

Charlotte Skinner Thurston and I traveled together to our Lake Forest College 50th Class Reunion. After the reunion Annie came down and drove me to Ripon for an overnight visit to meet my four-month-old grandson, Lawrence Wilson Peabody. Then I was back on a train for Montclair and found everything going well on my return. *I am such a stealthy grandmother.*

When I met Agnes and her husband on their return from Europe, Agnes came down the dock in a wheelchair. "She had a hard voyage with her pregnancy," Hal said.

"Miserable," Agnes added.

Agnes recovered for a few months, and we celebrated Thanksgiving and Christmas with Rose's family, but by January Agnes was not well and was in bed most of the time. When the time for the birth seemed imminent, I brought the bassinette down from the attic and called Hal at work. He came home and rushed Agnes to the hospital.

The baby was stillborn.

Wanting to comfort my daughter I took the bus to the hospital rather than waiting for Hal to come home. When I arrived, I asked for her room number, but a nurse caught my arm and prevented me from entering. She escorted me to a small waiting room. When Hal came in, the sight of his red eyes and ghostly pallor caused my diaphragm to seize.

"I was beside her when she waved her arms frantically in the air, gasping," Hal said. "I ran for the nurse, but when we returned, Agnes had passed away."

"What? What on earth?" I exclaimed, not believing what I had just heard. "I must see her immediately."

"It happens once in a thousand cases of childbirth," Hal said in a choking voice, "an embolism went to her lungs. One in a thousand cases, the nurse said it was an embolism." Hal covered his face with his hands and wept.

"Why?" I exclaimed. "She was with us yesterday!"

Only when the doctor came and gave his condolences, repeating what Hal had told me, did I start to believe. "But I have lost too many children already," I protested. "This cannot be."

Before going to the hospital, I had taken Hal's children to Rose's house. There, Hal and I gathered the family together and relayed the tragic news. Margaret was nine years old, and Polly was six and they clearly understood the permanency of death but could not fathom how being motherless would change their lives. Agnes had been a devoted mother, and their children adored her. The girls suffered a traumatic loss.

For five years following the death of my sister Sophea, my mother had taken care of her Dulles grandchildren, and I was ready to take on a similar role with Agnes' children. I found Hal in his study reading letters of condolence. "Hal, I want you to know that I am thoroughly prepared to take on Agnes' responsibilities for the children," I said. "Afterall, I have served in that role on multiple occasions while Agnes attended social functions, when you were out for entertainment, and on your trip to Europe."

"No," Hal responded curtly. "My sisters Grace and Mabel have offered to help and are closer in age to Agnes, so they are better substitutes. Grace will quit her teaching job and be the primary caretaker."

"Very well," I said and started to leave.

"Wait," Hal exclaimed. "There is something else. After the school year is over and Grace is available to be here full-time, you will be relocating to the Dodd's house. Rose and Ned have agreed that it is their turn."

I swallowed hard. "I understand that this decision was made jointly," I replied stiffly.

Agnes' death was a crushing blow that I would never recover from.

The tragedies came in threes again: the destruction of the mission station in Urmia, the death of my dear childhood friend Anna Holt Wheeler, and the death of my daughter, all within a few years. After my best friend's death, I prayed to God to have mercy on the third one.

"What a cruel God You are!" I declared.

Chapter 42

1933 — Montclair, New Jersey

Easter Monday, April 17ᵀᴴ, my friend Edna Austin and I gave a tea, and surprised our friends and neighbors by announcing the engagement of my son Robert to Edna's daughter Louise. No one suspected a thing, as Louise was secretly meeting Robert in New York. The wedding was September 28ᵗʰ.

"My last child is married," I said. "And now I am officially without children."

Robert and Louise moved to a big brick house with an apple orchard on the outskirts of Washington D.C., where Robert took a job as counsel for the Reconstruction Finance Corporation. It was established by Congress during the Great Depression, and I was proud that my son was helping people through those struggling times.

In summer 1934, Fred and Ida Coan visited me in Ripon, Wisconsin. "We have been on a tour visiting grandchildren," Ida said.

"I have ten grandchildren," I replied. "Ten is a good number to have; not too many to forget their birthdays, their favorite colors, and what grade they are in."

"Grandchildren keep one busy."

"Any word from Persia?"

"Over the last three years the mission in Tabriz lost four of our colleagues," Fred said. "Last year Mary Shedd withdrew and returned to America. In 1931, Helen Jessup resigned and has been living in Tabriz where she has property and an adopted daughter. Will Vanneman died of pneumonia at the end of October, and his wife Marguerite retired."

"Helen Jessup should be commended on her commitment, staying at the mission twelve years after her husband's death," I said. "Marguerite wrote me about the death of her husband, and it made me quite sad. I hope to see her when I return to Montclair this fall."

"Charles and Lucille Pittman and Lillie Beaber are in their sixties and still working at the Tabriz station," Ida said.

"Life for the non-medical missionaries in the field is becoming more and more challenging," Fred said. "In 1932, the Persian government ruled that all elementary school classes, first through sixth grades, must be conducted in government owned and operated schools. It effectively eliminated seventy-five percent of the students at mission schools across Persia."

"Lillie Beaber must be disappointed in the low enrollment," I said. "I expect she will withdraw or retire and return to America soon."

On Nowruz 1935, at the suggestion of the Persian legation in Berlin, Reza Pahlavi Shah asked foreign delegates to refer to Persia as Iran, meaning "the land of the Aryans." Many Persians opposed this change as damaging their cultural heritage and aligning them with pro-Nazi sentiment. A. V. Williams Jackson, our friend and expert on Zoroaster and the *Avesta*, had told us that since the time of Zoroaster, the Persian people have referred to their country as "Arya." I was glad that he was still alive to witness the "re-naming of Persia."

The more things change, the more they stay the same.

1937

The Sunday after Thanksgiving, Andy Stewart sent a telegram to tell me that Ella, his mother, passed away. She was my favorite sister-in-law, and we had become close friends while I lived in Pasadena. Her passing was like losing a sister, and I was sad not to be able to attend her funeral service in Pasadena. All Sam's brothers were now deceased: John died in 1928, Rob and Andy in 1930, Dick in 1932 and Harry in January 1937. When Harry died, Jenny wrote to me: "The Wilson family headstones now encircle the central Wilson family monument. Fortunately, they left room for me."

It is a time gone by.

In the summer of 1938, I was staying with Annie when she announced, "We are leaving Ripon and moving to San Jose."

"When?" I exclaimed.

"Don't worry, we will not move until October," Annie said.

"But I have enjoyed coming to Wisconsin every summer for the past five years and watching your children grow up," I bemoaned. "I've been witness to Larry's exploits — getting into the flour bin and coming out covered with flour, painting the kitchen floor, turning on the faucets in the neighbor's bathtub and flooding their house. Wherever will I find such amusement in Montclair?"

"After we settle into our new home in San Jose, we expect you to come and live with us," Annie replied.

And so, it was decided.

Reverend Stephen Peabody, Annie's husband, was minister at the Congregational Church on the corner of 3rd and San Antonio Streets. Annie and Stephen rented a house on 17th Street, a mile and a half away from the church. I had my own suite that the previous owner had built for his mother. The house was open and airy and decorated almost exclusively with furniture, pictures, and tapestries that Annie and Stephen collected during their missionary work in China.

In the dining room a blue Chinese rug covered the floor. The square cherrywood dining room table and chairs were carved with panels of fruit tree blossoms. A matching round tabletop stood against the wall behind the sideboard that could be placed on top to seat twelve. The sideboard contained Annie's blue Canton chinaware and on top of it were brass candlesticks and a samovar. The living room was decorated with Chinese Fette rugs, a carved floor lamp and a wrought iron lamp from China. In the center of the room was a chess table for playing *Xiangqi*.

"The Chinese chess table is Stephen's pride possession," Annie said. "When he asked the seller how much the chess table cost, the vendor told him that he would only sell it to someone who could beat him in *Xiangq*i. Stephen watched men playing in the streets for months and learned to play. He then took the vendor's challenge. Somehow Stephen emerged victorious from the match and the man was so impressed that he gave it to him."

Life at "the Manse," as I called their house, was constantly filled with social gatherings and overnight guests, missionaries and relatives. There was a small backyard, where Annie had a rose bed and she planted a climbing rose bush in the front, a family tradition since our house in Pasadena. Many evening meals were served picnic style with guests on a long table in the backyard. In summer we moved to Lake Tahoe, where Stephen was a minister at the Zephyr Point Presbyterian Conference Center. They had a cabin with a view of the lake.

After dinner when I offered to help dry the dishes Annie informed me. "We let God dry the dishes."

When Annie was born, I told my namesake that she would care for me in my old age, and my prediction came true. I loved my new life in San Jose with my daughter. I was living "like a cow in a field of clover."

In the summer of 1941, I was excited to receive Fred Coan as a visitor at the Manse, who I had not heard from since his wife Ida passed away.

"What do you hear from Persia?" I asked.

"I forgot that I did not write to you," Fred said. "In 1939, two weeks prior to the beginning of school, the order came from the Persian government that no foreign schools would be allowed to operate during the 1939-1940 academic year. The government's announcement came like a thunderclap. Students had been matriculated, boarders were moving into the dormitory, books had been purchased."

"Did the government officials seal the doors of the missionary schools?" I asked.

"No, not this time," Fred said. "The missionaries petitioned through the Board to be allowed to teach that year, agreeing that the students would transfer to the government schools in 1940. The Persian Ministry of Education gave them another year."

"And now?" I asked.

"The Persian government purchased the mission properties and buildings from the Board for $1,200,000," Fred replied. "The missions in Persia are officially closed."

"And the missionaries?"

"Over the past few years many of the missionaries that you knew retired or withdrew," Fred said. "A few of our brethren were taken by God to higher service. Lillie Beaber retired in 1938, and the Pittmans are retiring this year and moving to Southern California. They will no doubt come to visit you."

"What has happened to the schools in Tabriz?" I asked.

"They are now government schools," Fred replied. "The Persian government particularly admired the Boys' School building in Tabriz. It has been renamed the Avicenna School and the Girls' School was renamed the Pleiades School."

"What happened to the medical facilities at the mission?"

"The Persian government also took over the hospitals and dispensaries. They allowed the medical missionaries to stay on and teach in the government medical schools, at least temporarily."

"And the church and cemetery?" I asked.

"In Tabriz, I suspect they will honor the sanctity of the church and cemetery," Fred replied. "Even the plundering Kurds honored the sanctity of the beautiful Presbyterian cemetery on Mount Seir. While all of the buildings in the mission were damaged or destroyed, the cemetery was left untouched. The Persians even replaced the wooden picket fence surrounding the Seir cemetery with an adobe wall."

"Someday I must go back and see the Tabriz cemetery," I said. "That is where my husband and three of my children are buried." Tears welled in my eyes.

Fred put his arm around my shoulder. "We are all grieving the loss of our mission stations," he said, "and our missionary friends and loved ones."

In 1945, the United Nations held their first convention in San Francisco, bringing delegates from sixty countries. I was thrilled when I received a letter from the head of the Iran Delegation, Dr. Sadeq Rezazadeh Shafaq, one of our former students at the Boys' School in Tabriz. He had founded the newspaper *Shafaq*, meaning "Dawn" or "Light." In 1911 he led a procession of students to the Foreign Consulates to protest the Russian invasion of Tabriz. As a result, his name was on the proscribed list, and he went into hiding to avoid being executed.

After Shafaq fled to Constantinople, he taught Persian at Roberts College, and visited Rose during her assignment for Near East Relief. Later he received his doctorate degree from the University of Berlin. He was now a Professor at Tehran University and a member of the *Majlis*. Before coming to California, he visited Rose in Montclair, and she gave him my address.

When he visited me in San Jose, I said, "I always wondered how you were able to escape from the Russians in Tabriz. We heard rumors that you were arrested and hanged."

"It was Princess Ehteram who helped me," Dr. Shafaq replied. "After her husband was assassinated in 1911, she sent a message that I could join her caravan to Russia. When I asked her why she was helping me, she replied, 'My husband was going to divorce me because I was childless. My sister Princess Ezzat advised me to seek counsel with *Khanum* Wilson, who came to me and said she would try to help. She asked you to meet with my husband. You argued with him in the Bazaar about the evils of divorce

and he decided not to divorce me. For that I am indebted to you.'
Once I reached the Caucasus, I took a ferry across the Black Sea
to Constantinople."

"The following year when we returned to America on furlough, we were so relieved to hear from you," I said. "Sam was
delighted to write a letter of recommendation for your position at
Roberts College."

"I also appreciate your sending me a photograph of Dr. Wilson
after his death," Dr. Shafaq said. "I can never forget his prayers
for Persia at morning chapel. It was what inspired me to return to
Persia and do what I could for my homeland."

I cried after Dr. Shafaq departed, and for years I was moved
by his last words. He was living proof that Sam's devotion to his
students made a difference. *We made a difference.*

1951 — San Jose, California

This year I turned ninety and have been wondering how long I
will continue to live. Mary Labaree died in 1941. My dear friend
Fred Coan died in 1943 and Marguerite Vanneman died in 1945. It
must be close to my time too. I find I wear the *nazar* that Princess
Essat gave to me more frequently to protect me from the "Evil
Eye," but the hand of God is likely undeterred.

In Genesis 9:29, it says Noah lived to be nine hundred and fifty
years old. In Deuteronomy 34:7 we are told Moses lived to be one
hundred and twenty. I do not think I will live as long as Noah, and
when Moses died "His eye was undimmed and his vigor unabated."
My eyes are starting to feel the dimness of age, so I do not think
I will live as long as Moses did.

After I placed a stone on the ceiling of Noah's tomb, God
answered most of my prayers. Among the things I prayed for was

a lasting Memory. In Deuteronomy 8:2 Moses tells us: "And you shall remember all the way which the Lord your God has led you." I feel blessed that at ninety I can remember all the wonderful things about my life and those I have loved.

On February 1, 1952, Annie Dwight Rhea Wilson was taken by the Lord for a higher purpose. She was buried in the Rhea plot in Mountain View Cemetery, Altadena, California next to her mother Sarah Jane Foster Rhea and her brother Foster Audley Rhea.

Annie Rhea Wilson, 1949

APPENDIX

Glossary of Foreign Words	
Native Persian/ Russian Language	English
abandar	a water tank
Ahrab district	a ward west of Lawala
Aji Chai bridge	an ancient bridge northwest of Tabriz that was part of the Silk Road leading to Europe
Al hamd ul illah	"Praise to God"
Ala Gapi bridge	a bridge leading to the government center of Tabriz, "the Divine Portal"
Ali Illahis	another name for Yarsanis
Allah askar	"God is great"
Amir Khiz district	a Muslim ward on the northwest edge of Tabriz
anam	a fee or tip for a legitimate service
anan	the Islamic call to prayer
anderoon	the women's apartment, "harem" or "forbidden place"
Anjuman	local representative assembly
anjuman	a representative in a local assembly
arak	alcohol distilled from raisins
araqchin	a dome-shaped rimless skullcap
Ashtook	a game with eight rocks
at	"horse" in Azeri
Bagh-i Shah	the King's Garden in Behshahr near Tehran
Bagh-i-Shamal	the Vali Ahd's summer palace and the North Garden in Tabriz
Baharestan	the House of Parliament building in Tehran
bakh	"look" in Azeri

Bakhtiari	an ancient Lur tribe from the west central mountains of Persia
bakshish	tip or alms given to beggars with respect and veneration
balakhana	a second-floor room in a caravanserai
Baron Avak district	an Armenian ward named after Avak Avakian east of Lawala
bast	refuge
basti	a person taking refuge
bastinado	torture by caning the soles of the feet
beglar-begi	the mayor of the city
Bezhenets	"Refugee" in Russian, a newspaper in the Caucasus
booq-e javaz	a horn announcing the bath in the bath-house is ready
cajavahs	baskets carried on either side of a horse or donkey to transport young children
calguz	guano cakes
caravanserai	an inn for travelers with a central stable for livestock
chai	river
chai-khana	tea house
Charharshanbe suri	Festival Wednesday
charkh	A threshing sledge with sharp flint stones sticking out of the bottom side
charvadar	a muleteer
chenar	a plane tree
chesma	a hole from which water surfaces from a kariz
chuddar	a two-yard square piece of cloth that a woman warps around her body from head to ankle as street clothes

daha	"more" in Azeri
Daria-i-Noor	"Sea of Light," one of the largest cut diamonds in the world
dava	"fighting" or "brawl" in Azeri
Davachi district	a district on the northern edge of Tabriz, "camel-men's quarter"
dervish	a Muslim who has taken vows of austerity who tell stories or perform rituals for alms
dolmas	dumplings of ground meat and rice encased in grape or cabbage leaves
Dorugh-e Sizdah	"Lie of the Thirteenth," when Persians play tricks on each other
droshky	an open Russian carriage drawn by one horse
dua	"prayer" in Azeri
Eid mobarak	"May your feast or festival be blessed"
esfand	wild rue seeds
et	"meat" in Azeri
faragi	accommodations for foreigners
farsag	a Persian unit of measure of distance equal to about four miles
fidai	a member of the Volunteer Nationalist Army of Tabriz, a "devotee"
Gala district	a predominantly Armenian district west of Lawala
ghottab	crescent-shaped pastry filled with nuts
gini	"wife" in Armenian
Hadid	"Iron" or "Keen One," a Tabriz newspaper
Hafez	Xawje Shams-od-Din Mohammad Hafez-e Shirazi, a Persian poet who used the pen name Hafez

Haft sang	a game with seven rocks, one team knocks over a pile of eight rocks with a ball and tries to reassemble it as the other team tries to tag them out with a ball, like dodgeball
Haftsin	a Nowruz table with seven dishes, each containing something beginning with the Persian letter S, or 'sin'
Hajji	an honorific title to a Muslim who has made Hajj to Mecca
Hakim	physician
Hakim Khanum	Madame Doctor
hammam	a public bathhouse
hijab	the covering of women in public, according to the customs of Islam. In 1900 in Iran, women wore shalwar, baggy pants, chuddar, a large square cloth covering wrapped around the body from head to ankle, and a veil with embroidered eye slits to allow one to see.
Ishkan	Lake Sevan trout
it	"dog" in Azeri
jamadani	Kurdish turban
Jashn-e Melli	National Celebration
jihad	a holy war
jinns	bad spirits
kabin	the price to divorce a wife
kahgul	a dervish's alms collection box, often an Indian nutshell
Kala district	the old district of Tabriz
Kalabegi	a local government official who oversees several districts
Kalantar	the "mayor" and chief of police of a district and responsible for taxation

kanda kuda	the village chief
Kara Goynlis	"Black Sheep," a Kurdish tribe
kariz	an underground channel carrying water from wells
Khabar-dar	"Look here," "Attention," "Be wakeful"
khalat	a loose, long-sleeved silk or cotton robe
Khalat	a robe of honor, often worn first by the giver of the robe, particularly if it is the Shah or Vali Ahd
Khan	formal address to a noble man
Khanum	formal address to a noble woman
Khanum	polite title for a woman
Khoda be kheyr kone sevomisho	"God have mercy on the third one"
Khoda hafez	"God be with you"
khoncha	a wooden tray, typically 2' by 4', carried on a man's head
Khoresh Gheymeh	lamb and split pea stew
Kiaban district	a district east of the central district of Kala in Tabriz
kibitka	a covered Russian wagon drawn by four horses
kiny	"wine" in Armenian
Kuh-e-Nuh	Mont Ararat
laboo	boiled beets
Lake Gokcha	Lake Sevan
lavash	a thin leavened flatbread baked on the sides of a tandur
Lawala district	A central district south of the central Kala district where the Presbyterian mission in Tabriz is located, half a mile south of the Arg

Majlis	the National Parliament or its delegates
Masruta	Constitutionalism
matzoon	yoghurt-like fermented milk
maydan	a square outside the Baharestan
Mayrig	"little mother" in Armenian
Mosavat	"Equality," a newspaper
mudakhil	official or socially acceptable swindling
muezzin	a caller to prayer in Islam
mujtahid	a chief mullah and an authority of Islamic law of Shia Muslims
mullah	a high priest of Islam who wears a white turban
Nadim-bashi	principal of the government school
nazar	an amulet worn to protect one from the 'Evil Eye'
nazmiyya	a policeman
Neda-ye Vatan	"Voice of Nation," a newspaper
ney	a Persian end-blown flute, one of the oldest musical instruments still used
Nowruz	Persian New Year, which occurs on the vernal equinox
ojak	a fireplace built into a wall
Osmanli	Ottoman (adjective)
padishah yoshasun	his majesty's long life
peeshkesh	a gift to a superior to obtain a favor
peshwaz	a cavalcade of townspeople, traveling one to three days journey to meet travelers from afar
peskel	sheep or goat manure cakes
phaeton	a sporty, open four-wheel carriage

pillou	boiled rice with butter
qalyan	waterpipe or hookah, kalean
qiran	the currency in Persia between 1825-1932, when it was replaced by the rial
Rakhsh	Rostam's horse in the *Shahmaneh*
Rasteh Kucheh	Straight Street
Rostam	a hero in the *Shahmaneh*
sabze	sprouting wheat
Sadrazam	Prime Minister
Sahib	polite title for a man
sakka	a water porter
salam alakum	"Peace be with you"
samanu	wheat germ pudding
sangak	a thin leavened flatbread baked on a bed of stones
santoor	a trapezoidal-shaped zither
Sarabi	an ancient Persian sheep dog
Saranjam	the sacred book of the Yarsani
Shafaq	"Light" or "Dawn," a newspaper
sargin	cow dung cakes
sayyid	a male descendent of Muhammad, who wears a green turban
sayyida	a female descendent of Muhammad
seeb	apple
seer	garlic
senjed	Persian olive
serkeh	vinegar
Shahnameh	the national epic of Persia by Ferdowsi
Shahsevan	tribal fighters, historically "protectors of the Shah"

shalwar	baggy trousers worn by Persian women as street clothes
Shams ol Emareh	the palace of the Vali Ahd, or Crown Prince, in Tabriz, the royal compound called Dar-ol-Khalafeh
sherbet	fruit drink made from fruit syrup and water
shorba	a thick mutton stew with potatoes and herbs
Simurgh	a giant bird from the *Shahmaneh*
sin	"S" in the Persian alphabet
Sipahdar	Field Marshal
Sipahsalar	an army commander
Sizdah Be-dar	Nature's Day when Persians picnic outside
sogat	small gifts to relatives and friends
sokmeh-doozy	fine needle lacework
somaq	red sumac berries
Sur-i-Israfil	"Archangel Israfil" a newspaper
takhtarevan	a traveling chair or throne
takhtcha	a wall niche
talaq	divorce, "triple talaq" invokes divorce
Tamaddan	"Civilization," a newspaper
tamasha	a sight or event of interest
tambur	a string instrument, the sacred symbol of the Yarsani
tandur	a clay oven in the floor or ground, sometimes free-standing in a yard
tarlan	"hawk" in Persian
tasbuh	Islam rosary
teriak	raw opium
tonbak	a goblet-shaped drum
tuyul	an ancient land allotment system in Persia

Vali Ahd	Crown Prince and heir to the throne as Shah of Persia
Vali	Turkish governor
xiangqi	Chinese chess
Ya hak	"Oh truth"
Ya Yaradan Allah	"O Creator God"
yapma	manure cakes
yeddi luvn	a festive collection of dried fruits and nuts
zaptieh	Turkish soldier and guide
Zardi-ye man az toh, sorkhi-ye toh az man	a Zoroastrian fire jumping song , "my yellow is yours; your red is mine"

NOTES

General Sources

Wilson, Annie Rhea. *My Memories*. unpublished, 1951.

Wilson, Samuel Graham. *Persian Life and Customs: with Scenes and Incidents of Residence and Travel in the Land of the Lion and the Sun*. London: Oliphant, Anderson, Ferrier, 1896.

Wilson, Samuel Graham. *Persia: Western Mission*. Philadelphia: Presbyterian Board of Publication and Sabbath-School Work, 1896.

Coan, Frederick Gallup. *Yesterdays in Persia and Kurdistan*. Claremont: Saunders Studio, 1939.

Jewett, Mary. *Reminiscences of My Life in Persia*. Cedar Rapids: Torch, 1909.

Wilson, Annie Rhea. *Illustrations of the Bible from Persian Life*. Pamphlet, New York: Presbyterian Church, 1900.

Shedd, Mary Lewis. *The Measure of a Man: The Life of William Ambrose Shedd, Missionary to Persia*. New York: George Doran, 1922.

Speer, Robert Elliot. *The Hakim Sahib, The Foreign Doctor: A Biography of Joseph Plumb Cochran, M.D. of Persia*. New York: Fleming Revell, 1911.

Aro, Margaret Packard. *Hakim Sahib, "Sir Doctor": The Great Adventure Story of a Missionary Surgeon and Sometimes Diplomat to Persia Dr. Harry P. Packard, 1874-1954*. Colorado Springs: Box, 2003.

Ponafidine, Pierre. *Life in the Muslim East*. Translated from Russian by Emma Cochran Ponafidine. New York: Dodd, Mead, 1911.

Johna, Samir. *Twenty-five Years in Persia: The Memoirs of Mary Allen Whipple*. Bloomington: The Whipple Family, 2003.

Arpee, Edward. *Lake Forest, Illinois: History and Reminiscences, 1861-1961*. Chicago: Donnelley, 1964.

Kelsy, Susan L. and Miller, Arthur H. *Legendary Locals of Lake Forest*. Charleston: Arcadia, 2015.

Browne, Edward Granville. *The Persia Revolution, 1905-1909*. Cambridge: Cambridge University, 1910.

Browne, Edward Granville. *Letters from Tabriz: The Russian Suppression of the Iranian Constitutional Movement*. Manuscript edited by Hasan Javadi. Washington: Mage, 2008.

Karimi, Linda Collen. *Implications of American Missionary Presence in 19th and 20th Century Iran*. Master's Thesis in History. Portland: Portland State University, 1975.

Zirinsky, Michael. *American Presbyterian Missionaries at Urmia During the Great War*. Proceeding of the International Roundtable on Persia and the Great War, Tehran: Iran Chamber Society, 1997.

Davis, Matthew Mark. *Evangelizing the Orient: American Missionaries in Iran, 1890-1940*. Doctoral Thesis. Columbus: Ohio State University, 2000.

Presbyterian Historical Society: the National Archives of the PC(USA): https://www.history.pcusa.org

Davis, Matthew Mark. *The Legend of Howard Baskerville: American Missionaries and the Iranian Constitutional Revolution, 1907-1911.* Columbus: Ohio State University, 1997.

Presbyterian Church in the U.S.A., *The Annual Report of the Board of Foreign Missions of the Presbyterian Church in the United States* (Annual Report BFMPC). New York: Presbyterian Church.

1886, v. 49: 78-92.
1887, v. 50: 73-83.
1891, v. 54: 162-177.
1892, v. 55: 199-212.
1893, v. 56: 179-195.
1895, v. 58: 158-174.
1896, v. 59: 186-198.
1897, v. 60: 160-167.
1898, v. 61: 184-197.
1899, v. 62: 192-209.
1900, v. 63: 198-208.
1901, v. 64: 243-256.
1902, v. 65: 226-237.
1903, v. 66: 258-270.
1904, v. 67: 246-263.
1905, v. 68: 284-302.
1906, v. 69: 301-316.
1907, v. 70: 315-330.
1908, v. 71: 334-337, 355-369.
1909, v. 72: 350-359.
1910, v. 73: 332-342.
1911, v. 74: 321-330.
1912, v. 75: 358-368.
1913, v. 76: 358-334.

1914, v. 77: 335-348.
1915, v. 78: 321-333.
1916, v. 79: 298-303.
1917, v. 80: 303-312.
1918, v. 81: 336-343.
1919, v. 82: 271-280.
1920, v. 83: 322-332.
1921, v. 84: 339-347.
1922, v. 85: 373-378.
1923, v. 86: 231-236.

Chapter 1
Wilson, Annie Rhea. *My Memories*. pp. 1-2; Marsh, Dwight Whitney. *The Tennessean in Persia and Kurdistan: Being Scenes and Incidents in the Life of Samuel Audley Rhea*. pp. 336-350.

Chapter 2
Wilson, Annie Rhea. *My Memories*. pp. 2-7; Fain, John N. *The Sanctified Trial: The Diary of Eliza Rhea Anderson Fain, a Confederate Woman in East Tennessee*. Knoxville: University of Tennessee Press, 2004, pp. 70, 280, 309-310, 318, 369.

Chapter 3
Wilson, Annie Rhea. *My Memories*. pp. 7-11.

Chapter 4
Wilson, Annie Rhea. *My Memories*. pp 11-13.

Chapter 5
Wilson, Annie Rhea. *Illustrations of the Bible from Persian Life*. p. 23; Wilson, Annie Rhea. *My Memories*. pp. 15, 84; Wilson, Samuel Graham. *Persian Life and Customs: with Scenes and*

Incidents of Residence and Travel in the Land of the Lion and the Sun. pp. 40-49; Coan, Frederick Gallup. *Yesterdays in Persia and Kurdistan*. p. 60.

Chapter 6
Wilson, Annie Rhea. *My Memories*. p. 15; Wilson, Samuel Graham. *Persian Life and Customs: with Scenes and Incidents of Residence and Travel in the Land of the Lion and the Sun*. pp. 47-51.

Chapter 7
Wilson, Annie Rhea. *My Memories*. p. 15; Jewett, Mary. *Reminiscences of My Life in Persia*. pp. 27-29, 42-44; Wilson, Samuel Graham. *Persia: Western Mission*. pp. 30, 104-108, 110-129, 158, 224-225; Ponafidine, Pierre. *Life in the Muslim East*. pp. 290-429; Wilson, Samuel Graham. *Persian Life and Customs: with Scenes and Incidents of Residence and Travel in the Land of the Lion and the Sun*. pp. 52-70.

Chapter 8
Wilson, Annie Rhea. *My Memories*. pp. 16, 20-21; Wilson, Samuel Graham. *Persia: Western Mission*. pp. 197-221, 200-205; Jewett, Mary. "Far Away Persia," The Nebraska Journal, December 25, 1888, p.5; Jewett, Mary. *Reminiscences of My Life in Persia*. pp. 83-85, 95-100.

Chapter 9
Wilson, Samuel Graham. *Persian Life and Customs: with Scenes and Incidents of Residence and Travel in the Land of the Lion and the Sun*. pp. 52-70, 243-253; Wilson, Annie Rhea. *Illustrations of the Bible from Persian Life*. p. 25.

Chapter 10

Wilson, Samuel Graham. "The Influence of Medical Missions," Church at Home and Abroad, 1887, v. 1: 379; Wilson, Samuel Graham. _Persia: Western Mission._ pp. 207-212, 286; Jewett, Mary. _Reminiscences of My Life in Persia._ p. 100; Annual Report BFMPC 1888 v. 51: 83-85; Annual Report BFMPC 1889 v. 52: 84-86.

Chapter 11

Jewett, Mary. _Reminiscences of My Life in Persia._ pp. 97-100; Ponafidine, Pierre. _Life in the Muslim East._ pp. 300, 327; Wilson, Samuel Graham. _Persian Life and Customs: with Scenes and Incidents of Residence and Travel in the Land of the Lion and the Sun._ pp. 262-263, 309; Wilson, Annie Rhea. _My Memories._ pp. 20-21.

Chapter 12

Wilson, Annie Rhea. _My Memories._ p. 16; Wilson, Samuel Graham. _Persian Life and Customs: with Scenes and Incidents of Residence and Travel in the Land of the Lion and the Sun._ pp. 268-277; Ponafidine, Pierre. _Life in the Muslim East._ pp. 294-298.

Chapter 13

Wilson, Annie Rhea. _My Memories._ p. 16; Wilson, Samuel Graham. _Persian Life and Customs: with Scenes and Incidents of Residence and Travel in the Land of the Lion and the Sun._ pp. 109-124; Wilson, Samuel Graham. _Persia: Western Mission._ pp. 291-294.

Chapter 14

Wilson, Annie Rhea. _My Memories._ pp. 16-17; Wilson, Samuel Graham. _Persian Life and Customs: with Scenes and Incidents of Residence and Travel in the Land of the Lion and the Sun._ pp. 171-172; Wilson, Samuel Graham. _Persia: Western Mission._ pp.

164-166, 179-181, 212; Johna, Samir. *Twenty-five Years in Persia: The Memoirs of Mary Allen Whipple*. p. 118; Annual Report BFMPC 1891 v. 54: 162-177; https://history.pcusa.org/blog/2018/08/scandal-salmas-marriage-and murder-shushan-oshanan-wright.

Chapter 15
Wilson, Annie Rhea. *My Memories*. p. 18; Annual Report BFMPC 1892 v. 55: 199-212.

Chapter 16
Wilson, Annie Rhea. *My Memories*. p. 19; Wilson, Samuel Graham. *Persia: Western Mission*. pp. 295-313.

Chapter 17
Wilson, Samuel Graham. *Persia: Western Mission*. pp. 188-192, 218-220; Annual Report BFMPC 1892, v. 55: 179-195; Annual Report BFMPC 1893, v. 56: 179-195; Jewett, Mary. *Reminiscences of My Life in Persia*. p. 101.

Chapter 18
Wilson, Annie Rhea. *My Memories*. pp. 22-23.

Chapter 19
"The 1895-1896 Armenian Massacres in Harput: Eyewitness Account," Etudes armeniennes contemporaines, 2018, v. 10: 161-183; Annual Report BFMPC 1895, v. 58: 158-174; Annual Report BFMPC 1896, v. 59: 186-198.

Chapter 20
Wilson, Annie Rhea. *My Memories*. p. 36; Browne, Edward Granville. *The Persia Revolution, 1905-1909*. pp. 59-97; Annual

Report BFMPC 1897, v. 60:160-167; Annual Report BFMPC 1898, v. 61: 184-197; Annual Report BFMPC 1899, v. 62: 192-209.

Chapter 21
Annual Report BFMPC 1898, v. 61: 184-197; Annual Report BFMPC 1899, v. 62: 192-209; Jewett, Mary. *Reminiscences of My Life in Persia*. pp. 136-142; Wilson, Samuel Graham. *Persian Life and Customs: with Scenes and Incidents of Residence and Travel in the Land of the Lion and the Sun*. pp. 140-142.

Chapter 22
Wilson, Annie Rhea. *My Memories*. pp. 17, 20, 24-25, 27-29; Wilson, Samuel Graham. *Persia: Western Mission*. p. 212; Allen, Thomas Gaskell and Sachtleben, William Lewis. *Across Asia on a Bicycle: The Journey of Two American Students from Constantinople to Peking*. New York: Century, 1894; Annual Report BFMPC 1900, v. 63: 198-208; Annual Report BFMPC 1901, v. 64: 243-256; Wilson, Samuel Graham. *Persian Life and Customs: with Scenes and Incidents of Residence and Travel in the Land of the Lion and the Sun*. pp. 86-93; Coan, Frederick Gallup. *Yesterdays in Persia and Kurdistan*. pp. 166-175.

Chapter 23
Wilson, Annie Rhea. *My Memories*. pp. 25, 86; Annual Report BFMPC 1901, v. 64: 243-256; Annual Report BFMPC 1902, v. 65: 226-265.

Chapter 24

Wilson, Annie Rhea. *My Memories*. pp. 25-27, 29; Annual Report BFMPC 1902, v. 65: 226-265; Annual Report BFMPC 1903, v. 66: 258-270; Annual Report BFMPC 1904, v. 67: 246-263.

Chapter 25

Wilson, Annie Rhea. *My Memories*. pp. 30-31; Shedd, Mary Lewis. *The Measure of a Man: The Life of William Ambrose Shedd, Missionary to Persia*. pp. 79-80; Speer, Robert Elliot. *The Hakim Sahib, The Foreign Doctor: A Biography of Joseph Plumb Cochran, M.D. of Persia*. pp. 259-262, 265-268; Annual Report BFMPC 1904, v. 67: 246-263; Annual Report BFMPC 1905, v. 68: 284-302.

Chapter 26

Wilson, Annie Rhea. *My Memories*. pp. 27-28, 32; Annual Report BFMPC 1904, v. 67: 246-263; Annual Report BFMPC 1905, v. 68: 284-302; Annual Report BFMPC 1906, v. 68: 301-316; Browne, Edward Granville. *The Persia Revolution, 1905-1909*. p.112; Coan, Frederick Gallup. *Yesterdays in Persia and Kurdistan*. pp. 224-227; Shedd, Mary Lewis. *The Measure of a Man: The Life of William Ambrose Shedd, Missionary to Persia*. pp. 72-78; Speer, Robert Elliot. *The Hakim Sahib, The Foreign Doctor: A Biography of Joseph Plumb Cochran, M.D. of Persia*. pp. 257-258, 265-287.

Chapter 27

Wilson, Annie Rhea. *My Memories*. pp. 20, 32, 36; Wilson, Samuel Graham. "Political Progress in Persia," *The Presbyterian Banner* v. 93 (December 13, 1906), p 885; Annual Report BFMPC 1908, v. 70: 297-298, 315-330; Browne, Edward Granville. *The Persia Revolution, 1905-1909*. p.119-133; Browne, Edward Granville. *The Press and Poetry of Modern Persia*. Cambridge: Cambridge University, 1914, p. 75.

Chapter 28

Wilson, Annie Rhea. *My Memories*. pp. 31, 36, 38; Browne, Edward Granville. *The Persia Revolution, 1905-1909*. pp. 142, 144-145, 151-153, 172; Annual Report BFMPC 1908, v. 71: 334-373, 355-369; *Punch*, Sir Owen Seaman, ed., 1907, v. 133, p.245; Jewett, Mary. *Reminiscences of My Life in Persia*. pp. 14-23, 101-102.

Chapter 29

Browne, Edward Granville. *The Persia Revolution, 1905-1909*. pp. 198; Annual Report BFMPC 1909, v. 72: 333-336, 350-359; Wilson, Samuel Graham. "Inside News from Tabriz Persia," *The Westminister* v. 33: 20 (August 22, 1908); Wilson, Samuel Graham. "The Fight for Constitutional Liberty in Persia," *The Presbyterian Banner* v. 95: 688-689 (November 5, 1908).

Chapter 30

Browne, Edward Granville. *The Persia Revolution, 1905-1909*. p. 270-271, 249-250; Annual Report BFMPC 1909, v. 72: 333-336, 350-359; Annual Report BFMPC 1910, v. 73: 332-342; Wilson, Samuel Graham. "The Second Siege of Tabriz, Persia," *The Presbyterian Banner* v. 95: 1692-1693 (June 3, 1909); Wilson, Samuel Graham. Copy of correspondence with Mr. Baskerville, 1909, pp. 1-3; Davis, Matthew Mark. *The Legend of Howard Baskerville: American Missionaries and the Iranian Constitutional Revolution, 1907-1911*. Columbus: Ohio State University, 1997, pp. 15-18.

Chapter 31

Annual Report BFMPC 1911, v. 74: 321-330; Browne, Edward Granville. *The Persia Revolution, 1905-1909*. p. 275-278, 292-323, 330; Browne, Edward Granville. *Letters from Tabriz: The Russian Suppression of the Iranian Constitutional Movement*.

p. 19; Browne, Edward Granville. *Press and Poetry of Modern Persia*, 1914, p. 319.

Chapter 32

Wilson, Annie Rhea. *My Memories*. pp. 39-42; Annual Report BFMPC 1911, v. 75: 358-368; Davis, Matthew Mark. *The Legend of Howard Baskerville: American Missionaries and the Iranian Constitutional Revolution, 1907-1911*. Columbus: Ohio State University, 1997, pp 15-17, 39; Letter from J.N. Wright to Robert Speer, Tabriz, Persia, April 22, 1909, v. 204, West Persia Correspondence 1909, Princeton Theological Seminary, Presbyterian Historical Society; Browne, Edward Granville. *Letters from Tabriz: The Russian Suppression of the Iranian Constitutional Movement*. pp. 24-25, 29, 57, 91, 139-146, 180-181, 184-258, 260-261, 267; Browne, Edward Granville. *The Reign of Terror at Tabriz*, pamphlet, October 1912, Taylor, Garnett, Evans, p. 1-15.

Chapter 33

Wilson, Annie Rhea. *My Memories*. p. 43; Annual Report BFMPC 1913, v. 76: 358-334; Browne, Edward Granville. *The Reign of Terror at Tabriz*, pamphlet, October 1912, Taylor, Garnett, Evans, p. 1-15.

Chapter 34

Wilson, Annie Rhea. *My Memories*. pp. 43-45; *Letters from Tabriz: The Russian Suppression of the Iranian Constitutional Movement*. pp. 41, 246; Journal of Agnes Wilson, 1913, unpublished; Annual Report BFMPC 1914, v. 77: 335-348; Annual Report BFMPC 1915, v. 78: 321-333; "Philip Howard Wilson." *Princeton Alumni Weekly*, 1913, v. 14 (1): 30; "Derailment at Glen Loch, PA." *Railway Age*

Gazette v. 53 (23): 1086-1088; Letter from Rev. Frederick N. Jessup in *Women's Work* December 1912, v. 28: 271.

Chapter 35

Wilson, Annie Rhea. *My Memories*. p. 45; Annual Report BFMPC 1916, v. 79: 298-303; Coan, Frederick Gallup. *Yesterdays in Persia and Kurdistan*. pp. 250-260; "First Exodus from Urmia, January 1915." Letter from Reverend Robert M. Labaree to Hon. F. Willoughby-Smith, pp. 105-109. Rockefeller Foundation Digital Archive.

Chapter 36

Wilson, Samuel G. "To Persia Around the War Zone." *The Missionary Review of the World*, 1916 v. 39:683-684; Hill, Richard. "Letter from Richard Hill to Samuel T. Dutton, 1915 December 12; "Refugees in the Caucasus: Letter dated Erivan, 29 December 1915 from Rev. S. G. Wilson to Dr. Samuel T. Dutton." pp. 1-4. Rockefeller Foundation Digital Archive; Wilson, Samuel G. "Report on Armenian Relief Work, March 1, 1916." Letter to Prof. Samuel T. Dutton. pp. 1-3; Wilson, Samuel G. "General Report on Relief Work Among the Armenians in the Trans-Caucasus, March 6, 1916." pp. 1-2. Rockefeller Foundation Digital Archive; Wilson, Samuel G. "Letter dated Nalband, Caucasus, 12 March 1916 to Agnes Wilson." unpublished.

Chapter 37

Wilson, Annie Rhea. *My Memories*. p. 46; Journal of Agnes Wilson, 1916, unpublished; "Death of Dr. S. G. Wilson." *Princeton Seminary Bulletin* (November 1916) v. 10 (3):29-32; Labaree, Robert M. "Dr. Samuel Graham Wilson." *The Fourth Church* (1916) v. 4: 306-307; Labaree, Robert M. "The Priceless Offering." *Men and Missions* (September 1916) v. 8 (1): 20-21;[*]

Speer, Robert E. *The Mission World* (1917) v. 7:191-195; Annual Report BFMPC 1917, v. 80: 303-312.

Chapter 38

Wilson, Annie Rhea. *My Memories*. pp. 47-48; Journal of Agnes Wilson, 1918, unpublished; Coan, Frederick Gallup. *Yesterdays in Persia and Kurdistan*. pp. 263-272; Fulton, Ruth Coan, *Coan Genealogy 1697-1982: Peter and George of East Hampton, Long Island, and Guilford, Connecticut with their Descendants in the Coan Line as well as other Allied Lines*. Portsmouth, NH: Randall, p 340; Annual Report BFMPC 1919, v. 82: 271-280.

Chapter 39

Wilson, Annie Rhea. *My Memories*. pp. 48-50; Coan, Frederick Gallup. *Yesterdays in Persia and Kurdistan*. pp. 273-278; *Woman's Work* (1920) v. 35: 90-112; *The Wisconsin Alumnus* (April 1938) v. 39 (9): 206-207; Aro, Margaret Packard. *Hakim Sahib, "Sir Doctor": The Great Adventure Story of a Missionary Surgeon and Sometimes Diplomat to Persia Dr. Harry P. Packard, 1874-1954*. pp. 106-115; Annual Report BFMPC 1920, v. 83: 322-332; *Women's Work* (December 1913) v. 28:272.

Chapter 40

Wilson, Annie Rhea. *My Memories*. pp. 49-52; Aro, Margaret Packard. *Hakim Sahib, "Sir Doctor": The Great Adventure Story of a Missionary Surgeon and Sometimes Diplomat to Persia Dr. Harry P. Packard, 1874-1954*. p.133; Annual Report BFMPC 1921, v. 84: 339-347; Annual Report BFMPC 1922, v. 85: 373-378; Annual Report BFMPC 1923, v. 86: 231-234.

Chapter 41

Wilson, Annie Rhea. *My Memories*. pp. 53-60; Coan, Frederick Gallup. *Yesterdays in Persia and Kurdistan*. pp. 282-283; *The Wisconsin Alumnus* (April 1938) v. 39 (3): 206-207.

Chapter 42

Wilson, Annie Rhea. *My Memories*. pp. 62-82; Karimi, Linda Collen. *Implications of American Missionary Presence in 19th and 20th Century Iran*. p. 68; *The Wisconsin Alumnus* (April 1938) v. 39 (3): 206-207.

BIOGRAPHIES

Annie Rhea Wilson's Family

Parents
Sarah Jane "Sallie" Foster (1835-1918)
Rev. Samuel Audley Rhea (1827-1865)

Siblings	Spouses	Children
Annie Dwight Rhea (1861-1952)	Samuel Graham Wilson (1858-1916)	Samuel Rhea Wilson ("Rhea") (1890-1891) Mary Agnes Wilson ("Agnes") (1892-1932) Rose Dulles Wilson (1894-1960) Esther Thompson Wilson (1897-1901) Andrew Wilkins Wilson III (1899-1902) Annie Rhea Wilson, Jr. (1901-1980) Robert Graham Wilson ("Bobby") (1903-2000)
Foster Audley Rhea (1863-1920)	none	none
Robert Leighton Rhea (1864-1865)	none	none

Sophea Perkins Rhea (1866-1907)	William Dulles (1855-1915)	Dorothy Winslow Dulles (1893-1969)
		Edith Rutledge Dulles (1897-1985)
		Foster Rhea Dulles ("Rhea") (1900-1970)
		William Winslow Dulles ("Winslow") (1903-1963)

Samuel Graham Wilson's Family

Parents
Anna Graham Dick (1833-1912)
Andrew Wilkins Wilson (1826-1897)

Siblings	Spouses	Children
Harry Wilkins Wilson (1854-1937)	Margaret Patton (1854-1889)	Harry Wilkins Wilson, Jr. ("Lad") (1886-1946) Margaret Patton Wilson (1889-1963)
Robert Dick Wilson (1856-1930)	Ellen Conway Howard (1865-1954)	Philip Howard Wilson ("Howard") (1890-1913) Eleanor Stuart Wilson (1892-1956) Sarah Bruce Wilson (1894-1980) Anne Elizabeth Wilson (1896-1986) Jane Pope Wilson (1898-1989) Julia Roy Wilson (1901-1922)
Samuel Graham Wilson (1858-1916)	Annie Dwight Rhea (1861-1952)	See above for Annie Rhea Wilson
John Loughery Wilson (1861-1928)	none	none

Andrew Wilkins Wilson, Jr. (1863-1930)	Bessie Gladys Sansom (1864-1946)	Sarah Sansom Wilson (1890-1959) Anna Graham Wilson (1891-1983) Elizabeth Wilson (1893-1895) Gladys Margaret Wilson (1898-1996) Ella May Wilson (1900-1991)
Ella May Wilson (1865-1937)	George Rippey Stewart (1847-1937)	Andrew Wilson Stewart (1892-1946) George Rippey Stewart, Jr. (1895-1980) John Harris Stewart (1899-1906)
Annie Elizabeth Wilson (1868-1961)	Alfred Hamilton Barr (1868-1936)	Alfred Hamilton Barr, Jr. (1902-1981) Andrew Wilson Barr (1905-1997)
James Dick Wilson ("Dick") (1870-1932)	Clara M. Wagner (1885-1968)	Andrew Wilkins Wilson (1913-1983)
Jane Pearson Wilson ("Jenny") (1873-1952)	Robert McGee Mullen (1871-1950)	Robert McGee Mullen II (1908-1951)
Mary Agnes Wilson ("Agnes") (1877-1967)	Stacy Heater Smith (1878-1919)	Stacy Heater Smith, Jr. (1906-?) Jane Wilson Smith (1908-1989)

Annie Rhea Wilson's Friends

Anna Holt Wheeler (1860-1930)
Anna Holt lived across the street from Annie Rhea in the Holt estate, "The Homestead," in Lake Forest and was her best friend throughout her life. She married Arthur Dana Wheeler (1861-1912), Annie Rhea's classmate at Lake Forest College, who became a successful lawyer in Chicago.

Charlotte Eliza Skinner Thurston (1862-1943)
Charlotte Skinner was Annie Rhea's classmate at Lake Forest College. In 1891, she married Henry W. Thurston (1861-1946), a high school teacher in Chicago, who became the chief probation officer of the Juvenile Court and then the head of the Illinois Children's Home and Aid Society. He became head of Children's Work at the New York School of Social Work, and they moved to Montclair, New Jersey.

Princess Ezzat-ed-Dowleh Qajar (1872-1955)
Princess Ezzat was the daughter of *Vali Ahd* Mozzafar ad-Din. She married her father's treasurer Abdol-Hossein Farman Farmaian (1857-1939) and they had six children, including Prince Abbas in 1890. Annie Rhea Wilson gave Princess Ezzat music lessons until her father became Shah in 1896 and she moved to Tehran. Her husband sought to become premier but a coalition against him forced the family into exile in Egypt and Baghdad until 1903. In 1907, the family returned to Tabriz when her husband was appointed governor of the Azerbaijan province. After Reza Pahlavi gained power, her husband and two sons were imprisoned, then placed under house arrest.

A.V. Williams Jackson (1862-1937)

Abraham Valentine Williams Jackson was a scholar of ancient Persian language, religion and literature and professor of Indo-Iranian languages at Columbia University from 1895-1935. He visited Persia in 1903, 1907, and 1911 and stayed with the Wilsons in Tabriz. During his visit in 1903 he climbed the cliff at Mount Behistun and photographed the trilingual inscription by Darius I, considered to be the "rosetta stone" for Near Eastern languages. He was an authority on Zoroaster and the *Avesta*.

Eva Francher Wishard (1861-1947)

In 1884, Eva Francher married Luther Deloraine Wishard (1854-1925) who attended Princeton and Princeton Theological Seminary as a classmate with Samuel Graham Wilson. Her husband launched the intercollegiate Y.M.C.A. movement and provided the impetus for the Student Volunteer Movement, recruiting students to serve as foreign missionaries. During 1888 to 1892, they made a world tour to contact foreign missionary groups. They later moved to Pasadena and were Annie Rhea Wilson's next-door neighbors. They had three children: Janet (1898-1911), Winifred (1899-1973) and Margaret (1901-1999).

Missionaries

Note: This is a partial list of missionaries at the Persia Western Mission stations. For a comprehensive list of Persian Presbyterian missionaries see: Karimi, Linda Collen. *Implications of American Missionary Presence in 19ᵗʰ and 20ᵗʰ Century Iran*. Master's Thesis in History. Portland: Portland State University, 1975.

Urmia Station: "Mission to the Nestorians"
Missionaries during Annie Rhea's Childhood in Urmia:

Rev. Justin Perkins (1805-1869) — "Grandpa Perkins"
In 1833, Justin Perkins and his wife Charlotte Bass Perkins (1808-1897) came to Tabriz and were the first Americans to live in Persia. They founded the Urmia mission in 1835 with physician Asahel Grant (1807-1844) and his wife Judith as part of the American Board of Foreign Missions, which was transferred to the Presbyterian Board of Foreign Missions in 1871. Justin Perkins served as evangelist and educator from 1833 to 1869, Charlotte withdrew in 1857.

Mary Susan Rice (1821-1905) — "Aunt Susan"
Susan Rice served the Urmia station from 1847 to 1869 as teacher and principal of the Fiske Seminary, the Girls' School.

Rev. Samuel Audley Rhea (1827-1865) — Father
Samuel Rhea served the mountain station in Gawar in the Kurdistan and Urmia station from 1851 to 1865. His first wife Martha Ann Harris died in 1857. He married Sarah Jane Foster ("Sallie") in 1860 and returned to the Urmia station on Mount Seir. He died of cholera in 1865. Sally continued at the mission as a teacher at the Fiske seminary until 1869, when she returned to America with their children. Their daughter Annie Dwight Rhea Wilson returned to Tabriz as a second-generation missionary.

Rev. Joseph G. Cochran (1817-1871)
Joseph Cochran served the Urmia station as an evangelist from 1847 to 1871. His wife Deborah Plumb Cochran (1821-1893) served as evangelist and matron to the hospital from 1847 until her death in 1893. Their son Joseph Plumb Cochran, M.D. and

daughter Emma G. Cochran returned to Urmia as second-generation missionaries.

Rev. George Whitefield Coan (1817-1879)
George Coan and his wife Sarah Payson Coan (1821-1887) served the Urmia station from 1849 to 1874, when they withdrew and returned to America. Their son Rev. Frederick Gaylord Coan returned to Urmia as a second-generation missionary.

Rev. Benjamin Labaree (1834-1906)
Benjamin Labaree served the Urmia station between 1860 to 1906. His wife Elizabeth Woods Labaree served until she died in 1898. Their sons Benjamin Woods Labaree ("B. W.") and Robert McEwen Labaree returned to Urmia as second-generation missionaries.

Rev. John Haskell Shedd (1833-1895)
John Shedd and his wife Sarah Jane Shedd ("Jennie") served the Urmia station as evangelists from 1859 to 1895 until his death. Jennie Shed withdrew the following year and moved to Los Angeles. Their son Rev. William Ambrose Shedd returned to Urmia as a second-generation missionary.

Missionaries at the Urmia Station during Annie Rhea Wilson's Tenure at the Tabriz Station:

Name (b. – d.)	Years of Service	Spouse(s) (b. – d.)	Spouse's Years of Service
Dr. Joseph Plumb Cochran (1855-1905)	1878-1905	Katherine Hale (1853-1895)	1878-1895
Rev. Frederick Gaylord Coan (1859-1943)	1885-1924	Ida Speer (1861-1939)	1885-1924
Rev. Benjamin Woods Labaree (1865-1904)	1893-1904	Mary Schauffler (1868-1954)	1893-1905
Rev. Robert McEwen Labaree (1867-1952)	1904-1916	Mary Fleming (1880-1941)	1904-1916
Rev. William Ambrose Shedd (1865-1918) "Moses of the Assyrians"	1892-1918	Adela Myers (1870-1901) Louise Wilbur (1868-1915) Mary Lewis (1873-1962)	1894-1901 1899-1915 1903-1933
Mary Kinau Van Duzee (1843-1915)	1875-1914	none	
Dr. Emma Thornton Miller (1864-1932)	1891-1909	none	
Dr. Harry Phineas Packard (1874-1954)	1906-1944	Frances "Julia" Bayley (1875-1924) Jean Wells (1889-1982)	1906-1924 1916-1944

Tabriz Station: "Mission to the Armenians"
Missionaries at the Tabriz Station during Annie Rhea Wilson's Tenure:

Name (b. – d.)	Years of Service	Spouse(s) (b. – d.)	Spouse's Years of Service
Mary Jewett (1843-1931)	1871-1907	none	
Rev. Jeremiah M. Oldfather (1841-1910)	1872-1891	Felicia Rice (1848-1942)	1872-1891
Rev. William Levi Whipple (1844-1901)	1872-1879* 1899-1901	Mary Allen (1850-1937)	1872-1879*
Dr. George Washington Holmes (1841-1910)	1874-1899	Eliza Wisner (1846-1890) Dr. Lucy Hale (1856-1849)	1874-1890 1892-1899
Rev. Samuel L. Ward (1850-1944)	1876-1887	Irene Briggs (1887-1965)	1876-1887
Loretta Turner Van Hook (1852-1935)	1876-1894 1902-1916	none	
Rev. John Newton Wright (1852-1923)	1878-1911**	Mary Caldwell Shushan Oshanna Mattie Evans (1858-1948)	1878-1879 1885-1890 1892-1911
Margaret Yandes Holliday (1843-1920)	1883-1920	none	
Dr. Mary Elizabeth Bradford (1857-1935)	1888-1909	none	

Dr. William Summerhill Vanneman (1863-1933)	1890-1933	Marguerite Amy Fox (1866-1945)	1890-1910
Rev. Turner Goe Brashear, Jr. (1866-1940)	1890-1899	Anna Hewins (1868-1916)	1890-1899
Lillie Belle Beaber (1868-1961)	1899-1938	none	
Rev. Charles Read Pittman (1874-1953)	1900-1941	Lucille Drake (1867-1956)	1902-1941
Rev. Frederick Nevins Jessup (1875-1919)	1903-1919	Helen Grove (1885-1965)	1910-1931
Rev. Leon Frederick Vauthier ("Paul") (1876-1957)	1906-1911	Lucy Woodward	1906-1911
Dr. Edna Edgerton Orcutt (1884-1914)	1911-1914	none	

*Bible Agents 1880-1899
**Salmas Station 1885-1895

Shahs of Persia 1848-1979

Name (b. – d.)	Reign	Notes
Nasar al-Din Shah Qajar (1831-1896)	9/5/1848-5/1/1896	assassinated
Mozaffar ad-Din Shah Qajar (1853-1907)	5/1/1896-1/3/1907	died during reign
Mohammad Ali Shah Qajar (1872-1925)	1/3/1907-7/16/1909	deposed

Ahmad Shah Qajar (1898-1930)	7/16/1909-12/15/1925	deposed
Reza Shah Pahlavi (1878-1944)	12/15/1925-9/16/1941	abdicated
Mohammad Reza Shah Pahlavi (1919-1979)	9/1/61941-2/11/1979	deposed

Persian Military Leaders

Name	Army	Notes
Baqir Khan	Nationalist, Tabriz	head of the *Kiaban* district forces, died 1916
Satter Khan	Nationalist, Tabriz	head of the *Amir Khiz* district forces, died 1914
Rahim Khan	Royalist, Tabriz	tribal chief of Karadagh, executed 1911
Mir Hashim	Royalist, Tabriz	head of the *Davachi* district forces, executed 1909
Samad Khan	Royalist, Tehran	head of the Shah's army, executed 1200 Tabrizis
Ayn al-Dawla	Royalist, Tehran	Commander of Shah's army
Sardar Assad	Nationalist, Tehran	Leader of Isfahan Bakhtiari march on Tehran
Samsan al-Saltana	Nationalist, Tehran	Leader of Isfahan Bakhtiari march on Tehran
Sipahdar	Nationalist, Tehran	Leader of Rascht march on Tehran
Agha Petros	Urmia Assyrian	Leader of Assyrian army defending Urmia 1917-1918
Simko Shikak	Salmas Kurds	Chieftain, massacred Assyrians in Salmas 1918-1920

Famous Students from the Memorial Boys' School

Sadeq Rezazadeh Shafaq (1892-1971)

Shafaq was a student at the Memorial Boys' School in Tabriz who became the editor of the Tabriz newspaper *Shafaq*. After he led students to protest the Russian occupation in 1911, his name was on the proscribed list to be hanged. He fled to Constantinople and became a teacher at Roberts College, earned his Ph.D. from University of Berlin and became a professor at University of Tehran and a delegate to the *Majlis*.

Sayyed Hasan Taqizadeh (1878-1970)

Taqizadeh was a student at the Memorial Boys' School in Tabriz from 1899-1900. He was elected as a delegate to the first and second *Majlis*. He continued to be an influential politician and a diplomat, as ambassador to Britain and France.

Writings from the Wilsons

Before her departure from Lake Forest, the following was presented to Annie Rhea Wilson by her mother with reference to her
father, Rev. Samuel Audley Rhea:

"From out the grave of one
 Who laid his weary body down to rest
 In Persian soil, methinks I see a spirit rise,
 Who like the Macedoman angel stands and cries,
 "Dear child, we need thee, come!

"A vision then I see
 Of those who gather round the great white throne,
 With songs of praise, 'With joy exultant now I raise
 My song to thee,' says one, 'to thee be praise'
 'Glory and honor be.'

" 'Thy promises how true
 At home with thee, I from my labors rest
 In joy and peace! The precious child thou gavest me
 Returns to bless the land of her nativity,
 Through her I work anew.'

"So we send thee forth.
 Rejoicing that the Master fills thy heart
 With love for Persia
 As patient teacher, Christian wife,
 Christ's faithful lover, may thy earnest busy life
 Reflect thy parent's worth."

— Sarah Jane Foster Rhea, 1886

(Wilson, Samuel G. Persia: Western Mission. Philadelphia:
Presbyterian Board, 1896. pp. 154-155.)

Letters Between Howard Baskerville and Rev. Samuel G. Wilson
April 1909

Tabriz, Persia March 30, 1909

Dear Dr. Wilson,
Please accept my resignation from the position of teacher in the Memorial School.
Sincerely yours,
Howard Conklin Baskerville"

Tabriz, Persia, March 30, 1909

Dear Mr. Baskerville, In reply to your letter of resignation from your position of teacher, allow me to say that I regard your contemplated course of action as unwise, rash and impracticable, as founded on a grave error of judgement and certain to lead to serious consequences to yourself and others. I as a friend, must advise you strongly against such course of action if you acknowledge my authority, I would enjoin you from it for the common good. I regard your first obligation as to the school, and still look to you to fulfill your contract as teacher. Yours sincerely, S.G. Wilson.

Tabriz, Persia, April 1, 1909

Dear Dr. Wilson, I must go. I have gone. Please forgive me for not taking your advice. You have my resignation. Sincerely, Howard C. Baskerville.

Tabriz, Persia, April 2, 1909

My dear Mr. Baskerville, I am holding your resignation under consideration and will reply in regard to it later. Meanwhile I should be glad to see you and talk over the matter again. Come today if you can. With *salams* and prayers. Yours, S.G. Wilson.

Tabriz, Persia, April 2, 1909

My dear Dr. Wilson,
It seems to me that talking the matter over any more can only lead to pain and possibly bad feelings. I must do this. I should be exceedingly glad to stay out of it but cannot. Mr. Moore and I are in it for better or for worse. May God overrule it all for the best. I feel overwhelmed by a tremendous burden which I cannot shake off and talking would only distress me. With many prayers and *salams*. Believe me. Affectionately yours, Howard C. Baskerville.

Tabriz, Persia, April 2, 1909

My dear Mr. Baskerville, In accordance with your request I regretfully accept your resignation from the position of teacher in the Mission School, assuring you of our appreciation of your energy and devotion to your work in the past. I trust that God will bless you and keep you from temptations and from danger seen and unseen. Numbers VI: 24-26. We appreciate your motives and self-sacrifice but feel that you have erred. I remain, yours sincerely, S.G. Wilson 'Principal.'

Annie Rhea Wilson's Letter to Rev. Henry Baskerville and His Wife Emma (with minor edits).

Tabriz, Persia, April 20, 1909

My Dear Dr. and Mrs. Baskerville,

You have learned long before this letter reaches you that your dear boy laid down his life. It is almost three weeks since he left us, and he has come to see us six times since. The last time was last night, just before starting to battle. He told us it was a desperate attempt to open the road into this starving city. We had prayer together, Mr. Wilson praying only for his protection and commending him to God's care. Mr. Baskerville himself prayed only for others, "this city to be relieved," "the dear ones of the Mission to be kept in safety, and for peace to be obtained" — not a word of himself. In the night a soldier brought a note from him, "Dangerous rumor that the Europeans will be attacked to secure immediate intervention, don't be on the streets today."

The first Sunday after he joined the army he came to the church and sat down in his usual seat — the second in front — and had quite an ovation afterward, the men pressing around him to shake hands. That afternoon he came to see us. I begged him not to be reckless, saying "You know you are not your own." "No," he answered. "I'm Persia's." The name the patriots have adopted for themselves is "*fidai*," meaning "one devoted." And when the movement first began, they marched through the streets in white, as if in shrouds, devoted to death. He, dear boy, has thus devoted himself with them.

An attack was planned last Thursday, and he came in at ten o'clock just before starting, quite confident that they would take the enemy by surprise and "clear them out." We brought him a lunch and he drank milk, laughing at such a drink for a soldier. The expedition was futile, because Satter Khan, the General, failed to send cannon. They went out and found no cannon, tho' he promised it would be ready. They telephoned and got replies that he was coming but waited in vain till dawn and marched back. Then he and Mr. Moore felt the cause was hopeless with such leaders. Some say Satter Khan was drunk. He was very ashamed and gave an excuse that he was afraid of being shot in the back by traitors and didn't care to go out in the night. At any rate, it seemed futile to fight after that as the enemy would be on their guard and the city reached its last day's supply of wheat.

Mr. Baskerville and Mr. Moore urged them to ask the intervention of the Consuls to get as good terms for them as they could from the Shah. Such a telegram was sent Saturday to Teheran. Yesterday afternoon (Monday) late, after the plans for renewed fighting had been made, in despair of intervention and on account of bread-riots in the city, the answer came that the Embassies would try to persuade the Shah to make peace. The leaders still were determined to fight, in spite of Mr. Baskerville's and Mr. Moore's advice. Mr. Moore said he would go with them, but not to fight, only a war-correspondent. Mr. Baskerville, although doubtful of the possibility of success, said he would lead his men. He has been drilling 150 — "the pick of the lot," some of them young noblemen and some of them his pupils. He thought that they had more spirit than the others, and that the only hope for success was for him to lead them — they would not go without him. "It would be dastardly to desert them now," he thought.

The news was brought to us early this morning by Khachador, one of the boys, who takes care of his horses and room, who had risen at four o'clock to go out and see the battle and especially to bring news of Mr. Baskerville, as he himself had asked him to do yesterday afternoon, saying he might fall and wished us to know at once. The boy came running in, tears streaming down his face and the well-known brown riding-leggings in his hand, which Mr. Baskerville had borrowed from Mr. Vauthier. He said they were bringing the wounded to the rear, and he did not at first recognize the body, till he saw those leggings. They put him in a house and would not let the boy bring him home as he wished to do.

Mr. Doty, our Consul, at once got a carriage and sent a guard with one servant and the boy to bring the body. He wanted to go himself, but we dissuaded him, as the Consul's lives have been threatened. While we waited, I wrote the above to you, distracted with the grief and shock. They returned very quickly and the boys rushed to the gate to carry him in, all sobbing and lamenting. We carried him to our room and laid him on our own bed, and Mrs. Vanneman and I washed the dear body with the blood staining through his shirts and covering his breast and back. We found the bullet hole in front and back, having passed clear through, so small, so fatal. It had entered from the back and come out just above his heart, cutting a large artery, and Dr. Vanneman says causing instant death. His face was bruised a little on one side, where he had fallen. We dressed him in his black suit, and when all the sad service was done, he looked beautiful and noble, his firm mouth set in a look of resolution and his whole face calm in repose. I printed a kiss on his forehead for his mother's sake. A white carnation is in his buttonhole, and wreaths of flowers are being made. Our children made a cross and a crown of the beautiful almond blossoms in bloom.

The Governor came at once, expressing great sorrow and saying, "He has written his name in our hearts and in our history." The *Anjuman* (local assembly) sent a letter, saying they wished to share in doing him honor, and asked that the funeral be put off till tomorrow. The boys in little groups have come in and gone up stairs to our room, where we laid him till the coffin is ready. They recalled his Christian example, his love of the Church which he always attended, although he could not understand the service, his love of prayer and the Bible, which they say they often found him reading. They are deeply affected. "Greater love hath no man than this, that a man lay down his life for his friends." It was a good chance to say to them, "May each of you be ready as he was, when your hour comes," and as I began to say, "We can be sure Jesus said to him 'This day thou shalt be with me in Paradise.'" They repeated the verse with me. The merchant, who brought the cloth to cover the coffin, said "We know he died for us. He wanted to save these poor, starving people."

I must give you his last message. He came in one Sunday after-noon and said there would be fighting during the week, and if any-thing happened to him he wanted me to write to his mother, "Tell her I never regretted coming to Persia, and in this matter I felt it was my duty." On his birthday, just a week ago, I sent him a note wishing him "many happy returns of the day," and telling him I was preparing my prayer meeting on the subject, "Self-Sacrifice" and "a certain young man was in my thoughts a living example of it." Alas, he is slain, a dying example. He tried "to save others, himself he could not save."

It was decided to have the service in the church tomorrow morning at 9 o'clock. Notice is being sent to all the Europeans and the Armenian bishop and others. The women are waiting to cover and line the coffin. We feel toward him and treat him as one of our own children. He has endeared himself to us all. The chil-dren are overcome with grief. He was very kind to them, giving them much pleasure in taking them horseback-riding. Mr. Wilson is much crushed and laments his ending to a life which he foresaw had great prospects to usefulness and success. He often said of him: "There are few like him." His devotion to Christ and to the Mission cause was the ruling motive of his life. We always loved to hear him pray in our family-prayers.

8 P.M. We covered the coffin with black broadcloth and lined it with soft, white muslin and laid him in lovingly with tears. It was then just 5 P.M., the hour of our week-day meeting at the church. To our surprise the church was full, many Muslim young men, besides our own people. The coffin was in front, with cross and crown of flowers upon it. We sang "Heaven is my Fatherland" and "read of the house not made with hands." We arranged the seats and opened the prayer-meeting room partition in readiness for the crowds that will come tomorrow.

This evening four men from the *Anjuman* came to express sympathy and make arrangements for the funeral. This letter came from Mr. Moore and I send it entire. I am sorry we had no picture to send him. May I ask you to send us one? We would prize it highly. Mr. Moore is an Irishman and correspondent for the "Daily News." He came here several months ago sent to report and felt such sympathy that he joined the Nationalists at the same time as Mr. Baskerville did, as far as we know, each independent of the other. They have stood by each other, and we were glad he had this friend.

Wed. 11 A.M. April 21st. The funeral procession has just passed, and never did foreigner or Christian have such a funeral before this war. The service at Church was beautiful and impressive. Mr. Jessup first read and prayed in English, then Mr. Pittman did the same in Azeri. Mr. Wilson then spoke on the comfort we found in this bitter bereavement from "our brother's faith and character and our sure hope that he had entered into glory." The boys sang, "There is a Happy Land" in Azeri, and the benediction was pronounced. The coffin, in the front of the platform, was covered with exquisite floral wreaths, from the Boys' School, the Girls' School, the Armenians and ourselves, in front sat members of the *Anjuman*, at the right the English, Russian, French and American Consuls, and all the Europeans, at the left the Armenian Bishop, Muslims and Armenians filled the church, many standing in the rear and women and girls in the gallery. There was perfect order, and all were most respectful.

You cannot realize what a marvelous and unprecedented thing this is. In all the history of missions in Persia never did one have such honor from all classes. It would have pleased Mr. Baskerville to know that Christ was lifted up before the multitude as He has never been before in the history of Persia. The testimony of his truth, purity, piety and faith was one they could corroborate, for he had lived right among them these last three weeks. So he witnessed a good confession, and being dead yet speaketh. The nobility of his character was ascribed to its true source — his Christian faith.

We slipped out before the crowd and came to the school roof, overlooking the street through which the procession passed to the cemetery. After a long wait, we saw them, a dense mass of people filling the street. The leader was a stern old man on a splendid horse with drawn sword. There was a man with a banner first, then the band playing the Persian military funeral march. They stopped at the school-gate for the drum-taps. Then came several led horses, the one he rode and others sent by the general. Then came the men in uniform he drilled. The coffin was preceded by 16 boys carrying the wreaths. Mr. Jessup and Mr. Wilson were beside it, the older boys carried it, and the Armenians surrounded it, singing martial airs. The spectacle was wonderful. I cannot tell how many passed, but it showed that the city was deeply stirred. Two carriages with members of the *Anjuman* brought up the rear. How little he, in his reserve and modesty, expected such honor and glory so soon! He counted not his life dear unto himself, and these people recognize and appreciate his self-sacrifice.

I have just read this from Carlyle ("On Heroes, Hero-Worship and The Heroic in History – Six Lectures, by Thomas Carlyle, Willet, New York, 1859, Lecture II: "The Hero as Prophet," p63): "It is a calumny on men to any that they are aroused to heroic action by ease, hope of pleasure, recompense, sugar plums of any kind in this world or the next! Difficulty, abnegation, mar-tyrdom, death are the allurements that act on the heart of men." To the sneer that these people were not worthy of his sacrifice, we can only say: "While we were yet sinners, Christ died for us." (Romans 5:8). "Nor is a true soul ever born for naught; Wherever any such hath lived and died, there hath been something for true freedom wrought, some bulwark on the evil side." (James Russell Lowell, Sonnet XI)

Let me tell you a little of Mr. Baskerville's life among us these nineteen months. He seemed from the first to feel at home and well content in our society, entering into all our family and social life. He especially enjoyed our reading together Friday evenings. We read Roseln, Henry Remond, the Virginians, Vanity Fair, Old Curiosity Shop, Pickwick Papers, Bleak House, Nineteen Christian Centuries, Dr. Trumbull's Life, Jungle Folk of Africa, Chinese Characteristics and a volume on the Reformation, Friday and Sunday evenings. He himself read nearly all of the three volumes of Hodge's Systematic Theology Sunday afternoons and at other times 4 vols. of "The English Poets." We read French one winter Monday evenings, and he would join us to get the pronunciation. He was ambitious to learn French and Turkish.

His music books gave us much pleasure. He and I sang together many of the duets which he and his mother used to sing, and he was very fond of singing hymns with us Sunday afternoon and at Sunday morning prayers. He played tennis and taught all the children to ride horseback, taking the girls out in turn, giving them his gentle horse and riding himself our more spirited one. He often played with the schoolboys too, running races and winning their admiration for his "wind." As I wrote to his brother, he had a definitive plan to see the boys socially, going to their homes and having one or two at a time come to his room to drink tea. He always tried to have religious conversations and tell us what "a good talk" he had with this or that one. He felt greatly restricted in language, but there are quite a number who can understand English.

We shall always remember his Thanksgiving sermon, it was so patriotic and he closed with, "Breathes there a man with soul so dead, Who never to himself said, This is my own, my native land!" (Sir Walter Scott). He enjoyed Christmas and remembered us each one and all the children of the Mission with gifts. In his stay he showed a generous and affectionate spirit. Do not feel that he died among strangers, for we loved him and he loved us.

He was well all the time except for two weeks of fever in the summer, which at first seemed like typhoid. I had the privilege of being his nurse and his appreciation more than repaid me. These three weeks I have sent him boiled water as a safeguard and he kept well, while Mr. Moore, who lived with another Persian, was sick several weeks. He enjoyed the Persian dishes, especially the *lavash* bread. And always preferred it at our table. In school he was always faithful, prompt and devoted to his work. He was specially good in mathematics, and kindly taught our girls geometry four months. He made a success of a selection from "The Merchant of Venice," enacted by his highest English class last commencement. Only his persistent drill got them ready for it. Dr. Wright and Mr. Jessup kindly offered to help the school, when he left, as the war restricts their touring and they have time to teach, while kept in the city.

I often said, "I liked him best in his prayers." He took his turn in leading our evening prayers in English. All last Winter he, Miss Holliday and I met half an hour Monday evening for prayer. His faith and spiritual longings and love for souls were an inspiration. He always attended chapel prayers at school, Tuesday prayer meeting and Sunday morning service in the church, though in Azeri, which he could not understand, because he said he wished "a place among God's people."

Last summer he made a short visit to Urmia with Mr. Wilson and enjoyed meeting the missionaries there, but hearing of disturbances in Tabriz, he insisted on returning "to help defend the others" if there was danger. His unselfishness was shown when he said during that visit, before he expected to fight, "It is a terrible thing to lead others to certain death." Even then his thoughts were of others. "I need not tell you how this place appears," as the Persian say, in our home. He has never been unchristian in word or deed.

If we mourn for him, we can realize how much greater your bereavement is. In the service at the church, you were tenderly commended to "the God of all comfort." Let me say in Lincoln's words: "I feel how weak and fruitless must be the words of mine, which should attempt to beguile you from the grief of a loss so overwhelming. I may that our Heavenly Father may assuage the anguish of your bereavement and leave you only the cherished memory of the loved and lost and the solemn pride that must be yours to have laid so costly a sacrifice upon the altar of freedom."

Thursday, April 22nd. I keep writing, for there is so much to say and I cannot settle down to any work, my thoughts are constantly with you and with his. We went out to the grave yesterday afternoon, finding the long mound covered with flowers. He is the first man of the Mission buried there. We have sometimes said perhaps the harvest could not come in Tabriz till there was such a grave: "Except a corn of wheat fall into the ground and die." (John 12:24) We sang "Safe in the arms of Jesus," "Sweet Bye and Bye," and "Shall We Gather at the River?" That evening at station-meeting we sang his favorite hymn, which he introduced to us, often calling for it: "Thy Banner over Me is Love." The words seemed wonderfully fitting, none could be more appropriate.

I went out to his room for the first time I had entered it since he left. His trunk was unlocked, and I found the family-group and his own class-picture, which we were very glad to see. I will try to have it copied here, but if the negative is at the photographers in America and you could send us a few copies, they would be comfort to his friends here. Mr. Doty said he would have it enlarged and present it to the Memorial School as a memento. The boys will cherish it. Will you please write us what you wish done with his things? I will enclose a list.

Mr. Vauthier went yesterday and brought back his horse, watch and field glass we lent him, his valise and the coat in which he fell. In the pocket was $60 of money. We are most grateful that the dear face and body were not mutilated, nor his pockets rifled. Put this down to the credit of his comrades that took such care of him and his belongings. We took the liberty of reading his last letter to you, written Easter Sunday, as it was left open. If the mail had been going, he would have doubtless written often. But with no hope of the post getting out, we have all stopped writing, as he did. It was a bitter trial to him not to have home letters for so long. We have received only two mails in three months.

Friday, April 23rd. I spent all yesterday afternoon alone in the room he occupied in the school dormitory, making a list. Everything was in good order, but it was an ordeal to see all his things and think he no longer would use them. His shoes reminded me of his "quick-stepping" feet, as Mrs. Wright said, when she saw him lying so still and two Armenian women, who came to call, spoke of how they admired his swift springing walk, so different from people here. He was too quick for Persia. He could not "hustle the East."

The clothes in which he was brought to us have been washed and show little signs of battle, except the fatal bullet-hole. His trunk tray is full of your letters, as appears from the post-marks. Do you want these burnt or returned to you? Also two little books, a jot-diary? Do you wish these? The *Anjuman* wish to send his musket. One bullet only is gone from his cartridge-belt. Do you want the musket? The wreath of artificial flowers with its inscription, and the ribbons of the other wreaths I will send you. We will sell his horse as soon as possible. What about the saddle and bridle?

The boy, who went with him first from the school, as translator, has a sister in the Girl's school, who wept and entreated him so that he came back after 4 days (he has been sick with typhoid ever since.) Mr. Baskerville said to him, "I have a sister, too." Four Muslim women have just been to see me to express condolence and sympathy. They went with great emotion and said no other death had affected them so much. They wished me to send to you the sympathy of "all the women of Tabriz," and tell you that he was not a foreigner but would always be cherished in their hearts as a brother. A very brave officer was shot the same day by the enemy, as his head just appeared above the parapet, and his funeral at the same time drew a crowd, but the women said, "We forget even such a loss in our grief for Mr. Baskerville." They, too, were so glad that he had not fallen into the enemies' hand or been mutilated. The Lord certainly watched over him and suffered not this greater disaster.

There was a telegram to the English and Russian consuls, in answer to their intervention, that the king gave an armistice of 6 days and permission for provisions to enter the city, while peace negotiations were taking place. The English Consul's adjutant went out to the camp to see the King's General, who told him he had no such orders, but he gave an order for 2500 lbs of wheat, which a rich man had donated to the city, to pass. News came of this and there was great rejoicing, but the horsemen did not allow it to come in, saying they did not acknowledge the General's authority — just what Mr. Baskerville wrote in his letter to the Consul. A mob of 100 women went wailing through the streets to the *Anjuman*, saying "We want no *Anjuman*, we want bread." A soldier threatened to fire on them, and they scattered. So the anarchy he feared has begun. The result of the fight in which he fell was to push the enemy back a little and so far, delay their entrance into the city.

Mr. Wilson went to see Satter Khan yesterday. They both wept, as they met. He expressed great sorrow and said he had not expected the foreign gentlemen to fight, only to drill, and had warned them to go slow. Of course, now he wishes to shirk the responsibility, but he insisted on the attack, against their judgment, because the lot cast was favorable! Perhaps that may account for his failing them the other time, for the Persians are very superstitious about casting lots. He said the most appreciative things and told them he would put a monument over the grave.

Mr. Wilson also visited the General at the other side of the city, who said, or they all do, that Mr. Baskerville had made a place for himself in their hearts. He also seemed to be ashamed, but defended himself, saying "Persian war was won by strategy not straight attack." We hear that they said to him that, after the war, he must stay here and they would give him a high position, but he had said that he had no other purpose then to return to America, continue his studies, and become a minister.

Dear friends, I cannot tell you how deeply this has affected us. I have been so oppressed that it seemed almost unbearable. You knew him well and will understand that we could not dissuade him. I find comfort in the belief that God will overrule it all and, when I think of the dear boy at home in his "Father's House," forever safe and blest, I find relief.

Monday, April 26th. Yesterday at church Mr. Jessup preached a beautiful sermon on "Greater love hath no men than this," the love of Christ and His sacrifice, in which he made allusion to "the one, who the last week had laid down his life for us," and the longing we had to express our love and admiration and gratitude to him, so he urged us to show Christ our love and devotion, in turn for His Great Love. In the afternoon at our hour of singing, which he always enjoyed so much, the girls played Beethoven's and Chopin's funeral marches on piano and organ, and we sang the beautiful hymns we had so often sung with him and Mr. Wilson prayed, especially remembering you. At the Armenian service following, one of the teachers also prayed "for the parents and friends of our dear brother" very warmly and lovingly.

In the evening, at my meeting with the 12 older boys, I had versions written out for them to read on Self Sacrifice, and then told them all I know of his life. One of our boys, now in the bank, who had translated for him at a banquet given by Armenian soldiers, Easter Eve., told how he had made a speech of great eloquence there, eliciting enthusiastic applause. He began, "I hate war," and described the evil, saying that only necessity and a greater good could justify it — in this case the protection of the city and the cause of constitutional liberty for which he was ready to die. He also hoped that religious liberty would come with civil liberty. They cheered, "Long live Baskerville" and drank to his health and he sang for them one verse of "My country tis of thee." In our little meeting there seemed a very tender spirit. In the short prayers, that we always have at close, the petitions were all for "such unselfishness" and "such nobility of character." His death will impress on these boys his words and example. I read them the "White Cross Pledge" I found among his papers. Last week two of the soldiers were shot for kidnapping girls. His purity, his honor (keeping his word even "to his own hurt") his intrepid bravery, show him to have been "a good knight, without fear and without reproach." Again and again the boys repeat, "We will never forget him."

Friday, April 30th. This month that began with his joining the army closes with the occupation of the city by Russians. I have referred to the anarchy that threatened. The Russians were specially menaced, and all took refuge in the Consulate, building a barricade and having bags ready. The atrocities in Turkey also made the Consuls apprehensive, so they urged the sending of Russian troops to restore order. The generals were blustered, but it was all a bluff. Yesterday the Russian soldiers entered singing as they marched and were unmolested. Their camp is outside the city at the river, and squads of guards every ten miles to keep the road clear to Julfa. Provisions are brought in, and wheat has fallen, and the people rejoice, though the political leaders are sad to have Russia come in.

Satter Khan came here to call two days ago with thirteen soldiers as attendants, who stood outside, and five who came into the room with him. His call was purely condolence. He expressed great sorrow and regret. He has received a new title and a robe of honor from the King's General. It is so like Persia to have sudden changes. Many think he will receive an office but be secretly dispatched with treachery. The brigand-leader, who held the road to Russia, who Mr. Baskerville referred to as amenable to no authority, has been removed, and his fate is uncertain. They say he is summoned to Tehran to answer for his crimes.

We can hardly believe that the three-month siege is over. At the last it seemed so easy, when England and Russia really took hold of the affair, but it had to reach a desperate crisis before they would. The people say of Mr. Baskerville, "He was a sacrifice for us. His holy blood ended the war." Mr. Doty is going to take us this afternoon to see the fatal spot, now occupied by troops, and it will seem incredible that only ten days ago it was a scene of fighting and bloodshed. Mr. Moore leaves today for England. The two boys who were interpreters are about well, and one back in school. Our children keep the grave covered with fresh flowers. We shall always be glad we knew and loved him.

Again commending you to the God of all comfort, believe me.

Yours in sorrowing sympathy,

Annie R. Wilson

Ingram Content Group UK Ltd.
Milton Keynes UK
UKHW021956130323
418485UK00014B/760

9 781662 843778